TURNING THE WHEEL

Other books by Sandy Boucher

Heartwomen
The Notebooks of Leni Clare
Assaults & Rituals

TURNING THE WHEEL

American Women Creating the New Buddhism

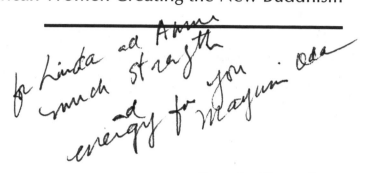

Sandy Boucher

With Photographs by the Author

Harper & Row, Publishers, San Francisco

Cambridge, Hagerstown, New York, Philadelphia, Washington
London, Mexico City, São Paulo, Singapore, Sydney

For my teacher, Ruth Denison,
for Treelight, with whom I began this journey,
and for Barbara, with whom I continue it

Cover art: silkscreen by Mayumi Oda entitled
"Goddess Hears People's Needs and Comes"

Photographs by the author except:

Deborah Hopkinson by Michele Hill
Barbara Horn by Barbara Lubanski-Wenger
Dhyani Ywahoo © Sunray Meditation Society, 1985
Peace Pagoda by Paula Green
Tina Turner by Paul Cox

Library of Congress Cataloging-in-Publication Data

Boucher, Sandy.
    Turning the wheel.
    Bibliography: p.
    Includes index.
    1. Women, Buddhist—United States—Religious life.
2. Buddhism—Social aspects—United States.   I. Title.
BQ734.B68   1988   294.3'088042   87-45689
ISBN 0-06-250097-X

88 89 90 91 92 HC 10 9 8 7 6 5 4 3 2 1

CONTENTS

ACKNOWLEDGMENTS

A book of this type grows from a community; it is a forum of experience and opinion, and it can be written because the members of that community recognize the importance of communicating with each other, because they hunger for knowledge of each other's experience and wisdom and are therefore willing to share their own.

The idea for this book came in 1981 when I decided I wanted to investigate the experience and views of women spiritual teachers. Through the various permutations of that concept during the next several years, a number of women gave me guidance and support, among them Clare Fischer of the Graduate Theological Union in Berkeley, Mary E. Hunt (now of WATER, Women's Alliance for Theology, Ethics, and Ritual), Laurie Ludwig by her convening of an early workshop on Women and Buddhism. When I presented my first proposal to Harper & Row I was aided by letters of support from Jan Willis of Wesleyan University, Suzanne Bowman, then of the Providence Zen Center, Sharon Salzberg of Insight Meditation Society, Deborah Hopkinson of *Kahawai*, Susan Murcott, Joanna Macy, and Jane Augustine, as well as novelist Marilyn Coffey and feminist author Sandra Butler. Judith Simmer-Brown of Naropa Institute and Rita Gross of the University of Wisconsin offered suggestions for making the project more representative. Further support was given by Paula Gunn Allen of the University of California, Sallie Gearhart of San Francisco State University, and Tillie Olsen.

The book was actually researched and written from 1985 to 1987, but all of the discoveries and dry runs which I had made since 1981 contributed to its maturation. I appreciate the help of those who gave advice or support during that incubation period. I also want to thank Marcia Angus for her conversation with me in early 1985 that directed me to the subject of my very first interview.

I spoke with over one hundred women. Not all of their portraits or opinions appear in the following pages, but the effect of our conversations is felt in the richness of context they provided. These women were generous of their time and thought, and those who spoke of delicate or controversial matters were brave in allowing their views to be published. Some of those whose stories I was not able to include, such as Zen teachers Cheri Huber and Judyth Weaver, Tibetan Buddhist practitioner Jane Augustine, author and former Buddhist practitioner Vicky Noble; and others such as Teresa Foudriat, Carol Rankin, Anita Noble, Helen Pelton, Sabina Klein, Vicki Gabriner, Jane McLaughlin, Nina Wise, Mayumi Oda, Carol Wilson, Louise Stanton Sichel, Adeline Alex, Leslie James, Phoebe Van Woerden, Ando Mueller, Margaret Clyde, Komei Larson, Daniella Kis, Doris Katagiri, Laura Boxer, Jan Spring (Cedar), Carolyn Gimian, Cindy Shelton, and Barbara Raif I thank for contributing to my understanding of women's experience of Buddhist practice.

As I traveled the country in 1985 many people extended their hospitality to me and generously aided me in contacting women to interview, as well as orienting me to the particular Buddhist practice environment in which I found myself. Among these were Ann Spanel, Maurine Stuart (formerly Freedgood), and Bobby Lev in Cambridge; Ruth Klein at the Providence Zen Center; Jeanne Ann Whittington at Insight Meditation Society; Paula Gray in Washington, D.C.; Barbara Dubois at Sunray Meditation Society in Vermont; Paula Green and Carla Brennan in western Massachusetts; Karen Thorkelson, Judith Niemi, and Carol Iwata in Minneapolis; Susan Edwards, Denny Robertson, and Buncie Shaddon in Boulder; Rita Gross in Eau Claire, Wisconsin; Ruth Denison in Los Angeles. More people than I can name helped me with introductions to their friends, dinners and transportation and the kind of information a traveler needs, as well as the sharing of their views and experience. Each of those contributors was important in the production of this book.

My Harper & Row editor, Jan Johnson, proved to be a supportive, sensitive, and knowledgeable guide in the shaping of the various drafts. I also want to acknowledge Clayton Carlson for his belief in the project. Then there were those who saw me through the months of transcribing tapes, writing, editing—the daily labor that creates a manuscript—by listening to me, now and then feeding me dinner or giving me a massage, most of all by believing that this book would be useful and was worth doing: my partner Barbara Wilt, Julie Wester, Ann Hershey, Osha Hibberd, and the women of the Women's Sangha. Catherine Dunford and Alex Alexander helped with the secretarial work in the later stages, and Grace Harwood offered technical assistance. The students in my writing workshops kept me cheerful. And while they were not directly involved in helping me with this book, my sister members of the planning committee of the March 1987 Celebration of Women in Buddhist Practice showed me we could manifest in the world what I was discovering in my writing. They include Anna Douglas, Stephanie Kaza, Cornelia Schulz, Lane Olson, Lenore Friedman, Yvonne Rand, Carolyn North, Barbara Wilt, Sue Schmall, Marion Tripp, Julie Wester. Sister Ayya Khema of Parappuduwa Nuns Island clarified certain aspects of my delineation of Theravada Buddhism.

In working with the material I received the help of women who came forward to provide me with facts, to correct my misperceptions, and to fill in important aspects that I had neglected. I thank them for their effort and the spirit of cooperation in which their suggestions were offered.

Some lesbians talked frankly with me both about their acceptance by Buddhist teachers and groups and about their experience of stereotyped responses and images among their sangha peers. However, when these women saw the typescripts of what they had said, several of them refused to let those comments be included, because they felt that would place "too much emphasis" on their lesbianism. As I worked on this book I was surprised at the level of homophobia present in our culture, in our Buddhist centers, and in ourselves. This prevented any but the most brief and oblique discussion in my book of lesbian women's relationship to their Buddhist centers, which was a topic I had hoped to address more fully. I thank the few women who *were* willing to let their views on this subject be published.

Some friends who helped me by commenting upon parts or all of the manuscript of this book were Valerie Miner, Sandra Butler, Estelle Jelinek, Barbara Wilt, Julie Wester, and Ann Hershey. Cathie Cade aided me with her usual skilled and enthusiastic assistance in the preparation of the photographs. Barbara Gates made valuable last-minute suggestions.

Exhaustive as the above acknowledgments may seem, they mention and thank only a fraction of the hundreds of women and a few men whose comments, behavior, support, ideas, articles, books, meditation courses, and retreats helped me to mature in my own understanding of the purpose and scope of this book and to deal with the complexity of the task. While in the end it was a solitary task, as writing almost always is, there was a great deal of communication and compromise involved in the preparation. I am so grateful for all of that, even when it was difficult, and I apologize for not being able to personally thank every individual who participated in the process with me.

Except for Brenda, who appears in "Childhood Sexual Abuse" of the section called "Bridges," all names I have used are actual names.

1.

Brave Beginnings

In the hills overlooking the blue expanse of San Francisco Bay, in a Protestant sanctuary rented for the purpose, 165 women have gathered. They sit in silent meditation, come together to perform a full moon ceremony, engage in a loving-kindness meditation. They meet in small groups to share the stories of their own spiritual practice and its effect on their lives. They convene in other small groups to discuss the relationship of Buddhist practice to authority and power, social service and political activism, addictive behavior, parenting and motherhood, intimate relationships and sexuality, and other concerns. Among them are female monks and longtime lay Buddhist practitioners, mothers and students, lesbians and old women, feminists and other political women who may only recently have come to Buddhist practice. The teachers who have chosen to participate in the gathering take an equal role with the other women in the small groups. There are no speakers, no panels, no voices of authority.

This is "A Celebration of Women in Buddhist Practice." It was conceived and organized out of the participants' understanding that they are involved in creating the new American Buddhism. It draws upon the consciousness developed in the women's movement in the last seventeen or eighteen years, the ways of women being together, working together, and trusting each other that grew up in that movement. And it answers these women's need to share their experience, their information, and their vision in a safe, respectful environment.

Women are coming together in groups all over the country. We are moving to create a distinctly Americanized, feminized, democratized form of Buddhist spiritual practice. In this effort lies the possibility for the creation of a religion fully inclusive of women's realities, in which women hold both institutional and spiritual leadership. This movement offers opportunities not found elsewhere.

But the more basic appeal of Buddhist practice to women resides in the fact that Buddhism posits no god, creates no I-Thou relationship with an all-powerful father figure. A central tenet is that one must trust one's own experience above all else. Nothing—no tradition, belief, or direction from a teacher—must be accepted unless it can pass the test of experience.

Buddhism is primarily a method for the investigation of reality. In this it corresponds to feminist insistence on the rigorous questioning of every assumption. The practice of Buddhism entails hours of meditation and other activities designed to reveal the nature of one's physical sensations, one's thoughts, and one's feelings. The state of mind achieved by these efforts awakens compassion for all beings and receptivity to the underlying truth of existence. While there is more than one definition of feminism, the one I understand most deeply comes from my own seventeen-year commitment as a feminist and some years of political activism. Feminism is *not* a dogma, a creed, or a faith. It is, preeminently, a tool for investigation, grounded in the belief in women's right to full realization of our potential. We look at a situation and ask, who has the power here? That is, what are the *true* dynamics of power underneath the shared fantasies, the naive beliefs, or the outright lies of the participants? Where do women stand in this? Are the needs of women, family members, mothers, considered and met? Are we given the same opportunities as men to actualize our potential? This inquiry and the actions emerging from it to change social structures and redefine and redistribute power are feminism.

Buddhism presumes that most of us are blinded by a veil of ignorance of our true nature. Feminism presumes that we exist within a hoary power structure of lies and misconceptions about the nature of human beings. Both systems allow us to tear aside the veil, dismantling the forms that hide from us the true beauty and potential of human beings. And the goal of both is liberation from limiting ideas and conditions. These correspondences explain the attraction of Buddhist practice for women and its potential usefulness. Many women see this practice as a way to augment or continue their own process of self-discovery and activism, for it offers techniques designed to awaken us and bring us fully present to life. And there is a growing number of female teachers and women-defined groups that provide encouraging environments in which to practice Buddhist meditation.

Many women committed to work for social change have come within the last few years to recognize a need in themselves for something deeply sustaining and nourishing with which to enlarge their lives and support their commitment. The struggle for peace, equality, and a humane society is long and can often be disheartening. To sustain it some women need to reach to a place in themselves that can be called "spiritual."

They may participate in rituals designed to celebrate women's unique connection with nature and all beings. But they may also feel the need for the stability, power, and precision of a tradition and a practice that have flourished unbroken from their inception and thus begin to practice Buddhist meditation.

Once involved in Buddhist practice, they find themselves confronting a tradition that has always held women to be inferior. They find Asian cultural forms that conflict with American values. And they find the usual sexist assumptions and behavior of the American men practicing with them. However, looking carefully, they also see that because its history in the United States is so short, its practices here not yet firmly embedded in the cement of tradition, American Buddhism offers unique opportunities for the incorporation of women's experience and the alteration of forms to encourage female participation and leadership.

A dramatic movement has grown up in the last five years among women who practice the several forms of Buddhist meditation. It involves not only women new to the practice, but those who have been meditators for many years. Nineteen eighty-three brought events crucial to women's full participation in, and transformation of, Buddhism. During that year, several of the principal male Zen spiritual teachers were exposed as sexual adventurers and abusers of power. Soon the revelations reached other groups whose male leaders were implicated. Outrage, pain, and disillusionment raced through the Buddhist communities. Most practitioners came to realize that the old hierarchical models brought from Asia do not, in the long run, serve Americans well. Authority was questioned, structures challenged. And women particularly became visible and articulate. These events served as a great impetus to students of Buddhism to examine their behavior and their loyalties. Painful as the phenomenon was, it offered an *opportunity* to change the direction of American Buddhism, open it up more fully to the needs and contribution of women.

Many women left the centers run by men and went to study with women teachers; some women formed independent groups for study, practice and analysis; those who remained in male-led groups began to question. Women just coming to Buddhism and those who had participated for many years shared their experience and insight in local and national conferences. Buddhist practitioners who only recently had awakened to women's concerns and the feminists and other women who had just begun Buddhist practice began to work together.

While keeping the essence of the Asian-developed forms of Buddhism, American women are altering the expression of that essence to accommodate their needs and vision. Some weave in strands of Native American rituals and reverence for the earth; others draw from the teachings of the women's spirituality movement—the deep exploration of woman's unique spiritual capacities; some bring training in psychological techniques which honor the emotions. All are guided by the investigative urgency of the spirit of feminism.

This activity and this urgency rest upon a crucial decision that a woman may make: to take herself seriously as a human being; to believe the messages she gets *from her own deepest, most authentic experience* rather than believing what is told her about herself; to go past her own internalized sexism in order to respect and join with other women for support and possible collective action.

Some Buddhists have stated that this inquiry and activity are not appropriate in the Buddhist context because they create contention and "make opposites," or because in the enlightened state male and female are transcended. These arguments assume that the realm of spiritual activity lies beyond distinctions and conventions/contention. Certainly it does, and yet we are here in our bodies, which happen to be female, living our lives with other human beings and subject to the conditions affecting all women. Enlightenment is here with us too. But being women who do a Buddhist practice does not mean that we need be fools, doormats, or victims; that we cannot move to change the conditions of our lives. In fact, because of its insistence on our being fully *here* in our experience, Buddhism offers an opportunity for women to see clearly and act skillfully in our own behalf.

This new Buddhism coming into being is not a women's religion but a spiritual path encompassing both male and female needs. It arises out of the shared visions and energy of women scholars, political activists, monastics, mothers: people engaged in looking deeply into themselves to discern the contours of the new spirit-creature who is now being born as American Buddhism. All over the country, we are challenging the old ways and male institutions and beginning to live the new. From these isolated foci of activity, a net is weaving itself together—a net strong and resilient enough to lift American Buddhism out of its sexism and narrow imitation of Asian forms to create the new Buddhism that will mirror our quintessentially North American tradition and harvest the fruit of the experience, analysis, and activism of American women in this century.

MY PART IN THIS

In the 1940s, in Columbus, Ohio, my grandfather took my sister and me each Sunday to the Methodist church. Dapper and bespectacled, he had hair of the same snowy whiteness as his neatly ironed shirt under his dark suit. With his narrow face and thin-lipped mouth, he might have been a preacher himself or a schoolmaster like his Vermont forebears, but instead he had done everything from raising dogs to running a grocery store to working as a carpenter. At church he enjoyed himself, chatting with the ladies after the service.

After Sunday school sometimes we would join grandpa where he sat in the balcony of the sanctuary, looking down on the rows of fancy hats and balding heads, and we would endure an hour of hard bench, somber music, a funereal voice from the front of the room, and the sight of a nearly naked man nailed in an agonized posture upon a cross, his sweet, suffering, bearded face gazing down from heavy-lidded eyes.

Looking at him Sunday after Sunday, I felt a melting, a swooning. There was something awesome in this utter vulnerability, something so passion-inspiring in his bleeding hands, his spiky crown, the gash in his tender flank.

But the image that struck even deeper was given to me in Sunday school where the teacher read to us the story of the Good Samaritan. Listening to that tale of a traveler who goes out of his way to lift up and care for an injured man, I was filled with a sort of joyous strength that I had never felt before. There was a fullness, a completeness in this experience for me.

I mention these first religious experiences because who I am now, and my particular relationship to Buddhist practice, are grounded there, just as the experiences of other women in this book are grounded in their, predominantly, Jewish or Christian training. Even women who received no religious training and consider themselves agnostic or atheistic grew up within the context of our Christian/Jewish culture.

In the intervening years of school and college, and ten years of marriage in San Francisco, I searched for ways to know myself, to connect up with my own wisdom. I read the great Hindu mystics Ramakrishna and Vivekenanda and mystical books like *Transcendental Magic* by Eliphas Levi and *The Secret of the Golden Flower;* I taught myself to do hatha yoga, and took L.S.D. But the next profound and transforming involvement of my life came in the women's liberation movement. I had been working as a secretary and performed most of the duties of a traditional wife for my husband, who was studying for his Ph.D. At work I lived with others' belief in my inferiority, as expressed by inadequate pay and demeaning treatment; at home I was expected to be solely responsible for housework and providing emotional support. It was not a satisfying existence, especially as I was struggling to develop my capacities as a writer.

Then women's liberation arrived and gave a name to my discontent. Soon I was involved in sharing my experience with other women, discovering the injustices and limitations of most women's lives, coming to understand my commonality with other working women and wives, with mothers, women of color, old women, battered women. I began to give my time and effort to effect change: going out to demonstrate at TV stations and newspapers, helping to set up an office from which activities could be coordinated. This was 1970, 1971, and I was in my early thirties. I

remembered Eliphas Levi's injunction: "Before opposing ourselves to a given force or current, we must be well assured that we
possess the contrary force, or are with the stream of the contrary
current; otherwise we shall be crushed or struck down." I left my
former life of marriage, job, and "straight" existence. Plunging
into the stream of the women's movement, devoting myself to political work, I found a strong, empowering belief. We came together so enthusiastically, so trustingly, to save the world.

From women's meetings and evening demonstrations, my
roommates and I would return to our little rented house on Ber-
nal Heights in San Francisco, where we looked in on our sleeping
children before staying up most of the night to paste up our newspaper, called *Mother Lode.* This periodical, which investigated
such issues as women in prison, women's health care, family relationships, and lesbian motherhood, was distributed at gatherings
and political events. Two of us were welfare mothers, three of us
came from working-class backgrounds. Women's liberation was
no abstraction to us but the chance to create more humane and
egalitarian conditions, a chance to improve the lives of all women,
including ourselves, and to alter the world so that our children
could grow up peaceful and fulfilled.

After a few years of tireless activity, we learned that the creation of social change is a much more long-term endeavor than
we had imagined. And the demands of earning a living and raising a child reasserted themselves. Eventually all of us left our collective household and went back to work at jobs, living with
children or lovers or alone, doing our political work as best we
could.

I now understand that the experience of politics is a step toward
the infinite, because it requires and fosters identification with
more than the self, sets one upon a quest for meaning beyond privacy. My next steps, very tentative, came in the late seventies when
I met people in the community of feminist healers in the San Francisco Bay Area. They were therapists and body workers, whose
healing included a spiritual dimension. I began to attend group sessions with a young meditation teacher named Margo Adair and became involved in a relationship with Treelight Green, a healer,
whose exotic name did not blind me to her humor and compassion.
I began confronting the questions of how to live, of how to break

old, crippling life patterns. And this led, when I was a few years over forty, to the practice of Buddhist meditation.

My first acquaintance with Buddhist sitting took place in one of the most beautiful and sweetly secluded settings in the United States: Tassajara Zen Buddhist Mountain Retreat in the Santa Cruz mountains. I had been taken there for a two-day vacation by Treelight. The monastery, which opens its gates to guests during the summer months, offers hot mineral baths, swimming in a bright rushing stream, mountain walks, delicious food, and rustic cabins in which to rest after all that pleasure. The monks also offer instruction in Zen meditation for those who are interested. At the meditation hall Treelight and I were shown how to sit cross-legged, how to position our hands and our eyes, and we were invited to rise the next day at 5:45 to attend the early morning sitting with the monks.

The next morning I sat facing a white wall in the predawn silence and coolness. Candles flickered, causing my shadow to hover like a nervous ghost before me. Behind the row of monks in which I sat, a black-robed figure carrying a long stick paced slowly, its shadow falling across each of us in turn. But I suffered no apprehension, because it had been explained to us that guests would not be hit unless we specifically requested to be made more alert in this manner. Outside in the darkness Tassajara Creek rushed by, singing. As the blush of dawn light began to appear in the open space between wall and roof, birds chirped tentatively, as if trying out the new day.

Inside we sat without moving, and the meditation hall held a deep silence to which we all contributed. Although my legs stiffened and at moments I shivered, I wanted never to leave that place, for I experienced a profound peacefulness.

When I returned to the Bay Area, I began to sit every morning before I began my day and soon noticed the benefits of increased steadiness and calmness in my life. It did not occur to me to seek out a Zen group to sit with. But I wanted to understand the basis for Buddhist practice, the content, the rationale behind it. So I began to attend classes at the Nyingma Institute, a Tibetan Buddhist center in the Berkeley hills. Treelight and I went there together to chant and meditate.

Above this brightly painted building, festive prayer flags snap in the wind, and in its garden a giant prayer wheel groans and thumps as it turns. In this ornate environment so different from the Zen austerity of the elegantly bare meditation hall at Tassajara, our study began dramatically. One Sunday it was announced that after the meditation and dinner a lecture would be given on the subject of samsara. Reading that word, I felt tremendous excitement and urgency. Not that I understood it, though I had heard it before and knew that it meant our "ordinary existence" or "this world" or "the cycle of rebirth." Gripping Treelight's arm, I insisted we stay for the talk.

I do not remember what the lecturer said that night. I think he described the great wheel of being, that endless cycle of interdependent origination that the Buddhists believe constitutes our life. But I felt that with every word he was describing my own attempts at mastery or liberation, my own failures; and it was excruciating. I left Nyingma Institute that night with a pounding heart.

In the car going home, I knew I had to find out all I could about this point of view, and I made the decision to take the course called Dharma Theory I. "Dharma," I knew, meant "truth" or "the teachings" or "what is."

The class consisted of a presentation of the Abhidharma, the so-called higher teachings of Buddhism, its philosophical and psychological infrastructure. While this is considered by many to be dry-as-dust material, I found it so exciting that the Wednesday night class at Nyingma became the pinnacle of my week. We sat on pillows on the floor scribbling in our notebooks while the teacher, an earnest intellectual, filled a blackboard with lists and definitions and charts. The Four Noble Truths, the Eightfold Noble Path, the Divine Abodes, the formulations of traditional Buddhist thought were given to us. Then a second teacher took over. He might make a casual remark, tell a classic Buddhist story, or relate a contemporary incident, after which we would sit in meditation for the last half hour. Although the stories bore no obvious connection to the information we had dutifully written in our notebooks, they produced a curious effect. Sometimes it would be as if, listening to him, I watched a tiny door open and I *saw* something I had never seen before. At other times I was electrified, as if my body were under pressure or had been briskly shaken.

So the teachings were powerful. But in the process of taking the classes we came up against the reality of Buddhism as a *religion*. Here it was, with all the machinery, the ritual, the accumulation of dogma of an institution that has existed for 2,500 years. And in its language and assumptions it seemed heavily male supremacist and male chauvinist, as are all the other world religions. "Why no names of great women practitioners?" Treelight and I asked our teacher, and he had no answer. While people stood in the lobby on Sunday evenings after meditation, a gong was rung to announce dinner. "Why doesn't a woman ever ring the gong?" we asked, and we were told that traditionally only men could do so. A look at the hierarchy of the institute revealed men to be in the conspicuous, decision-making positions, while women for the most part played supporting roles. In the building of the country center, we were told by one participant, women were expected to restrict their labors to kitchen work, until our friend vigorously objected. Treelight and I found ourselves in a quandary. We were strongly drawn to the teachings but repelled by some elements of the context in which they were transmitted.

At home I meditated each morning before I went into my study to work on the book I was writing. The meditation helped me maintain the clarity with which I awoke each morning and plunged me deeply in myself, aiding my concentration. Writing had always been the most important endeavor in my life. This Buddhist meditation I viewed simply as an aid to my work.

During this time Treelight discovered a woman Buddhist teacher whom she respected and loved; she urged me to experience this teacher, Ruth Denison, who operated from Dhamma Dena, the Desert Vipassana Center in the Mojave Desert east of Los Angeles. ("Dhamma Dena" or "Dhammadinna" was a member of the original order of nuns alive during the Buddha's time and was renowned for her ability to teach. This name was given to Ruth Denison by her Burmese teacher, we discovered, and she gave it to the center she founded.) Here was a type of Buddhism different from the Zen and Tibetan forms I had experienced. "Vipassana" means "insight meditation" and is taught by the Theravada Buddhists, whose practice began in India but is now mainly centered in Burma, Sri Lanka, and Thailand.

At Dhamma Dena, where I went with Treelight for a seven-day retreat, I encountered wide empty skies, low concrete block buildings on sandy desert soil, and a teacher who was unique. Ruth Denison, a woman in her sixties wearing a long full beige skirt, an embroidered white blouse, and a caplike scarf over her head, met us and immediately, in a thick German accent, began telling us to put our sleeping bags *here*, our suitcases *there*. She seemed to be doing everything at once—directing the kitchen help, feeding the dogs, writing up the schedule for the week—all with great verve and good humor.

The next day I discovered why she was considered innovative and controversial, for between the formal periods of sitting meditation, Ruth led us in sessions of movement, improvising slow sweeps of arm or leg, careful bendings and turnings, all designed to sharpen and quiet the mind by investigating the sensations experienced in the body. This was uniquely her expression, a method of engaging our distractible Western minds and strongly focusing them.

During the meditation sessions I had great difficulty sitting still. My body was at war with me, demanding activity; my mind screamed at me to provide it with diversion. I was driving myself crazy. And yet on the fourth day, suddenly, after a weeping jag, I broke through to a condition I had never experienced before. I sat on the desert earth before a creosote bush, staring at its spindly jointed branches, and I felt immense space open around and inside me. My mind was still, with no voice chattering, and completely receptive. I felt a subtle joy like a glow suffusing me, and there was absolutely nothing I wanted beyond this moment.

Even after such experiences as this it did not occur to me to think of Ruth Denison as *my* teacher, my stance toward authority having always been one of defiance. But my admiration was awakened by the absolute equality with which she treated each person. And I appreciated her willingness to teach all-women retreats and to accommodate the preferences of some of her more feminist students, even though she herself was not consciously a feminist or political in any way.

Soon after the retreat, one morning as I meditated in my apartment, I realized that a change had taken place in me. It was hard for me to believe or accept, but it was obvious that I was no longer meditating in order to prepare myself for the day's writing: I was doing this meditation practice *for itself.* And further, I felt in myself that this Buddhist practice had actually become as important to me as my writing. This was a stunning realization.

Then, in the summer of 1981, a historic event occurred. The first Women in Buddhism conference was held at the Naropa Institute in Boulder, Colorado. It was organized by Judith Simmer, cochair of Buddhist Studies at Naropa, and was attended by about fifty women who came from twelve states, Canada, and England.

Treelight and I drove across the desert to Boulder to attend this conference, and in the car I read I. B. Horner's *Women Under Primitive Buddhism*, a discouraging look at the conditions under which the Buddhist nuns alive during the Buddha's lifetime in sixth century B.C.E.[1] India existed. One of the most shocking rules required nuns even of long seniority to bow down to every monk, even the youngest and newest. Diana Paul's *Women in Buddhism* was every bit as sobering. A delineation of the exclusion and denigration of women in the Buddhist texts, the book told of early beliefs, one of which was the idea that women could not reach enlightenment in a female body, but it also offered a look at the evolution of the views of the feminine into the relative acceptance of women and the feminine element in later texts.

At the Women in Buddhism conference, which was beautifully organized and integrated, talks and group meetings alternated with workshops in poetry, calligraphy, flower arranging, and other arts taught by Naropa women artists. Lectures and workshops addressed questions of women's participation in Buddhist practice, the intersection of Buddhism with feminism, as well as issues such as the effects of hierarchy and the combining of Buddhist practice with motherhood. One clear and uncompromising feminist voice at the conference belonged to Rita Gross, a practitioner of Tibetan Buddhism and professor of religion at the University of Wisconsin at Eau Claire. Another distinctive personality with much to offer was Susan Murcott of the Diamond Sangha in Hawaii; and the periodical *Kahawai Journal of Women and Zen*, produced by women of the Diamond Sangha, was introduced to us.

We returned to California with the sense of being connected now to women who questioned and analyzed their own situations and were making serious moves to change them.

In the summer of 1982, Treelight and I drove across the desert again to the second Women in Buddhism conference at Boulder.

Attendance had nearly doubled. Enthusiasm ran high. But near the end of the conference a participant dropped a bombshell by asking Judith Lief, dean of Naropa, in a formal session, what she thought of Buddhist spiritual teachers initiating sexual relations with their students. The Boulder women were sensitive on this point, as their teacher, a renowned Tibetan former monk, was notorious for his many sexual liaisons with students. The subject opened, the visitors began to give their opinions, share their experiences, vent their anger and disillusionment. Here in Boulder we were acting out a preview of the fateful events and disclosures within the Zen world that would come the following year.

In 1983 a Women and Buddhism conference was held for the first time at the Providence, Rhode Island, Zen Center. Here women began to confront the issues recently raised by the disclosures that some male Zen teachers womanize, use alcohol unwisely, and abuse power. Susan Murcott presented some stunning revelations from her travels to Zen centers where she had been asked to speak throughout the country. In most of these places women came to her with stories of sexual advances made to them by the male teachers.

In December 1983 I was in the desert once again, working a shovel into the dry crumbly earth. I bent to dig, lifted, bent again. Around me the miles of chaparral stretched out on every side, the mountains rose brown and tumbled in the distance, the low houses lay scattered out across the earth. Not far away stood the concrete block meditation hall, and beyond it the little red bunkhouse that had been a garage, the main house, the converted chicken coop in which Ruth Denison lived. The raked dirt of the yard lay innocent of footprints; a breeze romped through, toying with the bell that hung outside the dining room. Everyone rested now after lunch. But I toiled on, digging deeper into this dry earth, bending and lifting, drawing the clear dry air into my lungs. Behind me stood the privy for which I dug this hole, a little tarpaper shack papered on the inside with colored magazine pictures of animals and crystals.

This labor comforted me, for I had been experiencing that year the hurt of my father's final illness, the breakup of my relationship with Treelight, the financial difficulties brought on by trips to the Midwest to be with my father and a stint in jail for participating in antinuclear civil disobedience. It had been a year of struggle and loss. Now I had nothing more to lose, it seemed, and so a new willingness was born in me.

In the meditation hall where I sat later that afternoon, grateful just to be still in this atmosphere of intense practice, the quibbling, the criticisms, the holding back that had prevented me from fully receiving Ruth Denison's teachings cracked like a weakened wall and fell into rubble. As she led us in a painstaking investigation of our bodies, I found myself completely receptive to each direction she gave to attend to the sensation in my throat, my shoulder, my knee; and soon I began to experience the flesh and bone of my body as living tissue, as cells vibrating with a life of their own and participating in the constant flow and change of all life. In the meditation hall, with the noises of the desert entering briefly—the barking of a dog, the roar of a jet passing overhead—the silence rested dense and almost palpable, and in it came Ruth's voice like a lifeline drawing me deeper and deeper into the adventure of this collection of bone and tissue I call my body.

My surrender to her guidance and my focused concentration allowed me to penetrate more deeply than I ever had before into the actuality of my physical being. When the meditation was over, I sat looking about the room at the other meditators, young men and women sitting cross-legged, wrapped in shawls and blankets against the cold, and I was filled with a great welling tenderness for each of them and for all of humanity who share with me the condition of this body that is only briefly here, neither solid nor permanent.

The experience of those seven days of the retreat changed me, awaking the recognition of the interpenetration of all beings, all life, plunging me into a more dynamic relationship with my practice and my teacher.

I came home to pick up once again the project I had begun several years before of researching a book on women spiritual teachers, but now I began to view the subject differently. For years I had been interested in the whole phenomenon of women's participation in Buddhism, not just that of the teachers but of the practitioners too. Now the time had come when the sparks struck at Boulder in 1981 were growing to a conflagration, fed especially by the revelations of male teachers' sexual misconduct. Buddhist women were examining their situations, arriving often at great pain, great disillusionment, and great resolve. Already I understood some of the issues involved, but I wanted to sharpen my thinking and awareness, so I determined to attend the second conference at the Providence Zen Center, entitled "Women and American Buddhism."

In the wake of a hurricane, as torrential rains lashed New England, over a hundred people gathered at the large gray Providence Zen Center set like a comfortable country estate in a green meadow near Cumberland, Rhode Island. The organizers at the center had so underestimated the interest in this conference that they were forced to rent a tent at the last minute to house some participants, and when that accommodation was made unusable by the rain, guests slept on the floor in hallways and lounges. Women and a few men had come from as far away as California, Canada, and Texas to hear the speakers and gather in small groups and workshops to express their concerns.

This conference was quite a different matter from the relatively peaceful Naropa conferences of years past. The rage, pain, and tremendous excitement expressed; the coming-to-awareness that went on in individuals within the workshops; the speaking of personal truth that characterized most of the exchanges: all this showed me that something deeply wholesome and constructive had awakened in these women. I was delighted and hopeful that at last we had within us the capacity to challenge and resolve the contradictions present in our chosen spiritual practice.

BASIC BUDDHISM

Buddhism began in the sixth century B.C.E., when an Indian nobleman's son named Siddhartha Gautama left his palace in order to investigate the causes of suffering, old age, and death. After years of searching and practicing austerities, he turned away from asceticism. Sitting alone under a fig tree, he attained "enlightenment," which can be described as "a direct, dynamic spiritual experience brought about . . . through the faculty of intuition . . . ."[2] or, more simply, "seeing clearly."

Siddhartha Gautama's enlightenment (which entitled him to the appelation *Buddha*) occurred without the help of a deity or even an earthly teacher, simply as the result of his own efforts. After it, while he could have remained in a state of solitary bliss, he chose to give to others what he had learned, and he spent the next forty-nine years of his life traveling throughout India and teaching the "Dharma" (the truth, or the way). That his early disciples came from all social classes indicates that he stood in open opposition to the Hindu caste system as it then existed. He was also revolutionary in allowing women to join the monastic order he founded.

Now, 2,500 years later, the teachings he gave are followed by somewhere between a third and a fifth of the earth's people. Chief among the observances they perform are generosity, moral conduct, and ceremonies expressing reverence. Meditation in order to achieve the goal of liberation or enlightenment is engaged in by smaller numbers of more intensely motivated practitioners. In the West it is meditation practice that is usually emphasized, and in some instances Buddhist meditation techniques are taught independent of all religious trappings.

The Buddha taught three universal qualities of human existence. The first is the *impermanence* of everything as it flows from birth to death or creation to dissolution. Next is the *suffering* in human existence. This concept has been variously translated, and one of the more inclusive interpretations is "the general unsatisfactoriness of life." Some explicators have used the image of a wheel set slightly askew on its axle, so that it rubs and wears as it turns, always just a little off balance, as *we* are almost always a little off balance in our lives. The third quality is *the nonexistence of the self*, a concept difficult for Westerners. In the unceasing flow of phenomena, the self is seen as having no solidity, no separate existence. It is viewed as an artificial construct, merely a tool for accomplishing actions in the world. When told to let go of belief in the self, contemporary western women especially react with outrage, pointing out that most of us need to *build* ego-strength and selfhood, not to destroy it. But this resistance arises from a misconception, for what one gives up are the qualities in oneself that obstruct and hinder, and cause pain—the impediments to full realization, such as greed, hatred, and delusion. In experiencing oneness with all phenomena one taps into an unshakable strength far deeper than the capacities of personality.

The *Four Noble Truths* form the foundation of Buddhist practice. They are:

1. We suffer.
2. The cause of our suffering is our craving, primarily for pleasant sense contacts and for survival—a craving that can never be satisfied because of the impermanence of the body and the transience of any particular mental, physical, or emotional state.
3. There can be an end to the suffering.
4. The means to that end is provided in the Eightfold Noble Path.

The *Eightfold Noble Path* is generally broken down into three sections under Wisdom, Morality, and Concentration. Wisdom is comprised of Right Understanding and Right Thought (that is, purpose or aspiration). Morality requires Right Speech, Right Action, Right Livelihood. Concentration is reached through Right Effort, Right Mindfulness, and Right Concentration (that is, meditation). This Eightfold Noble Path is called the Middle Way, for it avoids, on the one hand, losing oneself in sensual pleasures, and, on the other hand, giving oneself over to asceticism and self-mortification.

An almost universal practice in Buddhism is *taking refuge.* Often this begins a practice session or retreat. One "takes refuge" in, or invokes the protection of, the Buddha, the Dharma, and the Sangha (community of enlightened ones), which are known as the Three Jewels or Three Gems. In Western language, one takes refuge in the enlightened mind (Buddha), in the way leading to it (Dharma), and in those who achieved enlightenment by traveling this path (Sangha). Usually in American Buddhism the sangha is interpreted more broadly as the community of all those who practice, and this is the sense in which it will be used in this book.

The *Divine Abodes,* another mainstay of Buddhism, give an idea of its gentle and benevolent moral foundation. The four qualities to be cultivated are: Loving-Kindness, Compassion, Sympathetic Joy, and Equanimity.

As Nancy Wilson Ross has pointed out, "Buddhism recognizes no sacred and revealed Scripture and no Divine Personality existing outside and beyond man and his world. Buddhism is not a revealed faith but a religion of accumulated wisdom, and each generation is free to add to it without fear of the charge of heresy."[3] In this spirit, Buddhism was taken from India to other countries in the East, and in each new country its practitioners interpreted it through their own cultural forms, translating the texts into their own language, devising ceremonies appropriate to their needs.

There are two major strains or families within Buddhism: *Theravada* and *Mahayana*. (The name *Hinayana*, or "lesser vehicle," sometimes used to denote Theravada, was invented by practitioners who broke from the original teachings to forge a new path and who called themselves Mahayana, the "greater vehicle." Thus the term Hinayana is considered to be denigrating, and Theravada, or Way of the Elders, is more commonly used.) Theravada Buddhism is based upon the Pali canon, an extensive body of scripture first written down by the monks of Ceylon in 80 B.C.E., several hundred years after the Buddha's death. Pali is an Indo-Aryan dialect of the Buddha's time. Theravada Buddhism was originally dedicated to the ideal of individual salvation and set forth monasticism as the way to that end. While it has taken quite liberalized forms in the West, its practice in Southeast Asia can be seen as the "fundamentalism" of Buddhism.

The *Mahayana*, which matured in northern India during and following the first and second centuries C.E., is based on the Sanskrit version of the scriptures, and comprises all the forms developed after Theravada, principally Pure Land and Zen as they are practiced in China, Japan, Korea, and other countries, and Tibetan Buddhism. Sanskrit is the traditional sacred and scholarly language of India. The Mahayana proposed the ideal of salvation for all and developed forms of popular devotion and universal secular service to humanity. The term *Vajrayana* is used to indicate Tibetan Buddhism, and some practitioners think of the Vajrayana as a separate strain in Buddhism, but it is generally seen as a type of Mahayana manifestation.

One important distinction between the Theravada and Mahayana is the role of the *Bodhisattva*. In Theravada Buddhism, the Bodhisattva is one who has set himself or herself on the path to enlightenment or Buddhahood. In this endeavor he or she will practice the paramis or perfections, including loving kindness to-students most of these Zen centers have survived and grown to be financially and spiritually viable institutions. Korean Zen has also taken root in this country through the efforts of one particularly energetic teacher, Seung Sahn (or Soen Sa Nim), whose headquarters is in Providence, Rhode Island.

Tibetan Buddhism, as its name indicates, developed in the tiny isolated country of Tibet. Because of the harsh and mountainous conditions of its homeland and the resulting culture of its practitioners, as well as the folk traditions from which it drew elements of its practice, it is in some respects quite different from both Theravada Buddhism and Zen Buddhism. It places strong emphasis on loyalty to a teacher, and it employs techniques of visualization and other mystical practices. While Theravada accoutrements are usually fairly minimal and Zen in particular tends toward extreme simplicity, Tibetan ritual and trappings are elaborate and colorful. There are a number of different schools of Tibetan Buddhism, with their respective leaders, but the best-known representative is the head of the Gelugpa school, the Dalai Lama, who was also the secular ruler of Tibet. Because of his flight from the Chinese invaders in the 1950s, his establishment of a government in exile in India, and his several visits to the United States, he is well known to the West. The Tibetans, who have no homeland, are very active in establishing themselves in other countries: several Tibetan sects maintain successful centers and educational establishments in this country.

In addition to the above three types of Buddhism, with which most of the women in this book are associated, several other forms are vigorously pursued in the United States.

The *Pure Land* school of Buddhism, which developed in China, rather than relying on meditation uses recitation of the name "Amitabha" (the name of a historical Buddha) to qualify the practitioner to be reborn in the Pure Land after death.[5] From the Pure Land it is possible to reach enlightenment.

The Japanese versions of Pure Land Buddhism are *Jodoshu* and *Jodo Shinshu*, the latter being presently the largest denomination of Japanese Buddhism. Jodo Shinshu has established many centers in the United States, organizing itself under the name "Buddhist Churches of America." It maintains a *Fujinkai* (Women's Association) in most congregations.

ward other beings. With full cultivation of these perfections, h
or she will become a Buddha and will enter Nirvana at death. I
Mahayana Buddhism, the Bodhisattva is a person who has th
same wisdom and virtue as a Buddha but who delays the eventu;
entry into Nirvana in order to stay in the world to help all sentier
beings achieve enlightenment.

Most of the types of Buddhism practiced in the world tod;
have found their way to the United States, where it is estimate
there are several million Buddhists.[4] Three major forms follow
by Americans are Zen, Theravada, and Tibetan Buddhism. Al
practiced here are Pure Land and Nichiren Buddhism.

Theravada Buddhism is the oldest form, having arisen withir
few hundred years after the Buddha's lifetime. Considered t
most austere path, it thrives in Southeast Asian countries such
Sri Lanka, Burma, and Thailand, and it has some foothold still
India. The Theravada path is a gradual one, in which throu
meditation and study and the following of an ever more scrupul
moral life one eventually gains enlightenment. Although there
been considerable Theravada activity in this country for the
ten years, with the establishment of one large teaching center
several smaller ones, and at least one functioning monastery
ordains monks and nuns, it has operated in relative obscurity.

Zen Buddhism grew up in China, then was taken to Korea, Ja
and other countries. It expanded upon, and in some of its m
ods and ideas diverged from, the Theravada tradition. In Zer
tuition is the faculty most valued, and it is believed
Buddhahood is not something to be achieved or developed
exists in each of us right now. The effort then is to realize our
already preexisting condition of enlightenment. Undoub
Japanese Zen is the best-known form of American Budd
having been picked up and written about by the beatniks i
late fifties and widely popularized by writers such as Alan
D. T. Suzuki and Nancy Wilson Ross. Many Zen centers we
tablished in the sixties and seventies on both coasts, most of
headed by Japanese Zen masters and peopled with young c
dropouts disillusioned with their parents' middle-class life
their appetites for spirituality whetted by experimentatio
L.S.D. and marijuana. As the Japanese type of Zen enco
tremendous industry and commitment, through the efforts

Nichiren Buddhism is a Japanese form with various subsects (two represented in this book are *Nichiren Shoshu Soka Gakkai of America* and *Nipponzan Myohoji*), based upon the teaching of a thirteenth-century Japanese named Nichiren. It includes no silent meditation but uses the chant "Nam myo ho renge kyo," and adherents dedicate themselves to the goal of world peace, often engaging in social and political action. Nichiren Shoshu of America, alone among Buddhist sects, vigorously proselytizes and recruits members.

As might be expected, the majority of Buddhist activity takes place on the coasts, with New England, New York, and Washington, D.C., having many important Buddhist centers and California having perhaps the most Buddhist activity. But there are many Buddhist groups and centers in the Midwest, the South, and the West, one of the largest being in Boulder, Colorado.

The picture of American Buddhism can be a confusing one. For example, some women are drawn to Buddhism because it has so little ritual, while others indicate that they chose it for its rich liturgy. The reader will have to bear with such seeming contradictions, understanding them to indicate the diversity of practices that fall under the category of Buddhism.

The language or languages of Buddhism can be similarly bewildering. Preeminent is Sanskrit. But Theravadin Buddhists adhere to the Pali terms. The Chinese, Japanese, Koreans, Sri Lankans, Burmese, Tibetans, and other national groups translated the original Buddhist texts and developed their own forms in their own languages. Where an English term would work as well, I have avoided the foreign word. Words like *dharma, sangha,* and so forth I have defined when they first appear in the text, or if that was not possible, have footnoted them. I have included a glossary, (page 393), to which the reader is encouraged to resort if she forgets the meaning of a word or encounters a new one.

My hope is to make the contents of this book accessible to readers with no previous knowledge of Buddhism.

DIRECTIONS

Seduced by a fascination with orientalism or a taste for the exotic, or programmed by their female training and family background, some American women practicing Buddhist meditation have accepted situations inimical to their own good and insulting to their common sense and human dignity. But the honeymoon is over, and the actual dynamics of the marriage are becoming increasingly more apparent. We are Americans, with a heritage of egalitarianism and resistance to authority, as well as a history of women's effort to define ourselves and realize ourselves fully in religious as well as secular life. None of this is inconsistent with the essential teachings and practice of Buddhism. In fact, as Joanna Macy suggests below, it may allow for the manifestation of the true intent of the Buddha's original teachings, which have been distorted by 2,500 years of male-centered interpretation.

Joanna Macy, Buddhist practitioner, scholar, and activist, gives this opinion: "When the Buddhadharma [teachings of the Buddha] came to this country, it was rooted first in the old cultural forms—Japanese or Thai or Tibetan. Now, as they did in every culture, the teachings are beginning to adapt. You see, when Buddhism moved to the other cultures—Sri Lanka, Tibet, Mongolia, all of that—they were still in patriarchal hierarchical societies. *Now* the teachings move to the United States at a time when there is a profound revolution in perception and understanding going on about the structure of reality. This flies in the face of old patriarchal notions. What this means is that what is central to the Buddhist perspective can come out now: one might wonder when in the last two thousand years a situation has been so propitious for some of the core perceptions as taught by the Buddha to be revived."[6]

This book questions the prevailing structure of Buddhist reality and alters our understanding of American Buddhism by filling in the dimension of women's participation, women's insights and visions. In its analysis, interpretation, interviews, and biographies, it is meant as a segment of history and a tool for change. As the distinguished historian Gerda Lerner has suggested, speaking of women's studies, "What we have to offer, for consciousness, is a correct analysis of what the world is like. Up to now we have had a partial analysis. Everything that explains the world has in fact explained a world that does not exist, a world in which men are at the center of the human enterprise and women are at the margin 'helping' them. Such a world does not exist—never has." The knowledge that both men and women have built the world and that women are central to it is "a force that liberates and transforms."[7]

This book brings together the experience, insight, and wisdom of women culled from over one hundred interviews on the East Coast, the West Coast, and in some midwestern and western cities. It investigates the whole phenomenon of women's participation in Buddhism in the United States today, an inquiry in which the views of the secretary in the office of a meditation center are as important as those of a spiritual teacher. Some women in this book consider themselves Buddhists; others do the practice without identifying with the religion; some have left Buddhist practice behind; but in each case the woman's recounting of her experience and reflection upon it offer a unique revelation of the nature of the Buddhist experience for women.

Six major issues and concerns leaped out at me when I attended the Providence conferences and grew in significance as I talked with women throughout the country. They form the basis for the organization of this book.

1. STRONG VOICES FOR CHANGE

Considerable scholarship and independent thinking on the question of women's place in Buddhism has been pursued. This material provides a rich source of inspiration, for it not only offers a coherent critique of women's participation in Buddhist historical and contemporary situations, but also brings out visions of possible new forms of communication and practice conditions. Strong feminist consciousness wedded with deep Buddhist practice can give birth to a profoundly humane and creative worldview.

2. NUNS, MONKS, AND "NUNKS"

A number of American women have chosen to enter Buddhist monastic life. This choice throws into high relief the dilemmas facing, to a lesser degree, all women who do a Buddhist practice because (1) female monastics in some sects are forced to struggle for recognition, for the right to receive training, and for physical support; (2) female monks face the issues of celibacy versus intimate relationship; and (3) they must seek to incorporate an ancient, very specialized lifestyle into the hustle and pressure of modern American life. In many of us, at moments, there is the yearning to live the highly simplified and focused life of a nun. These women give us accounts of that experience and their own assessment of what may be possible.

3. LIGHTING THE WAY: WOMEN TEACHERS AND WOMEN-LED CENTERS AND RETREATS

The question of how to respond to authority is brought into an arena of some clarity when one studies with a female teacher, for the usual male-dominance dynamic is absent. The women in this book report that women teachers *do* relate to their students with less ceremony and more warmth, and they are often especially practical in adapting traditional teachings to contemporary settings, flexible in devising new techniques where needed. The importance of a woman teacher as a role model is enormous, for she allows us to visualize ourselves achieving mastery or liberation and to create ourselves in the image of someone fundamentally like us and therefore in harmony with our most profound potential. Yet the role of women teachers in the changes taking place in American Buddhism may be limited, ironically, by the very training and character traits that allowed them to win through to positions of authority.

4. CONSPIRACY OF SILENCE: THE PROBLEM OF THE MALE TEACHER

The abuse of power, sexual as well as other kinds, is usually examined from the point of view of the misdeeds of the teacher who has betrayed his ethical responsibility. However, to look instead at the experience of the *women* involved is to face the full human significance of those actions. The question of trust in the relationship of student to spiritual teacher leads to an examination of the place of sex in religion and the conclusion that, generally speaking, the rigid hierarchical stance of many Buddhist teachers fosters hypocrisy in the teacher and others. Because of it whole groups are drawn into patterns of denial and secrecy that mirror the dynamics found in patriarchal families, in which the man defines the reality and women are sometimes severely damaged. Yet many strong women make their way through this anguished experience into greater spiritual depth and wisdom.

5. BRIDGES: THE LINK BETWEEN BUDDHIST PRACTICE AND POLITICAL ACTIVISM

Eastern religion is commonly thought to foster a withdrawal from ordinary life or an acceptance of unsatisfactory conditions that precludes political awareness or activism. This view is sharply contradicted in Buddhism not only in this country but in countries like Sri Lanka where the Sarvodaya movement applies Buddhist principles to the making of grass-roots social change. Buddhist questioning and activism in the United States confronts issues of peace and war through individual and group work and concerns itself with the humane treatment of animals. It reaches into the sordid corners of human experience to touch the phenomenon of rape and examines the effects of childhood sexual abuse, a symptom of the powerlessness of children as disenfranchized, victimized people. Realities of race and social class also enter into Buddhist practice and assumptions.

6. LIVING TOGETHER: INTEGRATION OF BUDDHIST PRACTICE WITH FAMILY LIFE, JOB, AND COMMUNITY

Many mothers who have engaged in Buddhist practice in America have found their needs neglected, their practice and training interrupted or minimized during their years of caring for their children. The male monastic requirements of the Buddhist tradition have in the past prevented communities from fully accommodating practice schedules to mothers' schedules and responsibilities. Yet, as in the Asian model where practice for many laypeople consists of attention to their daily lives, some American women make motherhood itself a spiritual path and bring practice into every moment. In the Buddhist communities presented in this section, some participants make efforts to better meet the needs and realize the potential of women, as well as to accommodate people's intimate relationships and work in the world.

The following pages present a gathering of voices and faces, a partial map of women's participation in Buddhism in this country right now. My own views on the issues, and sometimes my own experience, appear at the beginning of each section. Then we move to visit and listen to the other women. In a book such as this, some people contribute through the intellectual content of what they say, some with the information they give, others by the experience of their lives, still others through what they stand for or embody. To enhance this differing significance, I have presented some women in full portraits, others in briefer treatments, some as part of a group.

Most of the women in this book fall between the ages of thirty and fifty. The vast majority are white and middle class, with many Jewish women, some Asian, several black women, one American Indian. While the majority of the women are heterosexual, some lesbians are represented in these pages. (It may be that lesbians are drawn to Buddhist practice because as homosexuals in a heterosexual homophobic culture, we have learned to take nothing for granted, to question everything, and to create a path for ourselves. Buddhism, a method of investigating absolutely everything, is thus familiar and compatible with our position in the world.)

It is said that in the countries in which Buddhism has taken root, a period of from three to five hundred years elapsed before it developed its characteristic and enduring cultural form. Given this perspective, and the fact that Buddhism in America as a religion involving significant numbers is a mere thirty or so years old, it is no wonder that it falls prey to the stumblings, the pratfalls, the convulsive castings-about to be expected from a being just newly experimenting with its capacities. As women, we can view this awkwardness as an advantage, for it gives us the opportunity to establish our presence strongly.

We are engaged in a great task, some of us quite unwittingly, some of us conscious of the implications not only for ourselves but for generations of American women to come. This endeavor puts us in conflict with powerful forces and asks of us clarity and strength. In the words of feminist theologian Mary Daly, speaking within a Christian context, "The work of fostering religious consciousness which is explicitly incompatible with sexism will require an extraordinary degree of creative rage, love, and hope."[8] As women engaged in Buddhist practice, we might choose different words, but the imperative stands out sharply: to bring our best and most honest faculties to bear, to awaken our hearts, to trust our experience and each other.

NOTES

1. B.C.E. (Before Common Era) and C.E. (Common Era) are used to avoid the Christian bias of the more familiar B.C. and A.D. and indicate the same time periods.
2. Nancy Wilson Ross, *Buddhism: A Way of Life and Thought,* p. 15. Other writers have given thoughtful and moving accounts of the Buddha's life and teaching. Two of the books in which these accounts can be found are *How the Swans Came to the Lake* by Rick Fields and *Living Buddhist Masters* by Jack Kornfield.
3. Ross, *Buddhism,* p. 47.
4. The largest estimate was made by Dr. Kevin O'Neil of the American Buddhist Movement, who wrote in 1985, "As far as we can determine there are around ten million people who consider themselves Buddhist within the United States. This is based on our contact with Buddhists nationwide. Since most organizations do not publish their numbers there are no hard facts." Other observers estimate a smaller number.
5. According to Buddhist thought, there have been a number of Buddhas who existed in the world, one following the other in succession.
6. Interview, 1985. More of Joanna Macy's thinking appears in the "Bridges" section of this book.
7. Interview in *Ms.,* September 1981, p. 95.
8. Daly, "After the Death of God the Father: Women's Liberation and the Transformation of Christian Consciousness," in *Womanspirit Rising,* edited by Carol P. Christ and Judith Plaskow.

2.

Strong Voices for Change

The women in this section are working to reconcile the high level of energy and self-consciousness of American women today with a 2,500-year-old religious tradition. While Buddhism provided a radical alternative to ancient Hindu culture, it still had to exist *within* that strongly male-supremacist milieu. These contemporary women move beyond that narrow context. In studies that give attention both to the texts (and as we will see, women in Zen, Tibetan Buddhism, and Theravada Buddhism refer to different Buddhist sources) and to their actual application in existing American Buddhist institutions. All of these women, for reasons they describe in the following pages, have done significant thinking and writing about the relationship of women to Buddhist thought and practice.

Within the context of our uniquely North American experiences, women interested in Buddhism are well aware, as Rita Gross, Buddhist-feminist scholar, reminds us, that not all of the repressive structures or attitudes arrive from the East. The sexism of both men and women in *Western* culture, she points out, also keeps us from full access to and development of our spiritual potential.

Some of the women in this section discuss the meeting of Buddhism with the cultural patterns and beliefs inculcated in our Christian/Jewish culture. They are attempting to distinguish between aspects of Buddhist practice that truly reflect the original intent of Buddhism and elements that are culturally more appropriate to an Asian country. They are seeking to discover or invent ways of viewing, practicing, and presenting Buddhism that will make it a spiritual path more harmonious with the lifestyles of American women, a path which honors our reality.

As Tibetan Buddhism is the form that most encourages its participants to study, it is no surprise that of the nine women presented in this section, four follow a Tibetan Buddhist practice. Three of these women are academics. Rita Gross teaches at the University of Wisconsin and has made especially incisive statements on the meeting of Buddhism and feminism in her books and articles. Jan Willis, chair of the religion department at Wesleyan University, has written of the historical relationships of women to Buddhist practice and has taught classes and workshops on this subject. Judith Simmer-Brown, who is cochair of the Buddhist studies department at Naropa Institute, organized the first Women in Buddhism conferences, held in Boulder, Colorado. Tsultrim Allione authored the important book on Tibetan Buddhism, *Women of Wisdom*.

But the first voice to speak out strongly on the subject of women's position in Buddhism was that of a Zen teacher, Reverend Roshi Jiyu Kennett, O.B.C., Abbess of Shasta Abbey, a Zen Buddhist monastery in California. (*Roshi* means Zen master.) In a 1976 issue of *The Journal of Shasta Abbey*, in an article entitled, "Do Women Have the Buddha Nature?" Kennett-Roshi wrote that the controversy over the ERA echoed the debate in many religions for centuries over the spiritual potential of women. Do women have souls or not? This questioning, she stated, "whenever it got anywhere close to being settled, was carefully shelved just in case women should know their true birthright of spiritual equality." She herself left the Church of England because of its repressive treatment of women. Buddhism, she found, "teaches, and has always taught, that all share in the Buddha nature equally. Dogen Zenji, in the twelfth century, wrote the 'Raihai Tokuzui' [see Glossary] making it absolutely clear that women's spirituality is identical with that of men . . . ."

But Dogen in the twelfth century was many centuries removed from original Buddhism, as Theravada Buddhists know, and long before Zen was invented the early texts, many of them attributed to the Buddha himself, told a different story about women. Jan Willis writes and speaks of these early attitudes and the changes that followed as Buddhism met different cultural imperatives. The most important book on this subject was published in 1979 by Diana Paul, a Zen practitioner, who was at that time an assistant professor at Stanford University. Her *Women in Buddhism* traces Buddhist attitudes toward the feminine through selected texts from the earliest extremely negative images to later affirmative ones. A meditation teacher, Jacqueline Mandell, in 1983 challenged the most ancient conventions when she gave up her association with the Theravadin school of Buddhism (but not Buddhism itself) because of her recognition of the sexist practices of that particular tradition. By this act she provided inspiration to other women to examine their conditions and challenge discriminatory structure and assumptions.

Two periodicals were created as a forum for women practicing Buddhism. *Kahawai Journal of Women and Zen* has been extremely important in addressing issues central to women, in offering female role models both historical and contemporary, and in chronicling the Women in Buddhism conferences as they take place in various parts of the country. *Kahawai*, begun in 1979, continues to appear, meeting the needs of women now practicing in Buddhist centers or alone. One of its founders, Susan Murcott, is at work on a volume of material composed by the earliest Buddhist nuns.

The Newsletter for Buddhist Women of North America, a more modest and shorter-lived publication (1981-1983), was put out by women in Washington, D.C. Karen Gray, one of the creators of the *Newsletter*, is a scientifically inclined woman who, in her speculations upon the possibilities for women inherent in American Buddhism, draws upon many fields of knowledge to offer original alternatives to present-day practices.

All of these women ask questions, envision change, and speak strongly for what they believe. In their efforts they encourage flexibility and innovative thinking. Whether they are committed Buddhist practitioners or they have made a decision to put aside that involvement, they add their honest and informed voices to the growing investigation of how one brings together a female perspective with this ancient practice and study.

JOY OF THE DHARMA

Jan Willis, scholar and Tibetan Buddhist practitioner, has some illuminating things to say about the reasons for the misogynist cast of the earliest texts, many of them attributed to the Buddha himself, and the ways in which they were altered over time to arrive finally at the later approach, which asserts that outward form, including one's sex, has no bearing upon one's access to enlightenment. She traces the development of the role of motherhood in Buddhism, from early rejection of it as personifying attachment to worldly things, to acceptance of it as embodying qualities of compassion and nurturance; and she emphasizes the important function served by laywomen in the establishment of Buddhism. A full professor and chair of the religion department at Wesleyan University, Jan does not define herself as a feminist, saying that as a black woman she has met the strongest discrimination in the area of race, but her scholarship and her classes on women in Buddhism raise and clarify the issues that other Buddhist women are addressing.

The broad green lawns of Wesleyan University in Middletown, Connecticut, sparkle in the autumn sunlight as Jan Willis and I leave her office and cross Church Street to her house. An energetic woman with large expressive eyes, who talks fast and laughs often, she tells me she does remember our first meeting. It occurred at Vajrapani, a Tibetan Buddhist center in the woods near Boulder Creek, California, in 1983, where she was teaching a weekend seminar on "Women in Buddhist Literature: Beyond Dualities."

In Jan's house I am struck by the elegant Tibetan rugs and note her altar in the corner of the living room. As we settle down on the couch with glasses of Pepsi, I discover that she was born in a little town in Alabama thirty-eight years ago. Her exceptional abilities and passionate ambition in the midsixties, when northern schools were searching for qualified black students, led to various prestigious fellowships, scholarships, and prizes at Cornell, to study in India, and at Columbia University in New York, where she completed her Ph.D. in Sanskrit and Indic-Buddhist Studies. She is the author of *The Diamond Light: An Introduction to Tibetan Buddhist Meditation* and *On Knowing Reality: The Tattvartha Chapter of Asanga's Bodhisattvabhumi*. A third book, *Enlightened Beings: Early dGe-lugs Siddha Biographies*, will soon be published by Wisdom Publications in London.

She met her teacher in Nepal, in the person of Lama Thubten

Yeshe, a man known for his loving-kindness as well as his great intelligence and learning. Lama Yeshe bubbled with joy, and Jan's smile when she speaks of him mirrors that abandon and delight.

As we talk, Jan becomes many people in turn: scholar, teacher, tough politico, loving devotee, and perhaps most predominantly, someone who likes to be here fully in the moment and enjoy herself. Again and again I see her eyes change, reflecting the mood of the story she tells.

Some of the stories are harsh ones, as she speaks of racist incidents in her home town and her civil rights activism in the sixties.

In her senior year, she says, she had to make a decision whether to join the Black Panthers or go back to Nepal to the Tibetan monastery to study with her teacher, Lama Yeshe. "I just really wasn't ready to lose my life, you know, I didn't feel very brave at the time," she explains, "so I ended up going to the monastery. And I'm glad in retrospect about that choice."

There followed a wonderful time when she and two friends lived with Lama Yeshe and studied with him. She and the lama became fast friends and scholarly colleagues. Then she returned to the United States to get her M.A. in 1971 and Ph.D. in 1976.

It was at the monastery in Koppan, in 1979, that she was encouraged to look at the particular situation of women in Buddhism by the questioning of an American student, Barbara Wilt.

Smiling, Jan sits back on the couch and begins her story.

"I was invited to give a little lecture on Asanga, who was the author of this fourth-century text I translated—the founder of one of the two big Mahayana schools of philosophy. So I talked about the life of Asanga and Asanga's view of voidness, and I mentioned that Asanga's mother had been cursed to be born a woman. And the next day Barbara came up to me and said, 'Well, what *do* the texts say about that? *We heard that*—she was cursed to be born a woman! And we hear that there are some Buddhist texts that say we can't attain enlightenment in a woman's form.' And I said, 'Oh, *come on*, look at Lama Yeshe, look at your own experience, have you ever experienced that?' I said naively, before I looked into things. I mean, it was true that Lama Yeshe treated everyone the same, but I gave this easy answer at first. Then I started thinking about it, and then I started reading the texts and preparing stuff on it, and the seminar came out of that.

"And when I got back to this country, Diana Paul had published *Women in Buddhism* in 1979. So, there were other people thinking about this. I use her text all the time when I teach the course on women in Buddhist literature, and a number of other books, including Horner's *Women Under Primitive Buddhism.* So now I teach that course. I did a weekend seminar at Vajrapani and I've done a ten-day series on women."

"How about the weekend at Vajrapani?" I ask. "What was your experience in teaching there?"

"Oh, it was terrific. I knew the people who run that center and they're just wonderful anyway, that whole setup, the kids, their parents, the whole organization. So it's great to go there any time. In the middle of the course in '83, which was Lama's last time there, we were all practicing hard, and I think it was at the end of that summer that people said, Let's do this little extra bit on women and Buddhism. So I did, and there were forty-odd of us. First we met at Vajrapani about how this thing should be organized. I told them, well I could do these talks, I had read this material, but what did people want to hear? So it was one of those open sharing kinds of things. One person just wanted to hear more positive things about female energy, wisdom, and meditation."

Vajrapani, a rustic practice center in the mountains just outside the town of Boulder Creek, California, was established by Lama Yeshe's students about ten years ago. It has always been a place where families lived and where women shared equally in the spiritual practice and management. In this rugged setting the women had to be strong.

"We had workshops that didn't focus just on women and Buddhism but on subjects like parenting and practicing the Dharma, for men and women," Jan goes on. "It came together so beautifully. At Vajrapani the women were so open. In Nepal the women would come up to me and ask, 'Do you think Tibetan is really a hard language?' and I'd say, 'Well, no, it's easier than Sanskrit!' And they would say, 'These guys tells us it's impossible to master.' 'Now, don't be ridiculous, tell those guys *of course* you can study Tibetan if you want!' At Vajrapani I started to hear that too, but at Vajrapani those women straighten those guys out, they work *together* there. It's taken years.

"One man said, 'All I can do for this weekend is do the food and maybe do the dishes so all the women can be freed up,' but we encouraged him to lead a meditation. It was a guided meditation and it was called 'Being a man.' So he talked about it—an incredibly clear, honest statement—and after an hour everybody was boohooing, guys were sobbing—there were two other guys who were taking the course. And one of the women there talked about giving birth, in guided meditation. You know the thing that says think about the love you feel for your mother and apply it to all beings—but that can give some Westerners a hard time because they don't have that love for their mothers—well here's this woman, she talked about *giving birth* in this guided meditation. We all felt our waters break. And then she said, 'Now instead of thinking about the love you have for your mother, think about the love you have for this little one that you just reach down and pull up to you.' That's the way to generate that love thing the Buddhists are talking about. It was wonderful."

Speaking of Vajrapani reminds her of some music they used to play there, and we break to eat cookies and listen to Jan's tape of the record "Awakening." It is a sometimes hilarious, sometimes inspiring half hour, for these songs on Buddhist themes are set to rock 'n roll rhythms, folk, and twangy Western-style music. They are written, sung, and accompanied by Buddhist nuns of the City of Ten Thousand Buddhas in Talmage, California, and they express the beliefs of Pure Land Buddhism.

Jan is delighted by her find, light and playful as we listen. Especially she directs my attention to the mournful-funny lyric "My Body," which is based on the Buddhist view of the impermanence of our physical selves. Jan's eyes gaze mischievously at me as we hear a nun sing,

> My body was the cutest thing
> Gave it the best of everything
> Plenty of fresh air and exercise
> Vitamins, minerals and apple pies
> Plenty of sleep, plenty of friends
> Rode it around in a Mercedes-Benz
> Then it came time to die
> Left, and never said goodbye.

As the singer goes on to detail the disintegration of the rotting corpse, we cringe and groan.

. Other, sweeter cuts praise the Buddha and encourage the cultivation of meditation. Jan and I listen quietly to the final soaring song, "Great Is the Joy," which is based on the overwhelming happiness of an early seeker when he finds that he too, one day, will become a Buddha.

"The sea of suffering is deep and wide," it finishes. "A turn of the head is the other side . . . . Great is the joy within my heart."

Jan tells me she cried when she first heard this song.[1]

Now it is time to delineate Jan's findings from her scholarship in the area of Buddhist texts: her theory on attitudes toward women as they were expressed there, from the earliest negative images through some surprising transmutations to the later more positive treatment.

"After that first questioning of woman's place, in Nepal," I ask, "when you started looking into the texts what did you find?"

Jan leans forward intently, elbows on knees, and now it is the scholar, serious and controlled, who talks to me.

"Well, most interesting for me was to find that generally the negative statements about women are clearly there, even misogynous statements. None of these texts are signed, but we know they were all written by men. Even the one text that is *about* women, the *Therigatha*, was codified and edited by the monk Dhammapada. In fact no Buddhist text that I know of is signed by a woman.

"Very generally speaking you could look at Buddhist literature as Diana Paul has done, noting that there is a typology there going from more negative to more positive imaging of women, of females, of femininity altogether. It is more negative at the beginning because the Buddha initially founded a celibate male monastic organization. And then Maha Prajapati asked to be ordained. She had raised him from the time he was seven days old. The Buddha was hesitant. 'My goodness,' Ananda, the Buddha's disciple, says to him, '*Come on*, this is the woman who *raised you!*' Well, the Buddha held back at first, but still he did the radical thing. He did admit women. Mahavira of the Jains [see Glossary] had done it just a few years earlier, so the Buddha had additional reason for hesitation because he saw that when Mahavira opened the gates, women had flooded the Jains and traditional society was falling apart. He didn't want to go around overturning everything. I mean you have to be practical too. So it wasn't an easy decision, nor should he have jumped to it, I suppose, to admit Maha Prajapati. And it is good that he finally did admit her. You have to recognize that it was sixth century B.C. India, and if you think that way it was quite a radical decision to finally admit women."

She settles back to explain this to me.

"The misogyny comes, I think, out of the whole psychological change that has to take place in order for men to leave mothers and wives and children and take up a monastic lifestyle. They developed this negative image of women to make that easier. In some texts *woman* is made to be a synonym for samsara [ordinary life, the round of suffering]. And if she is *that,* you want to get away from her altogether. But then women are allowed to come in. What's interesting to me is this funny transition period when you have women here, in robes, and you have these misogynous texts, and you're not quite at the full Mahayana that says sex has nothing to do with accomplishment. You've got this time where various texts are trying to include and reject women at the same time. And they come up with some great funny episodes, you know, in which they say, 'Well, all women can attain enlightenment but they have to become men first.' Just outrageous things, and they're usually quite humorous.

"But then you get the Prajnaparamita [perfection of wisdom] texts in the Mahayana, where the Buddha says, himself, that the outward forms, even those indicating sex, have ceased to matter.

"But some texts still gave a negative view of women, even a negative view of motherhood. *Now* we think of compassion as being a quality of mothers, but at first mothers were seen as embodying attachment and greed. And then over time the Mahayana tried it various ways, and eventually you have the more positive bent that females have the qualities of mothering, nurturing, growing, which is what the Buddha did for his congregations."

She pauses to think, obviously excited by the evolution of ideas she is describing, in which texts, philosophical arguments, and images change. And she points to the particular significance of laywomen to early Buddhism.

"Actually in terms of Buddhist history and socioeconomic kinds of factual data, women lay patrons became very important to Buddhism in South India. There the cult of Prajnaparamita as the mother of all the sangha originated, out of Greek influence and under a matriarchal society in India, one of the last remaining ones, and so the female was quite important anyway. Queens patronized Buddhism—they're very important to it. So you get sutras [scriptures] like the Srimala Sutra in which the protagonist is this queen who speaks, she doesn't need the Buddha to be there, she *is* a Buddha and *she* gives the discourse."[2]

But Jan loves most to talk about her time in Nepal and her association with Lama Yeshe, who sent her and her two friends to his own teacher, Geshe Rabten, for an initiation in which she would receive her new name, Joy of the Dharma. She tells the story with great enthusiasm, and when it turns into a joke on her, she is as amused as I.

"Geshe Rabten was going to do this ceremony just for the three of us. We were so proud. So he explained that at the ceremony you begged for these vows, and part of that ritual was bowing on one knee, and so you get down on your right knee. He said, 'Of course you don't have to stay like that because the ceremony goes on for some time. So you start out that way, as a symbol of requesting the vows, but then you sit comfortably.' Well, I'm tough, see. Willis is hard, I'm tellin' you. So the three of us get down on one knee, and after a while into it I see my friends sit back on their behinds. I go, 'Hah, not me!' Two and a half hours later, on this mud floor out in the middle of a field, it's over, and we all have new names." She laughs. "And my friends get up. Of course I cannot move! I'm frozen. I mean my leg's been numb for more than an hour and a half, right? So my friends have to lift me. Then the cook comes in and Geshe Rabten calls him, 'Come, look at this!' And the Tibetans are howling, and I ask, 'What exactly is being said about me at this point?' (That was before I knew Tibetan.) And Geshe Rabten says, 'What a perfectly great name you have, it was wonderfully chosen, Joy of the Dharma, look at all this joy you're causing!' "

The scene is so delicious that we let ourselves laugh for a while. Then I wonder whether, given her seriousness about Buddhist practice, Jan ever considered becoming a nun. My question occasions a final story that wonderfully illustrates the complexities of the meeting of East and West.

"Oh yes, I was ready to do it," she answers. "I went to Geshe Rabten and told him I was going to take the vows to become a nun. So we set it up for me to do a couple of days of special teaching and orientation. It was to be done by a German monk, very nice fellow. So he talked to me for a day, and I argued various things, and I was wondering about how limiting it would be to be back in the West. I was even then thinking about teaching.

"Of course, I had my 'fro. It had been a big year in the United States that previous year! So when the German got to talking about how you cut your hair as a symbol of something, when he touched my hair and said that, I said, 'Hey wait, it's *already* a symbol of something. This is an *Afro!*' So right then I changed my mind, and I never did become a nun."

ON THE MOVE

In her identification of and turning away from the sexism within the Theravada Buddhist tradition, meditation teacher *Jacqueline Mandell* (formerly Schwartz) became a role model for many women. She has stepped outside that tradition but has kept the essence of her Buddhist training intact and now works to translate it into contemporary American terms. Especially important is her exploration of the particular nature of spirituality as experienced by women, which she pursues in her own writing and in the context of workshops for women.

On October 16, 1983, Jacqueline met with her fellow meditation teachers at Insight Meditation Society in Barre, Massachusetts, and told them she was resigning. She makes it clear that she was not resigning from Buddhism but from the Theravada tradition. "I don't equate any tradition of Buddhism with Buddhism itself. So, in order to be precise: I left the Theravada tradition. I also honored my own position and integrity as a woman. As a woman, I could no longer represent a tradition which taught and believed women to be a lesser birth and life, and whose texts contained very clear passages of discrimination against women."

The changes that led to her resignation from Insight Meditation Society happened quickly, Jacqueline tells me, as we talk in a friend's apartment in Berkeley, adding that often in her life trans- formations take place with great speed.

"The process began in January of 1983, when I became aware of discrimination against women. That is, I *felt it.* Always before I had been aware of it, but not at all feeling a part of it. And in a sense for very good reasons. Being a woman for me had never limited where I was in Buddhism. No teacher had ever said, 'Oh, you're a woman, you can't do this practice' or 'you can't teach' or 'you can't do this or that.' Every teacher I had would go as far as I would want to go, and further. Yet of course I knew of some of the basic beliefs of woman as a lesser birth and, you know, com- ments about the woman's body, and all of that, but I didn't *feel* it. It wasn't even in my thought-realm. Because I was just function- ing as *myself.*"

A green-eyed thirty-eight-year-old with an observant manner, she speaks with great enthusiasm and animation.

"I began to be aware of instances of discrimination at IMS. When it started to affect me *personally* I started to realize what other women felt, and that these weren't *thoughts* or *ideas* about women's place in Buddhism or religion or the world but this was a *feeling experience.* From that experience I thought back and re- membered the texts and other times where maybe the men would be more a part of the decision-making process. Not because they totally took it, but because they just would naturally do that. And I would have a vote or a say, but I wasn't used to putting myself out that way. Even though when I *did,* change would happen right away.

"So I thought back on all of this, and I just started to feel the experiences that I never felt before, and then I wrote poetry about these experiences. I couldn't believe I was writing poetry! And then I shared it with people at IMS. It wasn't the most com- fortable thing to do because I was doing it in a context that had no condoning of this. 'This is not the practice,' was the message, 'This is not what we pay attention to.' Not only *that,* 'This is not *important!*'

"I have that programming myself, and I had programmed oth- ers. That's not the most appropriate word . . . well, what would you say . . . it's a training in the tradition. I was thoroughly trained in a tradition, and even when I studied in other Buddhist traditions there's still the same message. The whole heart of Buddhism is selflessness and emptiness and no distinctions. So I had to honor what was happening to me, alone. A lot of my journey has been done in an individual way. Whatever the reason, that is my own challenge."

Jacqueline gives the impression of extreme alertness, almost as if she is lifted up an inch off her seat to peer intently around.

"This was a whole subject arena that I did not want to have to deal with," she continues. "Then I couldn't get away from it. Wherever I went I ran into instances of sexism. And one thing I found was that even women who had been through the women's movement, who would identify themselves as feminist, still weren't bringing that awareness into their everyday decisions, often because of their unthinking acceptance of male authority."

Not finding other women Buddhist teachers at that time involved in a similar inquiry, Jacqueline began to look outside the tradition and found, "Wow, our *country* is more evolved than this system!" In her moving out from personal, spiritual concerns to political awareness and women's consciousness, she received the support of a few women therapists who had taken a similar journey.

"So then I went away for the summer to do some teaching and a lot came together for me at that time, which was that *I had a choice.* I could either stay and work this through in the system and help to effect change. Or I could move on with that knowledge and sensitivity. And I leaned toward the latter because I felt I could do much more work more quickly, knowing how slowly systems change, knowing how slowly *we* had changed. It felt right. This all took place more on a feeling level. And I did come to a place in myself where the hurt and the pain that I felt in the very beginning all just dissolved and metamorphosed into a greater awareness that then expanded beyond itself. So that I was more interested in teaching a broader group of people."

She leans forward and widens her eyes to emphasize her next words. "In my resignation from IMS there is no blame. I made my own choice for my own integrity and left a situation as it was. Completion with the tradition is still the best term to describe my own process."

And she adds, "I loved the tradition, and the amount that had been given to me was unbelievable, *and* the amount of service I had given was equal, so that my leaving, for me, was so clear. It happened in love, and with awareness. The fact that it was unprecedented in Buddhism was something else. There's no context for people to understand it, except for me expressing myself."

Jacqueline Mandell grew up in Cincinnati, Ohio, and after graduate school in Boston and work in the public schools as a reading specialist she set out in 1971 to travel around the world. Instead, she sat retreats with Theravadin teacher Goenka in India until February of 1974, while making short trips to see other spiritual teachers, and during these years she met Joseph Goldstein and Sharon Salzberg, who would become the founders of Insight Meditation Society. When she returned to the United States, Jacqueline lived on the West Coast, where she combined meditation with study of various mind/body therapies and taught meditation with Joseph Goldstein, Jack Kornfield, Sharon Salzberg, and Rina Sircar. Then she moved to the East Coast and taught intensively at Insight Meditation Society. While there she also studied Zen with Sasaki Roshi. In 1980, wanting to experience all aspects of Buddhism, she went to Burma to ordain as a nun and stayed there for several months; then, back in the United States, she ordained again at the Taungpulu Kaba Aye Monastery in Boulder Creek, California. (In Theravada Buddhism one can ordain for periods of months or even days.) And after that she began teaching her own retreats. She was one of the mainstays at IMS until her resignation.

This move brought Jacqueline Mandell to the attention of many women practicing Buddhist meditation who had never heard of her before, and it aroused curiosity and admiration and some criticism. After a period of study and assessment, she began to function as a guide to women in exploring their own particular spiritual potential.

She married in March 1984 and moved to Texas. During her first year there she spent a great deal of time alone studying, doing physical exercise, pondering the action she had taken. She read widely about women's place in Christianity and Judaism, finding parallels with her own situation, and she studied women's conditioning in society. And she began to write a book about her experience. Then she found that she was a resource for other women.

"I led some women's weekends, and that allowed me to be more exploratory. It was just another kind of freedom from form and an exploration of what is important for women, and an opportunity for women to come more into their own in whatever way they can."

Now she travels, teaching Vispassana meditation, emphasizing that "the heart of Buddhism" hasn't left her or she it. In her teaching, sometimes she finds it appropriate to use the terminology of Buddhism and sometimes not. "I started to be aware of myself as I was teaching and I started to be aware more of student response to that. So everything for me was called to investigation. It's not a black and white thing—I'm this and I'm not that—it doesn't have that kind of hierarchical or departmentalized way, but there's more expansion, a natural fluctuation that happens, wherein I can open to what is needed and I don't have to close down because of a certain idea. I can open and move with it. And a lot of times that's into unknown territory."

She elaborates. "There's no text to quote to a woman living on a ranch in Texas. Or people who might be very reluctant to learn a Buddhist practice but who really want to be aware in the here and now. It took my writing pages and pages to sift out an old language and go more deeply into what my own language would be, or to become sensitive enough to another person without thinking that they had to take on any other thing than what they needed in the moment. My own resignation was a freeing. So I can speak about my resignation, but the *true* aliveness is in where it's brought me."

She still sees a part of her path as teaching, although it is often in a more informal way—conversationally, or while taking a walk; and she still teaches meditation retreats.

"The women and spirituality retreats are a place for women to go through what they need to go through," she explains, "to be validated in their feelings and perceptions, and something more. I feel that women *know something*, and that the coming together in these workshops taps a new kind of knowing. So it's not just issue-related. My work with women is still evolving, so I don't have a basic statement to make right now, it's what I'm working on. And the women's spirituality—for me there's an exchange of energy. I don't walk in with an agenda. I walk in with as much awareness as I can and try to respond to what's there. And I'm also taking another step that's somewhat further than teaching meditation or teaching women's spirituality retreats, and I'm not quite sure what it is, because I feel on the edge of it, and that's come through with my writing."

So her exploration takes her further, and in some sense she takes us with her, for her sharing of her changes and her awareness with other women is an aid and enrichment.

KAHAWAI JOURNAL OF WOMEN AND ZEN

A few years after the early comments by Reverend Roshi Jiyu Kennett on women's relationship to Buddhism, the subject was publicly raised again, in 1979, by two young Zen women in Hawaii. Susan Murcott, *Deborah Hopkinson*, and others in the Diamond Sangha in Honolulu began to publish a mimeographed journal called *Kahawai Journal of Women and Zen*. The word *Kahawai* (pronounced Ka-ha-*wa-i*, as they patiently explained in their first issues) means, in Hawaiian, "little stream that moves boulders and uproots trees." For many years *Kahawai* has been the only publication of its kind (the *Newsletter for Buddhist Women of North America* lasted only three years), and it is read, studied, and passed around among Theravada and Tibetan Buddhist women as well as Zen practitioners. Unassuming in format and tone, *Kahawai* offers a forum for discussion of the concerns of Buddhist women.

The *Kahawai* collective has done special issues on childbirth, abortion, homosexuality, and sexual power abuse, and it has consistently published theoretical articles on Buddhist texts and koans (see Glossary) as they throw light upon women's role in Buddhism, as well as making available the talks given at the Women in Buddhism conferences. The influence of this publication is so pervasive that it can hardly be measured now, nine years after its birth.

To make the material in *Kahawai* more accessible (the 8½ by 11 mimeographed format of the journal's first years was not built to

last), the *Kahawai* collective culled the strongest or most significant articles from the mountain of material published in eight
years of existence and collected them in a book entitled *Not Mixing Up Buddhism: Essays on Women and Buddhist Practice.* (The title
is taken from a lead article by Deborah Hopkinson in the Winter
1984 issue.) With a handsome cover by Zen/feminist artist
Mayumi Oda, the book provides a realistic and sympathetic en-
tree for women into the world of Zen Buddhism. With its inclusion of articles from Tibetan and Theravada Buddhism, it will
also reach a wider audience.

One of *Kahawai's* founders, Susan Murcott, has moved to Massachusetts, no longer formally practices Zen, and is engaged in integrating the fruit of her many years of Buddhist practice and
study with investigation of her own Christian heritage. But Deborah Hopkinson remains in Hawaii where she still participates in
the writing and publishing of *Kahawai,* along with Michele Hill,
another early participant, and Lisa Campbell, who has been with
the journal almost since its inception.

Speaking of the creation of the journal, Deborah says, "One of
the motivations behind *Kahawai* was to reach the women who
might want to come to Buddhism through feminism, to make
Buddhist expression nonsexist so that women wouldn't get
turned off by it."

Across nearly three thousand miles of ocean, Deborah Hopkinson and I speak on the telephone about her involvement with
Kahawai, including how she and Susan Murcott started it.

"Susan and I met in 1978. She had come to Hawaii with an active feminist background while I had just finished a master's degree focusing on women in Japanese Buddhism. We began to
discuss ways to bring together our interests and our concern
about feminism in Zen.

"I remember vividly the day we went to lunch and simply decided to go ahead and do it during the upcoming training period we
were both attending. With our teacher Aitken Roshi's okay, we
were able to use a lot of the scheduled work time to develop
Kahawai. Without that initial time and freedom, we might not
have been able to do it."

How, I ask, does she see the function of *Kahawai* then and now?

"Originally, we felt there must be other people out there grappling with the same kinds of questions we were. We had an overpowering need to explore some of these issues: How do women come to terms with Zen as a tradition, which, at its very heart, is based on the full equality of male and female, but has gathered a patriarchal overtone? What is our heritage, as women, in this tradition? What will happen to that practice as it comes to the West at a time when the feminist movement is so strong?

"Now," says Deborah, "we have turned our attention to concerns about making Zen a truly lay practice, accessible to people with jobs and families."

Kahawai still operates at the forefront of this exploration, yet its publishers demonstrate a refreshingly modest approach to themselves and their work. Before we hang up the phone, Deborah invites me to come visit them at the Diamond Sangha. I reply that I don't think I can get to Hawaii but I wish I could, to see what the group there is like.

"Well," she tells me, "You've probably got a pretty good sense from reading *Kahawai*. We're kind of just folks."

SPIRITUAL REBEL

On the subway ride from Boston to nearby Newton to see *Susan Murcott*, I stare at the advertising placards, at the people dressed up for work and reading their newspapers, and I feel the overwhelming materiality of American life. When the subway car surfaces, I see out its windows the dirty brick facades of an industrial city. What place has Buddhism in this? I wonder.

And as I wait on a street corner near Boston College for Susan to pick me up, I think of the religious past of this region, its first manifestation in the beliefs of the native peoples whose land this was before the Mayflower touched its shores; then the Puritans, so conservative and shrewd and so convinced of the heresy of all other religions; the shameful story of witches tried and put to death. And the religions brought by the succeeding immigrants or invented here, as Mary Baker Eddy's Christian Science—here in the shadow of Harvard Divinity School and Boston College with their distinguished Christian scholars and ministers. What is the relationship of an ancient practice born in India to this wealth of religious precedent?

In Susan Murcott's living room I find that she is asking herself similar questions. A strong antidote to the exotic and hierarchical aspects of Asian-inspired Buddhist practice would be found in a firm grounding in one's own spiritual tradition, she suggests, so that one brings to, for instance, Japanese Zen practices, a thorough acquaintance with the Christian or Jewish tradition. And further, the American woman's spiritual Buddhist path, she maintains, grows in part out of the history of movements for liberation in this country.

Susan Murcott was raised in New York and New England and attended the prestigious Emma Willard School in Troy, New York. After she had been active in feminist and antiwar efforts, sojourned in Japan, and worked with Clergy and Laity Concerned in Boston, her spiritual quest led her to the Diamond Sangha in Hawaii by way of Australia. She says of herself, "I am both too private a person and too arrogant a person to take the conventional route to religion." Now, at age thirty-three, she has returned to the Boston area, where she lives with Ralph Coffman, attends classes at the Harvard Divinity School, and takes courses toward her B.A. at Wellesley College, and also teaches a course in meditation there. She is at work on a new translation of the *Therigatha*, a volume of enlightenment stories by the original Buddhist nuns.

In her large high-ceilinged living room, with its fireplace and beautiful red rug, chairs of green leather and dark wood, its flowered couch on which I sit, I see quite a different person from the woman I met at the 1981 Women in Buddhism conference at Boulder. Susan admits that she has left behind certain aspects of her counterculture existence and accepted this more conventional lifestyle. Instead of the long dress and bare feet of that earlier era, she wears a neat red sweater and tan slacks, her dark hair pulled back in a single braid. The same smile, however, and large clear hazel eyes light her face. She tells me how she came to Buddhism.

"There were two things that had to be prerequisites, for me, in a spiritual path. One, that in the theology or philosophy itself it was acknowledged that women could attain the same spiritual goals as men, that they had the same spiritual potential. Well, Christianity did offer that, stating 'We are all one in Jesus Christ,' or, equivalently, there is in the Gospels the basis for women's spiritual equality in Mary Magdalene and the other Mary at the tomb being the first to witness the resurrection. Second, women had to have the same authority within the tradition, and the same opportunities to exercise that authority. And I felt that while in Christianity there was a biblical basis for women's spiritual equality, in no way did women *in actuality* have the opportunities.

"So I looked at Tibetan Buddhism and I looked at Theravadin Buddhism, and they both said that the woman had to be reborn as a man before she could become enlightened. No good. Looked at Zen, and I encountered Dogen, and Dogen has a line in the 'Raihai Tokuzui' about how women and men have the same spiritual potential—we reprinted it in the first *Kahawai*—and further on in the same discourse he talks about women being teachers. And he wrote that in 1240 A.D.! So it was clear from his writings that he believed in both of those points I considered important. I was satisfied that here was a place that a woman could begin."

Much of Susan's questioning took place in Australia where she had gone to visit a friend and stayed to fall in love with a young Australian who was as serious about his Zen spiritual practice as she about hers. Later they moved to Hawaii to study with Robert Aitken of the Diamond Sangha; there they married and became house managers of the Koko An Zen Center in Honolulu.

She smiles as she speaks of this, her eyes bright and her face relaxed. "Our period of running Koko An was a very wonderful one, when we were very strong as a group. In that period we started putting out *Kahawai*, in 1979, and putting out the *Buddhist Peace Fellowship Newsletter*. The place was perfect for me. In those years everything came together, because I had wanted to integrate my feminism, my political activism, and my religious life, and here I was doing it. So it was heaven for me. I had nowhere to go and nothing to do but just what I was doing, forever. I just wanted to be a roshi [Zen teacher and leader] and that was all. And I loved my husband John passionately, and that was a part of the larger passion too. So my life couldn't have been happier."

Then, two and a half years after they had come to Hawaii, this life of tremendous fulfillment became laced with pain when Susan's husband began an affair with another senior student in the sangha. Having come from a family that stuck together through any and all adversity, Susan, partly unconsciously and partly because Zen, as a monastic tradition, offered no clear moral direction, responded to her marital crisis in the style of her family, sticking with the adversity, the ongoing humiliation of infidelity, and trying to see it through to a positive end. For two years, with much anguish, the triangle continued until the emotional costs became too great. Because neither husband nor lover would leave Koko An or Hawaii, Susan knew that she had to. "There was a feeling of having lost everything," she tells me, "not just my marriage, as if that wasn't enough, but my community of dearly loved friends, my work with *Kahawai*, my physical home, my religious home, everything I had worked for in my adult life."

Her former cheerfulness has been replaced by a look of strain, and her eyes have darkened. We are silent for a time, and I glance past her, out the window to the white frame garage, the spindly tree just showing its first buds.

Her criticism of Zen practice and the manner of people's living together in Zen centers comes partially from her own experience and partially from what she discovered as she went on a speaking tour to Zen centers on the mainland during this difficult period in her life. She spoke at the San Francisco Zen Center, where nearly a hundred people gathered to hear her. The Diamond Sangha was known for its innovative (to the Zen world) practices, and the SFZC people were curious about a center run so differently from their very conservative establishment.

"The San Francisco Zen Center," Susan says, "was so closed off that nobody had even talked *to each other!* So basically I was just a catalyst. Yvonne Rand and some of the other important women figures came down from Green Gulch, because that's where many of the feminists were.

"After I gave my paper I just opened it up to talk. And it was, like, whoooo! People started talking, and it just sort of sent this bolt of lightning through the community, as to what was going on, and must an authentic Zen practice be structured hierarchically? and women's anger at being mothers or cooks or whatever they were supposed to be doing in relation to practice—and just challenging all this inbred dogma, the way their much revered Japanese roshi had set things up in the first place—they just thought this was the way it had to be. It had become what I call 'Samurai Zen,' and it *doesn't* have to be that way.

"I stayed on in the San Francisco area for another three or four days, and each day someone would call me or come to me and tell me her story about having an affair with the then roshi, Richard Baker, and never telling anybody and how she had to tell someone, and I learned that there was this incident in 1965 when a woman tried to commit suicide because of an affair with him, and there was this, and this, and there was misuse of money, and . . . I was such an innocent. I loved the women I was talking to, I loved the affirmation I was getting as a spokesperson for women and Buddhism, and at the same time my own marriage was in shambles, and there was a part of me that was going through the same pain in relationship as these women."

Susan is silent for time, glancing out the window, her face showing some of the effects of that hard time.

Shortly after this speaking tour was finished, she came to the East Coast and decided not to return to Hawaii and to set to one side her practice of zazen (Zen sitting meditation), which had been the central theme of the last seven years of her life.

"I have not yet put together, I haven't wanted to put together, what practice means for everyday life," she says. "My concern now is that I used Buddhism as an escape from growing up. There were some values that I affirmed that I still affirm that are high ideals, it's not that I've lost those, but my practice was like a side-track away from growing up in some important ways. I'm speaking solely for myself here. The Zen practice is supposedly about awareness in everyday life but I had ignored some fundamental everyday life issues: for example, a job, a college education, money, health insurance. And it's my task now to take care of those things. I put in a lot of years, but I had neither authority to teach nor any credentials in the world I'd left.

"What I did, a very unfeminist thing to do, but I was terribly vulnerable, was to jump into a relationship. And it was, after all, *relationships* that were making the mess." She laughs. "However—and I give both Ralph and myself a lot of credit—we've turned our precipitous beginnings into a positive thing for both of us."

For now, Wellesley is becoming her community, particularly the continuing education students who are women of all ages.

"I've been trying to find what's positive in my culture of origin, and Wellesley connects back to my Emma Willard years, so that's a very integrative thing. I have an intellectual and scholarly bent that hasn't been fulfilled. Even though I've had to go back to completing my B.A., maybe I'll go on, maybe I'll have a baby, I don't know what I'll do. But I'm on a good path."

I ask about the spiritual dimension of Buddhism, and about the Buddhist community she has left behind. She shakes her head.

"There's a lot there. Zen practice and community is where my heart is and will always be. That's the part that can never die because I've known it, I've lived it, and it's me. I carry that forward no matter whether there's transmission or community in the present or anything. It was a yearning in me from childhood, to know where I've come from and where I'm going, and that has been fulfilled. I don't yearn anymore."

Susan gets up to make tea and brings it back to place on a low table before us. As we drink it she talks about the meeting of Western tradition and values with Asian forms. This is seen within a context of women's spiritual path, a reality that Susan is engaged in exploring and defining.

"The whole commitment of our sangha [community]—one of the things we represented to people in a lot of other sanghas, if anything—not that we were a vanguard or anything like that—is that we were making American Zen. We were talking about American issues, we were talking about feminism, we were talking about political activism, which are outgrowths of our Judeo-Christian heritage, outgrowths of our own tradition. You see, that's where, again, I'm back to my roots. Because I want to get that tradition from its own source, which is here, at Harvard and Wellesley and Boston College. You can't go to Japan and become a Japanese, but you can certainly take from what is the pearl of their tradition and meet it with your own.

"Then during my first year back here, we had a Buddhist women's group. We met once a month for nine months or so, with some wonderful women, Suzie Bowman and others, all strong and pretty long into the practice. Then Suzie and I worked together on the first women's conference at the Providence Zen Center."

Her book on the *Therigatha*—poetry by the first Buddhist nuns from the fifth century B.C.E.—she sees as an important document for women in Buddhism in America, and for Buddhism in general. The word *theri* means "woman elder," and *gathas* are verses.

"There are seventy-three poems that have come down in the Pali canon, Pali being the first language that the scriptures were preserved in," she tells me, and her enthusiasm is evident in her erect posture and shining eyes. "It's a unique document. There's nothing comparable in the Jewish or Christian traditions. So to my mind it's very precious material. They are enlightenment poems, and there is a comparable volume of poems by the monks."

Two translations of the *Therigatha* already exist, one done in 1909 by Carolyn Rhys Davids and one in 1972 by K. R. Norman. "Norman's is a very critical, scholarly edition," Susan goes on, "and Rhys David's was an attempt to be both scholarly and poetic, but its poetic style is very dated. What *I* have done is a contemporary poetic but straightforward translation, for the ordinary reader, so the work can become accessible."

She has combined her own translations of the poems with stories about the women who wrote them and has grouped them into the women's roles or their relationships to one another, giving the book a sociological-historical dimension.

"I want to point out that people don't become enlightened in a vacuum. Women don't become teachers in a vacuum. They become enlightened in a religious context and they become teachers in a cultural context. It's so airy to think that these things just sort of zap out of here and there. There are prescribed paths for becoming enlightened, and there's a practice; you do it for years, and you come to it. And then there are some rare individuals, of which the Buddha was one, and of which there are others, who become enlightened on their own. But people in society usually exist in interrelationship, and in that interrelationship they learn from each other.

"Women who have become teachers have done it in a tradition and in a lineage. But when you emphasize the *woman* part of it, to become a Buddhist roshi or teacher, you better not take a route that's not going to let you in. You need to find a place where there's the possibility that women will be given transmission."

Sitting forward on the couch, Susan speaks energetically. "Religious training is largely training in imitation. Just as learning to speak or write. You do those things with meditative practices. You imitate, and your woman teacher is your model. I feel strongly that women need models in the world, but also in the tradition. And especially those models from the very source of the tradition. The *Therigatha* material is so precious because there can never be more of it."[3]

She pauses to think and then gives her recommendation for the authentic orientation of American women involved in Buddhism.

"What I think is important about women in Buddhism is that the culture that supports the whole feminist issue has its roots in Western democratic liberation movements, and so *that's the lineage!* So, know that lineage. Know who the nineteenth-century feminists were, and know who Mary Wollstonecraft was, and know the democratic stuff in the French and American revolutions. Know that, because that's our intellectual heritage. If we're going to integrate it with Buddhism, it's also our spiritual heritage. And know what religious background you are coming out of and why you are choosing Buddhism. Why not Judaism? Why not Catholicism? Why not Protestantism? Why is *enlightenment* the path that you seek?"

DAUGHTER OF KALI

While *Rita Gross* is a true daughter of Wisconsin, land of cheese curds and beer and sturdy northern European folk, she claims allegiance as much to the Hindu goddess Kali (see Glossary) as to the German parents who raised her in a log cabin on a "marginal" dairy farm. A woman of great intellectual clarity and gritty courage, she is an important theorist in the area of women and Buddhism. She is outspoken in reminding Buddhists that the enlightened society they seek must incorporate changes in the roles played by men and women and the relationships between the sexes. And she urges feminists to look to Buddhism to take them past anger to attitudes more conducive to social change. Preeminently, Rita Gross is a teacher, always concerned that her students receive a clear and challenging view of reality, pushing forward her own thinking in order to enlarge and hone that view.

Here in this quiet university town of Eau Claire, where she is associate professor in the department of philosophy and religious studies at the University of Wisconsin, she lives in a comfortable white frame house among venerable trees. Her screened-in front porch is filled with plants; a well-tended vegetable garden borders a large lawn behind the house. Two big old cats, the black one named Krishna, the cinnamon longhair Vajra, are just learning to tolerate the newest animal, a small lively brown and white Shetland sheep dog named Lila. Inside the big old house, walls gleam with natural wood, and in the living room antique farm implements, rocking chair, and iron stove give an early American feel to the room, yet on the mantel dances a statue of Kali decked with her necklace of skulls. In the upstairs room in which I sleep are two elaborate Tibetan Buddhist shrines, evidence that Rita Gross is a senior student in Vajradhatu, a network of Tibetan Buddhist meditation centers headquartered in Boulder, where she is also a visiting faculty member at the Naropa Institute.

I am made welcome in this house, where I stay for several days with Rita. Previously I have seen her only in the formal settings of her lectures at the Women in Buddhism conferences at Boulder, where I remembered her as a woman in her late thirties who spoke briskly, with a focused intensity that revealed her confidence in herself and what she had to offer and her desire to communicate with great exactitude to her listeners. Here in her house I find her friendly and eager to have me know her.

Our first evening is spent at the Dharma Study Group that Rita founded, where she gives an introductory talk; the next evening finds us in deck chairs in her backyard. The dog rushes about, joyous in her freedom, as Rita cooks dinner on the grill for me, having insisted I must try some Wisconsin sausages while I'm here. (Not all Buddhists are vegetarians. Especially Tibetan Buddhists, whose teachers come from a mountainous land where farming was impossible and meat eating therefore a necessity, tend to eat meat.)

We have spoken of many things in my day and a half here, and I have learned about her growing up with parents who were Lutherans "of a rather strict and dogmatic variety." When she was a senior at the University of Wisconsin at Milwaukee, she was excommunicated from the Lutheran church for heresy, having questioned the authenticity of some of the New Testament. She had simply put forth some basic questions raised in biblical scholarship, which were, however, not acceptable to the Wisconsin Synod of the Lutheran church.

Rita goes to turn the sausages, her long soft brown hair falling forward beside her face. Her hands are strong, capable looking. She speaks with a confidence born of many years of lecturing before a classroom.

"I remember a particular confrontation with my minister," she tells me, "and I bring this up because it's really critical for my whole life pattern, for how I view religious pluralism, which is, along with feminism and spiritual path, the third issue I'm concerned with. The minister confronted me when he learned that I had begun singing in the choir at another kind of Lutheran church, and I said something like, 'But isn't it the case that Muslims are looking toward or striving to reach the same being when they pray to allah as we are when we pray to god?' And the minister said, 'Absolutely not, that's a false god, that's an idol, only Christians understand the true god, and really only Lutherans, and really only *Wisconsin Synod Lutherans.* Everyone else is wrong.' I just simply could not and *would not* accept that. That affinity for religious pluralism must have been very deep in me, because it was completely counter to everything I had been taught."

After earning her B.A. in philosophy, she went for graduate study in the history of religions to the University of Chicago, where she received a Woodrow Wilson fellowship.[4]

While we eat the crusty, spicy sausages and relax in the warm evening in her yard, Rita tells me that she formally converted to Judaism during her first year of graduate work. "The Unitarians were too purely intellectual for me," she explains. "I loved the Catholic liturgy but didn't want to get into another dogmatic trip. In my first visit to a synagogue I was surprised and moved not by the strangeness but by the *familiarity* of it.

"Then at the University of Chicago I was in the B'nai B'rith Hillel Foundation for years. I was a critical mover in many ways for getting the first traditional-format but sexually egalitarian minyan[5] going, in the late sixties. In 1966 I led the discussion one Saturday morning on 'Why don't women wear the prayer shawl and participate in every way equally in the service?' And that was the beginning of a new era at that minyan."

While writing her dissertation, she began to develop and critique the androcentric or male-centered model of humanity, a formulation that has been extremely important for feminist scholarship. "I was one of the first people who started using that term," she tells me. "It seemed to be a collective discovery of the term; I was using it before I read it anywhere. I developed the categories of the androcentric model of humanity and woman as object in androcentric thinking on my own despite the fact that so many other people also use them."

Her first touch with Buddhism came in a 1966 course in which Mircea Eliade[6] lectured on Tantrism. Leaving the class, she thought, "If I ever practice an Eastern religion, that will be it." Later she did academic research on Tantra (see Glossary). Also she did feminist theology, writing about Hindu goddesses as a resource for Western religions. And between 1975 and 1980 when she chaired the women and religion section of the American Academy of Religion, she edited *Beyond Androcentrism: Essays on Women and Religion* and coedited with Nancy Falk *Unspoken Worlds: Women's Religious Lives in Non-Western Cultures.*

While she taught courses about Buddhism, she had never practiced. Then in 1973, grieving over the death of a lover, she realized that the Buddha's Four Noble Truths really do describe our human condition. It was then that Rita decided that if she were going to teach Buddhism she should learn something about meditation. Within a few years she had begun sitting, gone to India, taught and studied at Naropa Institute, and found her teacher in Chogyam Trungpa Rinpoche, head of Vajradhatu. "I think part of the reason I was able to move so quickly from beginning to advanced practices was because of my former study," she tells me. "I had the appetite for it, I had the affinity for it, it's very much my home."

The next day, a peaceful Sunday, we settle on the porch and come finally to speak of the challenges Rita has presented both to the Buddhist community and the feminist community. Her eyes look out from behind her glasses with great intensity.

We begin by talking about her living here in Eau Claire, and she tells me she travels as often as possible to Chicago and Boulder to the Tibetan Buddhist practice centers there. "My situation is very odd, because I'm in many ways not just one of the senior students but because of my role in Buddhist-Christian dialogue and because of the very visible work I've done in Buddhism and feminism I'm one of the better known Vajradhatu people, at least in the academic world and certainly in the world of feminist thinking. So it's odd: I'm here isolated all by myself and yet I'm really out there working for Vajradhatu.

"For a long time I felt very poverty stricken about being in Eau Claire, but since I've become a senior student, in the last year or two, I feel much more that my work here is important and useful. In Eau Claire I'm able to work with people no one else would teach. I feel very strongly that other people should be willing to do what I'm doing instead of just staying in the more compatible situations."

Two nights before, in an upstairs room of the Unitarian Church, I had seen Rita give her introductory talk to the Dharma Study Group she founded. At the front of the room next to her chair was a minimal shrine. People sat in rows of folding chairs to listen, while some few sat on pillows on the floor.

Her talk, entitled "Calming the Mind: Meditation and Aggression," began with a description of aggressive behavior as coming from a tender place in us, a vulnerable place. She spoke of letting the aggressive thoughts rise, in meditation, and watching them, rather than letting them build to an action. The carry-over into daily life, she said, is the cultivation of *maitri*, loving-kindness or friendliness. "There is intelligence and energy bound up in the anger," she suggested. "Meditation is a way to unlock that and use it for enlightened action in the world." After her talk, students asked questions, and Rita responded with great gentleness and sincerity to them.

Two of Rita's students told me of their own experience of Buddhism as they have discovered it themselves and as she has presented it to them. One was a woman in her sixties who acknowledged Rita Gross for "opening the door and turning on the light" to her awareness of Buddhist ideas and practice. Toni Wile, a sixty-three-year-old widow who was persuaded by a friend to take a course at the university from Rita, soon began to sit at the Dharma Study Group and now studies and practices Buddhism with great interest and fidelity. It affects everything in her life, she asserts, and especially allows her to be joyful.

Ellen Alsterberg is a student in her early twenties who had experimented with goddess religion and Wicca before coming to
Buddhist practice. She is suspicious of Buddhism, having questions about "patriarchal structure, institutional structure," but
she is attracted to Buddhist practice. Recently she attended a
Shambhala (laypersons) training in Chicago. "When I was coming
back from that," she said, "I thought it would be a great boon for
feminism, if feminists would start sitting, in a secular way. The anger—becoming less angry as a political movement. Feminism
could really gain something by calming down a little, I think. If
you put all your energy into reacting against a system you hate,
then you inadvertently feed that system." And she concluded, "If
I were to become a member of a religion, Buddhism would be the
one. Its basic teachings make a lot of common sense. Reality, practical, whatever. You have to say, 'Well yeah, that's the way it is!' "

Now, on Rita's porch, we sit for a time, surrounded by plants,
Lila peacefully asleep on Rita's lap, and listen to the birds singing
in the trees outside. I mention the trend, as articulated by Rita's
colleague Nancy Falk, that in many religions there is a first generation that is open to women, followed by succeeding generations in which women are excluded or ignored. This is an idea
that will be pursued in the book Rita is writing on Buddhism and
feminism.

"Can you think of your book," I ask, "as a sort of wedge to keep
open the possibilities for women in Buddhism?"

Rita nods, fixing me with those serious, challenging eyes.
"That's one of the things I hope to do. I keep talking about this
tendril, the auspicious coincidence of Buddhism and feminism.
We talk in Vajradhatu about creating enlightened society. For all
of the stereotypes of Buddhism's not having a social ethic, and for
all of the pssivity that Vajradhatu has vis-á-vis social causes, there
is also very active concern with creating an enlightened society.
And *I* contend that it's pointless to talk about an enlightened society that does not consciously reform gender roles and relationships between men and women. I see a twofold agenda for the
book. First, I want to show feminists what Buddhist practice can
offer to provide some depth and grounding and some kind of

long-term energy. I think movements like feminism are very high on short-term energy, but they tend to burn out. I think that practice, and touching-in to that essential core of reality—the spiritual depth of existence—is what can provide feminism with vision and gentleness and sustained energy. Then, looking in the other direction, I want to show the Buddhist world that patriarchy and an enlightened society don't go together."

That morning I had looked at some of the more important pieces written by Rita in her effort to integrate her feminist thinking and experience with her Buddhist practice. At an American Academy of Religion meeting in New York City in 1979, Rita presented a paper entitled "Suffering, Feminist Theory, and Images of Goddess" in which she asked feminists to come to terms with that irreducible suffering in life that has nothing to do with patriarchy. Her academic colleagues were puzzled, and one friend commented, "Rita, this isn't an academic paper, it's a Buddhist sermon!" The implications her thinking may have for feminism are grounded in the understanding that while the altering of societal forms and attitudes may relieve suffering and should be vigorously pursued, there is ultimately no escape from suffering through action in a political or women's spirituality context. In other words, in a new world infused with feminist principles, in which everyone's material and psychological needs were provided for, people would still experience the outright pain and the nagging unsatisfactoriness of the human condition.

In 1980 her paper "Buddhism and Feminism" was published in *Kahawai*. I remember her reading it at the Women in Buddhism Conference in Boulder the next year and my being so delighted by her clarity and courage in delineating the deep similarities between Buddhism and feminism: (1) that both begin with experience rather than theory; (2) that this "allegiance to experience before theory leads to the will and courage to go against the grain at any cost . . . "; and (3) both are engaged in exploring how mind operates. I also appreciated her concern that we take steps to make Buddhist practice more accessible to women both in terms of role models, presentation of the teachings, and actual physical arrangements.

To date this is probably the most important paper written on the subject of Buddhism and feminism. A short version can be found in *Not Mixing Up Buddhism,* and the full-length article is in *Eastern Buddhist* vol. 19, nos. 1 and 2 (Spring and Fall 1986). Insights from both these papers are brought together in Rita's "Feminism from the Perspective of Buddhist Practice" *(Buddhist-Christian Studies,* vol. 1, no. 1 [Fall 1981]) in which she advocates Buddhist meditation as a useful tool for feminists. "Buddhist practice and teachings have suggested the possibility of transmuting anger and then utilizing its energy for more enlightened purposes," she writes, and she goes on to say that one can move on from anger to "some gentleness and humor, some spaciousness in the intelligence." She asserts, "Anger-filled reactions begin to seem like a luxury because one knows they have more to do with indulging one's own sense of being injured than with stopping the problematic activities." And she suggests that this transmuting of anger can allow one to be more effective in efforts for social change.

We talk on Rita's porch until the light fails and the cats come in to demand their dinners. Then, leaving our discussion for another day, we go out in the kitchen to make some dinner for ourselves.

PIONEER SCHOLAR

Until 1985, there were two basic texts on women and Buddhism. The first, *Women Under Primitive Buddhism,* published in 1930, was written by I. B. Horner, an Englishwoman who was a scholar and translator for the Pali Text Society. In 1979, *Diana Paul,* then an assistant professor of religious studies at Stanford who considered Horner to be her mentor in many ways, published *Women in Buddhism.* These two authors are in some sense the mothers of the burgeoning women's consciousness in Buddhism.

Women in Buddhism has contributed tremendously to our thinking about our possibilities within the institution of Buddhism, for it gives an overview of the portrayal of the feminine in Buddhist tradition, showing that this was not static or fixed but changed with the participation of women and the philosophical needs of the time. Diana Paul, an academic on her way to tenure when she wrote this book, performed a somewhat risky and independent act in publishing it, for the religious studies department in which she was the only female instructor did not consider such an investigation to be legitimate scholarship. While the book sold, and continues to sell, very well in academic as well as Buddhist circles, proving its usefulness, Diana's colleagues never recognized it as a worthwhile contribution to the field. Recently she fought a battle to be granted tenure at Stanford, where she taught for almost ten years, and filed suit against the school when she was denied it, on the grounds of discrimination.

When I arrive at her pleasant suburban house in Palo Alto where she lives with her husband and young daughter, Diana is jubilant, for she has just heard that her lawsuit has been settled out of court, with a cash settlement large enough to pay her lawyers and repay the National Women's Studies Association and the American Association of University Women, who sponsored her case. She herself is no longer interested in teaching at Stanford.

A round-faced, black-haired woman in her late thirties who radiates cheerfulness, Diana greets me and then leads me out the side door of the house and through the backyard to the little building in which she has her study. For women scholars, especially those who do research on women, it is not unusual to be denied tenure, Diana reminds me. She hopes that her victory will help to change the conditions at Stanford.

Diana Paul, who earned a Ph.D. in Buddhist studies and an M.A. in East Asian languages and literatures at the University of Wisconsin at Madison, who has taught everything from "Hinduism" to "Readings in Chinese Buddhist Texts" to "Women, Religion, and Politics," who has published and presented widely, and whose whole career has been pursued in the university, has now left academia to create a new career. She is the coowner of Interface Japan, a firm offering consultation on cultural matters to American businesses dealing with Japanese companies. For her consulting she uses her family name, Yoshikawa.

I ask her to tell me how she came to write *Women in Buddhism*, a very different book from I. B. Horner's study of the societal conditions under which women lived during the Buddha's lifetime in ancient Hindu India.

"It was way before women's studies was getting any popularity," Diana begins. "There'd been a few books out. Rosemary

Ruether and Mary Daly had written some of their first classics in women and religion, and I had read them.[7] In fact I had met Mary Daly when my husband and I were in Boston. She was at Boston College, teaching about Catholic church mythology and symbolism of patriarchy. She was talking about, basically, the death of female symbolism because of patriarchy. It was before I had gotten interested in Buddhism; at Boston College I was still in philosophy. I sat in on Mary Daly's course, and somehow things meshed with the symbolism in Hinduism, which I had begun to study. I saw how it would be interesting to apply the same kind of approach that she was talking about in the Roman Catholic church to the Hindu myths."

Having begun graduate school at Wisconsin in Hinduism, she soon switched to Buddhist psychology. One of her advisors told her of a story about a woman named Queen Srimala who had become a Buddha and suggested that since nobody had translated her sutra into English, and since Diana was interested in the psychology of Buddhism, this would be a fascinating text to try. It became her dissertation, and it was published as *The Buddhist Feminine Ideal.*

"As a result of that, I decided I wanted to do more tracing of the development of images of the feminine," Diana says. While doing her dissertation, she had amassed boxes and boxes of texts, enough for three books on the subject. "But I wanted to pick out a real spectrum of texts that were misogynous and texts that were sort of ambiguous as to whether women really did have capacities to be full-fledged human beings, and then the ones in which they considered them equal. By the time I started translating them there was a lot more information on women and religion. There was even a women's group by that time in the professional association called the American Academy of Religion, and Rita Gross was very involved in that, and Carol Christ.[8] So by that time there was a wealth of other religious studies material to allow me to do this book. So the timing turned out to be right for the publication of *Women in Buddhism.*"

Frances Wilson, whose name appears on the title page of the book and who wrote some of the material and translated some of the texts, was Diana's Sanskrit teacher at Wisconsin and helped her with publishing contacts. Diana explains, "When I first start-

ed research for the book—and it's still true among the real traditional types at Stanford in Religious Studies—we weren't sure
publishers would touch it because it dealt with a subject that people still thought was political and not scholarly, and that somehow
if you had strong feelings about what you were studying and researching it couldn't possibly be objective scholarship—as if humanities ever *doesn't* involve values! So Frances Wilson had
already had a reputation for very solid philological work, and she
was very interested in the project and happy to help me out with
her personal contacts to try to get it published. And the more we
started working on it, the more she herself personally was interested in the subject matter."

Then something wonderful happened. Diana received a note
from I. B. Horner in London saying she had heard of this work
and would like to read parts of it. When asked to write a preface,
I. B. Horner gladly did so—and the book thus received the bless-
ing of the grandmother of this field of inquiry. *Women in Buddhism*
came out in time for Horner to see a copy before she died in her
late eighties.

Women in Buddhism is a collection of Mahayana Buddhist texts
with commentary, arranged to show the development from the
traditional view of woman as an evil temptress to the later and
more popular images of women as Bodhisattvas, particularly
Kuan Yin (see Glossary). It ends with the *Sutra of Queen Srimala
Who Had the Lion's Roar,* a depiction of a woman who became a
Buddha. Paul's introduction and comments give a balanced and
scholarly view of the texts, and the stories themselves (some of
them translated for the first time from the Chinese or the Sanskrit by Diana herself) reveal a great deal about early Buddhist
attitudes on women.

Now, as Diana takes a short phone call, I look around her small
white-walled study to the cabinet of books, the Chinese scrolls, the
Apple computer. There is a certain disorder here marking the
transition from a scholar's study to a businesswoman's office. Diana
views the change without grief or nostalgia, telling me, when she
puts down the phone, "I served an important function for generations of students, and now I really want to try to apply a lot of that
same experience and knowledge to a larger segment of society."

Part of what has allowed her to survive the legal proceedings and make this transition, she says, is her meditation practice. She learned to sit zazen in Japan, where she went as a Fulbright-Hays scholar, and she has sat at the Kannon Center in Mountain View and at the San Francisco Zen Center.

"It was my practice that got me through litigation," she says. "I'm sure the university thought I was going to break under the cross-examinations. And I didn't. In fact, although it was stressful at times, in some sense it was empowering. Very satisfying. And at the deposition, my *colleagues* broke down. It was like seeing the real functioning of karma. It was just a dazzling and amazing validation of Buddhist psychology."

And it is the practice, she says, that helps her have the courage to be fully engaged in her new profession. "I believe people who do not practice some form of meditation or introspection are at such a distinct disadvantage whenever things get rough or when there's some kind of new challenge. My daughter knows how to meditate, she's very good at it. For a seven year old with lots of energy it's very hard, but she can do it for a certain period of time.

"The practice for me is the most significant benefit and reward of spending so much time studying Buddhism. It's the one thing that will not go away. Eventually my interest in these texts will dissolve, but the practice won't."

ORGANIZING, INNOVATING

It is a brisk, sparkling morning in Boulder, the massive bulk of the Rockies clearly visible as I walk the few blocks to Judith Simmer-Brown's house. I always feel energetic and excited here. No doubt it is the thin air of the over five thousand-foot elevation that brings on this mood.

Judith Simmer-Brown, cochair of the Buddhist studies department at Naropa Institute, came to her Buddhist studies with a background of feminist activism. It was she who in 1981 organized the very first Women in Buddhism conference to be held in the United States and a second conference in 1982. She continues, in her teaching and scholarly work, to bring together the issues of Buddhism and feminism. Especially at the 1982 conference that blending was accomplished. The organizers' and participants' confrontation of a difficult issue rather than avoidance of it led to a process that empowered the women to reach to deeper concerns, created understanding and respect, and freed their minds to concentrate on practice. It provides an example of the examination of a feminist issue from a Tibetan Buddhist perspective, in which *all* of life is seen as worthy of one's attention and use in the transformation of experience. As Judith Simmer-Brown remarked, "Genuinely gut-feminist issues came up and were dealt with in a very mature way, and genuinely Buddhist issues came up and were dealt with in a very mature way." This happened largely because of her flexibility and commitment to honest inquiry.

Judith has the WASP good looks and the confident manner of a junior executive. However, this is a modest living room in the small house she shares with her elementary school teacher husband, and she wears a casual T-shirt earned on her recent stint as an instructor on a round-the-world "Semester at Sea" sponsored by the University of Pittsburgh.

Like her friend Rita Gross, Judith came to her first interest in Buddhism while she was studying for her Ph.D., and her function at the Naropa Institute is an academic and administrative one. She was already sitting zazen when she earned her Ph.D. in Buddhist studies at the University of British Columbia, but she did not find in Zen any receptivity to her academic interest in Buddhism. Coming to Naropa in 1974 as a student, she found an acceptance of her intellectual interests as part of her Buddhism. She was teaching in Washington state in 1977 when Naropa offered her a job, and she made the decision to come here. "In Tibetan Buddhism," she says, "you learn how to bring together study and practice. When the two began to intermingle and enrich each other, it felt like I was a whole person for the first time as a Buddhist."

But the transition was not without its problems.

"During my last three years of teaching in Washington state," she tells me, "I taught half-time and ran a rape crisis center half-time. It was really the pinnacle of my feminist political involvement, because it was a federally funded grant and I was the director of the program and was responsible for the consciousness-raising of a whole region of the state. So I came to Naropa

from a world in which my real intensity of interest was in feminism, to a world in which nobody was interested in or cared about
feminism. I *was* ready for a change in environments, but I came to
a world of three-piece suits,[9] and it was a time when the sangha
was not very friendly and not very approachable. It was stiff-up-
per-lip and people buckling down to their practice. And so it was
very tough for me. I didn't find any women who felt at all the way
I did. I felt a little battle-torn, so I was ready to be exposed to
some new ideas, but I was not prepared for such a radical shift.

"In Buddhist studies at that time the students were almost all
men. I felt very amazed at the change in my life. Then, before I
was really ready to, I became director of the Buddhist studies department, and ran it alone for the next three years.

"It was after I had been here for several years that I got the idea
for the Women in Buddhism conference. I was surrounded by
men, I didn't have very many women around, and I really wanted
to know what people were thinking about feminism and Buddhism. Personally I wanted to bring those worlds together more
directly. So it was a very selfish motive."

While Judith was given the opportunity to hold the conference
at Naropa, she received very little support in doing it. And almost
none of her sangha sisters attended. However, it was well attended by women from all over the country, women who did Zen and
Vipassana practice as well as Tibetan. The conference promoted
a cross-fertilization of ideas, concepts, practices; investigating
how Buddhism and women's experience might not simply act
upon each other but interpenetrate and change each other. The
tempering of feminist thought and methods through the practice
of meditation, the opening up of Buddhism to the experience and
contribution of women, the finding within Buddhism itself of the
ancient female sources, the examination of women's experience
in their Buddhist groups, the delineation of problems: all this concerned the participants.

"That first conference surprised everybody here," Judith says,
"because it made some money. It didn't make very much—it
didn't cover my salary—but it certainly made a little money and
seemed to have some hot issues. It was very, very interesting.

"But there was something it didn't fulfill for me. Because an
awful lot of people there were very new to feminism, or new to

Buddhism, the real chemistry of feminism and Buddhism wasn't there in the first conference. There was not the real seasoned bringing together of the two."

The second conference, in 1982, occasioned an extraordinary sequence of events that led the participants through conflict and anger to honest sharing of their viewpoints, to the sort of meeting of mature feminist and Buddhist experience that Judith had hoped for the year before.

"In the second year I had a little better idea of how to do a conference," Judith says, "and I had a little more support. The second year was a real bombshell for Naropa and for our community because what it did was to bring out genuinely feminist issues. The issue of the role of the teacher was dumped in our laps in a way that we weren't prepared for. It was just before all the things were bursting out in the Zen community."

She refers to the disclosures of the sexual affairs of the Zen roshis that began to be made in late 1982 and early 1983. That second conference was attended by about ninety women, and the sessions were held in the Vajradhatu shrine room rather than in the classrooms at Naropa as they had been the previous year.

Judith describes the blow-up that changed the course of the conference and laid the groundwork for extraordinary honesty and growth of understanding in the participants. A woman who had heard rumors about the many sexual liaisons of Vajradhatu head Chogyam Trungpa Rinpoche with his female students announced to Judith Simmer-Brown her intention to raise this issue at a formal talk to be given by Judith Lief, dean of Naropa. The woman wanted to know how a sexual relationship between a Buddhist teacher and a student could be anything but exploitive, and if Trungpa's affairs *were* exploitive, what were the women of Vajradhatu doing about that. She was very serious about her question and the necessity of its being answered publicly. Judith Lief was informed that this question would be asked of her.

Leaning toward me on the couch, her face animated, Judith Simmer-Brown continues the story. "Judy arrived for the talk very late because she had been sitting downstairs trying to decide what to say. Everyone was very angry because she was so late, and everyone was marching around furiously. So things were pretty hot to begin with.

"Judy gave a talk that was quite abstract in a lot of ways, very short. People didn't get much out of it as far as I could tell. Then this woman got up and asked her question, and everything just began bursting everywhere. It was unbelievable, because it hit the nerve of all these Zen women there, whom she didn't even know, for whom it was the big issue. I had figured out there were eight different Zen centers represented in this group, and it was before any of these issues had been made public but everything was brewing.

"It just exploded. Judy answered the question by asking why did the woman assume it was always *Rinpoche's* initiative, that often it was the *women* who wanted to sleep with *him*. She said she couldn't speak for other people but that in her experience and understanding, she did not find it an exploitive situation because it was very mutual. No attempt was made to hide it or to use it in any way. And she fielded the question to other people from the community, who dealt with it with a great deal of humor. But all these Zen women began to stand up and yell at Judy, they were so angry. They were not going to be bought off by humor. They were furious and they began relating their own experiences. Obviously there was hurt in the room, and a lot of people were sensitized to it. Basically it blew the lid off, and the question came, is this always exploitive, or not? And what is the difference between an exploitive situation and a nonexploitive? So after this went on for a while, we agreed that we would consider how to pursue it the next day, because it was not resolved and people were just getting exhausted."

Thanks to Judith Simmer-Brown's courage and resourcefulness, a most extraordinary session followed.

"I beat the bushes to find some Vajradhatu women who had slept with Rinpoche, who would like to talk about how they felt about that, so that there would be some actual encounter there rather than people just dealing with everything indirectly. I managed to get enough women together on short notice. So, the next day we assembled and threw out our planned program and set up about ten small groups of about seven people each—little circles sitting around the shrine room—and devoted about two and a half hours for people just to talk about how they felt.

"It wasn't true-confessions time, but it was, you know, let's talk about how we really feel about this. The little groups were very, very intense. They were quite amazing, because there were people who were furious, some who felt fine about the whole thing, the entire range of emotion. The understanding also was that what was said was private, not to be repeated outside the group. And we tried to mix people up so there weren't two people from the same sangha in any group. They could say whatever they wanted to say.

"We talked, and at the end we made a big circle and passed a microphone around and everyone could say something about what they felt. There was an enormous sort of resolution in some way that people could talk this way. It wasn't that everybody agreed, but the feeling as the microphone went around was that the women in the group were tremendously relieved to have an opportunity to talk about it. The heat was no longer on Vajradhatu or Rinpoche particularly, it was a genuinely shared kind of thing. Several women said that they really felt afterward that the Vajradhatu women who were in their groups did not feel exploited and that this, while it was not a generalization, did indicate that the facts differed from situation to situation, and that they'd been very relieved to talk about it."

I am tremendously impressed by both Judith's and the Vajradhatu women's willingness to confront the question openly, when the impulse could have been to cover it up or sidestep it in some way. They showed exceptional trust in people's honesty and in women's working things out together.

"Yes, and it changed things," Judith says, "because from that point on in the conference what everyone wanted to talk about was practice: meditation and meditation experience and enlightenment—the kinds of things that I had really wanted everyone to get down to. So it was thrilling. And there was not a sense of obstacle at all. There was a feeling of vast space and tremendous inspiration and challenge to practice, and that whatever comes up is possible to deal with. It was so powerful, so fantastic. And at the end of the conference I was very moved. What I had hoped would happen had happened."

In our discussion of the third conference, which was to be practice-centered and which did not take place because of Judith's difficulty in scheduling with the Canadian female Tibetan Buddhist teacher Jetsun Kushok, we speak of the feminine principle as it exists in Buddhism. I am reminded of Jan Willis's pointing to the matriarchal influences in the Prajnaparamita, and of the work of Tsultrim Allione in her book *Women of Wisdom* in describing the female Vajra Varahi and the dakinis (see Glossary). Judith tells me that the style of feminism practiced by women in the Vajradhatu community has its roots in awareness of this female principle.

"You see, what do we mean by feminism? And what style of feminism has been developed by individual people in our community? It's not at all radical feminism, it's nothing like my feminism when I was director of a rape crisis center. There's something that's changed about it. Rita Gross and I have animated conversations on a lot of these things because she's more the textbook feminist than I am, in a lot of ways. I think that insofar as feminism falls into a poverty mentality, there's some basic misunderstanding of Buddhist teachings which are not poverty mentality in their basis at all. You know, Mahayana and Vajrayana Buddhism are grounded in some appreciation of feminine principle: there's nothing to chase after, it's much more actually coming to see what's there already. That, at least for me, is a style of feminism that you find in our community: it's not feminism as you might discover it in other places."

And she gives me her final thoughts on the matter. "In North America, because of our society being as it is, when we thoroughly understand the feminine principle and its role in mind, really coming to know who we are, there is the possibility of a nonpatriarchal Buddhism, a genuine one, being established here."

WOMAN'S PATH

One who recently made an invaluable contribution to women and Buddhism is *Tsultrim Allione*. Formerly a Tibetan Buddhist nun, now a mother of three who still seriously practices Tibetan Buddhism, Tsultrim authored a book called *Women of Wisdom* that, besides telling of her own Buddhist woman's journey, gives valuable and little circulated information on the female aspects of Tibetan Buddhism and provides biographies of a number of early female teachers. She envisions and practices the bringing of spirituality into everyday life and the integrating of women's ordinary wisdom into spirituality. She states that

"there is a vast untapped resource of female wisdom within so-called worldly life which could enrich our ideas about spirituality tremendously. Probably these resources have remained untapped because those who have defined the spiritual path for the last few thousand years have been men who associated spirituality with a separateness from nature and all that it represents, in terms of birth, death, children, and so on.[10]

Tsultrim Allione is in the San Francisco Bay Area because of her book, giving talks and seminars on the reawakening and reclaiming of feminine wisdom and teaching practices from the Tibetan Buddhist tradition. In a comfortable old Berkeley house on this warm October day, she is relaxed and pleasantly welcoming, casually dressed, with her short red-brown hair brushed back. As we eat lunch, she lounges on the couch, and as we talk I gradually realize that her languid manner and rather uninflected voice are not an indication of lack of interest but simply a characteristic style of presenting herself.

"Men have an inner knowing too," she says, "they have a feminine aspect as well. And what's happening now is that people, men and women, are recognizing that something that has been their birthright has atrophied and they are wanting to have that back again. The reemergence of the feminine is happening now because things have gone to such an extreme the other way. I see it like one of those toys that you wind up to a certain point and then it starts going drrrrrrrrrlllll and goes back. The masculine has taken over to such an extent, I think it reached its extreme a while ago, and that was when the suffragettes and all that started to happen."

She warms to her subject now, pushing aside her plate on the coffee table and relaxing back into the cushions of the couch.

"But the reemergence of the feminine is not just feminism and is not just women waking up: it's people being sick of living their lives in compartments and of being disconnected from their bodies and having their spirituality separate from their lives, and being totally disconnected from the earth. It's all those things, and a lot of things that are not labeled the reemergence of the feminine particularly, like natural childbirth. It has to do with connecting to the life process as sacred. The 'sacred' and the 'ordinary' become one."

Pausing, Tsultrim props her bare feet on the coffee table. And I ponder the thirty-seven-year journey this woman has made from her beginnings in New England through monastic life in Asia to her present situation as a mother of three living near New York City. Her life brings together the most intensive form of religious practice and the common female experience of childraising and family. "Tsultrim" is the name given her when she was ordained as a Tibetan Buddhist nun in Bodhgaya in January 1970. For three and a half years she lived as a nun, spending intensive periods in solitary retreat, studying Tibetan language and meditation practices, and making pilgrimages in India and Nepal.

Not long after this period, having given up the robes, she married and began to raise a family in the northwestern United States. And here, with two young children, she began to meet with a group of women. "Through this group I realized that being a woman was not a liability," she has written, "but rather that women had an ability to heal, to hear and support without judging and to have direct insight into situations. I began to love being a woman, being with women, and wanted to understand women more."

It was from this beginning that her interest in Tibetan Buddhist women's stories was awakened, and the seed for *Women of Wisdom* was planted. Later she taught at Naropa Institute, married an Italian, and went to live in Rome for seven years, where she gave birth to twins, one of whom died as an infant. Even as the busy mother of three, she manages to pursue a daily meditation practice. And she has written of her endeavor to integrate all her various disciplines and life experiences with women's spirituality and her present Tibetan spiritual practice, "I do not feel my path as a woman conflicts with practices I have done before but, rather, it is bringing forth other kinds of awarenesses."

In her book she has urged that "the path of a mother should be given its deserved value as a sacred and powerful spiritual path."

One of her more important contributions is the concept that

women's path to enlightenment may be different from men's. "Women need to become aware of what practices actually work for us, what practices are adapted to our energies and our life situations," she suggested. "We cannot be satisfied with just doing something because it is supposed to lead to enlightenment or blindly obeying the edicts of male teachers and administrators. We need to observe what actually works. Women need upaya (skillful means) as much as men need to balance their energies with prajna (profound knowing) and emptiness (sunyata)."[11]

Now, in this pleasant living room in Berkeley, over the remains of lunch, she sits cross-legged on the couch, her hands at rest in her lap, and we speak of woman's role as midwife, our connection to death and life, to the transitions. We speak of eroticism, and Tsultrim says, "If you are embracing the life cycle you are also embracing your senses, or your senses are seen as methods or as means, vehicles for enlightenment or for realization." In this she is expressing a Tantric approach, and she makes a distinction between traditional Buddhism and Tantra.

"Buddhism has the idea of renunciation and the monastic traditions and so on. That reality is very different from Tantrism (see Glossary). Tantrism involved living in cemeteries—these wandering yogis and yoginis, men and women, living together, waking each other up and using their sexuality as part of their spirituality. There's a very strong discipline in that, but not the kind found in an organized hierarchical situation. It is the discipline of confronting death, emotions, and sensuality every day, training the body, and using energy as a means to enlightenment.

"Because Tantra is a part of Tibetan Buddhism it's confusing. *Tibetans* are ambivalent about the feminine. They have very mixed feelings about women. I hear stories where a girl goes to India and meets the Tibetan lama, and he says 'Oh you're a dakini, come and sleep with me, and I'll transmit to you divine wisdom or whatever,' and if she says 'No,' then he says, 'Well, you women are just beings of lower birth anyway.' On the one hand they have this Tantra in which the source of the universe is the feminine, and disparaging women is called a 'root downfall,' and on the other hand the Tibetan word for woman means 'lower birth.' We don't know what Tibetan society was before Buddhism but it was probably fairly patriarchal, so they have that combined with Buddhist attitudes. I think it just makes for a lot of confusion.

"It's hard for me because I give these lectures and I say how Tibet has this wonderful Tantric tradition that really provides many different images of the feminine. So then women ask me, 'Okay, where are the women teachers?' I don't know what to say. The social structure reflecting the powerful feminine doesn't exist."

She has spread out on the couch now, propping her feet once again on the coffee table, and in her loose, light top and pants, sprawled as she is, she looks like a young university student at a late-night dormitory rap session.

She is critical of Buddhism for its emphasis on suffering and for the suppression of emotions that is often encouraged in traditional Buddhist settings where one is asked to separate oneself from and observe one's feelings rather than participate in them.

"If I was doing a retreat and a woman was crying, I would tell her to go completely into the sensations so that there's no separation, there isn't anybody who's observing it. It's very male, you know, to be there and say, 'What's my attitude toward this emotion?' I would tell her to go into it so that she would be actually *in* the color and the heat or the coldness or whatever it is of that emotion, so that there's no separation between herself and the emotion, and then it becomes a means of liberation. Everything does, you know."

One of Tsultrim's recent projects illustrates this attitude toward the emotions. She has begun teaching workshops designed to transform the "gross passions or neuroses" into wisdom through use of the energies of the five *dakinis*. In Tantric Buddhism, the dakinis are playful, wild, undomesticated female forces. By fully meeting and experiencing our emotions, Tsultrim suggests, we come to see the gift they contain and begin to heal "the split between good and bad in ourselves." She uses gestalt and other Western therapies and meditative awareness in order to help participants experience their feelings. Then workshop participants transform those emotions through the wisdom play of each of the five dakinis, using visualization, creation of a mask for each dakini, and dance/movement. Tsultrim states that these practices, while they may seem innovative, are very old; she quotes her teacher, Namkhai Norbu Rinpoche, who has said that before dance and mask-making were used for public performances, they were done by practitioners of Tantra to deepen and expand their understanding.

She emphasizes that her own spiritual practice is pursued within the requirements of her busy life. Some of her three or four hours of practice a day may be done while washing clothes or dishes or while sitting at a stoplight. "My boundaries of what is practice and what isn't are not so limited," she explains. "Often, female Tantric teachers were, for instance, washerwomen or prostitutes or winesellers. The whole idea was that you integrate with your life, you just keep washing your clothes only you're visualizing that you're purifying, and then suddenly at the end of twelve years you reach a deep understanding, a knowing called illumination.

"That's the ideal, to be just continually in the present and integrate the practice with whatever you're doing. And if you use mantras and visualizations, you're transforming, which is another method."

Her newest project involves a series of pilgrimages to the holy places of the earth, many of which are caves, to tap into the earliest sources of female wisdom. She plans to write a guidebook to these places. This plan grew out of her interest in the descent and reemergence myth, which is an important concept in *Women of Wisdom.* Major transformations and growth often involve a "descent" into darkness, suffering, death, after which one reemerges into the light, renewed. Such myths are found in many cultures and centuries and even appear in fairy tales in which the goddess of the underworld appears as Mother Hulda or Baba Yaga or the gingerbread house witch. The Greek Kore-Persephone and Roman Psyche myths are well known. But the oldest such story is that of Inanna, the Sumerian Queen of Heaven and Earth, who descends into the underworld where she encounters Ereshkigal, the Queen of the Great Below. The myth symbolizes one's return to the primal female life/death power of the universe and reminds us that in order to be reborn one must die. It mirrors the seasons and speaks of physical and psychological transformation, integration of the dark chaotic and infinitely creative elements of our psyches with the orderly, controlled tendencies.[12]

Tsultrim experienced her own "descent." New to Italy, where she had gone with her Italian husband, pregnant with twins, and much alone, as he was often away, she suffered loneliness and disorientation. The hospital where she gave birth would not allow her to take her twins home, and it was only after an agonizing struggle that she managed to do so. Then one day she found her baby daughter dead in her crib of sudden infant death syndrome. This was the bottom of the descent, the final killing blow.

From this devastating experience Tsultrim developed a passionate interest in the descent myths, and she began to think about and visit caves, which were often chosen as the sites of transformational and initiation rituals.

"They've done tests with parapsychology and found that it works much better in caves," she explains, "because caves are outside the electromagnetic currents on the surface of the earth. That may be a really strong reason why caves were used for rituals, and why the kivas [Pueblo Indian ceremonial rooms] were underground. Also it has to do with entering into the earth and being surrounded by earth. The vibrations may be affected by all that protection.

"The idea for the guidebook came," she says, "because I got so fascinated by that whole sense of going *down* for realization rather than going up all the time. And then decided that the whole path of pilgrimage—physically going to places—especially in America, has really been lost. Because we don't have an ancient Christian tradition as in Europe where all these Christian churches are built on old goddess places or on power places. So you get these totally void churches, with no spirit in them. Or else the Native American places, and most of those, because the culture is so whitewashed, have been lost. And so my idea was to make a guidebook to feminine power places, so that we could know where they were and how to get to them. What this would do would be to help to heal the earth, by people making pilgrimages to them, because they're like nerve endings or the nose, ears, mouth of the earth, places where she has opened somewhat. And also in going there *we* would be healed and benefited."

SHE WHO QUESTIONS

In Washington, D.C., lives a woman who believes that "In the next seventy years women will come to spiritual ascendance; if not, the world won't survive." She is one of the most radical thinkers in this book, a woman who tests all religious beliefs against standards of rationality, vigorously asserting that the route of the intellect is as valid an approach to liberation as any other.

Karen Gray, who holds a Ph.D. in theology and who works at the Smithsonian Institution, is attempting to envision a characteristically American form of Buddhism, something as yet nascent and tentative, which will constitute an alternative to institutionalized religion. Hers is a truly egalitarian vision, beginning with the rejection of all hierarchy, so that each person becomes her/his own teacher; and the use of contemporary technology, especially computers, to create a net of communication that will supersede churches and gatherings and allow for lightning-swift sharing of spiritual insight.

In her small apartment in the Foggy Bottom section of Washington, D.C., near the Potomac River, around the corner from the bulging facade of the infamous Watergate Hotel, Karen Gray and I sit at her kitchen table, talking for hours. With her neat dark-red bangs, her serious eyes behind round glasses, her direct manner, she gives the appearance of efficiency and the sense of someone who has arrived at a stable understanding of who she is. Yet as we talk she speaks of the changes happening so quickly to her and within her and the changes taking place in Buddhism in this country.

"The really big issue is, what is going to be born here in America in terms of Buddhism? I think what's going to be born that's really new will be born among women. Because for men the pattern is all there: the structures and the roots of climbing and gaining knowledge and gaining authority and all of those things, they have them all. Their full spiritual development already has a process laid out for it. Ours does not."

From New Hampshire Street NW far below this window rise

the sounds of traffic. The two-room apartment in which we sit is conventionally furnished, without extravagance or frills. It reflects its owner, who projects a sense of restraint bordering on asceticism.

She now begins to tell me of her three years of Theravada Buddhist practice at the Washington Buddhist Vihara, which she left because "we women must go out and see what's going to be born. When it comes to blossom, and we see what the nature of the flower is—its structures, its characteristics, its colors and forms—then will be the time for us to go to the men as equals and begin to build bridges and say, 'How can we help?' Because I think they're going to need our help then because they're going to have mimicked the path of Buddhism in Asia and they're going to be searching for their own liberation then. Of course our liberation wouldn't work for them, but at least we will then be a pattern and model.

"In five hundred years religions will have become defined by women, women will have the structures that will be the powerful structures. Because in fact power is leaking from the traditional religious structures of all the great world religions of today; they're becoming more and more impotent, less and less effective in people's lives. And what is born in women will become the new power structure symbol-wise, ritual-wise, etcetera. Five hundred years from now the men will be the ones who find themselves working within structures that will be female dominated. Assuming the species survives the next five hundred years, and that's an assumption I'm not prepared to make."

Karen gives the impression that everything she says has been carefully thought out. She wastes no words, makes no casual statements.

"I worry when you tell me that the Buddhist women teachers are doing their jobs so well," she tells me, "because it's very easy to mimic. I'm afraid most of the women are going to be inclined simply to seek out a teacher and follow her. That's not really what we need. What we really need is to do this very hard thing of looking inside of ourselves and saying, What *is* being born? What is it that is developing within us? And I deliberately use women's symbolism. I do think of it as a kind of fetus developing, that we are giving birth to something that will outlive us.

"That process of looking inside oneself is a painful and a hard one. I find it very difficult in myself."

I ask how best we can bring about change. Karen answers that communication is paramount and goes on to describe her idea of the most optimum form of this.

"What I'm envisioning coming about—and I don't know what it is, what its strengths and weaknesses will be, its formats and structures, myths and symbols and rituals, it's far too early to know that—whatever it is, I know it will come out of a group societal function of the species that is predominantly feminine, that emerges out of the feminine mind. I also believe in future technology being a part of this. How fast things happen depends on how fast communication occurs, and one of the things I believe in is that in twenty or thirty years if we women have computers and modems so that we can communicate with each other over the telephone on our computers, in that kind of thing the fullest, quickest, richest development occurs. We're still a decade or two away from that. At the moment we're just going at a snail's pace. And in a way it's too slow for me, I'm a little too frustrated with it.

"But that's part of the discipline we have to put to ourselves, is to not let ourselves just go off in a corner and do our own little thing, be silent Buddhists. The discipline is to get with each other and put our heads together. And when you find that there are great caverns of differences, and a person is fundamentally different from yourself in some really deep way, not to run away from that. For example, my tendency is to walk away from Zen Buddhist women and say, 'You're an alien Buddhism to mine, because your whole structure and format is antirational and mine is very scholastic and prorational, very verbal and yours is in fact prejudiced against that, so there's no way we can communicate.' The hard discipline is not letting yourself do that, saying, 'Even if there are these differences between us the fact remains that we share a feminine spirituality, and *that* is something that we don't share with the other half of the human species.' And out of that something very important is going to happen."

Her resistance to Zen, she admits, may come in part from her resentment of institutionalized religion, the result of the period of her life when, as a minister's wife, she had been very active in

the Episcopal church. Now she speaks of the demise of institutionalized religion and what might replace it.

"I don't know whether it's a fantasy of mine, but I find myself
saying often that all the great institutional religious structures of
the contemporary world are collapsing. They are becoming little
more than beautiful cadavers laid out to look very alive, but in
fact there is no life within them, no spiritual reality there. We
have to remember they were all born within a couple of thousands
of years of each other, and that that form and function of religiousness within human society may simply have run its full
course, and some new form will be born."

"People ask me, 'What's an alternative to institutional religion?' and I say I don't know. That's part of what's happening: we
don't know. It's like trying to imagine what the mind of a whale
who lives in a totally water environment and does not use words
but uses tones and sounds and body, what that kind of mentality
is. One can't make that transition. I don't know what future religiousness will be like, but I think it will tend to exist in computer
networks, for example, between *people,* and not in temples and
churches, not in buildings as such. It may become almost an elec-
tronic thing. I think there is more human sensing and sharing in
that than there is in coming together in a temple or church these
days where there is no spiritual reality and there is only ritual behavior and socially satisfying behavior."

Not only buildings are dispensable, she indicates, but teachers
as well. "I really believe that the *world* will teach me. That's one of
the reasons I'm a Buddhist. One of the basic teachings of the Buddha was that if you look at reality it will tell you the nature of reality: the Dhamma is right there in plain sight, all you have to learn
to do is see it. I believe this can be done without a teacher. My
experience has been that at a certain point teachers actually slow
you down, because their concern is to help you see and understand what *they* have seen and understood and to experience what
they have experienced. That always tends to be an effort to create
the banks through which your spiritual river will flow.

"I have to admit I've always been a radical. If there's some concept in Buddhism that is to me problematic—the doctrine of karma, for example—if I experience it as irrational and

unacceptable, then I lay it aside and go beyond it and I don't let myself get caught up in it. That means one is constantly making one's own way, finding one's own path.

"From my point of view, what will come about in the new religiousness is that there will cease to be this kind of vertical structure where there are the spiritually wise and knowing and there are the ones who have to learn from them. There will become a situation in which all spiritual beings see what they are truly doing, in a sense uniquely their own, and all of them are walking parallel paths. They share and grow from what each other gives.

In *The Newsletter for Buddhist Women of North America,* which she copublished, she elaborated on this idea:

The religions of the past come overloaded with powerful structures, hierarchically designed: experts/novices, leaders/followers, teachers/learners, advanced/beginners. I find this a profoundly male way of ordering things. Dare we break it? Dare we think of ourselves as *each* an expert on her own space/time perspective, experience and understanding? Dare we think of *all* of us as learners—just beginning a brand new journey into new spiritual forms—even, eventually, new social forms? (March 1982)

Now Karen has more to say about this egalitarian model of spirituality.

"The Buddha was quite right when he said, 'In five thousand years my way of telling the Dhamma is going to die,' only he was wrong about the time, it actually was about twenty-five hundred years. The telling of the Dhamma that Siddhartha gave is dying out and ceasing to be effective. I tend to suspect the new telling will not be that of a Buddha as such—maybe that whole period of human evolution has ceased to exist—and what it will be is a *group* telling. We will as a group generate what will never be as cohesive a statement as existed back then. What we will have in the future is our common experience.

"What there are going to be is perhaps much more like what we called 'primitive' religiousness, which wasn't primitive at all—and that is the deep spiritual experiences of a people shared among themselves. Perhaps early American Indian religiousness was closer to that too, and that's why some Indian religions and Buddhism are finding similarities. Buddhism I think will survive because it has the flexibility to grow into this. I am not convinced that the Levantine traditions of Judaism, Christianity, and Islam can."

On Sunday morning I go out to run and find the footpath along the old Chesapeake and Ohio canal. I pass the locks in the narrow channel, see the muddy water trapped there. In one section floats an old boat, wide bowed, low, and clumsy looking.

As I run I think of Karen Gray's history, how at a very early age, back in Spokane, Washington, where she grew up as the daughter of a truck mechanic, she was troubled by certain problems within Christian doctrine, particularly the concept of theodicy; that is, given a benign god, how can one explain the presence of so much suffering in the world? At her first contact with Buddhist teachings, she recognized them as being what she believed. But she went on trying to be a good Christian, through Harvard Divinity School where she earned the S.T.B. (Scientiae Theologicae Baccalaurei), fell in love with another Harvard Divinity School student, and went with him to become a minister's wife at a wealthy, prestigious church in Washington, D.C. In Edinburgh, Scotland, where she and her husband later journeyed to study for their Ph.D.'s, Karen went on struggling with her conflict in beliefs, coming to the realization that "If I took god out of the universe it became a beautiful, wonderful thing, because it operated by its own principles. I realized I was an atheist, or needed to become one."

When I return to Karen's apartment on this sunny Sunday morning, she is up and dressed, waiting to fix breakfast and willing to tell me of the next chapter in her life, in which, back in Washington after the breakup of her marriage, she realized she could not continue to be religiously split. She began to study at the Washington Buddhist Vihara, an institution housing Sri Lankan monks. These men she described as "happy and simple; scholars, but gentle benign scholars." There was immense relief in her finally beginning to practice and study with these men.

"Coming to Buddhism was a process of liberation," she says, "of just letting go of all the efforts to be Christian, of all the ways to try to find a god with whom I could make peace, to try to find meaning within the Christian doctrine. It's as if I had been wearing sunglasses and suddenly I said, 'Okay Karen, take the sunglasses off and look at things the way you know they really are.'

"Being a Buddhist is, in a sense, a coming to continual clarity. It is like having layers of colored glass taken off each day of your life. You feel you're seeing a little more clearly, more deeply, more fully than you did the day before. It is a continually trans-formational experience."

While we eat breakfast, Karen tells me that she insists on living her Buddhist practice at home and at her job.

"Every morning as I'm taking a shower and getting ready for the day I review the precepts and I think about how I am going to try to live them during the day," she explains. "The hardest for me in my job is the one which has to do with the proper use of language—not lying, not being harsh, not being deceptive—because the modern world functions on the basis of deception. The modern business world doesn't function well with honesty. Things break down when honesty is brought into that context. Trying to be a Buddhist in the modern world, in the sense of that precept, is extremely difficult. My coworkers are becoming more and more tolerant of the other ways in which my Buddhism affects my daily life—that I don't order a drink at a luncheon, the fact that I prefer not to eat meat—but the fact that I don't want to be asked to lie, or to mislead, or to use harsh language on somebody, that bothers them. And I can see that sometimes I affect the structures, I threaten them, I shake them, and when structures break down things don't go smoothly, so I cause trouble for them and for me. Sometimes I am not the most easy-to-get-along-with person on earth, as is often true of people seeking to actualize high ethical standards. But to me that is the challenge.

"I think that many of us, and perhaps even in the final sense all of us, do our own spirituality. We make our own paths and we make our own decisions and we don't apologize for them. I don't apologize for the fact that I have no connection with Buddhism and yet I consider myself a Buddhist. That's where I am now. And people have to accept that and if they can't, they must distance themselves from me so they are not caused pain by the way I am. And I think that will be true of all of us, that our spirituality will be highly individual, but somehow women like Sister Dharmapali [Karen's friend, with whom, along with Carol Hyland, she published the *Newsletter*], women like myself and women like you must still, over that, lay levels of communication, because otherwise this common river that we hope will come into being isn't going to exist."

I notice that many of the books on Karen's shelves are science books, and I ask her about this. She says she reads widely in math, biology, chemistry, physics, astrophysics, particle physics.

"I'm trying to understand them," she tells me, "and I'm finding that Buddhism fits them. There's not a lot of tension the way there was with Christianity. Whatever Buddhism is for me must be honest with science. I believe in the scientific mentality, in which you're always *in process* to your next definition. That is very consistent with what Buddhism is.

"And I love nature. I am very deeply concerned about the future of the earth, as a living organism. Much of science is turned in this direction.

"What we really need to be doing is to find the sense in which we are one with our earth. In that sense, perhaps, the Native Americans are closer to true spirituality than Buddhism is. But Buddhism has all that it takes to become that way: the core is there, the structure is there, the basic sensitivity and sensibility is there.

"Of course the Native Americans are very deeply developed spiritually but not scientifically. I like to think that I am learning to think scientifically, and to me that is part of the spiritual process: to learn to question, to be analytical, always to doubt that you've found the final answer. The message that you can never hold it and everything is always changing—aside from the fact that you're always only partially perceiving—the message is that the process of going through those continual transitions is itself the process of enlightenment.

"What I am trying to be is a scientific spiritual Buddhist woman."

A consistent bright thread runs through Karen's life of energetic effort and continual questioning and challenging of herself.

"I believe very much in joy. I don't think happiness is important. In my mind there is an enormous difference between happiness and joy. Happiness is fun and it comes and it goes and it's very ephemeral. And joy is something that you live with and you have all the time. It is there, even when you're sad. Since my liberation from Christianity into letting myself be Buddhist, I don't think there has been any time in my life when there has not been an undercurrent of joy. In my father's death, in the loss of some close friends, when I was deeply saddened, there has never been a time when there has not been a sense of incredible serenity and joy. Partly because I've made peace with the universe, but partly because the whole Buddhist way of living and growing is just so deeply helpful."

NOTES

1. "Awakening" is available on tape and record from Wondrous Sound Music, City of Ten Thousand Buddhas, Box 217, Talmage, CA 95481.
2. Jan has developed these ideas further in "Nuns and Benefactresses: The Role of Women in the Development of Buddhism," in *Women, Religion, and Social Change,* edited by Yvonne Yazbeck Haddad and Ellison Banks Findly.
3. Susan Murcott has written about and presented some of the poems from the *Therigatha* in her article "The Original Buddhist Women" in *Not Mixing Up Buddhism.*
4. Rita Gross has written of her life up until 1984 in "Three Strikes and You're Out: An Autobiography at Mid-Life" in *A Time to Weep and a Time to Sing: Faith Stories of Women Scholars of Religion,* edited by Mary Jo Meadow and Carole A. Rayburn.
5. A properly constituted group for a public Jewish prayer service, made up of at least ten Jewish males over thirteen years of age.
6. Mircea Eliade, professor at the University of Chicago for thirty years and until his retirement head of its department of religions, was a historian of religions, novelist, and playwright, author of more than fifty books, international authority on myth and symbol, and one of the great authorities on comparative religion.
7. Rosemary Ruether and Mary Daly are two prominent theorists on women in religion. Their early works include: Daly, *The Church and the Second Sex* (New York: Harper & Row, 1968) and *Beyond God the Father;* Ruether, *The Church Against Itself* (New York: Herder & Herder, 1967) and *Religion and Sexism.*
8. Carol P. Christ is coeditor of *Womanspirit Rising: A Feminist Reader in Religion* and author of *Diving Deep and Surfacing: Women Writers on Spiritual Quest* and *Laughter of Aphrodite: Reflections on a Journey to the Goddess.*
9. No dress code was ever imposed at Vajradhatu and Naropa, but Chogyam Trungpa Rinpoche began to dress as people do in conventional business settings and his students, in Judith's words, "followed suit."
10. Allione, *Women of Wisdom,* p. 20
11. Allione, *Women of Wisdom,* p. 17.
12. For a detailed investigation of the significance of the Inanna-Ereshkigal myth for modern women, see *Descent to the Goddess* by Sylvia Brinton Perera.

Jan Willis

Jacqueline Mandell

Susan Murcott

Deborah Hopkinson

Rita Gross

Diana Paul

Judith Simmer-Brown

Tsultrim Allione

Karen Gray

3.

Nuns, Monks, and "Nunks"[1]

My first glimpse of a Buddhist female monastic came in the summer of 1981 on a mountain in New Mexico. Treelight and I had been driving east from California across Arizona on our way to the Women in Buddhism conference in Boulder, Colorado. As we crossed the vast dream of desert, we draped wet towels on our heads and chests for a few minutes' relief from the staggering heat, and I read a book that hurt me in some deep way. It was called *Women Under Primitive Buddhism.* In the speeding car, now and then looking up to see the sacred land of the Hopi people, I read this patiently detailed description of the lives of the first Buddhist nuns in India. This account proved profoundly disillusioning to me as a feminist and a new practitioner of Theravada Buddhism, for it portrayed the Buddha as reluctant to establish a women's order and finally, under duress, establishing it with the stipulation that the women accept rules insuring their institutional inferiority and subservience to men.

Following an intuition of Treelight's we turned off the highway and drove into a Hopi village. In an open area a ceremony was taking place. Thirty or more male figures danced in a row. I call them "figures" because they seemed something other than mere people, with their faces dramatically hidden behind identical beaked masks, their bodies covered in feathers and bright cloth, their movements perfectly coordinated. Chains of absolutely alike figures danced a slow and unpredictable step in the cruel sun, on the baked earth. Standing in the heat, watching, I dropped out of time into some vast boundaryless realm. I could as easily have been in sixth century B.C.E. India, prisoner of Hindu culture, allowed onto the path of Buddhist liberation but hobbled by the oppressive regulations placed upon women and by the scriptures themselves.

Among the Hopis I felt that I was no longer in the United States or any other such limited delineation but had been transported to an ancient land and culture. The heat enwrapped and subjugated me. The sky flapped limitless above. This was not the place for rationalizations, or for the perception that most probably I am incapable of imagining the mental state of a woman in ancient India, where Hindu law and custom decreed her inferiority. As I read the description of those conditions and shared it with Treelight, she felt with me the slap of denial of self, the erosion of humiliating rules, especially as our major practice was Theravadin, direct descendent of the institution portrayed in the book.

Several days later, at the Lama Foundation in the mountains above Taos, New Mexico, I encountered a woman who had just come from six years living as a monk in a Zen Buddhist monastery in Korea. In the round meditation hall with its pale adobe walls, under the high star-shaped skylight through which the sun fell at noon in searing patches, Su-il sat at the front near the platform where the Indian Theravadin Buddhist teacher Munindra sat to lecture. A young blond woman, fresh and generously smiling, her hair grown out into a casual short cut, she was a gentle, benevolent, and silent presence.

Having found out her story, Treelight and I questioned her about her life in the last six years. Su-il was happy to talk with us. A native of Scotland, she had chosen Korea as a place to ordain because she understood that there she would be able to have the same monastic experience as the male monks. In fact she did, eating, sleeping, and meditating in the meditation hall, no distinction being made between male and female monks except in using toilet facilities. In that meditation hall, she told us, there was no Buddha statue on the altar, but in its place stood a large mirror.

We arranged for Su-il to speak to a group of interested participants of the Munindra retreat. There she told how uniquely valuable those six years had been and how she had decided now to return to the West, to a culture like her own, in which she hoped to apply the benefits of that intensive practice. She had received the permission of her teacher to let her hair grow, after six years of a cleanshaven head, and to assume Western dress. She had given up her monk's precepts—a hard decision for her—in order to be able to live and move and work effectively in this American environment. In Korea her months of formal sitting had alternated with periods of caring for sick and dying people. Now she was on her way to work at a hospice in New Mexico.

We were fascinated, and when we drove down off the mountain to continue on to Boulder, we talked for many hours about Su-il's choice and experience. To some extent it balanced the dour picture we had encountered earlier in *Women Under Primitive Buddhism.* This vigorous young Western woman had lived a monastic life in an Asian culture that seemed exotic and extreme to us but in no way denigrating.

From visits to Tassajara (Zen), study at Nyingma Institute (Tibetan) and regular Vipassana sitting (Theravada), we had come to understand that in looking at any particular aspect of Buddhism in this country one encounters a number of different experiences. Several variables come into play: the type of Buddhist practice, the Asian culture from which it has been brought, the particular teacher who offers it—whether that teacher is Asian or American, the sex, age, and life experience of the teacher, and so on.

The issue of monasticism for women may serve as an initial illustration of the diversity of Buddhist experience that we will encounter in looking at all the other issues in this book. It is also clear that Buddhist monasticism in this country is different in many ways from that phenomenon as it exists in the East and is very much in an experimental stage. In the process of its establishment here women are enthusiastic participants, although sometimes they face heavy odds.

The ancient order of Bhikkhunis (nuns or "female monks") lasted over a thousand years in India and then died out, long before the monks' orders were eventually decimated by a combination of Muslim invasions and the resurgence of Hinduism. The disappearance of the nuns is mysterious. In the absence of documentation it is attributed to economic causes or, in the case of the Sri Lankan nuns, to warfare.

The implications of this disappearance for modern women, not just those wishing to follow a monastic path but those practicing in Buddhist institutions generally, can be drawn from a statement by Nancy Auer Falk. In an article called "The Case of the Vanishing Nuns," Nancy Falk writes: "At the root, the major problem of the women's order probably rested in the Buddhist tradition's inability to affirm completely the idea of women pursuing the renunciant's role. This led to an institutional structure that offered women admirable opportunities for spiritual and intellectual growth, but not for the institutional and scholarly leadership that such growth should have fitted them to assume." And she goes on to say, "The nuns' troubles were compounded by an ambivalent image created in a tradition of Buddhist stories that sometimes praised their achievements but just as often undercut and attacked them."[2]

The conditions for Buddhist nuns today are difficult within Theravada Buddhism. Because the nuns' orders disappeared from the Theravadin countries, and because a nun must be ordained by another nun, technically there can be no full ordination within these traditions, and the male establishment is resistant to change or innovation. Without full ordination there can be no nunneries or real provision made for the support of nuns. Western women wishing to pursue a monastic life are allowed to take robes as novice nuns and live under eight or ten precepts. The only places where it is possible to receive the other three hundred or more precepts of the fully ordained nun exist in Hong Kong or Taiwan, in Korea and Vietnam. Some Theravada and Tibetan Buddhist women go there to receive the ordination, even though it is within the combined Chan (Zen) and Pure Land traditions, a different tradition from their own.

The question, however, is how to pursue a monastic discipline without the support of established monasteries. Theravada nuns, especially, are homeless people in this country. They are tolerated at the few male monasteries, but their existence there is complicated by the rules restricting male monks' contact with women. For instance, Theravada monks are not allowed to sleep under the same roof as a woman, so that in some instances a nun is not allowed even to sleep at the monastery. They live a precarious, marginal existence.

The situation for nuns in the Tibetan tradition is much superior in that their monastic commitment is supported by Tibetan Buddhist lamas and monks who encourage them to go to Taiwan or Hong Kong to ordain, and who are in favor of the establishment of a viable nuns' order in the West.

An American woman who has been working on this project is Ane-La Pema Chodron. At the Dalai Lama's suggestion, she has been investigating the lineage and vows she took in China to discover whether they can be traced back to the original order of nuns in India. If so, they could offer a precedent for the full ordination of nuns in North America. (The other Tibetan tradition for women is that of the wandering practitioners called yoginis, which is described by Tsultrim Allione in *Women of Wisdom*.)

The problem of a place to live and practice has also been addressed by Pema Chodron, who is engaged in establishing a monastery for men and women in Nova Scotia, under the direction (until his death in 1987) of the Venerable Trungpa Rinpoche of Vajradhatu in Boulder.

A woman determined to reestablish the Theravada nuns' order is nun and teacher Ayya Khema. An American citizen, born in Germany, with some years spent in Australia, Ayya Khema writes and speaks passionately on the necessity of reviving the Bhikkhuni Sangha and says that Mahayana ordination in Taiwan or Hong Kong is not an adequate substitute, as it lacks public acceptance and support in the Theravadin tradition. Instead, she proposes, "I would envisage a whole-hearted movement from the leaders in Theravadin Buddhist countries—spiritual, social, political—both men and women of foresight and integrity—who would want to be part of a religious renaissance that might change the consciousness of humanity."[3]

Not one to wait for others to act, Ayya Khema has established a nunnery for women of all nationalities run entirely by women, on an island in Ratgama Lake near Dodanduwa, Sri Lanka. The government leased the island to her for this purpose. At the official opening on September 9, 1984, some fifteen hundred visitors attended the ceremonies, and news and photographs went out to twenty-four countries. As Ayya Khema travels several times a year to the Untied States to speak and give retreats, a number of American women have gone to Sri Lanka to study and practice with her on what is known as the "Nuns Island." Ayya Khema was also a principal organizer of the first International Conference on Buddhist Nuns held in Bodhgaya, India, from February 11 to 17, 1987. There the Dalai Lama gave the opening address, expressing his support for the reintroduction of the Bhikkhuni Sangha.

The participants formed a worldwide organization of Buddhist women called "Sakyadhita" (daughters of Sakya, the clan to which the Buddha belonged) to work toward reinstatement of the nuns tradition.

Another project to address this need is the effort to create a Women's Dharma Monastery somewhere in the United States. It was begun by a group of Buddhist women in Washington, D.C., laywomen and "ordained precept nuns" of the Theravada, Mahayana, and Vajarayana traditions who wish to establish an "ecumenical Buddhist community/meditation center devoted solely to the development of women's spiritual life." Led at first by Ane Tsering Ch'odron (Martha Hamilton) and Sister Dharmapali (Martha Sentnor), the group has communicated with American Buddhist women through mailings and amassed information on women's needs and ideas with a detailed questionnaire.

Zen women do not face the same obstacles as Theravadin and Tibetan Buddhist women. Throughout its history in the United States Zen Buddhism has offered ordination for women, making no distinction from men, usually referring to both women and men as monks or priests. Some Zen women have been successful in taking institutional and intellectual leadership positions within Zen centers, a few achieving the title of roshi, which is conferred by a master only upon his most worthy disciples. But as one of the monk-priests in this section points out, Zen monastic settings have been predominantly male dominated and male defined. Women often find themselves either intimidated by the environment or engaged in a struggle for recognition that sometimes even results in expulsion.

A unique situation, however, exists in northern California, where a Western woman has established a monastery in which women and men are equally acknowledged and active. Reverend Roshi Jiyu Kennett, an Englishwoman who studied and received the mandate to teach in Japan, is the founder and abbess of Shasta Abbey near Mount Shasta.

One of the questions that particularly motivated me in talking with the women in this section is: What are the elements of personality and background, and of the Buddhist monastic experience itself, that caused these American women to become Buddhist monastics? Some of them were raised in Catholic environments, in which they wanted to partake wholly in religious life, and, denied this, found the door more fully open in Buddhism. Many who are older have lived worldly lives before taking robes, some having raised children, functioned in business or the professions. And I wanted to investigate the actual dailiness of being a Buddhist female monastic in a Western environment, or, in one case, a monastic situation created by a Western woman in an Eastern setting.

In spite of the difficulties encountered by many of these women, still their goodwill and good humor endure. Sincerely questioning, and exercising great patience, they are determined to establish a firm place for themselves within Buddhism, or in the case of the Zen women, to define that place as distinctly their own.

LOTUS TORCH OF DHARMA

"The separation between you and the world ceases to be very far and maybe ceases to exist at all. And therefore when something's hot, it really is hot, and it burns you up. Fire just burns you up, and wind blows you into a million pieces, and water drowns you, and earth buries you. And you're just not there anymore. At the same time, fire warms you, like it never warmed you before. And the wind in the trees is like hearing the sound of eternity. And the earth is your witness, and water is always moving and fluid and endless. And you're inseparable from all these things."

Ane-la Pema Chodron speaks from the front of a monastic hall, whose three glass walls open to the splendid scarlets and yellows of the trees in a Rhode Island autumn. Her clothing is every bit as colorful: deep maroon robe accented by a gold bodice. This is the robe of a nun in the Tibetan tradition.

Ane-la is the traditional title for nun in Tibetan and is translated as "auntie." *Pema* means "lotus" and *Chodron* means "torch of Dharma." It is a dramatic name for this fifty-year-old woman who speaks so gently and cheerfully to the women and men attending the Balancing of American Buddhism conference at the Providence Zen Center. She seems less a torch than a hearth fire, lively and steady, giving warmth and light to herself and others.

Pema Chodron is important for her central role in establishing a Tibetan Buddhist monastery in North America, for her sharing of her tradition with other religious leaders, for her perception that American Buddhism will have in it elements of the religious traditions already existing here. Always she balances her monastic commitment with the requirements and needs of our society, envisioning an American Buddhism that will fully embrace the laity and women.

As we talk at Providence, she laughs a lot. Her open suitcase lies on the floor between us; I am perched on one bed, she on the other. I had first met her in Boulder in 1982 at the second Women in Buddhism conference where she spoke to the group about her experience as a nun. I was struck by her ingenuousness, by some very available, unprotected quality in her, and by her joy. Today I see the same qualities, but she is more defined, stronger in her confidence.

She tells me how at age twenty-eight she "began to awaken spiritually." Before that she had done all the proper things expected of a daughter of an upper-middle-class New Jersey family. She and her lawyer husband and two children were living in Berkeley, where she went back to college, fell in love with another man, and began to participate in the exploration of the midsixties. Divorce and remarriage followed. After a second divorce, she chose to confront her extreme dependency on men, and she set out to create a different life for herself. She explored her sexuality and began to try various spiritual disciplines, beginning with scientology, gestalt, Hinduism. And always, of course, she was raising her children and earning a living. Finally she found Tibetan Buddhism, practiced in England, and began to study with Chogyam Trungpa in the United States. The "Ngondro" practices, an arduous program of prostrations, mandalas, mantras, and guru recitations, which are, as Ane-la puts it, "designed to bring everything up," helped her go through the residue of her relationship with her second husband. "I started to let go of the pain and become my own person." And while she was then in a good relationship with a man, she discovered that her "real appetite" was for her spiritual practice. "I didn't need to have lovers anymore," she says. "I began to be interested in being a nun."

She was thirty-seven years old when she took the robes as a novice nun in England, and she violated the expectations of her parents, who, she says, "had a conniption fit." Also, she was worried about the effect on her children.

"I wrote to the children and told them I was becoming a nun. It was just incomprehensible, of course, but I tried to make it sound as normal as I could."

"Interestingly enough, being children of the sixties, they thought I had done this incredibly far-out thing. When I came back, right away they started with great pride introducing me to all their teenage friends as Pema, and telling them that I was a Buddhist nun. Had this all happened five years later or earlier, they could have been humiliated beyond words. But it was just the right time in history; it represented in their minds that their mother had struck out on her own and was a woman doing her own thing. It's not quite as blissful as I make it sound, but essentially that was the taste of it."

"So, also, the fact that I couldn't live with them anymore could have been quite painful, but they lived with their father who had a great big house, who was a wealthy man, and I lived in one room at the Dharmadhatu meditation center. It wouldn't have worked for them to live with me anyway." [The issue of the meeting of motherhood and Buddhist practice, addressed throughout this book, is investigated more fully in Chapter 7.]

"I spent a lot of time over there at their dad's house and I got a job teaching school in San Francisco. So my first three years as a nun, I was sort of in disguise. I would go to school, teach every day, wear regular clothes, although I always wore maroon or brown, and my hair was short. Then when I would come back to the Dharmadhatu at night I would put on my robes. It was slightly painful, because it was so schizophrenic. And no one at school knew I was a nun, although gradually people began to find out, and it didn't seem to faze them at all. People began to come to talks I would give."

It is not hard to see how Pema Chodron could have made her new situation seem quite ordinary and acceptable to people. Her blue eyes look out calmly. Her fringe of brown hair feathers down onto a forehead that seems open and babyish. There is a shallow dimple in her chin, and her mouth seems most comfortable in a smile.

When her children were eighteen and twenty years old, she felt she could leave them, and she moved to Boulder, the seat of Vajradhatu. There she progressed quickly, serving as head of practice at the three-month "Seminary" for several years, during which time she worked closely with her teacher, Chogyam Trungpa Rinpoche, and then became codirector of Karma Dzong, the meditation center in Boulder.

"When I took on that job and began to work in Boulder, it was very gratifying to women," she says. "Women appreciated it a lot. And I realized that I had a role that way, as a spokesperson for these women."

She does not mention any difficulties she may have experienced as a woman in a male-dominated tradition. The day before, in her talk in the monastery building, she said that she regards "obstacles" as simply tools for practice. But she is quite willing to serve as a role model for women who may be more conscious of inequities.

We speak of her particular position as a "Bhikshuni," or nun, and the status of Tibetan nuns in this country.

"In 1980 I went to Hong Kong and became a fully ordained nun. In Tibet they had only novice ordination. They did not have Bhikshuni. But unlike in Theravadin countries where this is a political issue, when the Tibetan teachers came to the West, they saw that there was equality of men and women here and that there couldn't be this inequality in the Buddhist tradition. The only place this inequality continued to manifest would be in this lack of the Bhikshuni ordination. So we've been encouraged to all go off to Hong Kong to take the full Bhikshuni ordinations so that it's being preserved and can be revived in the Tibetan tradition through us. When we've been Bhikshunis for twelve years, some of us will be 'venerable,' older by that time and worthy of performing ordinations. Through us the Bhikshuni ordination will be returned to Tibetan Buddhism. We're lucky, because it's really encouraged by the male hierarchy, whereas the Theravadin women have to fight for it."

She points out that the Tibetan women teachers we may have heard about were not nuns but yoginis (independent women practitioners), and that there is a tradition of married lamas in Tibet, particularly in the Nyingma sect.

Now in the little sleeping room at the Providence Zen Center, Pema Chodron tells me about the last few years, in which she left her job at Karma Dzong to raise money, with stunning success, for the establishment of the monastery in Nova Scotia. In her travels to teach at Dharmadhatu centers around the country, she presented a slide show on the monastery project and was able to raise almost $175,000 in four months.

"This monastery project had a life of its own," she explains. "People are drawn to something powerful in the monastic tradition."

She is excited now, her whole face lively, as she talks about this endeavor that has so expanded her horizons.

"I'll tell you, I feel like I have found my place, that I've reconnected with a past karmic stream and that ever since this monastery came into being, I've stepped into a river that keeps going forward and keeps taking me out farther and farther. Because with the monastery project I'm suddenly not just going to the Dharmadhatus, I go to other Buddhist centers. I'm firmly grounded in my tradition, and therefore I find it so rewarding to experience Korean, Japanese, Chinese, Theravadin, all the other traditions, and the other Tibetan Buddhist traditions as well. Now is enrichment."

Gampo Abbey in Cape Breton, Nova Scotia, is now a reality, with the physical facilities in place. It sits on a beautiful spot of land sloping down to the sea. Everyone agrees, says Pema, that this will not be a copy of a Tibetan monastery but will be a place with a distinctly Western character.

"There are going to be men and women together," she says. "It wasn't the way in Tibet and it certainly wasn't the way in Japan or Theravada. But we feel that the combination and the balance of the energies really undercuts a lot of the neurosis that arises, and the pitting of masculine against feminine."

"Will you be the head of it?" I ask her.

"Yes, I think so. Right now I'm the only one who's directing it. The hierarchical structure is that Chogyam Trungpa Rinpoche and Thrangu Rinpoche, the abbot, are on the top, and then comes the Loppon, who's in charge of all practice and study at Vajradhatu, and then I'm the director of the place. Rinpoche has this vision of an enlightened society that he feels the monastery is part of: the whole enlightened way of living our lives, which includes schools and hospitals and how you handle old people and children and relationships and everything. The place of the monastery in that is as an inspiration to everybody, that certain people have committed their whole lives that way, and also as a place to go and stay for a while."⁴

Pema will be at the abbey during the intensive practice periods in the winter and summer, and she will be in charge of setting up programs. So far five nuns are connected with the abbey.

"The thing that's interesting to me about this monastery project," she tells me, "is that my field of experience is expanding and expanding, to all the other Buddhist groups but also to other religions. You get into this monastic network, and it just keeps growing." And here she points to a unique characteristic of American Buddhism.

"Father Thomas Keating, who always comes to the Buddhist Christian Conference at Naropa, had this yearning to have a conference where people would just sit around and talk about their spiritual experience. So we did it and it's very powerful. There are Native American women, there's myself as a Buddhist, and a Vedantic woman, and then there is a male rabbi, Father Keating who is a Trappist, a Greek Orthodox, a muslim, a Quaker, another Hindu teacher, a Native American man, and then one layperson. The sharing that goes on in this group is wonderful. We really talk about spiritual journey. We talk about prayer and grace and faith, all these things that Buddhism doesn't even have names for. You'd be surprised: with contemplative people there isn't this idea of god that you think of being the Christian or Jewish god, there's a lot of groundlessness and really being right out there."

And she emphasizes the interpenetration of influences in this country.

"The powerful thing is that Buddhism in America is going to embrace all these traditions that it's coming from. The role of the laity will be embraced totally and the role of women will be embraced totally. It will be organically eclectic, in the best sense.

"At the level of monasticism is where a lot of the mixing is going to take place. For instance, I thought Thrangu Rinpoche this summer would tell us how Tibetan monasteries work, but of course how can he do that?! Here we are, men and women— where they just had men—and it doesn't *look like* a Tibetan monastery, it's not set up like one. He said what's *not* needed is a Tibetan monastery, what's needed is a *Western* monastery. So he introduced us to a few of the formalities, but mostly he said that a monastery is a place to practice and study, that's really what it is. So he was interested in our just working on it.

"A Zen teacher could come and do a retreat and that would influence the place. Someone could come and do a Vipassana retreat, and that would influence the place. Teaching can go on in different ways."

She pauses, remembering, "Some of the best teaching that Trungpa Rinpoche gave me over the years was when he would stop me in the corridor or come up to me out of the blue and say, 'Don't be too religious. Just don't be too religious.' First I was insulted, then it was like a koan [a problem to solve], then finally it became real straightforward, *Just don't be too religious.*"

"I don't think you are," I tell her.

And Pema Chodron agrees with me, smiling.

UNLIKELY TRAVELER

A postcard arrives from Burma, showing two demonic warrior figures guarding the gate of a temple. On the other side *Shinma Dhammadinna* tells of public appearances she made with her teacher Taungpulu Sayadaw (a Burmese Theravadin master acknowledged to be a saint), of a clandestine walk through the jungle with a monkey as "my sweet and clinging companion," and she admits the heat is getting to her and she already has a touch of dysentery. It is like Dhammadinna to cover the gamut. Somehow she manages, in her own life, to span a number of identities and to look squarely at all aspects of her situation, even those that are painful and confusing.

Her story is a model of spiritual search, intriguing in her choice to live within a male monastic institution. Some uses of monasticism itself, and of celibacy, are made clear in Dhammadinna's reflections.

I first met her two years ago at the Insight Meditation Society in Barre, Massachusetts, the largest and oldest Theravada Buddhist center in the United States. There among us laypeople gathered for a meditation retreat was a brown-robed figure, her bald head pale in the dimness of the meditation hall. Of course I was curious about her but would not have thought of approaching her at this silent retreat.

Dhammadinna took matters into her own hands. One day there was a note for me pinned on the bulletin board in the entrance hall. (This board provides the only source of communication during silent retreat at I.M.S.) The note asked, "Are you the Sandy Boucher who has published stories in *Sinister Wisdom?*" I was taken aback, since *Sinister Wisdom* is a small feminist-lesbian magazine, hardly likely reading for a Theravadin nun. I left a message in the affirmative. The next day there was another note for me in Dhammadinna's somewhat spidery handwriting. "Let's talk after the retreat is over."

We did, sitting on Dhammadinna's mattress in the little room where her few objects were neatly and pleasingly arranged. Dhammadinna told me that before taking robes, as Erin Davis, she had been politically active as a local organizer for the National March on Washington in 1979 and had done concert production for performers such as Kay Gardner and the women's jazz group "Alive!"

She was easy to talk to, as we sat drinking tea, although at first I had difficulty reconciling her quick, informed, and hip style of speech with her nun's robe and her head on which only the faintest dusting of short brown hairs showed. How could one be a woman-identified, politically aware person and a Theravada nun at the same time? Dhammadinna managed this difficult balancing act, I was to find, by staying awake to the actualities of her situation, especially confronting the contradictions, and allowing for changes in herself.

It was participation in Al-Anon and Overeaters Anonymous groups that awakened her interest in spirituality. (Al-Anon is a self-help group for people whose partners are alcoholics, or who have alcoholics in their families.) In her early twenties she experienced a period of excruciating psychological pain when she became aware that she had been sexually abused as a child.

Shattered by this knowledge, she went looking for help in order to stabilize and heal herself. She began to attend Al-Anon meetings because of alcoholism in her family. As she was living in New England and some of her friends did Buddhist meditation, she tried a weekend retreat at Insight Meditation Society at Barre, Massachusetts, which she liked, she said, "because no one looked me in the eye and no one made me eat." In subsequent retreats at IMS she was influenced by Dipama, a woman teacher from Calcutta, recognizing "the power of her *metta*," or loving-kindness. During this time also she finished her B.S. in zoology and learned that there was a Theravada monastery in California named Taungpulu Kaba-Aye Dhamma Center.

As we talk, I notice how young she seems, although she is twenty-seven now, with something very eager and fresh in her face. Her brown eyes are extraordinarily bright, almost like small lights turned on me, and I wonder if that is the result of intensive meditation.

"I had exhausted how I related to the world and felt a calling to monastic life," she said, speaking of the period in 1983 when she came out to Boulder Creek to the monastery, formally took the robes, shaved her head, and began to live the life of a Theravadin monastic.

It was not easy, for the practices in the monastery, whether from Burmese social conventions or Theravada tradition itself, were archaic and oppressive. Her teachers, however, treated her with absolute respect, as a serious meditator, and did not perpetrate male-female bias. "I felt very empowered by their recognition and willingness to help me," she told me. "I trusted I would grow in wisdom and equanimity regarding the obvious inequality of the system. The form didn't have to interfere with my practice, I thought."

Dhammadinna, when I spoke with her, was in the process of exploring what the robes meant to her. She felt gratitude toward the tradition but no particular loyalty toward it. However, being in the robes helped her do her practice. "It keeps me on the beam."

A year after our initial conversation, Shinma Dhammadinna comes to Oakland, on her way to Taungpulu Kaba-Aye, where her teacher, Taungpulu Sayadaw, will be in residence for some months. I find I am very happy to see her again and have her stay in my home, where we engage in some hilarious exchanges, for her sense of humor is acute.

Sitting out in the yard in warm afternoon sunshine, we talk about her changing ideas about her spiritual journey.

"When I finally got out of retreat in January, this question became so hot for me: What is a nun? Because there isn't really a defined form for nuns, and even though my teachers always kept saying 'Don't worry about it, just do your meditation,' it was still such a *thing!* I felt nuts. There were no other nuns at Insight Meditation Society, and the rules I was following seemed to be the most arbitrary, ridiculous things in the world. That's how I felt. I fought the form, to within an inch of my life. What I experienced at the monastery, and also in retreat at IMS, was very deep feelings of isolation, confusion, and loneliness.

"Then came a point where I couldn't just watch my feelings of confusion anymore. I had to leave the silence and *talk* about my dilemma, read books about women's spiritual journeys, and seek out a monastic environment that would help me clarify my doubts."

She heard from a friend about the Nuns Island in Sri Lanka established by Ayya Khema, and she began to investigate it.

"It was a moment of gathering my resources and my commitment to come back to my original sense of purpose for taking the robes. Come back to square one, you know, and suspend the conflict. Come back to, why did I undertake a spiritual life and decide to stay on in the robes? Also it was very wonderful that at the end of the three-month course at IMS, the women really got together. It was powerful—the deep dialoguing—and I *loved* the space of that intimacy and the healing that happened. I felt undeniably called back to it, and I felt the maleness of what I'd been doing, and what it meant to me to be female. The level of protection that the robes had given me that was very appealing had now been satisfied. I mean not only protection from sexual advances. The more far-reaching protection is that a monastic is relieved from all worldly responsibilities, even the demands of friendship and family relations. No career decisions, no political involvements, no having to relate to American society. I didn't need that level of protection anymore, I needed to have a *reason* for *continuing on* in the robes different from my reason for *taking* the robes."

Later she decided not to go to the Nuns Island. "But what it did for me was to recommit me to my robes. I mean I had to decide that I was willing to travel halfway across the planet to go be on an island of nuns because I really wanted to investigate it further, I was not done with it."

Someone opens the gate and enters the yard I share with my neighbors, and I see the teenage son from the house next door on his way home from school. Before saying hello to me, he does a double take, glancing quickly at Dhammadinna and then away, and I think how many puzzled or shocked or hostile looks Dhammadinna must evoke out in the ordinary world. This is not something she ever mentions, except to say that in certain situations she covers her bald head with a shawl in order not to distress people too much.

"It was awkward for me at IMS to be in the monastic tradition," she continues. "In an American setting it didn't sit right with me that every day the monks go first to get their food, even though I've been in robes longer than some people who show up. One day I was just standing there waiting and I saw, 'This is *form* here and you can't turn away from it, it has a conditioning effect on the mind that every day the men go first and every day the nun goes second. They are boys and they go first *because* they are boys.' And I couldn't support it anymore.

"So I had to get out of retreat after this period, because it was time to meet challenges and tests and to dialogue and talk with people, and to build self-confidence. Because I was operating from a sense of fragmentation that was not going to get healed from intensive practice."

Dhammadinna read Tsultrim Allione's *Women of Wisdom* and found it empowering and energizing to think again about feminist issues. "Tsultrim tells how in Tibet nuns were independent and traveled by themselves, which does not happen in Burma," Dhammadinna says, "but I realized, 'Well, if it has been done, I can do it.' She said women made their own way and their own space within the male-defined system that they had entered, and it was very validating for me."

"Then I had this wonderful series of dialogues with my former theater teacher, Linda Putnam, who had been with Sufis. She mirrored or reflected to me the longings, aspirations, and difficulties I was encountering in my monastic situation. And I felt totally *seen* as a woman who was determined that my sanity is my self-affirmation, it's my own truth.

"I read more about Tibetan Buddhism because I wanted to learn more about this male-female principle that Theravada Buddhism does not acknowledge at all. It was mind-opening: ah, there's a *female principle* in the universe that some people think exists and some people think doesn't. Hmmm, that could be interesting. Then I read I. B. Horner's *Women Under Primitive Buddhism*, and it was depressing, but I was very happy to read it because it told me so much about who the nuns were, and it explained that *institutionally* the women were subordinate to the men. So I understood my experience at the monastery in a different way. I understood how this was my heritage in that institutionally women were *not* autonomous and had no opportunity to be leaders in the whole of the monastic community. I felt, 'Ah, now I *know* there was nothing. At least now I know this, and so I'm authorized to modify it as I go along.' I stopped worrying. All this that I thought I should be learning: it doesn't exist. Women have always come in through the back door, lived in the backyard.

"The Catholic women are talking about the same things. The Protestant women are talking about the same things. We just happen to be dealing it out in Buddhism, but it's happening all over.

"I got into reading about the Catholics. I read *My Beloved* by Mother Catherine Thomas, which was very provocative. It was written in 1958, before the reforms in the Catholic church, so I have no idea what the Carmelite nuns are doing now; but it seemed to me that the Carmelites are very strict and they do more ascetic practices than other nuns. Just as Theravadins see our tradition as the purest form, and we do the most difficult practices in the most direct way. It was the first woman's story of her monastic life that I read. With this reading I began to have a context, which is what I had wanted to go to Sri Lanka for."

Then Dhammadinna reread Starhawk's *The Spiral Dance*, a book detailing the rebirth of the ancient religion of the Great Goddess. "This is like sacrilege or heresy for a Theravadin." She laughs. "You just don't go read about sex and magic and willpower. But I felt there were some things that she was saying that were true, and even though I would define things in different ways than she did, there was an impact on me that was very powerful.

"So a lot of things broke down for me, and I saw that all things that are available I really can use, and I'm not, by fear and loyalty, bound just by what my Theravadin teachers have given me. And I'm not returning to them out of fear and loyalty but out of love and respect for their wisdom. And out of a need for mature guidance.

"Going back to the monastery, I feel so much more relaxed and accepting of what the limitations are. I feel so much more gracious about how limited we *all* are, understanding that what they do there is just par for the course of being human. And now I have a situation at the monastery that I feel will work for me."

Dhammadinna and I keep in close touch, and a few months later I go down to visit her at the monastery. Taungpulu Kaba Aye Monastery was established largely through the efforts of Rina Sircar, a female Theravadin teacher, native of Burma, who teaches in the United States both in an academic and a monastic environment. Dr. Sircar has taken the vows of a nun and wears the traditional brown robe. Her influence has been very important in bringing Theravada Buddhism to this country, for she started the department of Buddhist studies at the California Institute of Integral Studies in San Francisco. Now and then she takes students on a tour to Burma, and it was on one such tour in 1977 that she took her students to meet the Venerable Taungpulu Sayadaw. This visit led eventually to the establishment of the monastery in California as a place for Taungpulu Sayadaw to come and teach.

Taungpulu Kaba-Aye is a collection of pleasant frame buildings nestled among the redwoods near Boulder Creek. Having stayed at some Zen establishments, where the physical plant is meticulously cared for, I am surprised at the relative casualness of the buildings and large central yard at Taungpulu. But I remind myself that Theravadin monks are forbidden to dig in the earth and cut greenery, so that the care of the place falls to a few young American disciples and laypeople from the Burmese community.

Dhammadinna is radiantly pleased that I and a few friends have come to visit. Up in the tents on the hillside where we sleep we carry on a hilarious running dialogue ranging across everything from biology to geography to politics, with the major emphasis being Buddhism and what goes on at the monastery.

At dinnertime (the monastics eat one meal a day, about 10:30 A.M.), the monks come to the kitchen with their large wooden begging bowls. A row of smiling Burmese-American laypeople ladle food into the monks' bowls as they file slowly past before the table. (Serving the monks is a good way to accumulate "merit" [see Glossary].) Monks are not allowed to take food themselves but must be given it. It hurts to watch Dhammadinna stand back and wait until the monks are finished before she comes to be served.

In the shrine room sits a golden Buddha, and before it a fiber-optics sculpture like a big silver dandelion puff turning and changing colors from blue to yellow to red. A glass case to the side holds a second Buddha, and on the other side of the altar stands a model built of mirrors, of the beautiful white lacy pagoda up the hill. (A major patron of the monastery owns a factory where they make glass display cases for department stores: his generosity is apparent throughout.) Great bunches of roses and gladiolas flank the Buddha, behind electric candles. In here the monks take their place at the front before the altar to chant. It is hard to see Dhammadinna stay back with the laypeople.

"How can you *think* of going to Burma?" I ask, for she is making plans to accompany Taungpulu Sayadaw when he leaves to return to his homeland. Theravada Buddhist women in the Bay Area have been donating money for her and gathering supplies and medicines.

She grins, acknowledging my incredulity and laughing a little as if she too can hardly believe she's going. Then she sobers.

"When I first came to the monastery, I came for protection, really. You have to be very careful about this thing of protection. What do you pay for it? So often in the lives of women the price of protection is your personal integrity, your wholeness, your power." She pauses, then begins again in a burst of words. "It was useful for me, for a period of time. And I was treated somewhat like a child. That's somewhat inherent in the situation of being a nun in America if you're going to do the scene as it exists.

"So going to Burma is a natural next step. There I will be able to practice the form where it makes sense. I will live as a nun and I will not live as a child. I'll be able to meditate. I'll be able to do what nuns do, why they renounce the world."

We look at each other, boggled by the thought of her going halfway around the world, and she adds, "But, you know, I can't leave who I am at home. It all comes with me."

And I can imagine this, that Dhammadinna will not back away from any part of the experience or leave behind even a speck of who she is in order to make things more comfortable, and I remember her saying, in my yard in Oakland, "I feel so much that the path is one of moderation. How can I ever follow a path that doesn't reflect back my access to my own wholeness and my own common sense?"

In November 1985 Shinma Dhammadinna flew out of San Francisco International Airport will the Venerable Taungpulu Sayadaw and other monks, on her way to Burma. Before she left she gave me a few sheets of paper on which are her final impressions of her situation in the monastery at Boulder Creek. I offer some excerpts, for they express her inner struggle, her enthusiasm for the monastic life, and her hopes.

"The other afternoon Taungpulu Sayadaw called a group interview. As there was no one else there yet I sat up close. As the temporary monks arrived he motioned for me to move, indicating that the monks should sit up close. Although I have more detachment in these situations than I used to . . . there is still a stinging that I haven't been able to heal. . . .

"On a day-to-day basis I rarely run into problems with the monks (99% are Burmese). We relate as person to person, monastic to monastic, yogi to yogi. Living as celibates cuts through a lot of the usual male-female stuff. No one condescends to me. They treat me with the same respect with which I treat them. So it's an almost uncanny experience of there being no-man, no-woman, and on the other hand there appear these strongly sexist conventions. Sometimes they seem very transparent and meaningless and other times they can be staggering. . . .

"When I see the monks preparing for an ordination there is a lot of care and attention and excitement. This is the initiation into the sacred order. This is the 2,500-year-old order of Buddhist monks. They wear the original style of robes and follow the original set of rules. I watched a monk gathering the requisites for the newly ordained—the black bowl, the upper robe, the lower robe, and the outer robe. I saw that these are the symbols of his life, of the ancient holy life. There was a good feeling, one of self-respect and inspiration that I saw on the face of the one who prepared the requisites. And then the members of the sacred order sit up on the platform with Taungpulu Sayadaw. They're with him. They're in the same league.

"When I put aside my opinions and criticisms and looked objectively at what was happening, I saw that I have a great disadvantage. I have robes, but they aren't THE ROBES. I have taken precepts, but I wasn't ORDAINED. I'm in the entourage, but I'm not in the same league. It sounds so obvious.

"Before when I was coming only from a feminist perspective I only saw form. As a nun I only looked at emptiness. Recently I've been seeing the usefulness and the emptiness of the conventions all at once. I was always one for dismissing the conventions as empty rituals. It took me longer to see my envy and then to accept it as another empty mindstate. Accepting life on life's terms. I am appreciating the complexity of the problem and trying patiently to work with it."

THE NUNS ISLAND

Although there was a thriving order of "Bhikkhunis" during the Buddha's lifetime and for a thousand or more years after, never in the history of Buddhism has there been a nunnery for Western women founded and run by women. Yet in 1984 a Western woman created her own answer to the place of women in Theravada Buddhism by establishing Parappuduwa Nuns Island in Sri Lanka. Her action has significance not only in the struggle of Theravada nuns to gain full recognition, but also in her influence specifically on American women wanting to experience a monastic lifestyle, some of whom have already journeyed to Sri Lanka for shorter or longer stays on the island.

Ayya Khema is a sixty-three-year-old German-Jewish woman

whose family fled to China to elude the Nazis. They were put in a Japanese concentration camp, where her father died. She and her mother came to the United States after the war, and Ayya (then Ilse) became a U.S. citizen. Later she lived and raised a family and ran a farm in Australia, where she was ordained as a Theravada nun. Through her connection with the Island Hermitage, a monastery established in Sri Lanka by a German monk, she began to teach in Sri Lanka. In 1982 some laypeople there asked if she would be interested in establishing a nunnery on another island in the same lake. For the next two years work went on to clear and build on the jungle island, supported by donations from Ayya's Western and Sri Lankan students. In 1984 Parappuduwa Nuns Island opened as a nunnery for Western and Sri Lankan women.

Ayya Khema also teaches meditation courses regularly in California where she comes to visit her daughter. At the desert retreat center of her friend Ruth Denison, another Theravada teacher, I encounter her. She is a short, sturdy woman in a redbrown robe, with many tiny wrinkles at the corners of her eyes and mouth. In the meditation hall, shaded from the violence of the desert sun, she sits before us, her presence a strong and grounded aid to our meditation.

But it is her discourses that strike me most. She speaks with great energy, her large eyes wide open, and she smiles often. Her strong enthusiasm communicates to me almost physically, and I feel it as encouragement to persist in my practice. She speaks with precision and strict logic, and yet very simply; without any notes or books before her, she quotes from the sutras, supporting each point she makes with the words of the Buddha.

Certainly she deserves her name: *Ayya* is a polite form of address best translated as "venerable lady"; Khema was a nun during the Buddha's lifetime who was distinguished for her great insight and who was said to be wise, accomplished, shrewd, widely learned, and a brilliant talker.

When we meet that night on the back patio of the small plywood house in which Ayya Khema is staying, she comments that this heat is worse than the heat in Sri Lanka. We position our deck chairs on the flagstones facing out over the desert, hoping to catch a breeze if one should come our way.

"My nunnery is high energy," she tells me. "You've got to have both physical and mental energy." And I notice again her slight German accent and a hint of a lisp in her speech. "It's hot there, and the daily schedule is arduous."

As we talk, she chuckles often, especially as she describes some of the male chauvinist resistance she encountered in setting up the nunnery.

"The establishment of the nunnery was opposed because it was supposedly too near to the monks' island and the monks could swim over. And I said, 'Well, if that's what they're doing, they'd be too tired to do anything else.' " She stops to laugh wholeheartedly. "Then they said the bandits would come and rob us and rape us and kill us. But our girls are about twice the size of any of those bandits." Again she laughs, appreciating the absurdity of this. "So there's a lot of that going on, and the reason it's happening is because someone is feeling threatened. I mean, I'm successful as a teacher, so that's a threat."

She tells me that the island, leased to her by the Sri Lankan government, can accommodate twenty residents. At the moment there are Australian, Swiss, Sri Lankan, German, English, and American students there.

The nuns go on begging rounds every Monday in the surrounding villages. They could go every day, Ayya explains, but she doesn't want to take that much food from the villagers. "By our standard," she says, "Sri Lanka is very poor, but the villagers have enough, they all have their own coconut palm, banana trees, fruits, and vegetables."

A friend of mine wrote to me from Parappuduwa, describing it: "The island is truly idyllic—dense, lush vegetation, extraordinary sunrises and sunsets, and an army of sounds carried by the winds over the water—the fishermen singing or chattering early in the morning, the monks chanting from the nearby temple, the birds, lizards, fishes, and other inhabitants all contributing to this continual symphony of sounds.

"Even here there is never quite enough time—amazing isn't it? We certainly bring our mind-states with us. And at times the days really are packed with meditation, work, study, washing, watering, and a variety of extra things to be done that always pop up just when you're about to savor a few free hours."

Here in California, at the end of our talk, I ask Ayya Khema what she sees as the future of her work at the nunnery.

"What I have in mind is that some of these nuns can become teachers and can do what I'm doing—propagate the Dhamma—and that there will be more and more of them. That's what I hope," she tells me.

One American woman who spent time on the Nuns Island is *Treelight Green,* with whom I visit when she is only a few months back from Sri Lanka. It's good to see Treelight again, my old friend with her particularly contained and earnest manner. Her stay on the Nuns Island came after she had completed her Ph.D. thesis (which described a synthesis of hands-on physical healing with psychotherapy), because she wanted to immerse herself in the "spiritual foundation" she draws upon in her therapeutic work.

Since her principal teacher in her six-year practice of Theravada Buddhism has been Ruth Denison, a laywoman, Treelight is very much struck by the difference between the approaches of a monastic and a lay teacher.

"Ruth teaches the Dharma in daily life: how does your understanding of it permeate and affect your life. Whereas Ayya Khema is a nun. She has embraced a monastic lifestyle, and she has taken on a lot of formal vows. She is teaching people about renunciation. That's one of the main things she teaches. To renounce the worldly life, to renounce the ego, to renounce all the material things, all the things in life that give us a sense of identity, of who we are.

"Ruth on the other hand really wants people to embody and emanate the Dharma in life, to get out there and get in the institutions, be professional, go into the colleges, the courtrooms, everywhere, and *be* the Dharma in daily life.

"Those are two very very different things. It took me a while to catch onto that and to see that it made such a difference. For instance, there were some stray animals on the island, and Ayya Khema was talking about animals being a distraction and not to put any energy into them and you weren't supposed to stroke them because that was increasing sense contact. I was feeling very disturbed, because my teacher Ruth *adores* animals. She picks up animals in the road. She saves them, she mothers them. This was my first few days on the island. My mind was just having a head-on collision, you know. So I raised my hand and I said, 'Well, I think there's another point of view, there's another way to look at this—what about having compassion for all sentient beings?' I think in her answer Ayya said, 'Obviously, we did show compassion, we had three stray cats and we didn't kick them off the island. You need to understand that in Australia I was a rancher and I had sheep and cows and goats . . . ' She had this huge farm, and so it was not from a lack of love for animals, it was some kind of adherence to a monastic life. And a little later as I was trying to deal with my distress, I thought, Aha, *that's* the difference. Ruth is a lay teacher and a lay person, and that's more a lay response; whereas a nun, in keeping with the precepts and her understanding of not wanting to get distracted, would answer the way Ayya did."

Treelight says that while she sees the validity and the power in monastic life, she is not drawn to being a nun. She was, however, very influenced by her sojourn on the Nuns Island, where women staying short periods take eight vows and wear white; while the nuns, who take more vows and make a five-year commitment, wear brown robes.

"Ayya's whole thing is enlightenment," she says. "That's really what you're going after. And her thing is not being dependent on anything outside yourself for your well-being. I find that very influential. It does have to do with being whole, which is what we think of in the holistic health movement and the growth movement, but we think of *getting* everything we need so that we can be whole in ourselves, as opposed to *letting go* of *needing* anything external and totally calling on Buddha-Dharma-Sangha as the mainstay."

Western Theravadin teachers, Treelight points out, tend to stress the Eightfold Noble Path as a guide to living in the world, and put little emphasis on achieving Nibbana (enlightenment). Ayya Khema, she says, stresses the goal of "getting off the wheel" (i.e., getting free of this conditioned existence).

"When Ayya first started talking about this," Treelight says, "I felt aversion. I thought, What's so wrong with being *here,* that she doesn't want to be here?! It seemed like avoidance. But the more I listened to her the more I understood what she was saying."

"Do you think this is really a male trip," I ask her, "to want to escape from the earth, from natural processes, from the cycles?"

"No, I think it's really her understanding of what is Nibbana, what is enlightenment. I think she's loved the earth, she was an organic farmer, and she's loved animals; and she has two children of her own. I think for her it is penetrating a particular understanding that she thinks is the main thing about Buddhism. And I see her point! All our attachments in the world *do* produce suffering, produce karma. It doesn't make me not want to be in the world. I don't feel I need to have a disdain for life, and I don't feel *she* has a disdain for life. I still want to participate in the world, embodying the Dharma as much as I can. But it's caused a shift in me and I'm really reflecting on it. And I feel the difference, coming back to the United States, with my Dharma friends here. You know, the point at which people are pursuing the Dharma feels different from the experience I had and the way I want to pursue it at the moment."

"How could you pursue it that way here?" I want to know.

"I don't think I have to physically withdraw from the world to practice seclusion. I have thought about secluding my mind from entertainment, from music, from going to a lot of gatherings and outings, and the diversifications of the mind. Right now I feel like focusing on the Dharma, the teachings. I'm still in a period of seeking to fortify my depth and my understanding. And I think celibacy is one way to pursue that. And looking at some of the vows and considering them."

There were other differences, Treelight says, between her previous training and the guidance she received from Ayya Khema.

"She teaches samatha practice, which is concentration, absorptive states of meditation. That isn't taught in the West here by the Vipassana teachers. She does a combination of insight and samatha. So what happened for me was a much more formalized, methodical way of approaching my meditation, and I just made quantum leaps. It's a method of cultivating particular states of mind in a particular order. I got very specific guidance. I would have my meditation, go and report to her, and she would say, 'Fine, that's very good, this is what you've accomplished, now here's the next step; when you've accomplished that, come back and tell me.' I would work on it for a couple of days and I'd go back. I'm a veteran meditator, I know how to apply myself in that way. So I would go and do these things, and I had a sense of *progress!* This was just very well laid out.

"And cultivating particular states of mind, cultivating joy, happiness, equanimity. She would say, 'Okay, when you sit down, I want you to determine how long you're going to be in each state, and then as that dissolves note the impermanence of it. Then go to the next one.' "

As the afternoon mellows to dusk, Treelight tells me the significance of that particular practice for her.

"That was just very incredible to do, and it gave me a kind of wieldiness, a flexibility of mind. I've never cultivated happiness before. For me it was life changing, to really *value happiness.* And I feel much happier now!"

WOMEN'S DHARMA MONASTERY

Two Washington, D.C., women have taken the initiative in the establishing of a Buddhist women's Order of Nuns in the United States by envisioning a Women's Dharma Monastery. Their efforts began in 1985 and continue now as the major issues develop: whether to ordain in and bring over a traditional Asian lineage or to establish a new Order of Nuns in North America; how much of the Vinaya (monastic rules) it is possible to follow in an American setting; insistence on equality in application of rules to women and men. The Women's Dharma Monastery is seen as a place where laywomen as well as nuns will come to practice and study.

In January 1985, Ane Tsering Ch'odron (Martha Hamilton), a Tibetan nun, and *Sister Martha Dharmapali* (Martha Sentnor), a Theravada nun, sent out a letter to Buddhist groups, publications, and individuals, briefly describing their vision of "an ecumenical Buddhist community/meditation center devoted solely to the development of women's spiritual life" and asking anyone interested in this idea to communicate with them.

Two dozen women initially responded, mostly from the West-/Northwest and New England areas, with ideas and offers of support.

In July 1985, with Ane Tsering Ch'odron having gone to a Tibetan center in Germany, Sister Dharmapali continued the work of the Women's Dharma Monastery project, sending out a letter and two detailed questionnaires, one for all women meditators, the second for women who would support and/or join an Order of Buddhist Nuns. The letter and questionnaires were sent to three hundred people. More information was needed before a statement of goals could be formulated. More than 120 women responded.

Sister Dharmapali stressed the importance of this inquiry. "With newly emerging interest in Buddhist monasticism in the West, the topic is highly controversial," she wrote. "Basically, [the questionnaire for nuns] explores the prospect of perpetuating the traditional order of fully ordained nuns to the West—or to carefully shape a new concept for a modern order. This is a very serious matter. Even proposing a new order might seem presumptuous to some Buddhists who feel continuity of the order a primary factor; others may think the prospect of a new order long overdue. There is sure to be great divergence of opinion."

In a short history of the Nuns' Order and description of the issues involved, Sister Dharmapali pointed out, "The original teachings of Buddhism were strongly antiauthoritarian, and much freedom was given to the individual monk and nun in matters of doctrine and practice." She summarized opinions on the issue of the 227 rules for Theravada monks and the 311 rules for nuns.[5] "In informal discussion with over twenty monks and nuns in Asia and America, it is estimated a hundred or more rules are partially workable, or no longer operative. Certain rules are extinct, belonging to an India of twenty-five centuries ago, with many values inimical to women. Unity of agreement on the meaning of a few rules does not exist. Many monastics maintain rules of custom have always been open to interpretation." She adds, "Monks and nuns interviewed state that perhaps only the observance of the Ten Precepts, with a few other major Vinaya rules, is practical."

She says that in Asia monastics are less bothered by discrepancies between actual rule (which they pledge to maintain at time of ordination) and conduct in practice. They formally make confession twice a month, and they take the attitude that one should simply pay attention to one's meditation and let the structures remain as written. In this country (and often in Asia), however, it is almost impossible to follow many minor monastic rules, and some monks and nuns speak for change, arguing, "Let's look at the rules again, determining through actual practice, what works . . . or begin with very few rules in a community, and develop others as needed (which duplicates the original development of the Vinaya)."

Women responding to the first questionnaire wanted a center to which laywoman could come for retreats and study and/or to live; many thought it should be devoted to one tradition while open to all, and that it should be partially self-supporting.

The nuns' questionnaire occasioned careful, detailed comments. A major theme was the necessity for equality in the situations of nuns and monks.

One woman advocated a "female monastic establishment administered only by its membership, unless the monks are willing to admit women as authorities in their own midst as women (according to the old rule) were required to admit men as authorities. The Theravadin female sangha will need to address this problem immediately, and conflict with the male sangha, especially non-Western monks, may be expected." Another asserted, "The male sangha is inadequate to lead alone. It needs the balancing complementing coleadership of the fully ordained bhikkhuni sangha. Without this balance, Buddhist monasticism is just another oppressive political system. American females will not accept the Theravada male sangha as it is now set up." And another: "Many American women were able to become Buddhists only because they were open to new ideas: liberally investigative, independent, nonsuperstitious, progressive, free-thinking. Therefore, they include some serious feminists who will not placidly accept the constraints on bikkhunis which are not imposed in parallel upon the bikkhus. To lose, as monastic candidates, these women—who are among the best educated, most articulate and energetic—would be an enormous harm to the community."

Some respondents described a new order uniquely adapted to life in the United States: "My own vision is that there will be established a nunnery for all Buddhist nuns, regardless of tradition. One that would particularly care for the aged as an integral part of the daily life, provide a safe and productive environment, and be a place where each tradition can be experienced and preserved and where, perhaps, a 'New Age' Buddhism can unfold and blossom. This center would also offer laywomen a place where they can come and participate in the lifestyle." One woman wrote, "Women residents can create a new order based on experiences in all the various sects. Hopefully, feminist processing and other useful techniques will be encompassed." Another: "At this time, what I find myself wondering is whether it would be possible for the monastery to locate itself near a sizeable population of immigrants, particularly from Southeast Asia. The needs of whose women, especially mothers—usually the last among immigrants to be served—might be met."

One woman, who described herself as a Buddhist history buff, made this contribution: "The very early Buddhist sangha—a wandering band of monks and nuns—initially employed highly democratic procedures when finally establishing communities (majority vote, etc.). There was no abbot [or] abbess. No one person could dictate spiritual practices to each other, not even Dharma. . . . Actually, I would like to see the 'new order' become the 'old order' in that we get back to basics. Some confusion exists, I believe, because we haven't taken the time to learn, at least a bit, from Buddhist history."

In general there was a characteristically American concern with equality and a further feminist awareness of the hierarchically oppressive nature of Buddhist monastic systems in all the major traditions of Buddhism.

"The monks' rules can and do create an aristocracy and a servant's class," stated one woman, "a division between the pure and the impure. I feel this is extremely dangerous, especially when the system is based on the idea of enlightenment as goal; on the idea that the [practice of the] traditional Vinaya [alone] is a kind of mechanism for attaining that goal."

Sometimes the replies were adamant, often when confronting the importation of Asian cultural patterns disguised as religious dictums. In response to the question of whether the rule should be retained that a nun cannot become officially ordained by the Nuns' Order but must afterwards be ordained by the Monks' Order, one respondent wrote, "Absolutely not. This one factor alone has kept Buddhist lay nuns in Southeast Asia trapped in this predicament for over 1,000 years. We'll have our own problems: we need not import others." And on the issue of the laity supporting the monastic orders (in the effort to earn "merit") and whether that practice should be followed here, one woman replied, "Merit-making is an entrenched pattern in Asia, often as not, something like 'spiritual materialism.' We don't need such self-serving ideas exported to the West."

In her latest communication, Sister Dharmapali has announced the opening of a Buddhist nunnery and retreat center in Colorado. This nunnery, located near Denver, with facilities for residential meditation courses, has been established by Reverend T. N. Chan-Nhu, originally from Vietnam. Sister Dharmapali is coordinator of activities there. She invites all interested women to write to her at Chan-Nhu Buddhist Pagoda, 7201 West Bayaud Place, Lakewood, Colorado 80226. One wonders whether this facility may serve as a stepping- stone for a future Order of Nuns, and whether other women will go ahead in establishing an entirely separate and independent order, with no such affiliations.

MARTHA SENTNOR—SISTER MARTHA DHARMAPALI

The Buddhist Vihara Society (*Vihara* simply means dwelling place), established in 1966, is in the upper 16th Street area of Northwest Washington, D.C., which Sister Dharmapali refers to, fondly, as the "Buddhist ghetto" because it is the home of five other temples. We have spent the morning with Karen Gray touring the Smithsonian Institution and looking at Asian art in the Freer Gallery. Now we have left Karen and taken the bus to the Vihara.

Sister Dharmapali introduces me to several of the monks, Sri Lankan men wearing the traditional Bhikkhu robe that leaves one shoulder bare. Then we settle in the library with a cup of tea.

At age forty-eight, Sister Dharmapali has closely cropped hair lightly dusted with gray and intent blue eyes behind wire-rimmed glasses. She wears a modified brown nun's habit with a brown blouse under it, accommodation to her need to be inconspicuous on Washington streets and public transportation. Her speech is flavored with a vestige of the Bronx accent that indicates her origins.

The conditions of Sister Dharmapali's life, as she describes them to me, amply demonstrate the need for a Women's Dharma Monastery.

"I have since my ordination lived in temples where there are separate accommodations for women. I've usually been alone in these places as a Western nun. Of course, these temples are established by the laity who have come from Southeast Asian and other countries. You follow their tradition; if you're not happy there, you leave. You have to accept the whole package. Often it's not very comfortable because you are a Westerner. But these are worldly conditions. It is through these people's kindness and generosity that one is permitted to live there. In return, they expect you to conform and to 'look like a nun.' Your deportment has to be comparable with the monks, whom you simply observe and copy. You sit the way Asian women sit and learn how to conduct yourself around the monks."

"And you're not allowed to live here," I comment.

"This temple is for monks, not for nuns," she says, "so I have to make private living arrangements. Often I live with generous families or single women. It's preferable, however, to live in a temple or in a meditation center."

Sister Dharmapali's association with this temple is certainly not superficial, for she came down from New York City almost twenty years ago to help establish the temple and has been associated with it ever since in a voluntary, secretarial capacity.

"The temple doesn't support you as a nun?"

"No, I'm not resident here. I am not affiliated with any temple, per se. Most American Buddhist nuns have a similar dilemma. Unlike the monks, we need to be self-supporting, and many of us have jobs, which is against the rule. Because of these circumstances, it may be that our maturation in the Buddhist disciplines may be cut short in some ways. We often have to train ourselves, without the close association of a teacher, nor do we have the same training as the monks."

Referring to her work with the Women's Dharma Monastery, I offer, "You must feel a sense of community with the women who answered the questionnaire."

"Yes," she answers, "in that so many women responded in almost the same terms. 'It's about time' was a constant echo. 'It's something that's really needed now,' many said, and 'I'm glad to see somebody doing it.' It was very encouraging."

We talk about her problems in following the minor precepts in a Western environment.

"The precept about not handling money is practically impossible to keep in America and in Asia. Almost all monks handle money. The custom of eating one's main meal before noon is hard to follow. Actually the rule refers to midday—around 2:30 P.M.— but laity generally do not know that. Because our lifestyle is different here, as well as the climate, in cold weather I might have to eat what is permitted—yogurt, things like that—later on in the day. I try to keep the precepts as best I can under any given condition, determining my motivation as to purpose, suitability, and skillfulness. Though I prefer vegetarian food, I follow the custom of the temple and try not to make problems for laity. Sometimes it is difficult to keep the precept about correct speech for monastics because one is easily drawn into inappropriate conversations with laity. One has to use *upaya*, or tact, or it is very detrimental to spiritual growth."

Sister Dharmapali has told me that she is in transition, describing herself as Theravada based and using many so-called Mahayana styles, investigating the genesis of these forms within their Asian context and their applicability, if possible, to contemporary Western life.

"I try to understand and am sympathetic to ethnic monks. Their support comes from their own people, the majority of whom are traditional-minded. Manipulation occurs on both sides. Many monks would like to make certain adjustments, but most laity would not cooperate, so they resign themselves to the status quo. This is why I don't believe the present Theravada Buddhist form in America will make much impact. It has much to offer, though, as basic foundation, and for its precise and thorough delineation of early meditation techniques of Vipassana-Insight instruction as given by the Buddha himself."

"Does that leave you with the responsibility of inventing another form?" I ask her.

"In a sense, yes. But I'm not a leader. I'm very happy to help people whom I respect, who want to make some necessary innovations. Sending out the letter was the beginning of communication in this area."

She also sent out a detailed questionnaire to Buddhist nuns in different traditions, some of whom have been nuns for a decade. The responses described a multitude of difficulties and demonstrated how each woman in her particular circumstance has attempted to solve her problems.

I ask about Sister Dharmapali's treatment here at the Washington Buddhist Vihara.

"The monks here know me well and are personally very supportive. They wish they could do more, but there are limited resources."

"You're in such a strange position," I offer.

"Yes, I'm homeless, as a monk or nun should be. Actually that means having a nonattached attitude. It is preferable, however, to have some place to develop a practice."

"It's interesting that this happens to the most *committed* women," I comment, and ask whether her meditation teacher is supportive.

She answers that he is, but he would rather she spend much more time in meditation retreat rather than immersing herself in communication and organizing tasks. She agrees and has taken steps to be more selective. Helping her Dharma sisters, however, is important, and while doing that she integrates practice into her daily life. "Even if it's just a few minutes, there comes a point when the mind just naturally quiets, each day, and then there is a natural watching, if one is sensitive to its appearance. The formal sitting posture can become artificial—a rite and ritual, a source of attachment. If you just watch what's going on in your head, throughout the day and night, it's very revealing."

We talk about the necessity, soon, of her going out to find a job, and how she will have to modify her dress and grow her hair longer. I am very struck by the precariousness of her situation and the unlikelihood that it will change in the near future.

"Yours is a very insecure life," I comment.

"That's true," she replies, unperturbed. "It teaches all the basic lessons. American Buddhists are pioneers, especially the monks and nuns. Before I was a nun I would feel anxious about leading the monastic life, wondering where would I sleep, what would I eat—all ego centered. I now know that people are kind and help you in many ways, as much as they can. One then has a great responsibility to practice in the best way, refraining from self-indulgence and self-reproach. I try to discern the Middle Path. No one ever said it would be easy."

ZEN MONASTICISM FOR WOMEN

Zen Buddhism is vastly different from Tibetan and Theravada Buddhism in that since its appearance in this country it has offered an institutional role for female monastics. Women have been allowed to ordain alongside men and have been called priests or monks. They shave their heads and follow the same rules as male monks, and, theoretically, receive the same privileges and opportunity for advancement in the ranks. Japanese-style Zen is also distinctive in that monk-priests do not practice celibacy and usually marry. As the following stories indicate, this acceptance within a monastic institution offers attractions to sincerely religious women and may be especially compelling to women of Catholic background, who in a Zen monastery can live out the priestly role denied them in their previous religion.

Many American women in the last fifteen years have had the experience of Zen priesthood, as will become clear in the succeeding sections of this book. While the rewards of this monastic practice are often remarked upon, many women also feel a level of discontent, for Zen monasticism, while it allows women to participate, is a form of practice designed by and for Asian men. This particularly masculine orientation has created pain and confusion in some women who have followed this path. The two women whose portraits follow speak both of the satisfactions and of the frustrations and disappointments of priestly practice in Zen for women. Their stories point up the conflict between the Asian forms as practiced in most Zen environments and the particular nature and needs of American women.

ON THE FEELING SIDE

We talk in *Barbara Horn's* room in the giant brick former Catholic monastery that houses the Insight Meditation Society in the countryside outside the tiny town of Barre, Massachusetts. The setting seems fitting, as Barbara comes from a strong Catholic background and, if times had been different, she would have become a Catholic nun, and, if very different, a Catholic priest. Instead, she became a Zen Buddhist monk-priest-trainee and for three years lived a monastic existence at Tassajara Zen Monastery in the mountains of California.

She is here working on the staff of the Insight Meditation Society, on a leave of absence from her Zen practice at the San Francisco Zen Center where she had been a member for seven years. She is still very much a Zen student, however, and for our talk she puts on her rakusu (a biblike garment that takes the place of the larger traditional kesa or priest's robe). Behind her on the door hangs her black sitting robe.

Barbara is an earnest, highly emotional woman of thirty-four, whose irony and sense of humor enliven the story she tells me of her time at Tassajara. Her blond hair that falls in a mass of curls is so distinctive that seeing it I remember first noticing Barbara years before when she was serving in the dining room at Tassajara. Her blue eyes are passionate below a broad forehead often wrinkled in consternation as we talk.

Barbara had gone to an all-girl Catholic high school in Long Island, and she wanted to become a nun. But the upheaval of Vatican II had so affected the Catholic community that young women were encouraged to go to college before becoming nuns.

"Now it's just striking me that at a very early age I felt turned away by the church." Her voice is urgent, her words spoken in an intense clipped style. "I wanted to fully participate, I wanted to say mass! Yet I knew on an intuitive level that I, as a woman, couldn't be a full person in the church."

She attended a community college on Long Island, where she was involved in student strikes, and went to Washington to protest the Vietnam war. In the Unitarian church she found some solace. Then in her midtwenties, Barbara was staying for a period of time in San Francisco, and she went to Sunday service at Green Gulch Farm in Mill Valley, a Zen practice center and farm run by the San Francisco Zen Center sangha.

"I walked in and there were these little voices in the back of my head, you know, Sister Patricia Francis in grade school saying, 'Watch out for the pagans.' I saw these stone statues, I saw people bowing, and I went 'Wow, this is *it*, this is pagan headquarters.' But the *feeling* was wonderful: the respect and the composure. Part of it is I guess I just liked Japan, I didn't realize how much the culture of Japan was there—it wasn't all religion, but it was the embodiment of a religion in a culture, that had been transported to a barn in Muir Beach." She laughs. "The whole setting had so much power in it, had human life energy in it, it was just pulsing with *we are human beings, we are people, we're alive, isn't this a mystery!*" She pauses, then continues, almost whispering, "It was such a *relief*. I felt, I belong on this planet, and here's a place where people are talking about what's been going on in my mind and I have never heard anyone talk about."

Barbara began to do Zen sitting at the San Francisco Zen Center. She moved into the residence on Page Street and lived there for a year and a half, working nearby as a masseuse, then at the Tassajara bakery and in the SFZC accounting office. Then she went to the Tassajara Zen Training Monastery, a very special place to her.

"At Tassajara, if you're there for any length of time you take on meditation hall responsibilities, and I've done that. The ritual part was wonderful, I loved the service, and I like to sing, so then I got involved in the chanting part and leading the chants, and I loved taking care of the altar—being a good Catholic . . . " She laughs. "I had always wanted to be an altar boy.

"One of the things I like about Zen is the drama, the sense that everything *matters*, that your life is on the line at all times."

But still she was plagued by her Catholic conditioning, whole dialogues going on in her head about how these people practicing Buddhism were idol worshipers and pagans. She points to a book on her desk, *Love and Living* by Thomas Merton.

"This man made a big difference for me, in starting to translate Catholic contemplative life. I had no longer any great allegiance to the Catholic church at that point, so it surprised me how strong the voices were, because I was twenty-six and I hadn't practiced as a Catholic since I was eighteen or nineteen. I had a conversation with one of the senior Zen teachers there about soul—I couldn't get this bit about There is no soul, There is no self. He just expressed concern, he said he could understand that with my Christian upbringing I would be puzzled about the Buddhist idea of there being no soul. There was no attempt on his part to convince me. He just heard and acknowledged where I was. This detached, understanding response shook me. I felt like a door just opened, and I began to pay more attention to what was in front of me, which was these people who seemed to be living quality lives. I had heard Christ's words for many years, but I didn't see Christ's work. I couldn't put them together. At the Zen center there was much more of a correlation between what people were saying and doing."

At Tassajara, she tells me, she worked one training period with the children, then worked in the kitchen and was the baker one summer.

During the winter months, Tassajara is practically inaccessible, hidden in a deep canyon in the Los Padres National Forest and approached by a steep and tortuous dirt road. There are two three-month intensive training periods in the winter. In the summer guest season Tassajara transforms into a spa with hot mineral baths, swimming in the stream and a pool, and incomparable vegetarian meals prepared from the extensive, carefully cultivated gardens and lovingly served by the monks.

Having stayed at Tassajara in the summer, I imagine it in the winter, dark under the rain, with only monks in black robes crossing the arched bridge to the meditation hall. I ask Barbara what it was like and whether she feels she deepened through that intensive practice and has a more clear sense of herself.

"In one respect yes, and there was another part of me that ran into rather serious trouble. I'm not quite sure how much of it was canyon fever. I did start to notice every time I got depressed I walked up out of the canyon. Baker-roshi was fond of saying, 'You go to Tassajara to take yourself apart. You may decide to put yourself back together the same way, but this time it's by your choice.' I sometimes think what happened for me at Tassajara was

I took myself apart but I didn't know how to put myself back together.

"I was feeling the spiritual resources in the place and when it came time for a ceremony I usually shone. My strength appeared. But interpersonally . . . I would get really depressed. And I started to connect the depression with my menstrual cycle. Finally after about six months when I started to piece it together, I said to another woman there, 'Wow, I've just noticed that I get depressed in relationship to my period, and she said, 'Yeah, that's very common, it happens to a lot of women who come to Tassajara.' And I said, 'Why didn't anybody tell me?!' And from that point on I would tell women. I started to feel a softening, around the edges, from women; and started to hear women saying 'Give yourself a break.'

"Most of the people in charge during my time there were men. The guys just didn't know what was going on with me, and there wasn't talk about menstruation. Eventually just before I left we started to address some more practical issues. For instance, we had five straight days of sitting—tangariyo, it's called—the initiation period: when you first come to live at Tassajara for the winter training period you have to sit for five to ten days without leaving your seat except for very short breaks after meals—and what happens when someone gets their period during this, and you need to change your tampon?"

She mentions how much she liked the challenge of that five-day sit, along with many other things about Zen monastic practice, like the drama of the ceremonies, the formal meals. Yet something was wrong.

"Two things were happening," she explains. "Physically I think something was going on with my body, maybe an adjustment to the diet. Also when you get into a monastic schedule you get to observe yourself because you don't have the distractions— no phone calls, no music, no TV. At Tassajara you are stuck right there, you can't walk into town. So I think part of my problem was claustrophobia. Also, pretty early on, Baker-roshi tromped in one day with Brother David Steindl-Rast, who's a Catholic Benedictine monk. So all of a sudden, Catholicism resurfaced. I think Baker-roshi wanted us to check out our commitment, to look at our own heritage.

"Also there were a lot of families there, a lot of children and couples. It was confusing for me because I was going more and more toward celibate monk practice. Family life was all around me and so I felt a little bit out of sorts because I didn't have an intimate relationship or a close friendship.

"So I was getting hit on a lot of levels and I just didn't know how to cope. And I didn't know how to explore it. There didn't seem room for feelings, or womanness. What was being nurtured was *practice*.

"What happened was that I became very emotional and nobody knew what to do with me. Including me. I was shocked by the vastness of my depression, and I didn't know how to get out of it or how to approach it. And there's no therapy down there."

"But there were teachers down there with you, weren't there?" I ask.

"There was a head monk for the training period. It's slightly unfair to say they were all men. There were some women there, but you did not draw out the emotional stuff, you didn't dwell on it or look into it. And there wasn't a lot of time either. We only had an hour's free time a day: one-half hour after lunch and one-half hour or forty-five minutes after dinner."

I ask how the tasks were distributed among men and women.

"There were all these allusions to equality," Barbara tells me, "and there was an attempt at it. The men pretty much ran the shop . . . well, a few women ran it. I really wanted to do the weekly town trip, and I was rejected on that. The staff said we couldn't drive the truck because we didn't know how to run the chainsaw. You had to know how to do that because if a tree fell down— which did happen—when you were coming back, you had to be able to get out, use the chainsaw, remove the tree, so you could drive in. So we said, 'Well, we want to learn how to use the chain-saw!' And there was an uproar about that.

"When problems surfaced, people said, 'Why are you making an issue out of this? We are here to *sit*, not to explore emotions.' And at the time I felt there was some validity to that. And I also didn't now what to *do* with myself!" She laughs, this time painfully. "You know, I was experiencing trauma."

"I guess it comes down to who defines what's important," I offer.

She nods. "There were many mixed messages, because in a very deep way we felt how much we needed to care for each other. Baker-roshi would tell us, 'We have to take care of each other,' and make references to Suzuki-roshi saying 'We're like milk and honey, we've known each other for many lifetimes prior.' There's something about practicing together with that feeling. So the *big* connection was talked about a lot, but the regular everyday connections I didn't hear much encouragement about or notice much ability or competence amongst people to take responsibility for that.

"It happened that during the periods when I was having a hard time there was always a man in charge. I don't know if it would have made a difference if a woman had been in charge. it might've."

She had not wanted to leave Tassajara at the end of her three years there, but it was her turn to leave, so she had to go. She spoke with the two senior (male) priests of the Zen Center Council. And by this time her attitude and perceptions had changed.

"For the first time I walked out of an interview and I said, 'This interview was not good and the problem is that they are men and they are not in touch with their capacity for warmth.' I hadn't seen it before."

She came back to the San Francisco Zen Center where she stayed for several years, until the disclosures of 1983, in which it was divulged that her teacher had engaged in activities, sexual and otherwise, unbefitting a Zen roshi. The resulting conflict so confused and disillusioned her that she left to join the staff at Insight Meditation Society. Once so certain of her vocation as a monk- priest, now she has only questions: "Do I want to be married and have a family?—I just had never looked at that—do I really want to be a monk? and if so, well, what *am* I, am I a Buddhist or a Christian?" And I am reminded of Susan Murcott's assertion that Zen practice can sometimes serve as an escape from the challenges and complexities of life in the world.

WOMEN'S UNIQUE PRACTICE

Students from the Minneapolis Zen center have traveled with their teacher Katagiri Roshi down to Southern Minnesota to Hokyo-ji for a sesshin (meditation retreat). Hokyo-ji is a collection of small rough-hewn buildings in a grassy clearing surrounded by luxuriant trees. These few structures—kitchen and eating hall, meditation hall, and roshi's cabin—are the beginning of what will be a full-fledged Zen monastery. For now, the students sleep in tents pitched on the grass.

Even though it is an extremely hot June day, most of the students wear their black priests' robes for the opening session of the sesshin. Among them is *Teijo Roberta Munnich,* an attractive woman who looks younger than her thirty-nine years and who seems irrepressibly cheerful, even within the still, strict atmosphere of the meditation hall.

After the others have gone to bed, Teijo and I make our way out into the weeds by the stream in order to talk without disturbing anyone. Fireflies flicker around us, and a wind comes up to whip the grasses and tree branches.

Roberta Munnich, I discover, was raised as a Catholic in Minneapolis, and, like Barbara Horn, she wanted to become a nun. But unlike Barbara, she did enter a Benedictine convent, despite the changes in attitude brought on by Vatican II. After a year as a nun, she began to have problems in the convent, where her superior accused her of lesbianism, which not only was not true for her but was an idea, she says, that she "couldn't deal with." Her superior did not believe her, and the conflict could not be resolved.

"Finally I realized that was not the appropriate place for me. And I left with ideas about starting a convent. I remember thinking about them on the airplane on the way home. That was a revolutionary idea, in the Catholic church at that time, in 1967."

I ask her to speak more loudly, as the wind moans in our ears and lashes the long grass around us. How ironic that we had worried that our voices might disturb the sleeping people.

"Well, the next year," she shouts, "about half the convent walked out. Nuns and priests were leaving en masse during that time. One of the biggest conflicts was between nuns who felt we should be involved in social causes and nuns who felt like you should stay in the convent and pray. I was on both sides, that was one of the problems. I felt very much that it was important to begin with the contemplative life, and whatever comes out of that, in the way of action, is really authentic. I'm a Virgo, you know, so

ble with men. Of the approximately fifty monks who inhabit Shasta Abbey, half are women. Women and men wear the same robes and shave their heads. In the hierarchy women take on the same responsibilities as men, with a number of women having been given the title "roshi" by their teacher. Our retreat master was a woman. At that time construction was going on for the meditation hall, and many women as well as men ran the electric saws, climbed the scaffolds, hammered nails. Tasks were rotated irregardless of sex, it seemed. This created an atmosphere that was immensely freeing in its acknowledgment of our true humanity and capacity.

The abbey is a necklace of small stone cottages connected by covered walkways, whose most conspicuous ornament is the meditation hall, much larger than the other buildings and covered with aluminum siding. In the center of the cloister stand pine trees above short grass scattered with pinecones and piles of firewood.

Here I stacked cedar in the quiet afternoon, taking the lengths of wood from the pile in the yard and placing them against the wall of the cloister. It was hot in the pine-smelling, cedar-smelling yard. A sprinkler turned, sputtering at regular intervals. Through the window cut in the wall I saw Mount Shasta, a big brown presence now in summer, with an apron of dirty snow draping its side; it stood so high above us, like a patient old woman whose presence joined earth to sky.

The little stone houses were built in the 1930s by an Italian stonemason to be used as a motel. Reverend Kennett and her Order of Buddhist Contemplatives (then called the Zen Mission Society) acquired it in 1970. It was so near busy freeway I-5 that a few buildings had to be torn down to allow for the required space next to a highway. The firewood is important, for snow has been known to fall in every month but July at Shasta, where the treasurer refers to summer as "the season of free heat."

In the meditation hall sits a massive gold figure called the "Cosmic Buddha," a representation of a vision experienced by Reverend Master Roshi Jiyu Kennett. The high small windows of the meditation hall display stained or painted glass scenes, reproductions of the illustrations in the book *How to Grow a Lotus Blossom*—again, Roshi Kennett's visions as seen when she was near death and sat in deep meditation for many weeks.

Whether she is literally in residence or not, the presence of this most unusual woman and Zen master is strong at the abbey. On that first visit, I encountered her by surprise. I was working, carrying loads of small stones in a wheelbarrow to the site of the new zendo (meditation hall). (Work is greatly emphasized at Shasta Abbey as a form of meditation practice. The ideal is constant awareness and every minute practice throughout all the actions of daily life.) I saw a maroon-robed figure, standing just under the overhang of the roof. She was quite majestically proportioned, and her head was newly shaved. A commanding chin gave strength to a round cheeked, somewhat puffy face. As I pushed my wheelbarrow toward her, she looked at me with an expression of interest, pleasure, and surprise. Glancing at the load of stones, then up into my face, she said in a deep rich voice with a decidedly British accent, "*Oh,* thank you very much!" In those moments I felt her goodwill and also the sense of power strongly contained.

Roshi Jiyu Kennett, now in her early sixties, was born in England and educated in music there, working for some years as a musician in the Church of England. She began her Buddhist training at the London Buddhist Society, was ordained in Malaysia, and then spent seven years in Japan at Dai Hon Zon Sojiji Temple. There she became personal disciple to Koho Zenji and head of the Foreign Guest Department. She was declared a roshi by her master and served as abbess of her own temple for a time in Japan. Having come to the United States on a lecture tour in 1969, she stayed to found Shasta Abbey and has lived here ever since.

Now five years after that first encounter with her, I have come to the abbey for a week-long retreat with the lay ministers, and I am very interested in the chants we sing during services. Roshi Kennett has translated the traditional texts of the Soto Zen church into English and set them to Gregorian chants. They are sung to the accompaniment of organ music. While some of the language reminds me of Christian god worship, I find the whole effect immensely rich and intriguing, as it rings out into many associations, touching my earliest experiences of religion.

At the abbey many aspects of life are deliberately not Japanese. Monks are referred to as "Reverend." In the cloister they wear traditional robes (of different colors to indicate the level of their attainment), but when they go out they wear the clerical collars of Western priests. The woman monk who picked me up at the bus stop was wearing a wig over her bald head, a beige medium-length skirt and white blouse, hose, and "sensible" shoes. In the dining hall everyone sits at long tables and eats with forks and knives.

In this adaptation to Western mores, Kennett Roshi actually is doing what some Buddhist masters claim to be doing but aren't. Besides operating from her own natural insight and courage, she was aided in this effort by the specific direction and encouragement of her Japanese teacher, who was abbot of one of the chief training monasteries in Japan and an archbishop. To her book *Zen Is Eternal Life* (formerly *Selling Water by the River*), Reverend Koho Zenji contributed a foreword setting forth his thoughts on the transformation of Zen as it travels from culture to culture. He urged that the people of Western countries give to Zen their own "customs, ways and behaviour" just as the Japanese gave to the Zen brought from China their own particular cultural stamp. "Thus will Zen be reborn in the West," he says, and adds, "The Zen of the West must be born of Western priests in Western countries and not spread by Japanese who are unfamiliar with Western ways and customs."

Here at the abbey this time I have a deeper sense of the inner life. On my first visit I was struck by externals—the work, the bowing, the semiformal meals. This time I sense in the monks the effects of deep meditation over time. The ceremony is more powerful to me, and I feel the emphasis on service to others. In a conversation with one female monk, I discussed the purpose of monastic practice and its effect on the surrounding world. "A lot of the practice here—much of the ceremonial, and the ritual, the bowing, and so on." she answered, "is not only intended to help you get beyond self and be less opinionated and soften you, but also it is intended to constantly open you up and offer the merit of your practice wherever it's needed, so that you don't hold onto anything. The deeper you go in meditation the greater the reward, the spiritual fruits, are. All the offering of incense and the bowing is a way of always letting go and offering that up for the benefit of all beings. So a monastery is a little like a spiritual powerhouse, always sending out merit."

I speak with Reverend Roshi Jiyu Kennett in the backyard of the Berkeley Buddhist Priory, a modest house on a busy street, one of a number of priories staffed by priests from Shasta Abbey. She often comes to the Bay Area to lecture at the University of California, and this summer she has stayed longer because of health problems. I am greeted by a jocular-seeming woman in a brown robe who sports a short crewcut dappled with gray. She is as large and commanding as I remembered, flanked this morning by two male monks who stay with us throughout the interview and now and then interject a comment. We seat ourselves below a sun umbrella at a round metal table, and Jiyu Kennett begins to talk with the authority of one who is used to holding forth, in a strong voice that I can only describe as juicy, her stories underlined now and then by hearty laughter.

One story concerns her graduation ceremony in Japan.

"When I was in Japan, as a woman you could officially become a priest, but you didn't do it in public," she begins, "because that would mean that the emperor would have to recognize that a woman existed. So you paid him four times the price that a man did, to get the certificate, and you did it in private.

"My master said, 'We're going to do it in public, because this is totally wrong.' And he forced the issue. I have never done a ceremony with more terror inside me, than that one with twelve men down each side, each one with the curtains drawn over his eyes as if to say 'I'm not here.' Those were the witnesses. Try *that* sometime! That can be pretty scary—in a foreign country, in a language you're not one hundred percent sure of, with a lot of people who are hating your guts. And the reason Koho Zenji did it—and I've got it on tape—was for the benefit of women in his country.

"The weirdest thing was sitting on the floor in the guest department with the chief guest master chanting words in front of you as he offered you the big red teacup, and a look of total disbelief on his face. He could not *believe* this was happening. It would make a wonderful film."

She leans back to chuckle in appreciation of the scene and comments on the significance of it.

"As I see it, if women want to do this, they've got to make their minds up just what it is they're going into it for. Are they going into it because they want to become one with the Buddha and find their own buddhahood, or are they going into it because men say they can't?

"I've never had a fight with men. I've always loved 'em. I don't trust 'em, and I don't admire 'em, but I love every one of 'em. Fair enough? That's experience."

She has a way of taking an idea, spinning it out, then reeling it back in, closing it down, and snapping the lid shut on it. She has already told me how she made it through her difficult training in Japan, where she was discriminated against as a woman and a foreigner. The Buddha had said women could make it, she said, and as far as *she* was concerned, all the rest was simply trappings from the Indian culture of the Buddha's time. She tells the story of the monk Ananda's having asked the Buddha whether women who had gone forth into the nun's life could reach the highest level of attainment. The Buddha replied, "Women, Ananda, having gone forth . . . are able to realize . . . perfection."[6]

"Obviously a lot of women feel frustration and jealousy and hurt and pain because of what's happened to them. And I understand that. But in religion that's gotta fly out the window. What are we in religion for? Yes, in religion you have a lot of people who're insulting because you're a female, and a lot of people who won't come to you for funerals or weddings or the like, but that's *their* problem, it's not *mine*. Somehow or other women have to get to that stage, if they want true spiritual equality. They've gotta stop letting the men put them down.

"In my case, at Shasta Abbey, I have created, if you like, an oasis. Or I've *tried* to make an oasis—where people really are equal. That's bringing the *essence* of Buddhism rather than women shall walk three paces behind, we shall use chopsticks, we must all sit on the floor, chairs are illegal, going round with a loincloth instead of an ordinary pair of undershorts. I mean, my god, all of these things are not *us!* The norm for religious dress in this country is a collar turned backwards and a shirt. Why have we got to go around pretending we're Japanese or Chinese or Thai?

"When I was a child in England, you had the Ceylonese monks ordaining Britons to be Ceylonese monks in England, and it was illegal for them to wear anything other than the one sheet and a sarong. Have you ever tried living in one sheet and a sarong in England's climate? Think about it! You have gale-force winds most of the time, which means that you lost your sheet and you were left in the sarong. When I was a kid I looked at this and I said, 'They're daft!' One of them gets a yellow sweater, puts it underneath: the church throws him out! Now that's not Buddhism. That's stupidity."

And she returns to punch home the moral.

"You see what I'm talking about. We've got to stop worrying about the unessential things and worry about what we're really trying to do. We can bring about *social* change by legislation, but you're not going to bring about spiritual equality by legislation. What you're going to have to know is that you *are* spiritually equal, and the only way you're going to do that is if you march right by the laws of man and say, 'I'm only interested in the laws of the Eternal.' Fortunately the Buddha said it for himself. So, for that matter, said Jesus Christ, except Paul got in the way. I wish people would stop worrying about the goons who followed them and pay attention to what they themselves said. Because *that's* where it lies."

I ask whether some of the practices at Shasta Abbey are derived from the Christian tradition.

"Give me an example," she challenges. "You know, Buddhism and Christianity are not all that far apart, except from the savior point of view."

"The figure of the Cosmic Buddha in your temple, is that a correspondence to the Christian God?" I ask.

"No. The best way I can describe the unborn, the undying, the uncreated, and the unchanging is to say 'the Cosmic Buddha,' and they understand. It's a bad term, but I hate wasting breath."

"What about the use of the organ?"

"They use organs in Sojiji. They use 'em all over the East. I used to be a professional musician. I barely got to Malaysia before Reverend Kim Seng was moving in a large grand piano, saying, 'Now we can do it properly!' That's not particularly Christian. We've got recordings of the girls' school in Sojiji's choir singing with the piano and the organ and the orchestra. This is nothing unusual.

"Now the sort of chants we use—yes, they were thrown out of

the Catholic church. I thought it was very wrong to lose the baby with the bathwater. They were darn good chants. Everybody knew 'em. And all that *Buddhism* had done in the *Far East* was pick up the old chants of the previous religions! So we *use* them. It makes a wonderful bridge.

"As for the translations, I was *told* by Koho Zenji to translate the scriptures. And some of my translations are now the official English translations of the Soto church.

"There's a part of what I suppose can best be called the Buddhist Bible, the Tripitaka, which is scads of volumes long—and of which we were sent a copy which means we were officially on the map—in which they have a section called 'Patriarchs and Virtuous Ones.' To qualify as a patriarch or a virtuous one, what you needed to have done was translated so many volumes of the scriptures from one language to the language of the country you're in. And the entire list says, 'he translated etc., etc.,' and the next, 'he translated etc., etc.' That's the qualification of virtue. As soon as somebody with a different language turns up in a temple, the thing the priests do is sit you down to translate. To spread the teaching. They think we're very weird to be grooving, I think the term is, on oriental sounds. I don't doubt that those sounds are very beautiful. I enjoy them no end. I can *make them.* But that's not what the Asian priests want us to do. Except that some Japanese think that's the right way to go. Some Chinese think that. But a lot of them don't."

When I ask why she did not change the language to accommodate female pronouns she says she doesn't like using extra words and chose the briefest form, but that women are included in the masculine pronouns.

The service is going on right now in the front house, the chants sounding strongly. We stop to listen for a moment and I am reminded of the abbey. We talk now about how specific changes came about there.

"The thing is we didn't deliberately set out to alter anything," she points out emphatically. "We're up in Shasta and we're using chopsticks, and suddenly we can't find any. 'Better get some knives and forks,' says somebody. So we get some knives and forks. And somehow we never go back to using chopsticks. And we're getting on buses and stepping in our sleeves, and somebody says 'Why don't we shorten them a bit?' That's how things have happened—in response to the situation. There was a fair bit of time when we could not get, because of the distance away we were, Japanese stick and powdered incense. So I said, 'Why don't we get some of that stuff from the local Catholic church supply store?'

"I mean, it happens like that. We started off with all tatami mats. Everything was so traditional it was scary. And one day we said, 'My god, carpet's so much cheaper, we can't go on buying these things with the import duties and all the rest of it.' So it became carpeting. But there was no intention of getting rid of tatami mats."

"Has women's participation changed over the fifteen years the abbey has been in existence?" I ask her, and she answers by telling of a difficulty some women encounter in pursuing a spiritual path.

"It's been subtle. Most of them when they first came didn't believe they could do it. And I had to keep holding out my certainty, because I *knew* they could. And it became very obvious that they could, but they weren't totally sure of it. And therefore a lot of them have been slower than the men, simply because they had to *believe*. Now we have at least three senior females totally capable of doing any job that the men do in the temple. But it's taken a good five, six, maybe ten years, in some cases longer—simply because of the brainwashing that was done prior to their getting there.

"When I was in the Far East, they said, 'Women are much slower than men.' And Koho Zenji said, 'Yeah, they are, guess who made them so!' And the old boy was right. There were monks around who said he was mad. I mean, he wasn't like any other Japanese. No, nobody else was *archbishop* either! How did they think he got the job?!'"

From a discussion of the position of women in the Christian church she moves to the declaration that some of the problems of women within Buddhism in the West derive from Christian concepts.

"The Japanese word for monk-priest has both male and female forms; when you translate it as nun, what you have is a *Christian* thing that automatically puts the woman down. If you translate it as female monk or female priest, you immediately have a thing which is a distinction but not a put-down. The words *monk* and *nun* are Christian.

"You see what I'm saying. One of the big problems in this is that the people who originally translated the Buddhist scriptures were all Christian, so of course they made Buddhism sound very cold and unreal. Now we've got all those Victorian translations from early in the century running around. 'The Christian God is the only real god,' was the message, 'therefore anything else has to be wrong.' I can remember when I was a child in school, one of the hymns we sang: 'What though ye spicy breezes blow soft o'er Ceylon's isle/ Though every prospect pleases and only man is vile . . . ' " She gives a huge theatrical sigh. " 'From many a tranquil river, from many a palmy glade/ They call us'—'Us! Us *Britons!*' " she interjects—" 'to deliver their land from error's chain.' "And there was a Buddha from the museum sitting on the mantelpiece.

"That sort of mind was doing the translations! There's a particular book I think of, concerning certain of the teachings in Japan. Some of the finest pictures I've ever seen. You should *read* the text! It is nothing but insult and put-down to the teachings."

As a conspicuous and outspoken religious leader, and the only female head of a Buddhist monastery, Kennett Roshi is sometimes criticized by people who either disagree with her or misunderstand her methods or intentions. Among these criticisms is the assertion that she discourages sexual expression in her students. Indeed, she tells me, she does favor celibacy for her monks, and she gives her position on this persistently challenging issue in monastic life.

"Over here, when I first started teaching, I believed utterly that married priesthoods were possible. That was because in Japan that was all I saw. As I watched, I realized that you could have much better priests, male and female, of a much higher caliber from the point of view of the congregation, if they weren't married. And that if you wanted to go beyond a certain distance in spirituality, it didn't matter whether you *wanted* to be married or not, you *couldn't* be. That explains to me why a lot of the Chinese priests, who were celibate, seemed to be going a lot further in their spirituality than did the Japanese. I did not come to this conclusion easily. It took me something like fourteen, fifteen years to be certain of it."

"In your view," I ask, "is it because relationships take too much time and effort? Are they a distraction?"

She fixes me with an intent look.

"The scriptures say, 'If you want true spirituality, give up everything.' That means all attachments. Give up everything. The scriptures tell it as it is. Everything means *everything*. You have got to get to the state where it doesn't matter if you're dead—if you would go the whole way. You cannot even have the comfort of fondling another person, if you go the whole way.

"Now anyone and everyone, including the laity, can have what the Japanese call a first kensho, or enlightenment experience, and from which most of the priests teach. The first kensho is the first certainty of spirituality. You know in the Bible it says that many are called and few chosen. Buddhism has it that all are called and few answer. Sometime or other, in everyone's life, that call will come. If it is answered, it becomes a first kensho, and one has the absolute certainty of the unborn, undying, unchanging, and uncreated. You know in a way that you can never forget or lose, that this is so. It is from that certainty that a lot of priests teach.

"But in actual fact if you want to go on further than that in your spiritual training, you've got to understand this is like taking down the plaque from the door and sticking it up outside and saying 'I'm ready now.' You've got to go into the house and go through everything in the house . . . Do you see what I'm saying? If you're married, the singleness of mind, the devotion, the oneness with that eternal can't take place, because you're dividing it off for a member of the opposite sex or a member of the same sex, or whatever. If you're going to follow the eternal, *he's* the one you're gonna be fond of. He-she-it. *That's* the difference."

"Is there a loss," I ask her, "for people who are going to minister to others, in life experience, for instance, the experience of raising children?"

"I've not found it so," she answers. "But I personally think that it's probably wiser to go into the priesthood later in life rather than earlier. You come in at seventeen or eighteen when all your juices are flowing eagerly, and you can have an awfully rough time. A lot of Buddhist countries won't take people until they've been married and had children. So there is that side of it, but they *do* say you've got to be separated off afterward."

We can hear the melodic chanting from the meditation hall in the front house. The service is coming to an end now, to be followed by a meeting that Kennett Roshi must attend. We part amicably, and I stay in the yard for a few minutes to listen to that music reaching so deeply into the Christian experience, those English words that speak of the great Buddhist insights into the nature of existence.

NOTES

1. Although the term *nun* is used in Theravada and Tibetan Buddhism, some women are uneasy with its Christian associations. The Pali or Sanskrit terms, *Bhikkhuni* or *Bhikshuni*, can be translated as "female mendicant." In Zen, on the other hand, while there are nuns, most Western women have been ordained as "monks" or "priests" equally with the men. The word *nunk* was invented as a joke by a Zen Buddhist roshi, Venerable Gesshin Prabhasa Dharma, in answer to people's wondering if they should call her a monk or a nun.
2. Nancy Auer Falk, "The Case of the Vanishing Nuns," in *Unspoken Worlds*, edited by Nancy A. Falk and Rita M. Gross, p. 208.
3. Sister Ayya Khema, "Is the Bhikkhuni Sangha Necessary?" *NIBWA (Newsletter on International Buddhist Women's Activities)*, no. 4 (July-September 1985).
4. Since our talk, Chogyam Trungpa Rinpoche died, on April 4, 1987.
5. The larger number of rules for nuns came about partially as protection in response to threatening or exploitative situations. For example, when a nun meditating in the forest was raped, the rule was established that nuns could not meditate in the forest, and so forth. In addition there are the Eight Special Rules for Nuns, which cause a nun to be submissive to all monks in specified matters of daily life and ceremony. For a detailed discussion of the nuns' life and the original rules of the Vinaya, see I. B. Horner, *Women Under Primitive Buddhism*.
6. Quoted from the *Sacred Books of the Buddhists*, vol. 20: *The Book of the Discipline (Vinaya-Pitaka)*, volume 5 (Cullavagga), Chapter 10, p. 354, translated by I. B. Horner (London: Pali Text Society, 1975).

Pema Chodron

Shinma Dhammadinna

Rina Sircar

Ayya Khema

Treelight Green

Sister Martha Dharmapali

Barbara Horn at Tassajara

Teijo Roberta Munnich

Reverend Roshi Jiyu Kennett

4.

Lighting the Way: Women Teachers and Women-Led Centers and Retreats

In every Buddhist center there are women who function as teachers, whether officially, with robes and the mandate of transmission, or informally through their interactions with other sangha members.

The phenomenon of American women as teachers within the Buddhist tradition is an issue of tremendous importance, for until women can take institutional and spiritual leadership in Buddhist institutions, they remain marginal, their needs easily overlooked, their strengths and capacities readily coopted.

Many of us have found our way to women teachers, some because we preferred to study with a woman, some because we particularly responded to the teacher's style without reference to her sex. Some feminists sought out female teachers because they were used to honoring and working with women and because they wanted to receive the Dharma from a person with female sensibility and experience. Other women came to study with female teachers through accident of location or association. Some women went to female teachers after disillusioning experiences in male-run Buddhist centers, out of a desire to practice the Dharma in a situation safe from the sexual power abuse of male teachers and free from the strong masculine orientation of many centers. Often in women-run centers they developed a particularly strong appreciation for the warmth and accessibility of women teachers.

Most of these teachers have experienced repression and rejection in their training. Often when women begin to come into their own spiritual power within a male-dominated and male-designed system, they encounter suspicion and jealousy. As several of the women in this book have pointed out, male Zen roshis comprise a sort of "old boy" network not unlike that of business executives or Christian priests and ministers. This loose fraternity is, so far, impenetrable by women, even the few women who have attained the rank of roshi, so that the women find themselves functioning independently. A number of women who are now prominent teachers have been, in effect, disinherited by their own (male) teachers; they have been made unwelcome in the centers in which they trained and sometimes in the lineage itself. This phenomenon is not limited to Zen. A Western Theravadin teacher was dropped from the Asian lineage in which she had received her transmission because she insisted on introducing innovations to the traditional Vipassana practice in order to make it more accessible to the Westerners she was teaching, and because she taught men as well as women.

In Theravada Buddhism as it has developed in the United States, centers run by Americans show more receptivity to women, but participants still confront the usual American forms of sexism. Tibetan Buddhist women teachers are well-nigh invisible. Pema Chodron has become known through her work to establish Gampo Abbey (see Chapter 3); there is a Tibetan-born woman teacher in Canada named Jetsun Kushok Chime Luding who was given opportunities because she was the sister of a tulku or reincarnated lama. For the rest, even in the large Tibetan Buddhist community of Vajradhatu in Boulder, the women perform a number of teaching roles but none stand out. The one woman offering a Tibetan Buddhist teaching in her own center is a Native American medicine woman, Dhyani Ywahoo, who has recognized the spiritual kinship of her people with the Tibetans and incorporated Tibetan Buddhist practices into her own teaching.

To make their way through a system that placed obstacles in their path, to confront the sexism of their fellow students and sometimes their own teachers, and to transcend this to deepen and realize their full spiritual potential, many women teachers have developed heroic grit and daring. That struggle to win through adversity to mastery required extraordinary willpower and heart combined with belief in the individual's ability to triumph. This process has resulted in women of enormous presence, who embody the battle and the victory in themselves.

There are advantages and drawbacks to this accomplishment. Certainly it is encouraging to a student. There is the sense that these women's practice is built upon a rock, that no accidents or disasters can shake them; that is comforting and inspiring. They are deep Buddhist masters more than precious to us. And there are situations in which their heroic individualism works to the disadvantage of students, as in the group experience described below.

At the Balancing of American Buddhism conference at Providence Zen Center in September 1985, the questions being raised from the floor about sexual abuses in Zen centers, about the difficulties of pursuing a Buddhist practice while raising a family, about inequities in treatment in Buddhist groups, were being asked by young women who had absorbed the influence of the women's movement in this country in the last fifteen years. These women made certain assumptions: that a focus on so-called women's issues is necessary and useful, that by the sharing of experience women are strengthened, that it is through communication and group effort that wrongful situations are changed, individuals helped and healed. The experiences of communication, group process, horizontal structure, as practiced in feminist groups, were shared by many in the room. The teachers, however, coming as they do from an individualistic position, and to some extent ignorant of the changes in contemporary women's psyches, when confronted with the women's desire to investigate the issues in their own lives, were at first not able to answer to the needs of the group.

Because we receive so much from these teachers' guidance and are so heartened by their example, we assumed they would respond with an understanding of women's issues and feminist process; we forgot that our understanding is the product of a certain kind of experience, whether overtly political or cultural, that these women do not necessarily have. While we were living in the secular world, some of the teachers were living in monasteries where their every effort and concern was bent upon spiritual awareness, or if in the world, with a perspective so focused upon spiritual work that it ignored the politics of their situation and the surrounding environment.

Whatever the reason, while these established teachers are enormously important to us as guides on the spiritual path and as role models, it is not realistic to imagine that they will lead in conscious feminist innovation. It is some of the new teachers, and a few of the women teachers most affected by changes in the Zen centers, who are making the effort to incorporate feminist process and women's spirituality insights and experience into Buddhist practice situations.

But most important is the realization that reliance on *any* teachers to do it *for* us won't work. The task falls to the women practitioners who are informed, concerned, and determined to create new forms and relationships within Buddhism. This realization, far from discouraging, may indeed empower us, for, in good Buddhist fashion, it puts the responsibility back in our own laps and calls for energetic investigation and self-reliant action that will no doubt serve better than reliance on a teacher. And this drawing from our own experience and wisdom, where appropriate, may allow us to relate with a balanced and joyous receptivity to our teachers in a way destructive neither to ourselves nor to them. We can stand beside them in their own journeys to increased insight just as they participate in guiding us.

In general, the teachers in this section offer a particular flexibility and warmth, an intuitive directness, and an ability to touch the physical realities of human experience that is distinctively female. Some follow a relatively traditional path, but their very femaleness lends a different quality—a softer, more down-to-earth feel—to traditional practices. Some are innovators who follow their hearts and call on their wisdom to create new patterns and approaches to teaching. By far the dominant theme of their teaching is the manifestation of spiritual investigation and awareness in daily life.

These women amply illustrate the role of a teacher as one who can awaken the heart. That they are women lets us understand that we too can aspire to their honesty and dedication.[1]

TWO WHO CHALLENGE

It is a foggy Sunday morning at Green Gulch Farm in the Marin hills next to the green, rolling Pacific Ocean. In the long, high-ceilinged meditation hall, whose white walls are punctuated by dark rough beams, the meditators sit facing the wall. Interspersed among the black-robed priests and students of Green Gulch are many visitors from the surrounding towns and villages: some tanned, healthy-looking people in their thirties, counterculture types in drawstring pants and Birkenstock sandals, a surprising number of old people of both sexes. Many are obviously experienced meditators whose backs are straight above their black cushions, their bodies unmoving.

When the bell is rung to end the meditation, more people crowd in to sit on rows of folding chairs in the open center floor of the room, facing the front where the priest who is to lecture today will sit. A full-bodied middle-aged woman dressed not in the traditional black robes but in a gray blouse and black skirt enters from the back. She makes her way to the front to take the seat on the platform, then looks out for a few moments over the assembled crowd, which numbers now well over a hundred people. She seems perfectly at ease, her round face calm, her blue eyes intense and friendly. She crosses her hands under the little black rakusu (see Glossary) over her blouse, this the only outward sign that she is a Zen priest. Instead of having a shaved head, she wears her straight brown hair turned out slightly at the base of her neck.

This week at Green Gulch Farm *Yvonne Rand* has been leading a retreat designed to promote mindfulness in daily life, in which she has made it clear to the participants that she gives us nothing she has not tested in her own life. She had to make a difficult choice early in her training, for her teacher insisted that in order for a priest to become a teacher, she or he had to spend a period of time at the Tassajara Zen training monastery. Yvonne went to Tassajara, leaving her two children with their father, but she was called back to do fund raising. "After a year it was clear to me that I'd lost my chance in terms of my kids," she told me. "I arrived in this community and practicing Zen with my kids and I had a responsibility to take care of them, and if that meant I wasn't going to go to Tassajara until they were grown, that's what it would mean. Dick [Baker-roshi, her teacher] didn't agree with me. I just said, 'Well, I know you don't agree with me, and this is what I'm doing, I'm convinced that this is the responsibility I have. My kids will teach me, this is what my practice is, it's got to include taking care of them.' I made a clear decision to make my life as a house-holder, as a parent, as somebody who lived if not entirely in the world, with a real appreciation for people in the world, and that I would have to find some way to express my understanding of Bud-dhism, given all of that."

Yvonne, whose children are grown now, lives with her husband in a house down the road from Green Gulch and drives each day to her duties there. Three major teachers have influenced her: Shunryu Suzuki-roshi, founder of the San Francisco Zen Center; Harry Roberts, a Yurok medicine man who was an informal advis-er at Green Gulch; and Lama Govinda, Tibetan Buddhist author of *The Way of the White Clouds* and other books. Each of these men she took care of while he was dying, including the preparation of his body after death. She often works with dying people and teaches seminars on death and dying.

Now in the zendo at Green Gulch, Yvonne is finishing her talk on the Buddhist precept: 'A follower of the way does not possess anything selfishly." She ends with a directive given to the Mayan people: "The roots of all things are intertwined. When you cut down a mahogany tree, a star falls." She pauses, looks out across the people, lets the picture sink in, and then finishes, "Before cut-ting down a tree, ask permission of the guardians of the forest, ask permission of the guardians of the stars." The room is silent.

Later, in the Wheelwright Center, a carpeted meeting room where couches and chairs are arranged in a circle, more than half of the people who were at the lecture have gathered for discus-sion with the lecturer. When Yvonne enters, she takes a straight chair and settles herself, smiling and chatting with the people around her. Hers is a questioning face, with something stripped, essential, about it; this could be the face of a pioneer woman, at once stern and extremely kind.

When everyone has entered and the room grows quiet, a young woman raises her hand.

"You are changing so many things here at Green Gulch," she says, "but there's one thing I wish you wouldn't change."

"What's that?" ask Yvonne, her whole body alert and receptive.

"I want you to sit *up there!*" says the young woman and points to the couch at the front of the room where the lecturers usually sit. "I want you to sit *there* so I can have someone to look up to."

Yvonne leans a little toward the woman, but somehow manages to include the whole room in her answer as she explains that, first of all, she finds this straight chair more comfortable for her back than sitting cross-legged on that soft couch. Then she says that she does not want to perpetuate the illusion that she knows more than we do or is more worthy of respect.

The young woman argues. "But I want a godlike figure, someone who is perfect, to look up to."

"I am quite corruptible," Yvonne tells her. "I don't want to let you help me corrupt myself. I can really get off on sitting up there giving lectures and being important. If you keep reflecting at me that I'm perfect, I might begin to believe I am! But I'm not interested in separating myself from you. And I'm very much engaged in exploring my role as teacher. I have something to communicate, here; so do you."

She pauses and smiles slightly. "Here I am, leading a retreat on mindfulness practices this weekend, giving people techniques for being more aware in their lives, and I pull into the parking lot this morning and get out only to find that I've put my blouse on backwards. I won't go into all the things that transpired last night to distract me. The point is, I raised my hand to touch my blouse, and there was the label, in front. So there I was in the parking lot struggling to turn my blouse around: the big teacher of mindfulness. So this is what I am, too."

She talks about why she has chosen, just now, not to wear her robes as she lectures. "Think of what authority projections one puts on that priestly robe!" she says. "I don't find it useful right now to arouse those projections or deal with them."

"And as for teaching, the Dharma doesn't *belong* to me so that I can give it to you. We don't possess the truth here at Green Gulch." She tells about her trip last week to Los Angeles where she rode the city buses and was heartened by people's consideration and caring for each other. "Compassion, gratitude, kindness exist out in the world in many forms. They exist *in you!*"

She continues, "This idea of perfection is such a dangerous one. We've got to be aware of our mistakes. There must be room for mistakes. If you can't make mistakes—as a student, as a teacher—you move way back from that edge where growth occurs."

This time an older woman on the couch challenges her: "Don't respect and reverence go with your role as priest and isn't it your *responsibility* to accept that reverence that's given to you and deal with it however you can?"

And the young woman chimes in. "Yes, if everyone's just going to be equal, then what you're doing here will be no different from what people are doing 'over the hill' " (that is, in the city).

"It's *quite* different," Yvonne responds. "When I speak of being a spiritual friend, I am not talking about our being pals. I am suggesting a relationship that is not so easy to understand in this culture."

The discussion goes on, with the men mostly making pronouncements, the women asking questions. Questions about authority, about the nature of a spiritual teacher and our desire to enshrine someone as such.

Yvonne points out that there are four priests besides herself at Green Gulch who give Sunday morning lectures, some of whom wear full robes and maintain the strict Zen-teacher stance, so that the people who come can be exposed to a variety of viewpoints.

I ask how she deals with the projections that *are* put upon her, as a middle-aged married woman with children, for instance, or even just as teacher? She answers that she and several other people at Green Gulch meet regularly to talk about their behavior and the way people are behaving toward each of them. In this way they check each other and break down the isolation that can put a teacher into unproductive or harmful states of mind.

When the session is over, I realize what has occurred. Not only have some of the major issues facing American Buddhism been raised in a passionate and succinct way, but we have seen a teacher questioning her role, examining the meaning and uses of authority, exposing herself as a human being in process, in public. Having spoken with Yvonne privately and then having experienced her teaching in the mindfulness retreat, I now see that she has the courage to bring the same questions she asks herself privately out into the public setting of her teaching at Green Gulch, and my respect for her grows.

In this openness and willingness to risk lies the possibility of healthy change in American Buddhism. Another woman teacher who has understood the essence of Buddhist inquiry and expresses it in her teaching is *Annick Mahieu (Sunanda)*. In 1981 the Insight Meditation Society in Barre, Massachusetts, which prided itself on being nontraditional and flexible, was confronted with a teacher who challenged its most cherished practices and assumptions. With imagination and spontaneity, Annick introduced communication into the traditionally silent retreat situation, creating events to jolt the students into awareness.

Annick lives and works in Cambridge, Massachusetts. I find her in her studio, dressed in loose white pants and top, at work on a large blue painting of a nude man seated in a meditative posture.

We settle near the window to talk, Annick telling me about her growing up in France, her Buddhist training in Sri Lanka, her work with mentally handicapped children and their parents. In 1980 she became a nun in Sri Lanka and insisted on ordaining herself, even though the monks and nuns were horrified at this departure from the rules. She objected to the ceremony because it was conducted by monks instead of nuns and therefore implied her inferiority as a woman. So one early morning she shaved her head herself, gave away her possessions, and took the vows. Not wanting to separate herself from laypeople, she did not wear the traditional robes but wore the white clothing of a novice instead. Her name *Sunanda*, given to her by her teacher, Seevali Thera, means "the one who dwells in the heart."

After a year of teaching in Sri Lanka, she went back to France, where she was contacted by a teacher from the Insight Meditation Society who invited her to come to Massachusetts to help teach the annual three-month course. She had taught with two of the IMS teachers previously in Switzerland, and they had liked her innovative methods. So she accepted, and in September 1981 she came to the United States to teach at IMS.

"That's when I started to get in trouble!" she says, laughing, and explains. "My way of teaching has always been challenging and untraditional, but at that time it was quite radical. For example, each of us would take turns giving a talk. I noticed that the teachers were sitting on a little platform higher than the students. This came from the common practice in the East of having the nuns and laypeople sit lower than the monks in order to show respect for the Buddha. I always felt uncomfortable with that particular behavior because of its implication that women or unordained persons are inferior or less spiritually accomplished than monks. Personally, I felt that I couldn't sit higher than other people because I was one of the group, and I didn't want to support that kind of indirect communication. Also, I didn't think that it was correct for Hinayana Buddhism because it created a separation between people, and, for me, where there is separation there is conflict. And peace cannot exist where there is conflict."

Annick speaks with great animation, her eyes ardent. "I thought it would be a good idea to concretize that separation and have everybody look at it. So with some help I placed seven wooden poles upright across the room in front of the platform, and a white canvas was stretched on the poles from one side of the room to the other and from near the ceiling to the floor. Then a tape recorder was set in the middle of the room and three microphones were put in different places so that if anyone in the room wanted to, she or he could take the microphone and talk.

"That day the bell rang as usual for the sitting and the other teachers came into the room. They discovered then that they had the choice of sitting on the platform behind the canvas and out of view of the students or sitting on the floor with everybody else."

"What did they do?" I ask.

She laughs again. "They sat with the people! We all sat together in a big circle and for one evening the separation between teachers and students disappeared. I cannot really remember how I started the talk, but the aim of it was not only to let me talk, but anybody else who wanted to as well. They could share their feelings, scream, yell, jump, laugh, do anything, it didn't matter, as long as it was *experienced together*.

"Some of the teachers told me later that they thought that my doing this had created too much chaos. But, according to my understanding, that evening was the beginning of a real and honest communication between all the participants."

"Did the students talk?" I ask.

"Yes, *of course*. Some shared deep and beautiful life experiences. Some conveyed their fear or anger; some were disoriented by this break in the continuity of the practice; and some happily discovered that they were no longer alone in experiencing pain. When one begins to practice meditation a lot of questions, emotions, and suppressed feelings come up and one doesn't know what to do with them. In this situation, everyone else who was on the same wavelength could feel what one person felt. A sense of togetherness emerged from this openness—and a sense of honesty too. It takes guts to stand up in front of two hundred fifty other selves ready to give you their undivided attention and openly share your feelings."

"When one person started talking, other people felt the urge to share and, naturally, reacted to what someone else had said. Very soon, these sharings formed a group process: a *big* group process!"

"I felt very happy with what was happening in the room and very touched by people's willingness to open up and talk fearlessly. I didn't question the spontaneity of the situation for a single moment, nor did I ever regret taking the risk of creating chaos! At that moment it brought a sense of honesty, love, and connectedness. It was not meditators routinely practicing meditation or a teacher routinely giving a formal talk *about* the traditional themes, it was *alive.* It was a talk given by everybody and received by everybody. And *that is,* to me, the essence of Hinayana Buddhism."

Most of the male teachers at IMS were distressed by Annick's methods, finding that her behavior stretched the limits of acceptability there. When it was time for her to lecture again, she resolved not to be quite as radical but to continue to challenge the students and the teachers in a way that went beyond thinking and verbal messages.

"For the second talk, I had some of the books about religion, meditation, and especially the Buddhist scriptures, brought out of the IMS library into the meditation room and piled up in front of the teachers, so that all that the meditators could see was these piles of books and perhaps the tops of the teachers' heads over them." Both of us laugh at this picture. Annick continues. "Then from behind the books I read the first chapter of Jack Kornfield's book *Living Buddhist Masters.*"

She goes to her bookshelf to find the book, opens it, and reads a section presenting the Buddha's initial doubts about teaching, as he worried not that the Dharma is too complex to understand but rather that it is so simple that no one would believe it. "The Dharma is everywhere already," she reads. "East and West, the truth is the same." And she recounts a story from the book about a monk practicing under a teacher's guidance. "He leaves. After trying other methods he discovers that he could have as well stayed with his first teacher. But it is only by going away and trying other methods that he discovered that it was not necessary."

Annick comments, "My questions were: What are you learning? What do you think books are going to teach you? What do you think we, as teachers, are teaching the meditators? Through piling up all the books and reading from someone who comments on the scriptures and who was also a teacher at IMS, I wanted to challenge the practice as well as have people think about the roles they were assuming within the Buddhist system. I wanted them to understand that what meditation is, is Life!"

During another lecture session Annick talked about her personal spiritual experiences and the link with her childhood. She often sat on the floor with the meditators rather than with the teachers. She portrayed the Buddha as a young man in search of himself and his freedom, and who, like the meditators, experienced psychological pain. In staff meetings she was as challenging as in her talks, questioning sexual issues at IMS, one of the most sensitive areas, and she offered classes outside IMS.

"The idea of my Love, Sex, and Meditation workshop sprang from my discovery that some meditators on the staff who were married or already in a relationship were having difficulties. And that in spite of the 'no-sex-no-eye-contact' rule, new relationships were formed that sometimes included sexual encounters on the premises. These budding relationships or 'Vipassana romances' as they were called at IMS needed to be paid attention to. I didn't see 'Vipassana romances,' I saw people having problems in coming together as a couple because they were in a meditation center. Somebody had to take care of that. It felt natural and sane to deal directly with that issue. To me, there is nothing like love and oneness between two people. Sexuality is part of it. I have always respected and admired the Buddha as a revolutionary thinker and philosopher who dared to question a society based on the caste system, and who challenged its most deeply rooted religious practices and beliefs. But if he were alive today I would probably challenge the man Siddhartha about having to leave his wife and child to understand the truth."

"These workshops, which were designed for married couples

who had already been in a relationship for some time, proved to be very beneficial to them. They discovered that the support of the other person helped them both to develop individually and to grow together as a couple within the meditation practice. Because they began to realize how they could facilitate each other's process, this empowered them with the possibility of a greater independence from the system and the teachers.

"It is significant that these workshops were held outside the IMS premises. They were unacceptable to the tradition and therefore the teachers in authority rejected the idea of having them there.

"Since then this issue has been opened up to discussion among staff and teachers at IMS."

At that time Annick felt, as she had in many other such instances, that she became a catalyst for change; as she puts it, she was "trying to expand and liberate the self-contained energy of an established system." This was a difficult position to be in.

When she went out to Yucca Valley in California, a site in the Mojave Desert where the IMS teachers hold retreats, she continued to teach in a spontaneous style. She describes one particular instance when she was giving a talk. "In that space where whatever happens, happens in the moment, the bells of a church suddenly started to peal out a song. So I stopped talking and listened to these bells, knowing that everybody was doing the same thing. At that moment it was so beautiful that no other sound or word was needed. And I felt I had nothing else to say. So I said that and left.

"One teacher told me that that was not communicating the essence of Buddhism. I completely disagreed with this, because I felt I was doing just that, as well as expressing the essence of meditation and spirituality in general. Because meditation consists in being conscious of thoughts and feelings as they arise. Not to judge them in terms of good or bad, but to move with them. In that state of observation, one begins to understand one's own movement and the process of thinking and feeling. And from that understanding comes clarity.

"All my actions within the system were motivated by the need to bring that clarity to the situation and to enable the Buddhist system to progress. When I felt I had done what I could, I left my position in the institution. Despite the disharmony I had experienced with the other teachers and the inevitable separation from them, I sensed that, in my actions, I had responded to the situation according to the Vipassana teachings I had received."

And she finishes, "In challenging the system, I was not challenging any particular person or group. My primary concern has always been to work with people interested in comprehending life in its totality, and not only in some of its parts. To me, meditation has always been the art of fully accepting life as it is and living it attentively in *all* its aspects. Nobody can teach Truth/Love/God, because it simply exists like a fresh breeze wafting through an open window: you cannot invite the wind, or be taught to do so, but you can leave the window open."

TO SHINE LIKE A STAR

I have the luck to be in Los Angeles in April of 1985 for the ceremony in which *Gesshin Myoko Midwer,* in a splendid golden robe, receives the transmission of the Dharma Mind Seal in the lineage of Vietnamese Thien (Zen) Buddhism and is given the Vietnamese name Thich Minh Phap or, in Sanskrit, Prabhasa Dharma. At the colorful, bustling Vietnamese Buddhist center, amid the sounds of bells, gongs, and drums, chanting and waving of incense, The Most Venerable Dr. Thich Man Giac officially proclaims her a roshi, entering her name on the lineage scroll and giving her the Holy Dharma Instrument, a white short-handled whisk.

The next morning, a sunny smogless Monday, I find this middle-aged German-born American woman in a building belonging to the Vietnamese center, and I recall first encountering her at the Women in Buddhism Conference in Providence, Rhode Island, the year before. There she had communicated a traditional Zen message in a classical style. I was impressed by her clarity and depth of insight, her reaching down beneath the forms of religion to the essence of the teachings, and especially her relationship to death. She stands up in many situations, as a woman, to challenge male bias and demonstrate the attainment of a female teacher.

The Venerable *Gesshin Myoko Thich Minh Phap Prabhasa*

Dharma, Roshi, whom most people now know as *Prabhasa Dharma,* has left behind her a career as a painter, a marriage, and most recently her commitment of many years to Rinzai-ji, Inc., where she received her training and was ordained. But her training, as she likes to point out, began long before she encountered Zen in this country, when as a child in 1940s Germany she endured the horrors and privations of war. By the time she was eight years old, when asked what she wanted to be when she grew up, she answered, "I want to shine like a star." One of her Buddhist names, Myoko, means "brilliant light."

We are to talk in the small room that is the site of the International Zen Institute. The house stands a few doors down from the International Buddhist Meditation Society on a noisy street in a Los Angeles neighborhood of Asian and Latino immigrants. The International Zen Institute is an entity created in 1983 because Prabhasa Dharma's students wanted her someday to have a place to give retreats and an address at which to receive donations.

This morning she wears a robe of palest gray and her head is so closely shaved that the skin shines, reflecting the window light. Below the delicate line of her brow her eyes are direct, the upper lids downcurled at their outer edges, giving a vaguely oriental cast. She smiles at me, ushering me into a small room with two chairs beside a low table, a desk, a hotplate on a stand. In her serving of the tea, her lifting of a napkin from a plate of small pastries, each gesture carves out a small silent space. And I think of the word most used when describing Gesshin: impeccable.

We talk about the festivities yesterday and her acceptance talk in which she said that while this was a special day it was also a quite ordinary day on which she got up, made her bed, washed her face, ate breakfast, just as usual.

"Yes, I did very ordinary things, and very *consciously,*" she tells me now. "Step by step I did all the things. This is how I live. I liked in the Gandhi movie when he said, 'If you want to know my philosophy, come and see how I live.' That is exactly what I would have to say. Because that's what it means to be a master of yourself, to be a roshi—not master over other people, over *yourself.* Your mind is clear and calm, you live your daily life in that consciousness, and yet you deal with everyday things. Get up, brush your teeth, make tea—but with every act I am fulfilling myself in that act. And I enjoy myself in that act. Everything you do in that mind. It's all Buddha mind.''

She is willing to speak of her childhood in the war.

''The outer circumstances of war and destruction and from moment-to-moment being faced with death, at such a young age, led me on the right path, on the *inner* path. Actually it was obvious that the outer world was unreliable. One minute there was a house and the next minute there was nothing. Or a person. *People* disappeared. So that was totally unreliable, and so there developed in me a strong inner life. An intense meditation developed for me spontaneously.

''So in my life in the monastery in Japan, where I studied when I was an adult, when I looked at how the monks were being trained, I realized that I had received my monastic training *in the world,* just in the way my life unfolded and where I was at the time. I had done everything, and to a much harder degree, than the monks did.''

She pauses to pour me more tea, offer me the plate of pastries. I know that some women students find Prabhasa Dharma intimidating in her traditional Zen orientation. But here in her room, dressed in the dove-gray robe, she seems softened, vulnerable; and while she is always the teacher, instructing me, she is also a woman. I remember our talk, late at night in her room at the Providence Zen Center, about menopause, when we swapped stories and symptoms late into the night. I remember her storytelling that preceded that talk, when a number of us gathered with her in the night kitchen and laughed until our sides hurt. And yet certainly it is true that Prabhasa Dharma is always elegantly aware of herself, each gesture conscious and spare.

In a workshop she had led at Providence, there came a moment which electrified me. Discussing the Europeans' intense fear of nuclear war, Prabhasa Dharma had said, ''I'm not afraid to die, I've already died,'' and went on talking. In a few minutes one woman, with a puzzled face, asked, ''Could you talk a little more about how you managed to die?'' and there was uneasy laughter in the room. Prabhasa Dharma did not speak or look at the woman. She carefully took the cup of water before her, lifted it from the floor, drank from it, and slowly set it down. Then she folded her hands before her. Chills ran over my back. I understood her: that in each action we die. Each completed action is a birth, a continuance, and a death. And I appreciated the Zen mode of teaching without words.

"I like Zen practice because it always throws us back upon ourselves and the experience," she tells me now. "The Buddha used to say, 'Come and see.' Jesus incidentally said the same thing. First you think you see the other—the person, or the thing—but if you stay around for a while with a master, you suddenly begin to realize that what you see is *yourself.* You're always looking at your own consciousness activity. And then you see, what you thought of the world and what you blamed on others was just your own fabrication here in your own consciousness and what you projected out. *That* is the wrongdoing. This is what one might call ego."

"As for the true self, it is love. Especially in Christianity people are taught to love others, and it says, 'as you love yourself.' But most people don't know how to love themselves. If you approach this with the dualistic mind, naturally it comes out as ego. So first we have to enter into this profound deepening, looking deep, deep, deep inside, and it requires a lot of discipline, that's why Zen has that discipline. Because the habitual energies are so stuck and so deeply rooted, it takes a lot of force and power to uproot them, if you want to do it in this lifetime. You *can* do it in this lifetime."

Prabhasa Dharma entered Zen training at the Cimarron Zen Center in Los Angeles, which she helped start with her Zen master Sasaki Roshi. For fifteen years she worked and traveled with Sasaki and with him established Mount Baldy Zen Center. In 1983 she left that organization. Now she travels most of the year to teach groups of students in Europe and various cities in the Untied States.

She is an artist still, proficient in calligraphy and haiku. And she is an eloquent speaker, giving public talks often to audiences who are not necessarily followers of the Buddha's teachings. She emphasizes that what the Buddha revealed and experienced is something so profoundly human that it transcends our institutions and systems. "It is totally human in all aspects, including the inhuman, when we're in no-form: the totality of it," she explains.

And she elaborates, "I'm invited to give sermons in Christian churches. And I talk about the sayings of Jesus, not about Buddhism. Buddhism is to be *in everything*, to *realize everything*. When Jesus talks, if you have experienced the truth yourself, of yourself, then you understand what he says. I never understood it when I heard the interpretations of various Christian ministers, but today I understand profoundly because I have learned through Zen practice to go beyond the words."

TOUCHING THE EARTH

At Insight Meditation Society in Barre, Massachusetts, in Cambridge, and at the Providence Zen Center, Buddhist women spoke to me of a unique and powerful teacher, *Dhyani Ywahoo* (pronounced Da-há-nee Ee-wá-hoo). A medicine woman of the Cherokee Nation, Dhyani offers her ancestral teachings in conjunction with Tibetan Buddhist practices. Her major work is "The Peacekeeper Mission," which teaches a spiritual practice designed to promote individual and world peace and respect for the planet. This work is directed from the Sunray Meditation Society central administrative office near Bristol, Vermont. Having seen a photograph of Dhyani Ywahoo, I am surprised to hear that this woman who looks so young is actually a grandmother.

I make my way to northwestern Vermont where I am driven from the bus station in Burlington through gorgeous green country overlooked by mountains so long and gently rounded that they seem like great dozing beings about to wake and stretch. Shacks and trailers thinly scattered beside the road bespeak the economic depression of this area, while occasionally a palatial ski resort rises up out of the green: glossy outpost of more affluent folk.

The Sunray Meditation Society sits up high on a wooded hill under the rearing bulk of Camel's Hump mountain. (At the time I visit Sunray, it is still in this original site near Huntington.) Housed in a rambling lodge that formerly hosted the Rustler's Roost Steak House, it bears few reminders of that past in its glassed-in dining room looking out over the valley, the living rooms and offices upstairs, its large shrine room, the real heart of Sunray, where much of its practice is pursued. Four altars stand in the shrine room, placed in the four directions, each representing a particular energy and intention.

At Sunray, I am told, summer courses are taught, planting and harvesting celebrations take place, workshops are given by spiritual teachers of many sacred traditions, and there are special events for children and families. Sunray has been designated a practicing Dharma Center in the Nyingmapa School of Tibetan Buddhism.

I meet the inhabitants, women and men mostly under the age of forty, and many children. There is Barbara, in her middle forties one of the oldest persons here; there is Yaniya, a woman who has researched her African heritage by studying Yoruba practices; Rich, who wears long black braids and has five children; Phil, a visitor brimming with enthusiasm for wilderness survival training, which he has just experienced; Melanie, who studies physics; several other adults, two rambunctious preadolescent girls, and a number of healthy-looking children of varying ages. There is the familiarity and warmth of family at the dinner table here, and a sense of calm purpose. Dhyani Ywahoo is spoken of with great reverence. Her names, I am told, mean, respectively, "gift for the people" and "the great mystery." A visit with her will be arranged for me.

And I am anxious to meet her, for while others speak of the interpenetration of Buddhism with Native American influences, this woman actually embodies that hoped-for merging. Deeply grounded in her own tradition, integrating it with Tibetan Buddhist practices, recognizing the ancient connection between her medicine-people forebears and Tibetan monks and nuns, Dhyani Ywahoo has established her own center, in which female participation and influence is very strong, and has involved people all over the country in work for spiritual mastery and peace.

The next afternoon Barbara Dubois drives me the few miles through green rolling hills, past old barns and ponds, to Dhyani's house. A steady fine rain falls, with sunlight beaming through it. Suddenly, ahead, rises the tender arch of a rainbow, and we see that one end comes to the ground in front of a clump of trees, very close, making a luminous bridge under which we will drive. "Now we'll see what's at the end of the rainbow!" I joke. "That barn!" shouts Barbara, laughing, "That cow!"

As we pull up to the modern raw-wood house where a big black dog runs on a lead, Dhyani Ywahoo comes out to meet us on the

deck. She is a brown-skinned woman apparently in her early forties, wearing a green print granny dress. At first glance she does
not seem imposing, her hair pulled back from her forehead, simple gold hoops in her ears. But she greets me with a particularly
intense look that is benevolent and welcoming, and when she
laughs, all of her seems alight.

I am surprised to notice that her eyes are a light green, and that
she seems perfectly at ease standing on the deck in the fine rain.

"Indians," Dhyani tells me, "do not run from the rain, especially gentle rain like this, which is called 'female rain.' "

When we enter her house, she settles into a chair while I sit in a
corner of the couch, and I have a chance to take a good look at
her strongly molded face with its slightly prominent teeth and
deep open eyes. The communication that follows is not really a
conversation, for Dhyani has certain things she wishes to say to
me and she does so, in a strong, slightly nasal voice, with now and
then an eccentricity of diction that indicates she grew up speaking
the language of her Tsalagi (Cherokee) people. Sometimes she
ends a thought with a brief "yah" of completion.

"In this time it is wise to encourage the female teacher and
practitioner," she begins. "Often one is given the impression
through misinterpretation of the sutras or perhaps through a cultural vision that the Buddhist teacher or master is a male. Yet the
Prajna Paramita [heart of perfect wisdom, as in the Prajna Paramita Sutra] is female in her form as she's depicted as a meditation
deity in Vajrayana Buddhism, of which we are a part. It's important for us to recall the dignity of the female form and that innate-
ly the stream of wisdom and the emptiness of unmanifest
potential is the void within each of us. And through that direct
experience of wearing the female form, we have a clearer accessibility to understanding of the emptiness, and also to compassion.
Our heart is open, in that primarily our function is caretaking.
Our whole form is created in that way. And in this time it is good
for the female practitioners to be supportive of one another. It is
a time of great change. The idea-forms of what a teacher is and
the idea of hierarchy are very much changing. The old forms are
falling down very fast. It is for the wisdom-mind of those of us
who are wearing the female body at this time to make more clear
the inclusiveness of the circle so that the teachings might be lived

and experienced fully, in contrast to the idea of something you study and do *away from* society and/or family. True Buddhism is to be fully involved in the world."

Dhyani's motivation to connect with Tibetan Buddhist practices resulted from the directives of her grandparents and prophecies about red people who would come from across the sea. Certain signs given to her in her own meditations let her recognize the Tibetans as these relatives, who came to work with the native people here to bring about a new world through a change in consciousness. In her family and in her clan, the Ani Gadoah Clan of the Tsalagi Nation, they have always communicated, in their meditations, with monks and nuns meditating in Tibet. And she refers to the prophecy, made by Guru Padmasambhava, that in the time in which the iron bird flies and horses run on wheels the Dharma would come and flourish in the land of the red people. Another common factor between the Cherokee and Tibetan peoples was the appearance of a teacher among the Cherokee who, before he disappeared, hid his teachings, to be found at a certain time in the future; and the Tibetan story of the great teacher Padmasambhava who similarly hid teachings to be found at the appropriate time for the benefit of the people. All this Dhyani tells me with great intensity and concentration, so that I feel myself drawn into the radius of her energy.

"One might see Tibetan Buddhism as quite airy and male," I offer, "and the Native American culture is so very earth-based and female, so that the two coming together create a very satisfying whole."

"It does create a great clear stream of energy," Dhyani says. "It is as if there is a pool that is so deep, and yet one sees clearly through all the many fathoms of the water." She leans out to look down in front of her chair, as if she's peering down through the water, and I can *see* far down into the moving depths. The experience is so powerful that I am shaken. "That is an analogy for the meeting of the Native American stream and the Vajrayana Buddhist stream," she concludes. "It is quite beautiful. Yah."

Beauty is a word she uses often. Walking the beauty path. Seeing beauty. I have heard this concept spoken of by other Native Americans. Surely it speaks of balance, harmony, and a profound appreciation for the natural world.

In teaching, Dhyani is very practical and realistic. When Sunray was first established, she asked her students to begin by investigating and honoring their Christian or Jewish roots, even designating specific altars for that purpose, in order that they might better understand the path they have now chosen to walk.

"Is there a different role for women in the practice?" I ask her, "or do you see them differently?" I have noticed that the majority of the people here are women, including some lesbians.

"We think of our body as a robe," she answers. "You may lay down the male body's robe and take on the female robe, or you may choose to go through in the female form. In Tsalagi tradition, seven lifetimes is the maximum it takes to become supremely realized. One working diligently can accomplish it in one lifetime, and then make a choice to either be born on earth again to help or to become a planet or a star to give life to other people. Some people are already committed to becoming a parent to reality, to becoming an island to those in distress, and they are worked with in a particular way. For those people the distinction of male or female has no significance. It is just a matter of clothing or headset. In our medicine making, that is, the practical application of mind energy, there is a great joy in the female and the male forms and our working together. When we are making medicine for something to be seen in this world, say for healing or making shields to transmute ignorance, then half the circle is male and half is female and we are facing each other. So there are certain times when we do focus on the energy of the male-female polarity. And according to the person's evolution in practice at some point we recognize it is all an illusion and what does it matter, and those are practitioners who have made a particular commitment."

"You seem to draw more women than men," I comment.

"There are cycles. When I first began teaching, it was all male . . . for about three years. They were scientists. That was in the late sixties. Then there was a time of larger mixed groups, and then deeper teaching with all gay men. That was a period of three years. That was very interesting. It was when I was a guest lecturer at Southampton University on Long Island for a number of years. And from those meetings developed a core of people with whom to work. The gay men were very sensitive and attracted to the work."

"Are homosexuals more open for this kind of endeavor?" I ask.

Dhyani shakes her head. "I won't say that homosexual, hetero-sexual, male, or female is more anything. I think those lines create separation. People who are looking at art, people who are looking at the synergy of thought and action are more open to realizing the changing of the guard, and more willing to change forms; the issue is one's mind in a process of transition and seeing the world around in a process of transition. And those are people who are open to letting go of any attachment to illusions that are creating discord in one's own psyche and through resonance into the world around."

I ask what chance there is to protect the Indian lands, turn aside the nuclear threat.

"It only takes a small amount of catalyzing agent to make a change," Dhyani answers. "Enough people of clear mind in this land will transform it. It has changed a great deal. What we see now is the *reaction* to that change, seeking to take back what has been made right. Individual and group thought has a great deal to do with the environment and the outcome of all that goes on in this land, through this and all worlds. So how willing each of us is to put aside argumentation, to turn aside anger, that is the determining factor in our nation's evolution."

I find myself strangely affected by Dhyani's presence. It is as if I am buzzing with more energy than I can comfortably handle, and looking into her eyes at moments I blank out, forgetting what I had meant to ask her. Later when I mention this to her students they tell me it often happens to them. Barbara says that Dhyani's "vibratory rate" is faster than ours and takes people awhile to get used to. In groups, they tell me, the circle holds Dhyani's energy and makes it manageable, but individually sometimes her power is too much.

Now I ask Dhyani how it happens that she is teaching white Americans.

"Basically white, black, yellow, red, all of us are concerned about the same thing. We're concerned about clean water for our children, food for our families to eat, a comfortable, beautiful place to live in, or some people are thinking at the level of survival, not so much about beauty; nevertheless all living creatures have the same concern. We are no better than the bird in the nest, and it is wise to think about how carefully the bird considers what is making the nest. We have the same inclination to make things clear and beautiful for ourselves and one another. Somehow this inclination has gotten out of hand, from the idea of protecting the heart to protecting imaginary boundaries. It is this that calls for correction, by generating enough compassion in our heart to see those across the sea or those across the border as relatives. So when I travel around to speak, I am very happy to see the faces I see, and I'm especially happy when Native American people come to hear me. I notice they come out more to the Buddhist centers than to the universities when I speak there, because they feel the comfort of the Tibetan mindset as inviting to them. It makes me very happy to see the people, all of the people who are really committed, because each lecture is also a meditation. There is direct experience of what is being said. There's not just talk or theory. It's very practical. People directly experience and can take home and immediately apply attitudes to transform the illusions, and that is very beneficial, so as you see the faces lighting up, you can only be thankful. Yah."

Of her other centers, she says that in Washington state there is a community house; in Boston, people living together; in Colorado, the starting of a community; in Vancouver, a communal living situation; in Toronto, people who come together weekly and monthly. Wherever there are two or three peacekeepers studying, they offer a general introduction to meditation to their neighbors and friends. There are people in Kentucky doing the practice that she hasn't even met, and in other parts of the world also: Turkey, Nigeria, Australia, Germany, Switzerland.

This morning I had gotten up early to participate in the service. By far the most powerful altar in the shrine room was the north one, I noticed, where giant crystals balanced among a Kachina doll[2], a basket of weeds, various objects wrapped in cloth, ears of Indian corn, and other objects.

In the open center of the large room the women did a ritual dance, with vigorous, graceful repetitive motions. Afterwards we faced the north altar and sat to perform a series of chants in a Native American language, followed by a half-hour meditation.

Then we turned to the eastern altar with its large black Buddha flanked by Tibetan thankas or wall hangings. At the side hung the rawhide drum used to accompany the Lotus Sutra chant. Here we chanted Tibetan verses. Then the "Myo ho ren ge kyo" of the Lotus Sutra was chanted very quickly, and finally the Heart Sutra was read in English.

The morning ritual, Dhyani explains, grows out of the cosmogony of her people, which she describes:

"The three and the seven are very significant to the Cherokee people because in the beginning there was emptiness and there came forth the sound and that sound is light and that light in observing itself became two and then three. These are the three elder fires above, and from them spun forth seven stars and also hidden stars—they're actually vortices of energy, they're potential for worlds to be born—and once the form solidified, then the three elder fires returned to the seventh heaven, and it is our cycle of thought that maintains the process. That's the foundation of the teaching."

"What is the purpose of the crystals on the altar?" I ask.

"The crystals are amplifiers. They amplify so that the energy of our prayer, our practice, may go out to benefit many beings. Also they can be set for particular purposes, they make connections with all of the practitioners' shrines throughout the planet. It's like a switchboard. So our prayers all converge and are carried out in all directions. Most of our communication occurs telepathically. After the first class all of the students are able to practice telepathy. That is one of the gifts that are moved in this lineage: a very clear ability to teach it and to inspire and bring it to fruition in people. So a great part of our teaching occurs through telepathy and through meetings at night. Although we're in different time zones, when it's eleven o'clock anywhere we are of one mind. Once a thought has been brought to fruition, it flowers throughout the entire circle. Sometimes it's amazing: it makes us giggle a great deal."

Dhyani grew up in a Cherokee community in South Carolina and a Native community in New York City. The original reservation in South Carolina does not exist anymore, she says, most of the land having been stolen by the whites. Her relatives still retain small parcels of it, and she goes back now and then to visit.

"You're nourished by the land of your foreparents. There are certain energies that are necessary to your well-being in your homeland. So it is very good to be there. But when one puts aside the idea of dominating the earth or owning it, then one can feel good comfort and good relationship with it. Anyplace I go I feel at home. In Scotland, in England, anyplace!" She laughs delightedly.

She chose to locate the Sunray Meditation Center in this part of Vermont at the suggestion of her grandparents. The Green Mountains here, part of the Appalachian Trail and originally part of the Smoky Mountains, are significant to the Indians, and in seven- and nine-year cycles native peoples from the Southeast made their way up here for certain meetings to maintain the spiritual balance of things. It is the duty of the Cherokee, Dhyani says, to take care of the high places and to keep the ceremonies of the high places. She speaks of the fluidity of Buddhism, whose growth occurs in each country in harmony with the minds and needs of the people, mentioning the Christian influence in this country.

"When you look at the being who walked as Jesus Christ, you see a contemplative, you see a person who was a caretaker, a Bodhisattva, considering the needs of other people, and who practiced. There is really just one road, and we may take different side roads to get onto that main road. We are all walking that road together, and it's a road that leads to understanding, and yet we don't need to go anywhere because wherever we stand on it the face is clearly reflected. So it is a matter of our choice to see something as ism this or ism that. We're human beings walking on the beauty road, and it began in beauty and we are walking in beauty and it shall end in beauty. And with that mind we cast out the illusions of separate nations and the illusions of scarcity, and we see that we have the means to share what is needed and the earth will give to all when we take down the fences, and where are those fences *erected* but in the minds of *people!* Yah."

There is silence for a time as Dhyani looks at me, as if sizing me up, and then she says, "You're writing a book. How you put the words out, the thoughts you carry in your mind, they are like a fire, you can light a realization of right action in the hearts of thousands of people. The shaping of the form, the crafting of the word, is a small part of it. It's the energy behind that form that's most significant. In Native tradition, always three principles you take into consideration. First the will and the intention and how it will affect the people unto seven generations. Then the affirmative power of it, that it affirms and builds rather than negates and destroys. And third that it gives people the means to actualize that clear vision. That's your sacred duty. That's what you've chosen to do, and so you want to really be clear and let the triangle of pure mind shine through it."

When I leave, Dhyani is cooking dinner for her family. She wishes me luck, fixes me for one last time with those green eyes, and sends me on my way.

WOMEN PRACTICING TOGETHER

The Bay Area Women's Sangha was formed by Zen, Theravada, and Tibetan practitioners in 1982 to meet their needs for a practicing community of women. At that time it was unique in the United States—the only independent and teacherless women's sitting group. Here women who had been struggling in male-defined situations found the relief of doing their practice in a welcoming environment, and women new to meditation could begin to experience Buddhist practice in a setting controlled by their peers. A strong sitting practice has always been the foundation of the Women's Sangha, and it offers a place to tap into our potential in creating our own practices and rituals. While eventually there was the formal choosing of a teacher, that teacher's location and the infrequency of her visits have operated to preserve the Women's Sangha's independence from hierarchy. Most importantly, nothing happens at the sangha that is not generated by women, and this provides a validating and nurturing environment in which to meet the challenge of Buddhist practice.

In Marin County, California, on a summer weekend, thirty women who have come from Berkeley, Oakland, and San Francisco as well as Marin gather in a secluded house to meditate together. They sit in the large open living room of the house, they do walking meditation in the yard. Silence is strictly observed. There is no formally designated teacher present.

The Women's Sangha had asked each participant to bring an item of food for the meals. Everyone signed up for chores on a job sheet on the wall.

For two days, the women sit and walk. Shinma Dhammadinna, visiting from Taungpulu Monastery, sits at the front of the room during the meditation periods. A movement session is led by a meditator who is also a dancer and performer. A Theravadin meditation teacher from Insight Meditation Society, who happens to live down the road, drops by to give a short, respectful talk.

At night the women unroll their sleeping bags on the living room floor and go to sleep. On Sunday they take a silent hike up into the yellow foothills of Mount Tamalpais and sit for an hour in a high meadow. In the afternoon a woman leads some instruction in Vipassana meditation. To end the retreat, another woman guides the loving-kindness or metta meditation.

It is a peaceful, concentrated weekend in which women meditate and are silent together, prepare food, do other chores, each taking responsibility for some aspect of the retreat. On leaving, many women express their gratitude for this opportunity.

In an Oakland cottage surrounded by tall, delicate bamboo stalks, on every other Wednesday evening the Women's Sangha holds its regular sittings. Six to twelve people may attend. Silent sitting and walking are done for an hour and a half; after this the women drink tea and share information or inspiration. Technically the sangha has a teacher, Ruth Denison, but as Ruth is many miles south in the Mojave Desert, the sangha members lead the sittings and sometimes bring meditation audiotapes or written material to share. Now and then there are special programs, and at least once a year the sangha hosts Ruth Denison who comes to give an evening talk or a weekend retreat.

Treelight Green tells how the group came to be. "Numbers of women heard about Ruth Denison and started going to her retreats. I was among them. And Karla Boyd and I started having meditation sittings at our house very sporadically, generally around holidays. We would invite the women we knew who were sitting with Ruth, and some other women from the Tibetan tradition, or just women who meditated. Then in 1981 two Zen women, Denah Joseph and Jessica Barshay, started the Women's Zendo, which offered a sitting every Sunday evening, and celebrations of Buddha's birthday and New Year's. The next year, these two groups drew together and became one interdenominational sangha.''

At this time the Oceana Center in Berkeley was rented for regular Sunday night sittings.

"The strength of the Women's Sangha," Treelight says, "was that here was a place where women from any tradition could come and practice together. The weakness was that there was no one there who had received transmission, who had been through the lineage, who could provide a singular spark of inspiration and teaching. But there was good support to meditate together, and I think that is essential and that is still continuing with the Women's Sangha.

"There was always the question: what is the sangha for? Are we interested in outreach or in just sitting together? There was a feeling among some members that a small group who regularly came would meet their needs. Others wanted to make this available to all women."

"The high times of the sangha were the events," Treelight offers. "Buddha's birthday, New Year's, Buddha's enlightenment. The New Year's celebration we adapted from the Women's Zendo, which I'm sure comes from the Zen traditions. We would chant and sit and meditate, and then everyone would write down two or three things that they wanted to let go of. A cauldron was passed around and all the papers were put into this common bowl. Then the bowl was passed again and the papers were drawn out one at a time and each woman read aloud what was wanting to be released. I liked that because it depersonalized it so that everyone could relate pretty freely to what was written, as opposed to 'Oh, that's *that person's* limitation.' And then the papers were burned. Then there was a candle ceremony in which we would all walk around and we would put flowers on the altar and then light a candle and leave it on the altar, so there would be just all this light. Those were really unifying and strengthening times, when women really did join together."

When eventually the group decided to take a Theravada Buddhist as its teacher, the original Zen and Tibetan Buddhist women left. Then the steering committee dissolved itself and opened the Women's Sangha to new leadership.

The sangha as it now exists is open to anyone and is more loosely structured than the initial group. There is no steering committee. All planning and tasks are simply taken care of after the twice monthly Wednesday night sittings, and anyone may take responsibility.

"Something I want to mention," Treelight concludes, "is the appreciation I feel for all of us having created an opportunity for women to sit together. Because of that and Ruth Denison's women's retreats, the majority of my meditational group experience has been with women. I know from being up at the Nyingma Institute what it's like to sit in another kind of center. When we choose to sit with women, we don't have to be reminded all the time of dealing with a more heterosexist or heterosexual group and being invisible as feminists or as lesbians, either one. And I think that's an essential wonderful thing about the Women's Sangha. When people who had not had that opportunity would come, they felt so grateful, and it was so *refreshing*. They would say, This means *so much* to me to be sitting in this room with all of you women!"

A LION IN THE DESERT

Already the sun rides high, assaulting my eyes as I look out on the miles of low chaparral, the chalky round sage bushes, the tall creosote shrubs scattered among the sage, their skinny stems gray with black circles like the joints of a puppet's limbs. Above them a Joshua tree tilts at a wacky angle, opening prickly arms to the sky. Low brown-blue shapes of mountains rise, far out, wrapped in haze, always there at the horizon like friendly spirits who watch over one but never come close.

Here on Copper Mountain Mesa in the high desert of California, just north of Joshua Tree National Monument, stands the group of modest low buildings that is Theravadin teacher *Ruth Denison's* Dhamma Dena (see Glossary) or Desert Vipassana Center. Here Ruth Denison is constantly in motion, instructing, chiding, comforting, mothering. She strides vigorously across the desert, legs wide, back bent forward, arms held out at her sides. And yet when she leads the group in dancelike exercises, her body moves with grace and subtle control. In the meditation hall, a concrete block–walled former homesteader's cottage, she sits at the front wearing a long full skirt of a deep rust shade, a long-sleeved blouse with lace at wrists and throat.

Ruth Denison is one of the few women teachers to have established her own Buddhist meditation center in the United States. (She has also cofounded a center in Germany.) She has been a help and inspiration to many women students in her deep teaching and in her willingness to invent what is needed on the spot. Especially her work with the body is valuable; through movement and guided meditation she establishes a strong awareness of one's physical and mental being. And she was the first teacher to lead an all-woman meditation retreat, something she now does regularly at Dhamma Dena.

A native of Germany, Ruth Denison worked as an elementary school teacher and principal. When she came to the United States after the war, she married an American, Henry Denison, who was a psychologist and for five years an ordained monk of the Hindu Ramakrishna Order. With him she traveled to the East where he was to undergo further training in the Theravada tradition. In Burma, her own spiritual vocation soon became apparent to the Theravadin master U Ba Khin. She trained with him until he gave her transmission of the Dharma, which brought with it permission to teach. Because of political unrest in Burma, she could not stay with U Ba Khin, so she continued her practice in Japan in the Soto Zen monastery of Ryotako-ji under the Zen masters Soen Roshi and Yasutani Roshi. Later, in America, she continued practice with these masters in Los Angeles and opened her home to them for their first sittings.

Now in her midsixties, Ruth lives part-time with her husband in their home in the Hollywood Hills and part-time at Dhamma Dena, and she travels throughout the United States and Europe to give retreats in Vipassana meditation. She teaches regularly at the Insight Meditation Society in Barre, Massachusetts.

Here in the desert, as I walk toward the main complex of buildings, the wind races like a gang of adolescents through the yard, loud and playful and destructive, slamming the macrame hanging on the porch wall against the windowpane, lifting a discarded blanket and dragging it across the dirt to wrap it around a fence railing, shaking the aluminum siding of the tool shed.

It is perhaps two hundred feet from main house to meditation hall on a path out through the sage and creosote. In the hall, the women sit cross-legged, backs straight, eyes closed. Maggie, a woman in her fifties from Los Angeles, who has been ill, sits in a chair near the back wall. There is blond Cheryl, married and mother of two; Hope who is just recently divorced; Heather who teaches dance; Rae who directs TV and stage dramas. I see two women from the Bay Area with whom I was in jail after the Lawrence Livermore Laboratories demonstration, a woman who worked in the cotton harvest in Nicaragua to support the revolution there, an antinuclear activist who came to Vandenberg Air Force Base to protest launching of the MX missile, some longtime feminist activists. There are women from Oregon, from San Francisco, Berkeley, Oakland, from Sonoma and Mendocino, who earn their livings in everything from secretarial work to law. A number of these women, besides Cheryl, are mothers.

Now as I sit among them, eyes closed, I hear the sound of footsteps crunching on the dry crumbly earth, a rhythmic rasping that grows louder. In the desert all noises are magnified. The sounds stop as shoes are removed. The screen door squeaks and I hear the swish of Ruth's long skirt moving up among us. Then the silence settles again.

Some minutes later, the soft round tone of the bell sounds in the room. When I open my eyes, Ruth is seated on the platform on her wicker stool, reaching to lay the wooden bell ringer on the little rickety podium. Her dark blond hair sticks out in loose curls from under her scarf, around a face with stark high cheekbones under pale skin, blue challenging eyes, an impudent mouth that smiles now ruefully.

"Ah, I know some of you are angry that I disturb you in your deep concentration, hmmm? You were just about to reach enlightenment and then I came and rang the bell."

Some women laugh, and she joins them, lifting her chin. I know she is referring to the criticism sometimes leveled at her, that she talks too much and disturbs people's concentration.

Ruth surveys the room. "Maggie, I see you have found a chair to sit in. Very good." She looks back to the far corner where Hope, who is experiencing much pain in sitting, has built a little platform and backrest of pillows. "Hope!" Hope looks up. "Tell me, is there hope?" Hope frowns and shakes her head, and then, despite herself, smiles wanly. "Actually it's a little better today," she answers. "I think there may be hope."

"Excellent!"

This is one of the twice yearly all-women retreats that have been offered since 1978 and have become a tradition with many Bay Area and Oregon women. Ruth Denison gave her first such retreat at Womanshare, a women's farm in Oregon, in 1978, and since then she has offered them (in addition to her regular mixed retreats) regularly at Dhamma Dena. Many of her dedicated students are lesbians; Ruth is consistently respectful of their lifestyle and relationships.

While Ruth Denison always speaks with great veneration of her teacher and her tradition, she has not hesitated to innovate, and she is considered controversial in more traditional Theravadin circles. Since the beginning of her teaching she has used body movement as a mindfulness training, as well as the walking and sitting of the usual Vipassana meditation. She directs her students in slow, very concentrated movements not unlike sensory aware-ness exercises, but her deep penetration into Vipassana training causes this movement to be a true Dharma teaching, that is, it leads one to apprehend the reality of one's condition.

Students who have come from Vipassana centers where no such lively maneuvers are encouraged sometimes balk when asked to bend and stretch or lie on the floor and slowly lift their heads or wiggle their toes.

"It is in a way a humiliation," Ruth says sympathetically, "be-cause I'm very direct in it and sometimes playful. 'This is too childish,' they think. You know, Christ said, 'Unless you become as little children, you cannot enter into heaven.' And in this really you *do* become children, but it's not childish to move and express the body in the way they are asked to do. Since they don't know the difference, they feel awkward. We don't understand that body and mind affect each other profoundly. Mostly we are quite unaware of the constant interaction between body and mind and how that allows for changes."

She points out that in the last few years some other Vipassana teachers have incorporated movement sessions into their work, and she tells of her first experimentation with the use of movement. "I remember I had ninety-six students in the retreat in Santa Barbara in 1976, and I did a little bit of sensory awareness and movement, such as moving the shoulders. But in the walking meditation I felt more courageous, so I changed the steps and pace and rhythm. And that brought joy and the students tended to forget their attachment to the traditional form. Through joy one learns more easily."

She goes on to explain, "The Buddha expressed this emphasis on the body by saying, 'If the bodily processes are known and comprehended clearly, the mental processes issue rightly.' To achieve this mindfulness calls for dedication and thoroughness of procedure. It calls for more, often, then the traditional sitting meditation can avail us. So I came to see movement as an integrated part of Vipassana meditation simply in order to widen the scope of the development and cultivation of mindfulness and to support and safeguard its right practice. At the same time this active part of meditation provides us with many useful hints and suggestions for integrating mindfulness practice into our daily lives.

And she points out a more intrinsic advantage. "Observing and witnessing, being mindful to our body sensations, when we express it in movement lets us more easily connect and touch the level of atomic activity in our body. We can demonstrate through movements that there is the heat element, the element of vibrancy and extensiveness, or the qualities of hard, soft, solid, to be felt, which may for many bring the concrete realization of being a *process* in ever-changing patterns of energies or qualities of elements rather than a solid 'I.' "

She continues, "When I see that sloth, torpor, and resentfulness are dominating the students' minds and preventing further progress in the meditation, it is at such times that I will interrupt the quiet sitting meditation and make an invitation to an active one. Our nervous system responds quickly to the pleasant; consequently, when we move, sometimes rhythmically and expressively, being mindful of what we are doing is no longer a struggle, the pressure and frustration get vented, and the mind can be open. Our sense of density and the weight of gravity gives way to a sense of lightness, and that inspires a willingness to continue the practice in formal sitting meditation."

Something else Ruth does beautifully is the creation of ritual within the activities of mundane existence. Wherever she is, she gathers people and helps them experience the full value and significance of every simplest action.

Now in the meditation hall, as we sit, she leads us in what in Vipassana is know as a "sweep"—a meticulous guided journey through the body from the top of the head to the toes and back again. This guiding in physical awareness is Ruth's true genius. Her own apprehension of her physical being must be preternaturally acute, for she guides with great precision, always asking the student to be aware of the sensation in that part of the body, sometimes working in one area such as the throat (a particularly sensitive spot, as we breathe, eat, and talk through this aperture) for many minutes. This work can bring one to a direct experience of impermanence, and because of the depth of that awareness, to an all-inclusive compassion for one's sister beings, animal and human.

In one such meditation, Ruth guided us to such a strong perception of our bones that I felt my skeleton and especially my skull as the brittle, vulnerable matter it is; I saw my skull in thirty years' time lying unused in a coffin; I felt the tenuousness and change of my own existence so vividly that I came to a mingled fear and sorrow and tenderness for myself and then elation just at *knowing*, for the first time in my life, my true condition and being led to contemplate that. In these direct ways Ruth teaches the great basic truths of Buddhism: suffering, impermanence, and the insubstantiality of the self.

Her formal Dharma talks in the evening can often be so lengthy that one struggles with sleep; her frequent talking during meditation can be experienced as intrusive or bossy or insensitive; but in this guiding through the body she has no peer, and its value is so immediately felt that other small annoyances fade before its power.

Ruth can often be quite humorous, pointing out the absurdity of the human condition. She speaks with a thick German accent, with oddly accented English words firmly embedded in German grammatical sequence. Sometimes, I believe, the mispronunciation is intentional, for comic effect, used to disarm resistant or critical students. When she speaks of concepts like "the leak in the canoe," (in which just when we think we're floating safely down the stream, the canoe starts to fill with water), the meditation hall erupts with knowing chuckles. She is especially relaxed at her all-women retreats, where a movement session can develop into a circle dance out among the creosote bushes or a chain of fast walkers winding out through the desert. She lets each sequence of movements develop naturally until one finds oneself sometimes in outrageous postures, while maintaining strict attention to the sensations involved.

Her most profound message concerns living the Dharma in one's daily life, and the work done at the retreat, the manner of eating one's food, all actions are bent toward perceiving the truth of one's existence.

I remember one particular retreat with men and women, in which there was a young man so anxious that he could not sit still. Ruth did not require him to sit in meditation with us. She took him out behind the main house and showed him how to rake the sandy dirt of the yard in long curves, as if a lazy hand had dragged its fingers in the dirt. This activity, simple and necessarily slow, was agreeable to him, and at any time of day I might see him pacing the yard, guiding the rake with increasing care. Ruth had chosen the perfect activity, for it kept him in the area where all of us passed through and often sat to eat or be quiet, so that he was within the community; it had a concrete goal, his raked yard a thing of beauty and neatness; and most of all the motion of raking developed in him a beginning concentration. Soon he began to relax, and by the fourth day it was often clear that he was enjoying himself. On his last day, he came to each of us and said he was glad to have been here with us.

No doubt she thought to give him the rake because at one point in her life she had experienced a breakdown and had had to gradually retrain herself to pay attention by painstakingly accomplishing simple tasks. One of the reasons some people trust Ruth Denison so completely and follow her suggestions is that it soon becomes clear that she never asks anyone to do something she has not done herself. This teaching directly from her own experience gives great stability and power.

Sometimes she speaks of her experiences during the Second World War in Germany, where, after the defeat, she was incarcerated in a Russian concentration camp, an experience that did not create bitterness in her. "I have no revenge or need to pay back something what is done wrong to me or to my group," she says. "I could be really nasty to men, you know, I am raped and really violently handled by men through the war situation, by Russians and also Western men. So I could be having a real turn-off, but I don't see it that way. I was lucky to have a sense of justice coming from a deeper soul or ground, and a great compassionate feeling. I have a love for life, hmmm? which is bringing with it sensitivity and care, *real* care. Because you see that if you strike back you injure life, and you see how balance can best be attained. And so when you have that certain sense you cannot really be vindictive or unforgiving, no matter how much wrong was done to you."

Some of the women who study with Ruth are politically astute and active. Their attempts to get her to make connections between meditation and politics invariably fail, for Ruth's manner of being is so intuitive that she seems incapable of the logic of discursive thought. There is a certain innocence about her, so that all unwitting she may come out with a statement whose politics are so retrograde that her feminist students shudder. But her innate loyalty to women is profound, and the flexibility and essential compassionate humanity of her teachings transcend verbal messages and offer a grounding in the Dharma that is rare and precious. At other times she speaks strongly from women's consciousness; she has been known to invoke the four directions in Native American fashion and to refer to "the goddess within." No one ever knows what she is going to do. This spontaneity is part of the reason people travel long distances to attend her retreats.

I remember one weekend mixed retreat in Berkeley at which she met with the women alone afterward to answer questions. She asked everyone to write her question on a piece of paper. After she gathered the papers from the circle of women, she sent each paper across the room at random to a woman to answer. Thus we were asked to call upon our *own* wisdom to answer the questions of our sisters. I was astonished at the acuity of the answers and at Ruth's confidence that it would be so. With gestures such as these, she empowers women.

ZEN FOREMOTHERS

Two women who helped to create the Western Zen environment in which many women began to practice and some have become teachers are *Nancy Wilson Ross* and *Elsie Mitchell.* Both journeyed to Japan, where they developed a deep appreciation of Zen Buddhism. Both brought back with them something of the practice and the spirit of Zen, Elsie Mitchell by establishing the Cambridge Buddhist Association (now headed by Maurine Myoon Stuart Roshi), Nancy Wilson Ross by writing a number of books on Buddhism and other Eastern religions and maintaining a long supportive association with the San Francisco Zen Center.

A generation of Americans have been introduced to Eastern religions by *Nancy Wilson Ross.* Her ability to present the wisdom of the East in a form understandable to Western readers is amply evidenced in her *Three Ways of Asian Wisdom, The World of Zen,* and *Buddhism: A Way of Life and Thought.*

A novelist and world traveler, Nancy Wilson Ross developed her early interest in Zen when she became fast friends with Shunryu Suzuki-roshi of the San Francisco Zen Center. Her fascination with Eastern thought is grounded in her love of Asian art, of which she has many valuable pieces in her home in Old Westbury, Long Island, along with a fine collection of American paintings, including the work of Mark Tobey and Morris Graves, who were her friends. Irreverent, witty, amused by life, Nancy Wilson Ross has lived a rich, productive eighty-odd years.

Westbury, Long Island, is a forty-minute train ride from New York City. It is a small town of pastry shops and hardware stores and tree-lined streets. From here I take a taxi to Old Westbury where the old families have their vintage frame or shingle houses on wide green lawns under ancient spreading trees. On the Whitney estate I find Nancy Wilson Ross in a beautiful old shingle house and am ushered through the living room with its Asian screens and sculptures to her study, a large pleasant room dominated by a fireplace with an impressive mantel.

She sits in a chair, wearing pajama bottoms, a blouse, and socks, her hair uncombed. Clearly she has always been a "handsome" woman, as she would say; now in her eighties she is small, her face either disgruntled or startled when I meet her, as if age has sneaked up to surprise her, not happily. Her pale hair, somewhere between blond and gray, hangs mid-length and tangled beside the fine white wrinkled skin of her face. She looks as if she has just awakened—on the wrong side of the bed.

Greeting me, she grasps my hand in a narrow, warm, and firm grip, and she looks me over, her bright eyes taking in my whole face, my height, my clothes. And her face breaks into a smile that is at once knowing and pleased.

"Ah, you *look* like a Sandy!" she says in a voice that rasps just a little, like an old instrument not often played. "I was afraid you would be one of those New York City women!"

"Oh, not a chance," I say, grinning back at her, "I'm from California." And we are instant jovial companions for a talk that begins with tea brought by Nancy's attendant and the munching of Godiva chocolates, which Nancy pronounces "the best in the world."

She tells me about her growing up in Spokane, Washington, a town settled by new Englanders and retaining a decorous air, and of her exposure to Native Americans, Chinese, Japanese, and Koreans in that town. Faced with the conventionality and cowardice of her Presbyterian minister and Sunday School teachers, Nancy "gave up on the Christian religion." Later she began to read about Buddhism and found it more palatable. She went to study at the famed Bauhaus art school in Germany and in 1939 traveled to China, Korea, and Japan, where her passion for Asian art was born. After she had written several novels, traveled to Nazi Germany, and married, she was introduced to Suzuki-roshi in California.

"I felt that he was a pure human being," she says, "a really enlightened soul, and if he said something to me I would listen to it because I felt that whatever he said came out of his inner being. That was just good luck that I met him. And I began to think of myself as a Buddhist. Suzuki-roshi and I became great friends, and I think his book *Zen Mind, Beginner's Mind* is one of the great books. I've given it to many people and reread it thousands of times. It just made sense to me. Now not all Buddhism makes sense. When people start to quote Dogen[3] to me, I leave the room, usually running. I think there's just such nonsense talked and written about the great masters of Buddhism that it's as bad as Christianity."

"Did you begin to sit when you found Suzuki-roshi?" I ask.

"Yes, I did, and I sat alone, because I was not living in circumstances where I could sit with people. Because of the conditions of my life I've had to do it *all* alone, really. Study alone, everything else. It's just been my curious fate."

Her practice of meditation, she tells me, had begun many years before her meeting with Suzuki-roshi when she studied with the great Theosophist and mystic Alice Bailey,[4] whom she met while she was at the Bauhaus. "She took me on as a very young girl and trained me," Nancy said. "She thought I was bound for the higher spheres. I worked very hard with her and studied with her."

Nancy meditated with many teachers after that, some of them Indian gurus, but she was never "taken in," as she puts it, by a guru. Even her beloved Suzuki did not serve that function in her life.

"I thought of him as a wise old man who gave evidence, to my very blunted senses, of enlightenment," she explains. "I don't meet people like that very often. I felt he was more enlightened than Alice Bailey. She was an enlightened woman in the sense of having a very open and startlingly free mind. She believed in all kinds of things. She would have been more like Kübler-Ross than Madame Blavatsky, because she was a very intelligent woman, and her brain came first, really. To my amazement, in England today, people still absolutely worship Alice Bailey and were willing to just practically kneel at my feet because I had known her personally. In New York that school of hers on 42nd Street called the Arcane School still exists, and people still study her."

Nancy pauses, remembering. She sips her tea and gazes for a moment at the chocolates, then, smiling, turns to speak to me again

"Alice Bailey had a wonderful sense of humor and freedom."

We drink more tea, and talk a little of Nancy's books on Eastern religions. They are all still in print—evidence, she says, that people really do want to know about "these puzzling matters of spiritual thought and belief." When she wrote the books, Nancy had already been to India several times and to other Asian countries, and she used the art she had collected as illustrations in the books.

She confesses to me that she has never sat a full sesshin and is somewhat less than impressed by people who sit long retreats. One can probably learn as much by some prolonged sessions with a good analyst, she suggests. But she admits this may be a jaded point of view.

"That's probably the matter with me, you see. I've lived too full a life and nobody's interfered with my thinking or reading or believing any way I wanted to believe, and as a consequence I'm so completely free I don't have maybe enough mooring." She peers sideways at me from those bright eyes. "I'm being perfectly honest with you now."

We speak of how she was never really inside the institution of Zen or any other institution, noting that her relationship was with the ideas and with the practice rather than the hierarchy or groups of practitioners. I ask what she thinks of the carrying over of Asian cultural forms to the practice of Buddhism in this country.

"That's a terribly interesting question, and hard to answer, because I'm drawn to it, you see. I'm terribly drawn to the beauty of Asian forms, and it seems to me that I've learned a great deal from . . . well, for instance, Jizo." And she gestures to a small statue on a shelf near us. "To my mind that beautiful figure of the lover of babies and sick children and so on . . . that's just so marvelous, I can take that down and get a real reaction to it. That's the sort of stuff I responded to in Asian art. So I can't feel that it's been a total loss, in fact I feel that America could learn a great deal by looking at that art, and that's why I put as much of it as I did in my books and why I'm always glad when people speak about it. I never really realized how it could move me." And she adds, "Of course, Zen has the greatest meaning for me, even in its poetry. I get more out of a wonderful haiku than almost anything else in the world."

Nancy's attendant lets us know that lunch is ready. This young woman, Carol Melkonian, is a Zen student from the Mt. Tremper Zen Monastery who has worked with the Vietnamese antiwar activist monk Thich Nhat Hanh in France. She serves us soup and small open-faced sandwiches. Nancy suggests wine and Carol brings us each a glass of excellent Cabernet Sauvignon. I notice that the silverware has a substantial weight in my hand.

Behind the table where we eat stands a long Japanese screen, dark with age; stone statues regard us. A beautiful scroll, slightly damaged by moisture, is spread on the floor to dry. Laughing, Nancy tells the story of the hairdresser who, having looked at these art objects, said to her, "Well, Nancy, you're safe from burglars, because if they got in and saw all this old faded stuff on your walls, they'd realize you didn't have anything worth stealing and they'd leave you alone."

We speak now of women's position in Buddhism, and Nancy's brow wrinkles in irritation. "I've always been annoyed at that. But I was annoyed at the Catholic church too, and I was terribly annoyed when the pope got here. The way he refused those noble women who came forward with petitions. The way they presented them would bring tears to your eyes. And then that old fat man would just shake his head in an avuncular way and say, 'No, it's not for the girls yet.' You just wondered when 'yet' was going to roll around. I was infuriated by all that.[5] So naturally I'm infuriated by anything I see of the same kind in Zen.

"I discussed this with Ruth Sasaki by the hour. She was a woman with some money and some taste and a tremendous interest in Buddhism.[6] She was allowed to take over this temple in Japan and encouraged to do it and to become a priestess and then to become the abbess of this church at Riohanji, which she did. She was totally independent. I said to her, 'Ruth, didn't you ever have to cut your hair?' She had just masses of marvelous hair. 'Oh no,' she said, 'I refused right away.' I said, 'How did you get away with it?' She said, 'Well, I said, Everywhere I look I see pictures of Bodhisattvas with just miles of flowing hair, so I don't know why I should cut my hair.' She said nobody could ever answer that, so nobody made her cut her hair. I said, 'What about those earrings?' They were interesting, diamond and pearl. 'Well,' she said, 'they were given to me by my husband and I love them, I've worn them for years and years,' and she said again, 'I just said, Show me a Bodhisattva without dangling eardrops and I'll take my earrings off. Nobody ever brought me a picture, so I wore my earrings.'

"She became an abbess of great repute. So I decided you could get away with a lot more than most people believed." Nancy ponders this and adds, "She was helped by having a good deal of money."

Ruth Fuller Sasaki, she says, was a learned student of Japanese who wrote "one of the greatest books on koans [*The Zen Koan*]. She wrote it with a Japanese scholar, but she really did an enormous amount on it."

Speaking of the early days of Zen in this country, Nancy admits that she did really want Zen to take hold. "I thought it would be awfully good for us," she explains. "Because it was not so religious in the oozy-goozy sense, and it seemed to me we had gone as far with the oozy-goozy as we were ever going to get. I thought the other stuff really pulled you up short and made you question your own mind, and that's where I think wisdom lies."

She does a type of meditation, herself, though erratically.

"I believe you can quiet yourself and do a good deal for yourself by control of the breath, and I used this quite a lot when I was sick. I have to use it now because I have blackouts. I use breathing control to conquer that so I don't fall down on the floor, and so on. All that stuff is terribly useful."

When we leave the table to settle ourselves back in her study Nancy tells me of her long association with the San Francisco Zen Center, which grew from her friendship with Suzuki-roshi. This continued during the years when Richard Baker was roshi there. She helped Baker-roshi with fund raising and other efforts, and he became her friend. During recent years, he sent one of the Zen center students to serve as her attendant and help her with her work. When the great upheaval at the Zen center occurred, Nancy was extremely hurt and shaken. She became very ill shortly after and has not fully recovered her health. But in speaking of events at the Zen center, she cannot remain somber for long.

"These people have been through, you know, just French novels! It's so crazy, when you think about it—all in the name of religion! God knows I hope you can write it all perfectly openly."

She glances across the room at her attendant, Carol, whom she has taken great pleasure in shocking during our talk, and says with affection, "Poor Carol. Carol is really one of the purest and best people I've ever known in my life. Here she is, living with *me!* I'm sure every night she'd pray for my soul, if she believed in prayer."

When I say I have to leave, Nancy tells me, "Well, Sandy, I didn't want you to come at all, but I'm so glad you did. I enjoyed it! I hope I'll see you again."

I say I hope the same. When I tell her I will send her what I write, she shakes her head.

"I'll trust you. I'll be dead when your book comes out."

She looks at me from the side, her head tilted at a rakish angle, her smile knowing and a little tired.

On the train back to New York City, I realize Nancy never once spoke of the labor and dedication it must have taken to write her books, many of which required extensive research. It seems that she takes herself quite seriously without the slightest whisper of self-importance.

A few months later, Nancy sent me a copy of *Westward the Women*, a book of hers about women in the great pioneer migration, in exchange for my *Heartwomen*. A note from her read: "Enclosed is the book I promised you, emerging in distinguished paperback after so many years in print. Quite a record, of which I am very proud."

On January 18, 1986, eight months after our talk, a friend called to tell me Nancy Wilson Ross died that day in Florida.

A woman who knew Nancy Wilson Ross well, and who in her own right has contributed substantially to American Buddhism, is *Elsie Mitchell*. With her husband, Elsie Mitchell founded the Cambridge Buddhist Association, a sitting group and library that has existed for thirty years and is now led by a woman roshi. They brought from Japan tape recordings of the bells and chanting in one of the most venerable and distinguished monasteries. And most recently they created the Ahimsa Foundation, an animal rights and environmentalist group.

Elsie Mitchell today looks surprisingly like a photograph of her as a young woman wearing Zen robes and rakusu, kneeling before a Japanese scroll, which I have seen in a magazine. She greets me in her gray shingle house on Brattle Street in Cambridge, attractive in a soft white blouse.

It was in a house just around the corner that the Cambridge Buddhist Association was born, and in this house in which we meet that it continued until its move to its present home. We sit in a bright living room to talk, surrounded by a few elegant objects: a black oriental lamp, a white mantel on which balance three small pieces of china. We are joined here by Elsie's two dogs, a white Bichon Frisé and a small shaggy Chinese breed.

Elsie Mitchell had begun to be interested in Buddhism through her reading while she was still a young girl, she tells me. Then, as a newly married woman, she became an English tutor for the Harvard Yenching Institute's East Asia Program for visiting scholars, an activity that brought her into contact with learned Asians from several countries. Between 1957 and 1962, she made three trips to Japan to visit temples, zendos, and Buddhist universities. One product of these journeys was the unique and historic Folkways album of the Soto Zen chanting and bells in the temple of Eiheiji. She and her husband John Mitchell culled this two-disc album from their fourteen hours of recordings made under the supervision of Rev. Tetsuya Inoue and with the help of the Reverend Dainin Katagiri (now roshi of the Minnesota Zen Center). Elsie Mitchell was initiated as a lay member of the Soto school of Zen in Japan and later received the "Tokudo" initiation, in which Rindo Fujimoto Roshi accepted her as a postulant disciple.

As we sit in her living room, Elsie Mitchell tells stories of those visits to Japan, remembering especially Katagiri's well-developed sense of decorum and urging me to give him her greeting when I visit there. She has written engagingly of her adventures in Japan and many subsequent events and associations in her 1973 book *Sun Buddhas Moon Buddhas.*

In Cambridge in the late fifties, she remembers, through the influence of Dr. Shinichi Hisamatsu, a visiting Japanese scholar, several people joined with her to find a permanent setting for a Buddhist library and meditation room. They used the library in the Mitchell home on Craigie Street. Dr. D. T. Suzuki also took an interest in the budding Cambridge Buddhist Association and became its founding president, although he was never active there. The sittings were led at first by a number of different Japanese priests. Elsie Mitchell and her associates gathered books on Buddhism, Zen, comparative religion, and the relationship of religion and psychology, and over a thirty-year period this collection grew into the hundreds of books lining the walls of the present Cambridge Buddhist Association. Soon after the death of the Japanese roshi who had headed the association for almost ten years, Maurine Stuart (then Freedgood) was accepted as the teacher at the Cambridge Buddhist Association.

Mrs. Mitchell tells the painful story of the CBA's move to Sparks Street, after twenty-two years of peaceful existence in her home. The residents of Sparks Street, among them an MIT professor and an instructor at the Harvard Law School, became fearful at the prospect of a Buddhist establishment in their midst and persuaded the city council to ban the CBA's ownership of real estate, tax-exempt status, and occupancy permit. It required two years of meetings, letter-writing campaigns, and legal proceedings before the Supreme Court of Massachusetts ordered the city of Cambridge to allow the CBA to move into the house they had purchased. While they appealed to religious leaders in the area for help, only one Unitarian minister, Reverend Edwin Lane, responded with support.

Elsie Mitchell has written of this struggle: "A curious aspect of the episode was the fact that the people who originally objected to us were young to middle-aged professional couples or members of the academic community. A number of the older people, long-time Cantabrigians who were not members of academe, refused to sign a petition against us and welcomed us warmly."

She added, "Life is full of surprises. All the fuss seemed strange to me. I have lived in Cambridge for thirty years, surrounded by people fond of vaunting their liberal proclivities. It was remarkable how quickly they could forget their oft and loudly proclaimed idealism when actually presented with an opportunity to practice it."

Her days of sitting zazen are over, Mrs. Mitchell tells me as she cuddles the black dog in her lap. Now her practice is chanting. In Japan, she says, often older people switch from zazen to chanting.

"Here in this country, Buddhism is too much of a *practice*," she comments. "It's followed almost as an athletic discipline. Whereas in Japan it is deeply a way of life."

Her living of her Buddhist principles these days, besides her support of Maurine Stuart and the Cambridge Buddhist Association, finds expression in her work with the Ahimsa Foundation. Founded in 1981 with her husband and a few friends, this entity helps organizations devoted to abused animals and threatened species, promoting animal protective legislation, preservation of wilderness, sound ecological philosophy, and vegetarianism.

Our talk has been brief and pleasant, communicating to me the enthusiasm for Buddhism that prompted her pioneering work in establishing the Cambridge Buddhist Association. In providing a place for westerners to sit and study, Elsie Mitchell is a true fore-mother of Buddhism in this country.

MIND-HEART TO MIND-HEART

A few blocks from Harvard Square where the punks with spiked hair and chains lounge menacingly on the roof over the subway and scurrying students mingle with tourists and business people, in the backyard, so to speak, of Radcliffe College, the Cambridge Buddhist Association nestles inconspicuously among the trees of a distinguished old neighborhood. It is a brown-shingled house, large and gracious, behind a brown slatted fence. Upstairs where I sleep with four other women on mattresses on the floor, I look up to a window filled with a mass of dogwood blossoms hovering like a cloud. I am here to sit a sesshin led by *Maurine Myoon Stuart Roshi,* the teacher at the Cambridge Buddhist Association.

Downstairs we do our sitting and walking in the book-lined living room and dining room. Maurine says some people have been surprised by the lack of Asian decoration. She answers them, "We live in *New England!* This is not a Japanese-style place."

I first encountered Maurine Stuart (then Freedgood) Roshi at Providence the year before, where she was a commanding presence. A woman in her early sixties with substantial bosom and distinguished head, whose gray hair was twisted up behind, she began her talk by asking us to chant with her. This chant was obviously done with all of her body and self, for it came out in a deep voice that was powerful and richly tuned. In an atmosphere in which all the Zen trappings were being questioned, she wore her formal robes with dignity and explained that in following her Zen tradition she feels the utmost freedom.

Maurine Stuart is a major figure in the transformation taking place in American Buddhism. As president of the well-known Cambridge Buddhist Association, she is the person to whom many women have come after damaging or disillusioning experiences with male roshis. Again and again women told me that after leaving an oppressive Zen center or an abusive teacher, they began to sit with Maurine. Traditional in many ways, full of warmth and spontaneity and willingness to invent, she is counselor and role model to scores of women. As a practical, caring Western woman with a family, she provides inspiration to younger women struggling to coordinate Zen practice with life in the world.

Who is this woman with her dramatically arched black eyebrows, her intensely blue eyes the shade of hyacinth, her striking voice? This morning in the meditation hall, as we sat facing the wall, nodding sleepily, that voice came: *"Keep your eyes open. Wide open, if you're falling asleep,"* and I thought of the remark made by one woman that Maurine always speaks in capital letters. Now in the upstairs interview room, she sits before me wearing a white underrobe, a black transparent robe over it, a gold and turquoise brocade rakusu, her hair cut now in a short casual style. Her presence is so large that, across from her, I feel the invitation to arrive here, fully, myself. (This is the classic Zen presence, a solidity and calm, the person eminently visible, with nothing hidden or held back.)

Speaking from the podium at Providence last year, she had told a story about the thousand eyes of Avalokitesvara, the Bodhisattva of compassion, and went on to say, "Avalokitesvara with the thousand eyes and hands is all the different roles that each one of us here represents: Man, woman, artist, friend, mother, lover, child, whoever. Every single one without exception is one of these true eyes. It is the moment-to-moment experience of being here together that is so vital to all of us. This is the life-giving and wisdom-making process: our being here together, looking at how we are engaged with one another, heart to heart, hara to hara [see Glossary], mind to mind, and each one of us answering our 'why?' with the deepest expression of our own nature, our own experience, without any speculation about it."

So she has defined the challenge she presents to me in this room. She spoke of the "living dynamic spirit" of each of us that teaches us. Her warmth is like a strong supportive touch.

Maurine Stuart came originally from the great central prairie region of Canada. She became a concert pianist, married and bore three children in this country, and raised them while pursuing her career in music. In her early forties she discovered the Zen Studies Society in New York City.

"I was going one morning to take one of my children to school and came back along a street where I looked up and saw on the side of the building, 'Zen Studies Society,' and I said, 'Heavens, where did *this* come from?!' and walked right in. I asked the monk who was there, 'How do I get into this?' He handed me a schedule without saying a word. And I figuratively have been there ever since." That monk, she adds, was her first teacher, Eido Roshi, who was her good friend for many years.

This finding of Zen was the culmination of much searching and questioning and a spiritual sense grounded in Maurine's relationship to her grandfather. "The way he lived was a great inspiration to me when I was a little girl. He had a farm on the Saskatchewan prairie, and every single creature, blade of grass, flower, stone, everything on that farm, was treated with the utmost respect, and a kind of feeling for life and also for people that was quite exquisite. He was a pacifist, and it was very difficult to be a pacifist at that time; he was a socialist and so he believed in not hoarding things for himself and he shared with everybody. All of his way of being was quite extraordinary."

When she went to Europe to study music, she read about Buddhism, which reminded her of what she had learned from her grandfather. But back in the United States, it took her almost twenty years to find a teacher and a place to practice. When she did, she discovered that the very strong discipline required in Zen practice was familiar to her.

"Hours and hours of sitting on a piano bench practicing, with deep concentration, meant that sitting on a cushion was just translating this into another place. And the two helped one another tremendously. Playing changed, and as playing changed more freedom of expression came, and more freedom in the practice itself, and deeper understanding. I always say to people, 'I don't do calligraphy, but come up to my house, I'll play a prelude and fugue for you.' "

Maurine Stuart now teaches piano to a few students. I remember her speaking of the nature and fruits of discipline to a woman at the Providence conference. "I can't get up on the platform and play a Beethoven sonata unless I've worked at it for years. Then when I start to play, all thoughts about the music are gone. Just as with this chanting, this walking. You are so much *in it*, you're not conscious that you're doing it. you're just the vehicle for it. But the vehicle has to be trained, has to be tuned. And that's our freedom. *True* freedom comes from that strong, strong, strong discipline."

Even though it was hard to leave her children to attend sesshins (they were four, seven, and nine when she found Zen), she practiced intensively with masters like Yasutani Roshi and Soen Nakagawa Roshi. "I was very much a part of the Zen Studies Society in New York," she says, "and my training was really all done there, apart from in the kitchen of my own house, which was pretty good training too. Looking after children and cooking and doing all of that is good training.

"Fortunately I have always been blessed with good health and a good strong constitution and never required too much sleep, so I could do all these things: be the pianist, the mother, the Zen student—sometimes with difficulty, it was not always easy. But it *mattered* so much to me, and everybody in my family could see that. They also could see I was a lot easier to live with when I came back from this kind of thing. So it was good for all of us."

I ask her about the characterization of Zen as militaristic in its asceticism and harsh teaching methods.

"This is, of course, against the real spirit," she says, frowning slightly. "When it gets to be like that, I think it's dangerous. If I see that people are doing some kind of endurance test to bolster their ego . . . it's no good . . . that's not what it's about. If you are here for true insight, you don't do it as an endurance test, you do it out of your heart and your real desire for this.

"The militaristic part comes from the Samurai tradition, of course, and this *was* practiced for fearlessness, for mastery of oneself in the face of death. That part of it is not bad. If you look at it in this way of becoming fearless in the face of dying of cancer, or fearless in the face of old age and so on, it is very constructive."

When she and her family moved to the Boston area, she met Elsie Mitchell, at the suggestion of Soen Roshi. "Immediately we had a rapport that's grown into a deep friendship," she says. "She has been the most important teacher in my life, by how she helped me grow when I came here. She saw that I was lonely and felt desolate at leaving my group in New York, so she put me in charge of the zendo in her house that Dr. Suzuki and Dr. Hisamatsu had started. She had me conduct the meetings, she made me the librarian so I had to get to know all the books. She had me answer letters, so I had to study, I had to be busy and helping, instead of sitting in my house in Newton feeling sorry for myself.

"Even my ordination was because of Elsie Mitchell. She said, 'I think you really could be of service to the community. I think you should be ordained. You should go to Eido and ask him for ordination.' So ordination came because of Elsie. Then this house came because of Elsie." Maurine had started a zendo in her former house in Newton, also. Both groups grew until finally she suggested they merge and begin to function in a building set aside just for that. The securing of the house was accomplished by Elsie and John Mitchell. "Elsie doesn't come to sit," Maurine says, "but she's always available, she's always ready with help and support."

The Cambridge Buddhist Association is a nonresidential lay community of professionals, students, and homemakers, which has an equal balance of men and women from a wide age range. Over the years the association has inconspicuously provided people with books and travel aid as well as instruction. It is not specifically a Zen center, since other Buddhist traditions are very much included.

When I ask Maurine to what extent American Zen is a receptacle of Asian culture, she delineates for me her definition of Buddhism, emphasizing that it is not tied to Japanese or any other cultural forms.

"What is Buddhism but doing good deeds, having a pure warm mind, not hurting anyone or anything. All these precepts are basic to our culture, to *any* culture. I think Buddhism is very plain. It speaks clearly to all of us: what are we doing at this present moment? This moment affects what happens tomorrow as well as in the next hour. What are we doing *now,* how present-minded are we?"

As for the traditional Japanese Zen forms that we are practicing in the zendo, these are her tradition, she says, but "it is appropriate for any human being to sit down quietly, to move mindfully, to eat mindfully, to work mindfully." When I question the Japanese chanting we do, she says it is good to chant in a language other than English, so that one is not conceptualizing while chanting. This allows for a better meditative effect, she suggests, the sounds resonating not just in the head but in the whole body. And she points to the healing power of the sounds themselves.

Maurine Stuart was given the title *roshi* by Soen Nakagawa Roshi during his last trip to America, at Dai Bosatsu, the mountain monastery in New York. "I explained to Soen Roshi exactly what we were doing here at the Cambridge Buddhist Association, how it was progressing," she tells me. "He knew Elsie Mitchell very well. I think he knew that if she had confidence in what I was doing—and goddess knows he tested me enough during those days I was there—that I was ready to help in whatever way I could. This, I told him, was my life. So the roshi part is not so important. It's like wearing the robe, it's a mantle of authority, but it didn't change me. Everybody calls me Maurine, and I like it that way. I don't want to be put up in a special place. It's only for the sake of the work of the Cambridge Buddhist Association that it's helpful."

Does she believe, I ask her, that it is important for women to hold positions of leadership in Buddhist centers?

"I think we do have to worry about whether there are women in places of authority, for the sake of some kind of structure. For example, in this present situation, I am here to try to answer questions or to remind people to sit strongly whether they are alone or with others. You must do it yourself, but we do need somebody who says, here is the *place where you can do it* for yourself. You can't hang on to me or anybody else. But there must be a feeling that there is somebody to come to. *Yes*, we do need to be in these positions of authority."

The next morning I accept Maurine's offer to play for me, walking out Mt. Auburn Street by the Charles River until I come to her place just opposite the sweeping lawns and ancient spreading trees of the Mt. Auburn Cemetery. She lives in a modern brick, wood, and glass house, stacked on six different levels, from the kitchen and entrance on the ground floor up through study and living room to bedrooms on the top floors.

Maurine greets me wearing a long blue robe that matches her eyes, and a purple turtleneck. We sit at her kitchen table drinking orange juice and I tell her about some of my adventures in traveling about the country. She enjoys the stories tremendously and asks for more.

Upstairs in the living room, where a grand piano stands before tall purple drapes at a window, all is white walls and bold colors.

Maurine sits at the piano and plays—Bach, Beethoven—with great power, skill and sensitivity. I feel how immediate, how heart opening is this music, and how lovingly she performs it. When she comes to join me on the other side of the room, we speak of the emotional content that can be expressed in music, where one can say all without embarrassment. And I see the parallel with Zen, so essentially nonverbal, in which one gives everything.

This house is vivid and comfortable, a place where I move easily, feel welcomed. Before me on the coffee table stands an Eskimo carving of a hunter with a spear. Watching me examine it, Maurine offers, "There used to be a piece of rawhide on the end of that, but a little girl who was teething came to visit and she took it off and chewed it right through."

She shows me a watercolor by her chief assistant, Sheila La Farge, of people sitting in the zendo with Max the cat pacing behind them looking authoritative. It is a bright, funny little painting. Sheila La Farge is Maurine's "right arm," she says. The Cambridge Buddhist Association is overseen by a board of directors, of which Elsie and John Mitchell are part, but in the zendo Sheila is the person who helps Maurine most.

Maurine speaks of the flexibility of Zen and mentions Kosen Roshi, who in the nineteenth century taught that Zen should be open to laypeople as well as monks. "It was this Kosen Roshi who was the teacher of Soyen Shaku who was the first Zen teacher to come to America," she explains, "and it was that man who gave koan instruction to Mrs. Alexander Russell in San Francisco. *She* was the first Zen student in America. A woman! She didn't go to a Japanese monastery, and she practiced in her own intimate family situation. Kosen Roshi lived with them, he was a good friend. So already in this country it began within a different kind of form."

While Maurine believes in change, she tells me, she believes equally in the necessity to be firmly grounded in tradition. And this includes the questioning of the practice. "Almost the very first sesshin I attended," she says, "I went to the teacher and said, 'I don't understand all this hitting and shouting and telling people to get enlightened. I thought we were supposed to be here to get rid of our ego, and all you're doing is *inflaming* egos.' So he looked at me and said, 'Okay, do it your own way.' I said, 'Well, thank you.' I do not shout at people at the Cambridge Buddhist Association.''

I mention her recent trips to California where she led sesshins for women only, which were arranged by several California women who invited her to teach. One of the reasons she agreed to this, she says, was her desire to offer something to those Zen women who were so shocked and disillusioned by recent events in the Zen world. "This was to make a place for people to practice where they would not be threatened in any way. And it has worked very well. I don't know how many of the women who were there were women who had had bad experiences, but some were. One in particular was in a state of mental chaos. She came expecting to find some kind of wishy-washy not-so-strong sesshin where she could just sort of wander in and out as she pleased, instead of which I confronted them all as warrior women and said, 'Let's get to it!' And we did. I think it was very helpful to these women to get together and to feel that they could do good strong intense practice as women.''

This is part of a reassessing and healing process that must take place, Maurine says. "People have to realize that their *practice* is their teacher. As I've said, when you depend on a person for your practice, it's not true practice. This help from a teacher is fine, and we all need one another as helpers. Everybody's a teacher, *you're* my teacher. But to put one person on a pedestal is very dangerous. It will be healthy for people to see that you don't take this man's word for it, but find out for yourself. 'Sit yourself.' In this current situation, which is changing, as women become more involved they can stand up and say no.''

Finally we speak of the place of emotion in Zen, and Maurine says, "I think the coldness in our practice comes if people are insecure and are too clinging to the form. If they are hanging on so tightly to the form and forget that first of all we are living human beings with wonderful feelings, wonderful expansive lovingness in us or hate in us or whatever it is—to face that, accept that, look at that, and then know that there is something else there as well. We are not just emotions. We are this wonderful Buddha nature. We are Buddha from the beginning, men and women. No woman excluded.''

Maurine's communication with me here at her house comes less in what we say than in my sense of being sheltered and cared about, of her offering the immediate content and texture of her life as a woman, as a human being, in response to my being here. The piano seems still to speak in the room, and the colors are beautifully straightforward. Maurine tells me stories of her life with great gusto.

Then finally when it is time to go, we make our way down several flights to the ground floor. Saying good-bye, Maurine tells me of the calligraphy done by Soen Nakagawa Roshi. "It says mind-heart to mind-heart." As she enfolds me in a warm hug, I understand she is telling me that our communication has occurred that way too.

Leaving the house, I see across the street in the cemetery a tree that flames. It is a massive Japanese maple, its leaves many shades of red against a perfect blue sky, extravagant above the graves.

THREE VIEWS OF MAURINE STUART

I sit with *Sheila La Farge* at a metal table in the peaceful backyard of the Cambridge Buddhist Association. She is a fifty-year-old woman with hazel eyes and gray hair that waves back from her forehead, daughter of a distinguished New England family, who after a career in book translation now concentrates on developing her considerable gift for painting and fulfilling her duties at the Cambridge Buddhist Association. Her face intent, she tells me how she became more involved here.

"I saw that Maurine was doing everything, that there was so much to be done. I felt the thing to do was plunge right in, and if I didn't do something correctly, she would let me know. Her method absolutely fascinates me. At first Maurine didn't feel we were ready for lots of rules and guidelines, so she didn't provide them, but one by one we'd get the point and offer to help. For example, at first in the coatroom all the shoes were left in a great mess, but the more individual people arranged their shoes tidily, the more other people did too. Gradually more formal elements were introduced—more chanting, more bowing. But Maurine always keeps a fresh sense of experimenting with new and simpler ways of doing things, more tasty recipes for sesshin, a sense of fun as well as discipline. She is very encouraging, and people often comment on the friendliness of the community.

"Maurine and I talk a lot about change, what it is, what makes for the capacity. Sitting practice makes me really see that it isn't a question of becoming different but rather of letting go of hindrances, defenses, old patterns. This is the same issue for us as a group as it is for me or you. I am so grateful that I can come here."

Rhonda Postrel, a thirty-one-year-old librarian in an architectural office, takes some responsibility, along with Sheila, for the running of the Cambridge Buddhist Association. She arrived there three years ago, after a difficult time in which a male teacher in a religious community in New England, although he was a married man with children, pursued her so aggressively that she had to stop studying with him.

In her second-floor apartment above a busy Cambridge street, Rhonda offers me fruit and tea as we talk. She is a woman with curly dark hair, dark eyes, and beautifully shaped hands. Now she punctuates her talk with gestures of these hands as she tells me how glad she was to find a woman teacher.

"I used to sit with Maurine very early in the mornings, and not too many people would come then, and one of the mornings I said, 'I should tell you who I am and why I'm here.' So I explained to her, just briefly, the sensitivity I had about her being a woman and what I had been through with my other teacher. And that's when she put her arms around me and said, 'Don't think that you're *wrong* for feeling what you feel. It's a terrible thing, and a very impure thing for a teacher to do that.' I was so proud that she came out so strong. Oh, I just breathed a big sigh of relief and knew that that was the place for me.

"It was very important for me to have a woman teacher, although I wouldn't have gone out specifically seeking a woman teacher. I had grown up basically with my mother, because my parents got divorced when I was young, so I was used to a woman's energy. And many of my other teachers and role models in professions had been women. And I was living with a man who ended up beating me, which was why I left him. That was another reason it was nice to have Maurine as a teacher. And ever since, she's treated me so well."

Through sitting and studying with Maurine, she says, she has come to see her life as her practice. "I understand my relationship in the world as not something separate from it, but *as* it. I am a single person and I don't feel the least bit lonely. I feel like the practice has given me a confidence and a security that there's a place for everything, for all of us, and I feel like I have found that place for myself.

"The other thing it's given me is a sense that there's always going to be more wonder and more surprises . . . sort of the infinity or the open-endedness. Sometimes people talk of how much suffering is involved in Buddhism, but I really see the compassion as a very positive feeling that is not different from the kinds of things that women have been doing for centuries . . . the same thing as peeling the carrots."

A pianist and teacher of piano herself, thirty-year-old *Deborah Polikoff* was naturally drawn to Maurine Stuart, even though she had begun her Zen sitting at the Cambridge Zen Center across town.

"I toyed with the idea of moving into a Zen center," she says, pushing her mass of long dark hair back from her neck, "but I felt that it was set up for a sort of monastic life, and I wasn't prepared to put Zen center responsibilities first. I was an artist and I needed to explore that. So I found myself at the Cambridge Buddhist Association, and I started talking to Maurine. Here was someone whose way of doing things seemed closer to mine. She was a pianist, she had a family, she did not live a monastic existence, and yet she was this extremely powerful practicing Zen woman."

Deborah tells the story of her "Bach dokusan" (dokusan is a formal interview), an incident revealing Maurine's flexibility in teaching methods. "Last year I said that I wanted to do Bach dokusan. My koans [see Glossary] would be preludes and fugues. It's something I came to because there's something very pure and centering about Bach, something that transcends the personal. Maurine loves Bach; sometimes she uses his music for teisho [formal lecture] instead of speaking. I felt that music was a language we shared, and I was trying very hard to integrate the Zen practice and the piano practice at that point in my life.

"Maurine said, 'Fine.' I asked her to assign me a koan, and she chose the A minor prelude and fugue from Book Two of the *Well-Tempered Clavier*. I started a practice of waking up every morning and doing bows or stretching, then half an hour of sitting, and at least half an hour of working on the Bach. When I went over to her house and played it for her, she laughed. 'It's much too explosive! Slow down.'" Deborah herself laughs, remembering. "It was not a piano lesson; she did not critique my playing. It *was* dokusan, because I presented my koan and she directed a few words at the essence of what was coming *through* my playing. So I went back and worked on my koan some more, and she passed me and assigned me another one.

"She loves doing things that way. One reason I appreciate her so much as a teacher is the creativity and flexibility she brings to her vision of Zen practice.

"Another reason I like working with Maurine is that, like me, she works through the body. One of my other teachers used to say, 'Mind okay, Body okay'; and I have always felt just the opposite. I need to get my body okay before my mind can do anything. And the first thing that Maurine started talking to me about was my posture, my breathing.

"I've really enjoyed Maurine's ability to be physical with her students. I remember one time I had gone to an early morning practice. There were only about three of us in the zendo. She must have *felt* that the energy was difficult—I was having a hard time, and there was a woman next to me crying. And sometimes when that happens she'll just start talking. She gave us this whole speech which went right to the heart of what I was feeling. Afterwards—I didn't know her that well then—I went up to her and I said, 'Thank you for your teaching,' and she gave me this huge bear hug. It was great. It's so un-Japanese." Deborah laughs. "Maurine is able to integrate this wonderful, nurturing, female, highly individualistic Western energy with this really strong Japanese form—it's just amazing!"

NOTES

1. I have been able to include only a few of the many American women teachers in this book. I apologize to the teachers whom I interviewed and whose contribu-

tions I was unable to use, to those I have spoken with and worked with but did not interview, and to those whose names I did not yet know when I was interviewing for this book. Each of them has helped me understand the role of teachers as guides and models. Readers interested in finding women teachers near them might begin by calling the Buddhist centers in their area and looking for notices of meditation groups for women.

2. The Kachina is a spirit being of the Hopi Indians in the American Southwest which is often personified in a carved and painted wood doll.

3. Dogen Kigen, founder of the Soto Zen school in Japan in the thirteenth century.

4. Alice Bailey lived from 1880 to 1949. Her writing on metaphysical subjects can be found in *Works*, published by Lucis Publishing Company, and *An Unfinished Autobiography of Alice Bailey*, also published by Lucis (1951).

5. She refers to the pope's visit to the United States in 1979, during which a group of nuns petitioned him to allow a wider role for women in the church.

6. Ruth Fuller Everett was one of the principal supporters of the Buddhist Society of America in New York in the late thirties and forties. She married Sokei-an Sasaki, its founder. Her daughter Eleanor married Allan Watts. In 1956 she opened a branch of the First Zen Institute in Kyoto, Japan, to train Westerners in Rinzai Zen. In 1958 she was ordained a priest at Daitokuji. With Isshu Miura she coauthored *The Zen Koan, its History and Use in Rinzai Zen*.

Yvonne Rand

Annick Mahieu (Sunanda)

Gesshin Prabhasa Dharma Roshi

Dhyani Ywahoo

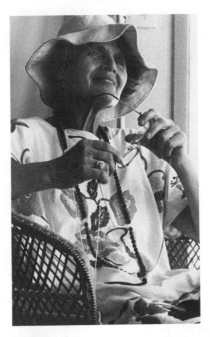

Ruth Denison

Nancy Wilson Ross

Elsie Mitchell

Maurine Myoon Stuart Roshi

Sheila La Farge

Rhonda Postrel

Deborah Polikoff

5.

Conspiracy of Silence: The Problem of the Male Teacher

Rage. Anguish. A vivid sense of betrayal. All this burst out when Zen women finally voiced the pain and disillusionment they had been suppressing, some of them for years. Two of the most important Zen roshis in the United States had been revealed to be men who regularly slept with and made sexual advances toward their female students while pretending to lead lives of utmost moral rectitude. Both were married, with children. In one case the disclosures were complicated by misuse of funds, in the other by alcoholism. Once these men's deeds became public (both admitted to their actions), stories from other Zen centers began to surface. Women began to share the experiences they had kept secret for years, and several other prominent roshis were revealed to be womanizers, one having gone so far as to fondle his female students during interviews at retreats.

These disclosures proved devastating to Zen students for several reasons. First, the atmosphere of Zen centers is one of extreme decorum, in which silence, modesty, and strict moral behavior are enforced; the structure places the roshi firmly in the position of spiritual master, according him almost superhuman status. Second, the relationship between student and Zen master is a delicate one in which the student makes her- or himself deeply vulnerable to the master, who in turn accepts the responsibility to act only for the student's good.

When it was disclosed that that trust had been violated, Zen students recoiled in shock. Many (both men and women) left the Zen centers these men headed, some bitter and angry, and badly damaged psychologically. The two major centers where this occurred, both of whose members numbered in the hundreds, have still not fully recovered and are still experimenting with new organizational structures, dealing with financial losses and diminished credibility.

While it was primarily Zen centers where these disclosures were made, other Buddhist groups also fall prey to this problem. One prominent Tibetan Buddhist master (recently deceased) was notorious for his drinking and having affairs with students; at least one Eastern Theravadin teacher, who was purported to be celibate, had a compromising encounter with a female student at a retreat center.

The extreme events at the Zen centers gave women (and many men) no choice but to look critically at their Buddhist environment and practice. In the harsh light of this heightened attention, they saw the hierarchy and the sexist dynamics governing much of what went on in Zen centers; they realized that the structure and atmosphere of these centers fostered the withholding of information, the manipulation of students, and other abuses of power. The Zen masters may actually have done Buddhist women a favor in that the stories of their transgressions blasted the secrecy and fabric of illusions holding some Zen centers together and caused the students to examine their own motives and behavior in ways they never had before.

The Zen form of Buddhism as it was brought from Asia is based upon strict obedience to a teacher. This tradition created Zen centers in the United States in which the teacher was the unquestioned authority on everything and was considered infallible. (After all, he's enlightened, isn't he? How could he make a mistake?) An arrangement that made sense in the highly structured, hierarchical societies of Asia, ironically held a special appeal in the looser structure of American society, especially during the social ferment of the sixties and early seventies. Young white middle-class Americans who had rebelled against their parents by taking drugs and engaging in free love and protest politics were attracted by the immediacy of Zen practice and also by its discipline, which offered a strong antidote to their chaotic lifestyle. They flocked to the Zen masters and began to build the meditation centers.

Many of these students were women. All of the Zen masters were men, many with little or no experience in relating to women, especially American women. They came from male monastic environments in Asia into coeducational Zen centers in the United States where young women were relying upon them for spiritual guidance. As Susan Murcott, author and former codirector of a Zen center, has pointed out, the Asian Zen masters in America live far from their own teachers and peers, so they have no support structure among themselves, no source of checks and balances to monitor their behavior and guide them.

The Zen center became a family for the young Americans, with the Asian roshi, or, in one case, the young American heir of a distinguished roshi who died, playing daddy. Soon the teacher became isolated, relating only to those who accorded him ultimate authority and respect—his own students. In this situation the teacher began to lose perspective on his own behavior and to give himself great latitude. He made sexual advances to one or another of his female students. The women, whether because of a need for his approval or a desire to share in his power, because they were in love with or intimidated by the teacher, sometimes gave in. (One young woman, seduced by a roshi when she was sixteen, said, "What do you do when God makes a pass at you?")

The inner circle of the Zen community carefully kept the secret of these affairs, hiding behavior that often continued over years. The damage sometimes done to the women involved was not seen as important or sufficient reason to confront the roshi with his misdeeds. In fact, it has been pointed out by therapists and some participants that several of these communities mirrored the dynamic of the alcoholic family, in which family members deny that there is a problem and protect the alcoholic father, while covertly encouraging his behavior. Such an addictive system requires dishonesty and promotes confusion and abnormal thinking processes.

The effects of these sexual affairs have often been negative, sometimes severely damaging both to the well-being and to the spiritual practice of the woman involved. As Carla Brennan, a critic of these conditions, points out, "These sexual relations are especially destructive to younger women because this contact can hinder development of a clear sense of themselves as women and of healthy relationships with men. Spouses and partners of the teachers and students have also suffered greatly from these situations. It is very common that the woman involved feels she must leave her community while the offending teacher remains, keeping his power and position."[1] Carla draws the parallel with the businessman-secretary, therapist-client, professor-student model of sexual power abuse, thus removing Buddhist teachers' misdeeds from spiritual or otherworldly justifications.

Often, while the actions themselves may or may not have caused problems, the secrecy shrouding the affairs of the teachers was the factor most destructive to students. This secrecy was maintained by loyal longtime students who hoped to preserve what was good in the institution and also to protect their home and livelihood. When it was breached, those who had not known about the teacher's actions felt they had been lied to and manipulated.

The rigidity of established groups and their resistance to women's questioning were sources of great pain to many women, even in cases where the teacher was not sexually abusive. Often the Buddhist practice itself was pursued in such a spartan, masculine fashion that women felt ill used and denied by the experience. The cultlike insularity of some groups, in which the feminist inquiry and activism going on in the outside world were denigrated, sometimes led to the defection of various of the more sincere and committed women students.

The women whose stories and comments follow confront some of the issues raised by relationships with male teachers. The events they recount and their ideas about the incidents are presented in order to bring to light the experience of women caught in oppressive or abusive situations, and especially to show the ways in which they survived these circumstances, often grew from them, and went on to pursue their lives and develop their spiritual practice.

This has been a difficult section of the book to complete, a fact that bears witness both to the continuing pain and problems created by these events and to the efforts still being made by some women students to protect their teachers and their institutions from criticism. Patriarchal culture maintains its institutions in part by withholding certain kinds of information about the behavior of leaders and participants. We hide what is going on for a number of reasons: to protect our teachers whom we see as deep

Dharma teachers and who have given us so much; to spare younger students the inevitable anguish and questioning that follows disclosure; to maintain the validation and power we get by associating with a powerful male teacher; to protect the institution that provides us with, in some cases, our livelihood, in many cases, our sense of purpose. For all these reasons, many women are reluctant to talk about the discord that has rocked their Buddhist centers as teachers' behavior was revealed, or to be forthcoming about the damage done to themselves in severely masculine settings.

Several times I wanted to abandon this section of the book, as it became more and more problematic. The reason I persevered is that I believe that as women we cannot afford any longer to maintain, by our silence, the conditions that disable us. In order to move skillfully through the challenges we encounter, we need information. This is information that only we can give to each other, for it will not be printed in the books written by men or in the brochures of Buddhist centers or told to us by those who welcome us to those centers.

I struggled ahead with this section, also, because of the bravery and clarity of some of the women in its pages who have chosen to speak as honestly as they possibly can about the events they have witnessed, the experiences they have lived. They have, again and again, articulated for me the importance of our letting in the fresh air of just-looking-at-what-really-is, in order that we may help each other to understand and change it.

UNMERGING, BECOMING ONESELF

Often the most spiritually committed women, who become teachers and spend a great deal of time with the roshi, are the ones who enter into intimate relationships with him. One might question what effect this has on their being given teaching responsibility and status, while recognizing that the situations are complex and contain many elements and motivations. The affair may become public, the teacher may take other lovers. How does the woman put her emotional life back together, how does she continue her practice and teaching?

One woman who has moved through this experience in an ultimately wholesome way is *Jan Chozen Bays*. In her life as a mother of three teenagers and a pediatrician-acupuncturist working in a clinic and teaching, she now spends little time in formal Zen environments, but works hard to learn more about herself and put her Buddhism into action with her patients and coworkers.

I first glimpsed Jan at the Women in Buddhism conference at the Providence Zen Center in 1984 where, in her formal black Zen robe, she was one of the teachers who lectured and gave a workshop. She had spoken principally of the dilemma of pursuing a Zen practice while raising children and working at a job, her candor and humor livening that difficult subject. She mentioned having "merged with" her teacher and now needing to pull away and define her own boundaries once again. I learned from other participants that Jan is the Dharma heir of Maezumi Roshi of the Los Angeles Zen Center, with whom she had an intimate relationship. Maezumi Roshi has been particularly open to women in Zen, ordaining women, including married women, as nuns. Two of his five Dharma successors are women. "In Japan this is unheard of," Jan later told me. "Married men can be monks, but married women are never nuns, and there are very few women who have been given Dharma transmission—that is, the passing down of the lineage and authority to teach—in all the history of Zen."

Jan Bays and I meet in the bright mirrored living room of her brother-in-law's apartment in the Mission District of San Francisco. She and her new husband are in town briefly from their home in Oregon. Perched cross-legged on the couch, dressed in a jersey and jeans, she seems perfectly relaxed, and not at all the stereotype of the forty-year-old professional woman she is. Her short reddish hair falls in soft waves, her eyes are blue and clear. She gives the impression of great gentleness.

First we talk about her initial work at the Los Angeles Zen Center, which until the events of 1983 included a full city block of single-family and apartment buildings and where more than a hundred students lived. (Because so many people have left the Zen center, those who remain were forced to sell parts of its property in order to meet expenses.) It is situated in a neighborhood inhabited mostly by people of Latin birth—Salvadorans, Mexicans, Nicaraguans, Chileans—many of them undocumented immigrants. Jan started a clinic for these people that offered not only Western medicine but acupuncture, naturopathic, and chiropractic medicine. For some years she pursued intensive Zen practice while working full-time in the clinic, maintaining her relationship with her husband, who also lived in the Zen center, and raising her children. In 1979 Jan was ordained, and in 1983 she officially became a sensei, or teacher, and received Dharma transmission from Maezumi Roshi.

When I ask if we can speak of her affair with the roshi, she replies that she is comfortable talking about it. Was the discovery of that liaison the trigger for the Zen center's blowing apart? I ask her.

"I wouldn't say it was *the* thing that blew the community apart," she objects. "It was *one* of the things. I think the community was building and growing to a point where it *had* to break into smaller units. It was too large. There were too many internal stresses. Roshi couldn't be personally available to people in the way they wanted him to be. At that time there were 150 people living on the block, living together within a 1 1/2 block radius. It was getting so big that Roshi couldn't possibly be available to that many people in a very personal way, and so the tensions were building."

She talks earnestly, meeting my eyes with a steady gaze.

"Zen is set up in a very individual way. It's face-to-face transmission. It's not just a teacher talking to a group of three hundred people, like Muktananda's or Rajneesh's or other ways of teaching. That private interview is the key, where the teacher really tests your understanding. Wherever he feels you're stuck he pulls the rug out from under you. So if that's not happening, you start to feel cheated."

And she elaborates, "In serious Zen study, the teacher and student meet alone in the interview room several times a week for ten years or more, in the most intense and intimate study imaginable. In koan study the student plunges into and becomes all aspects of existence and nonexistence: anger, love, hate, death, birth, emptiness, animal realms, male, female. The teacher continually strips away anything the student is clinging to, using any technique which works. The process is frightening, exhilarating, frustrating, horrible, and wonderful. The student and teacher become extremely close during this process, like people who have been through a war together. I think it's no wonder that this closeness sometimes takes a physical form, not that it *should,* but it does. In the old Zen monasteries in Asia, women and men were segregated and there wasn't a chance for this intimacy between male teacher and female student. In America there is, and we have to be trained so we are aware that the problem might arise, just the way psychotherapists are trained about the transference phenomenon with their patients and the risk of physical intimacy."

Other problems, Jan tells me, were inherent in the setup of a monastery that had married people, families, residents who were working outside, a situation of contradictory needs in which people were constantly pulled in two directions. "There's a monastic element in all of us," she points out, "that wants to retreat from the world and sink full-time into this desperate search for Who am I? Why am I here? Then there's another element that wants to be involved in the world—have a good time, party, dance, go to the movies, go see *Star Wars.* At the Zen center we thought we could combine them, but instead people got torn, back and forth, back and forth."

"What about your teacher's alcoholism?" I ask. "Was that causing problems?"

"Well, that was a funny thing, because we were all coalcoholics," she says, tipping her head to the side, smiling ironically. "When we realized that he was an alcoholic and we had the team come in and educate us about alcoholism, I know several of my friends and I just about fell out of our chairs when we saw the movies on alcoholic families, because it was *our large family of a hundred!* Saying the same words! The very words that we had spoken were there in this movie about an American family with alcoholism. We in subtle ways encouraged his alcoholism. We thought it was enlightened behavior that when he would drink, elements of Roshi would come out that we had never seen before. He would become piercingly honest. People would deliberately go—everybody did this—and see what he would say and do when he was drunk, and how he could skewer you against the wall. Because in Japan the society is very contained and very repressed according to an American way of thinking, so when you drink, those wild and honest elements are allowed to come out."

Jan and her fellow students had the common misconception that since her teacher didn't drink all the time and could function in his work, he was not an alcoholic. When they learned about alcoholism as a disease, it was obvious that he had the disease and that they were all contributing to it.

"What about your sexual relationship with the roshi?" I ask.

"To me the sexual aspect of it is very minor," she answers, "and Roshi would say the same thing too, if you talked to him. It really was almost *fusing* with another person. It's very difficult to explain. Most people see the relationship as a traditional 'affair,' and it certainly has aspects of that—you know everybody wants to be loved and part of your expression of love is physical—but that was really a minor part of it. It was becoming so close to this person that I really was fused with him in a way that my identity was submerged. That's part of Dharma transmission, to become one with your teacher so that you can see through their eyes. It became a reality in the sense that sometimes I would know what he was thinking. Once a strange thing happened. I was standing next to Roshi in the Dharma hall and someone took a sitting cushion and tossed it. With no awareness in my mind a voice came out of my mouth and said something like 'Don't do that. Treat your cushion with respect.' It was bizarre for me because it was *his* thought that came through my mouth. There were several instances of that, where there was a psychic merging."

She pauses, looks down at her hands, and then looks back up to me. "There's a real danger of trying to make a relationship more than it is. You know, to say this was a sacred relationship or a mysterious relationship or a mystic relationship—somehow to justify a relationship on that basis. I don't mean to do that. But it was a very profound, very special relationship. And it taught me a lot about love."

There is a particular silence in the room, both of us listening to those words in the air, acknowledging their significance. I glance out the window, down a street lined with Victorian houses, where cars pass noisily.

"Do you have regrets now?" I ask.

Jan nods, and says steadily, "I have regrets that people were hurt. His wife was very generous. I think more for her sake and for my exhusband's sake I don't like to talk about this, than for my sake or Roshi's. Because I feel that they were hurt. She's a remarkable person. About a week after the news came out that we had had a relationship that was physical, she agreed to talk with me and she was wonderful. I went to the house and she looked straight at me and said 'Come in and would you like some tea?' and we talked for a while. And I just thought, If I were in your shoes I couldn't be this generous or this forgiving! She really has tremendous capacity to forgive and to go on."

The disclosure of the affair happened in late 1983. In the summer of 1984, feeling that it was no longer appropriate for her to stay there, Jan left the Los Angeles Zen Center and with her children moved to Oregon. There followed a time of self-discovery.

"Because I had looked forward to a life where I would be merged with him and do whatever he wanted to be done," she explains. "Then I realized, 'No, I really now need to unmerge and become myself again.' That's actually what Zen practice is about, is to become more and more yourself. That's what Roshi is, he is *himself*, and either you accept that or you don't. To me that was the bottom line. That's what I felt during all the turmoil: 'Okay, here's who Roshi is, do you want to stay or do you want to leave? Fine. No big deal.'"

She still considers Maezumi Roshi to be her teacher, saying, "I can go to him and he can lead me clearly, know exactly where I am. He can say one word, sometimes even unintentionally, and it will just crack me open and take me to the next stage that I need to go. To me that means that's your teacher." Jan goes each year to meet with Maezumi Roshi and his other Dharma successors, to study together and share ideas and news.

We speak of the precepts, the rules that govern the conduct of Zen practitioners, one of which warns against "sexual misconduct." Jan admits that in her Zen center, "I think there were two sets of rules: one for what was really happening and one for what was *supposed* to be happening, and that's what caused the difficulty."

Her decision to move to Oregon was motivated partly because she likes colder climates and changes of season, partly because her sister lives there. And a deeper motivation: "At the time of all the upset at the Zen center, there were obviously things I wasn't looking at clearly and places where I had not studied myself, which is what Zen is supposed to be about. So it was time to pull back from the formal study of Zen and really look at and examine myself in a different context."

In Portland she was fortunate to find a job she loves, as supervising pediatrician in an outpatient clinic next to a private hospital, a job that entails some teaching.

She pauses, looking around the pleasant room, thinking, and then tells me, "Where I am now . . . you can call it love, or you can call it seeing the Buddha in everything. That's what I want to explore next. How can I experience constantly the presence of god or Buddha nature in everything. Boy, that's difficult."

"Does that happen with your patients?" I ask.

"We have a very difficult patient population," she answers. "Poor, depressed, angry people. That's the real challenge. We all talk about it, the group who work with this patient population, how can we keep going and keep supporting them, when to be firm, when to be yielding. To me this is Buddhism in action—or religion in action, however you want to say it. We have bodies for a reason. We're out there working for a reason. To me the warp and the woof of religion is, how does it work every moment in relationship to people?"

As she walks me to the door I ask her if she can see herself teaching Zen and leading sittings at this point.

"I just don't know," she tells me. "I feel like we're all teaching each other all the time, and I don't know if that will stay my framework for the future, where I just feel like there's a flow from everybody to everybody, or whether I will want to teach more formally." She adds, smiling, "I don't feel I'm *not* teaching.

A year after our talk, I learn from Jan that she and her husband have begun to conduct a sitting group in their house and that she gives a Dharma talk once a month.

SEVEN STRESSFUL YEARS

The attempt to speak out about women's concerns in a male-created, repressive environment can be a painful, discouraging experience. *Denah Joseph* lived in and participated extensively in the Rochester Zen Center under the direction of Philip Kapleau, a Japanese-trained American; this Zen center, she says, had "an extremely masculine orientation and masculinist expectations." Immersion in this environment from 1970 to 1977, a period when Denah's feminism and sexual preference were taking form, resulted in a great deal of conflict, turmoil, and damage for her.

Denah, a thirty-eight-year-old psychotherapist, mother, and lesbian, talks to me in her brown shingle house in East Oakland. Earlier, in the twilight, I had watched her playing on the sidewalk with her young blond son, chasing him while he ran screeching with delight.

A blue-eyed woman with an aureole of curly blond hair and graceful hands, Denah talks easily, although as her story becomes more painful her face now and then shows the stress of that life she was living and the transition from it. She begins by telling me how devoted she had been to the Zen center, which had felt like a family to her.

(When Denah saw this interview, she was dissatisfied with the tone of her remarks as she had spoken them. She sent me this revised version of what she had to say, some parts of which I have summarized in parentheses.)

"I had to do a lot of inner work later on to make sense of what happened there for me. Notice that I started by saying how devoted I had been 'to the Zen center,' not to the process of spiritual development, or even to the practice itself. Certainly these were important to me, but I'm afraid that my involvement, at the ages of nineteen through twenty-six, was much more motivated by psychological needs than a true understanding of spiritual practice. And I think that there were many young people at that time—the late sixties—gravitating toward Zen in a similar, somewhat pathological way: as a replacement for family, as an attempt to bypass the painful developmental tasks of individuation and identity formation.

"There were many young people—dedicated but basically immature—at this center. It was a very compelling place, providing round-the-clock structure, community, meaning. I embraced the whole thing, unquestioningly. I rarely left the grounds. I became a staff person, living in staff housing, receiving a small stipend in exchange for my work there. We sat many hours of zazen, on a rigorous daily schedule, including regular sesshin, or periods of intensive practice.

"I learned a great deal. The teacher was a Buddhist scholar and a brilliant speaker; his disclosures were exhilarating. But basically I think my motivations were quite immature and not particularly spiritual. I think if I were a teacher, I would have discouraged a lot of people from that level of involvement—including me— 'Just go out and live for ten years and *then* consider making this your life.'[2]

"The center was riddled with elitism, sexism, and homophobia. [She had laughed as she told me she eventually became the head housekeeper.] Although there were always a few token exceptions, the main line was women are the secretaries, cooks, and men are the gardeners, builders, craftsmen."

(She tells about the asceticism and physical challenge of the place, what one Zen woman has termed the "combat-boot mentality" of the teacher and his prize students. The monthly week-long sesshins were very rigorous, with extra sitting, or staying up with as little sleep as possible, favored as the best way to practice.) "During the sesshins there was tremendous emphasis on 'breaking through.' It was very traditional Japanese, with the stick [the 'kyosaku': see Glossary]. The roshi would speak very proudly about how his Japanese teacher used to break sticks on people's backs during sesshin. The pressure was relentless. And if you couldn't 'take it' then there must be something wrong, or weak, about you.

"The last year, or maybe two, that I was involved, I started having some very difficult experiences, I think because I was repressing so much. There really wasn't much room for questioning. If you questioned this way, you were seen as 'not into your practice.' There were a few women and I who started a women's group, for which we were derided and questioned. Therapy was very much frowned upon. Going to other centers was frowned upon. I have since heard fanaticism defined as 'repressed doubt' [Kathleen Speeth], and by that definition, this center was indeed fanatic. It was an extremely rigid, narrow, and closed world.

"Eventually I started to experience extreme physical pain during sittings—again, I think, because I was in so much inner turmoil, with no place to turn to deal with it. To want, more than anything in the world, something that I was incapable of having because the one way of having it I was failing at, was a thought that was beginning to assume delusional power within me. Slowly the realization began to grow that I was deteriorating, and I became very frightened. By this point my entire life was tied up in this: it was my community, my entire social world, my livelihood, my reason for being alive, my organizing principle. To let it all go was devastating."

(She left the staff and moved out of the center, and eventually she stopped going to the center at all.)

"When I finally left the Zen center, I didn't go back. I felt ashamed. And I couldn't sit zazen, after years of daily sitting. I was having dreams that I'd be in the zendo and wouldn't be able to find a seat, or walking in kinhin [slow walking meditation] in the wrong direction. I felt like a pariah and became extremely isolated. It was a very difficult time, to say the least."

(Having left the Zen center, she went back to school to get a master's degree in counseling, worked as a waitress to put herself through school, came out as a lesbian, and then had a baby. Her son's father is a gay man who is actively involved in the child's life.)

(Others had experiences similar to hers, and eventually such people began talking to each other. Denah told of several she knew who, having come out of comparable situations, found themselves completely dysfunctional and unable to cope with the outside world; but she did not experience that level of distress. In fact, her experience, in retrospect, taught her a great deal that she values: discipline, the ability to work, a more realistic attitude toward teachers. But it took many years for her to return to Buddhist meditation.)

"Very slowly, I started to sit again by myself. I went into therapy and began to deal with what I had been avoiding—the alcoholism in my family and the physical and emotional abuse I experienced as a child. I didn't deal with my experience at the Zen center, it was too soon. When I started to meditate again is when it all came back. When I would sit down on the cushion, my mind would become flooded with memories and feelings of shame, of having somehow failed at what I cared about most.

"But when I started to sit again, so much that was right about practice came back too. I had always felt a fit with the Buddha's teachings: the worldview, the ethic, the psychology—all of it had always sort of resonated with me. And slowly that sense of rightness came back. I'm grateful for that, because I thought I'd lost it all."

(Denah met a friend, Jessica Barshay, a former Zen student from a West Coast sangha, and they began to sit together regularly in 1981. Gradually other women joined them and formed the beginning of the Women's Sangha [described in Chapter 4, "Lighting the Way"]. Denah, who had always liked the Zen rituals and celebrations, led those for the group. Still, she remained tentative and was careful not to get too involved.) "At that point I had a pretty healthy case of skepticism about *any* organizational practice."

(She spoke of the Women's Sangha experience as a step in her healing and her coming back to Buddhism. She also studied Kum Nye, a Tibetan form of movement meditation, and found it extremely helpful in its validation of the body and access to a meditative state through movement. Then she attended a retreat led by Ruth Denison, her first contact with a teacher in six years.)

"That was quite momentous for me. I was very scared to go to a retreat, to put myself in a position of relating to a teacher, because I was very unsure how I wanted to do that. That first retreat opened me up. I had never had any Vipassana training, and it helped me to see that there were many other ways to approach spiritual training than the Zen way, and there were ways perhaps more suited to me. And though I didn't want to make any further commitments to this particular teacher, I was able to *separate* the teachings from the teacher, to understand that the teachings always have to come through the personality of a teacher, and that I could retain my commitment to the former without having to lose myself to the latter."

(In the last few years she has attended several retreats with different teachers.) "I'm still sort of watching my responses and tasting different offerings. Although this approach was derided in my original training, I think it is valuable and essential in my path now. I miss the support of a Buddhist community and hope someday to be able to experience that wonderful sense of sangha again. But for now I need to veer away from any institutionalization of the practice and focus on the practice itself.

"Before I left the Zen center, I talked with another woman

there who said to me, 'You won't fall out of the universe. Spiritual centers all have their own texture. You'll find your way.' I appreciated that she said that, because at the time I didn't know that for myself. I thought if I couldn't make it there, then that was *it* for me. Although that seems incredibly naive to me now, I don't believe it was just because I was naive that I thought that. That was also what I was taught, by someone I respected and trusted completely. Now I know there are many different teachers, all deserving of our respect and appreciation, for their efforts to teach the Dharma within the limitations of their own personalities. Even if I never find another teacher or community to work with as intensively as I did at the Zen center, I am certain that I will continue to go along in my own daily practice. It's been over sixteen years now that I've meditated, and it *has* really blessed me. I would never give it up!"

SECRETS

In most situations in which the teacher is having sexual relations with students, it is not the actions themselves that prove destructive, but the secrecy in which they are pursued. Students believe in their teacher and model themselves after him. A deep trust is established. When that is broken, much psychological harm is done. Also, the senior students usually know about the affairs, keep the secret, and thus the hypocrisy spreads. Certainly the teacher's participation in secret affairs affects his ability to give guidance to his students, especially in the area of relationships.

Often the sexual liaisons are only part of a larger picture in which a hierarchical structure results in some students feeling taken advantage of, as their unpaid labor built the Zen center and their loyalty allowed their Zen master to enlarge his domain of influence and function in a dictatorial manner.

Two women who recently have looked critically at their teacher's behavior and the context in which it occurred are Sonia Alexander of the Cambridge Zen Center and Loie Rosenkrantz of Empty Gate Zen Center in Berkeley. These institutions are branches of the Kwan Um Zen School headed by Korean Zen

Master Seung Sahn, called by his students Soen Sa Nim. (Others in the Kwan Um Zen School perceive their teacher and their institution quite differently and would like his actions to be kept private. Their views are represented later in this subsection).

Sonia Alexander, a small blonde woman who radiates friendliness and amused intelligence, was a director of the Cambridge Zen Center, which occupies several row houses on a street behind Central Square. She lived there with her husband and worked outside as a medical photographer. Now she believes that she was simply being used in order to build Zen centers and establish Korean Zen practice in this country.

Her teacher, Soen Sa Nim, has opened Zen centers in cities from New York to Berkeley; Lawrence, Kansas, to Lexington, Kentucky; as well as in South America, Asia, and Europe. All of these centers are guided by the Kuan Um Zen School at the Providence Zen Center in Cumberland, Rhode Island. The creation of these institutions has been accomplished by tremendous labor on the part of Zen students like Sonia Alexander.

When I first spoke with Sonia in Cambridge, the news of Soen Sa Nim's intimate relationships with students had not yet come out. Sonia, who knew nothing of these affairs, spoke of the example of pristine conduct set by her teacher. By the time I spoke with her again, on the telephone from California, her life had changed drastically. This woman whose whole existence had been based in the Cambridge Zen Center had moved with her husband to a condominium in Jamaica Plain and severed all official ties with the Zen center after learning that her teacher, whom she had been led to believe was a celibate monk, had several long-term sexual affairs with women in his Zen centers.

"When he was questioned on it," Sonia tells me on the phone, "he said he slept with the women because he needed someone in the Zen center he could trust. It wasn't love, it wasn't desire."

She and others were outraged at this news and began to take a hard look at the assumptions and procedures in their Zen center. They began to identify instances of questionable behavior that they had previously rationalized, and they saw the Zen center as a little world of its own, which functioned to exploit them and give them an unreal view of themselves.

"We bought into the 'mystery' of Zen," Sonia Alexander says. "And we created a closed community where we had status, where a lot of people are economically and morally tied in."

However, she still appreciates Soen Sa Nim as a teacher, she says, for he taught her to "see clearly and act well." She might go to him, even now, for interviews, but she would never again live in one of his Zen centers, for she believes that "the system he devised is a form that can't succeed in this country." She now sits Zen with Maurine Stuart Roshi at the Cambridge Buddhist Association.

A woman more deeply disturbed about the dynamics within the organization founded by Soen Sa Nim is *Loie Rosenkrantz*, who was at one time director of the Empty Gate Zen Center in Berkeley and representative to the council that oversees all of the centers under Soen Sa Nim's direction. She speaks particularly of the method in which deception is perpetrated, and she points out that it is our giving up of power in these situations that allows them to continue.

Loie, forty-five-year-old mother of a teenage daughter, meets me for breakfast before she goes to work as a gardener. When we have settled ourselves in a booth she fixes me with huge brown eyes and begins to talk about her experience.

"I was a participant in this community for a good eight years and had become one of the old-timers, and I never knew that Soen Sa Nim and the woman in Providence had slept together for five years and subsequently that he and another woman who lived at Cambridge Zen Center had been lovers, and perhaps there have been some other women . . ."

While certain events had seemed suspicious or repressive to her over the years, Loie had not questioned or investigated them. She tells how one can come to ignore one's perception that something is wrong. "Once you buy that this action is okay because it's a teaching, or it's helping somebody from the Bodhisattva point of view—which is what Soen Sa Nim says—and you take the approach that whatever your teacher does, you're devoted, you trust, you don't question; that they are somehow more than you are, they're more enlightened or they're more compassionate or they're more something; and you give away your clarity and your original perception that something's fishy there; from then on you're just dead."

When the information about Soen Sa Nim's intimate relationships reached Berkeley, Loie says, people responded with shock, confusion, and anger—and some relief in finding out that Soen Sa Nim was "not so perfect." Some men found it freeing not to have to live up to the model of the superfather anymore.

"For me a very big issue is: I really don't believe in telling lies. And I had to look at the ways I had colluded inside myself, psychologically, my own form of denial. Not that I had all that much information, but it made me very coldly scrutinize everything over the years. At the time of my coming to the community it was the seventies and there was a lot more freedom in terms of how people were sexually. I had been with Soen Sa Nim in sauna rooms and hot tubs—he would be nude with all the students, as we all were with each other—and there was one female student who told me that he had played with her in certain ways, and I didn't know whether to believe her or not, because she had a way of expressing herself very sexually and was very seductive. But as I look back at her in hindsight I just see that she was a confused person, and I didn't want to hear clearly what she was saying."

Loie herself had been practicing at Dharmadhatu (the San Francisco branch of Vajradhatu, the Tibetan Buddhist center) before coming to Empty Gate, and she was tired of the "partying, drinking, and sex" that she says was indulged in there, so that she was attracted to a practice led by a man presented to her as a celibate monk, at a seemingly sedate Zen center.

Her eyes are wide with outrage as she tells me about the letters to a friend of hers in which her teacher explained his actions.

"He said that he slept with this woman because she could be the core of the then Providence Zen Center and that sleeping with him helped make her strong." She adds ironically, "It took *five years* to make her strong! And he said the same thing about the woman at Cambridge Zen Center: that the Zen center was floundering, and by making her strong, it made the Zen center strong, and therefore he acted for the benefit of all the people. And *he believes it!*"

I think about the example of the San Francisco Zen Center, which pulled together to confront its teacher, and I ask Loie if her community could have done that. Her answer points up the reasons why Zen students often do not question their teachers, the tremendous amount they stand to lose if they do.

"No, this community can't do that, because, for one thing, it's decentralized. And the people who are in charge, none of *them* has really questioned Soen Sa Nim. If you live in these communities for years, it's not just how you feel about your teacher, it's your home, it's all your friends, it's where you're raising your kids—do you have enough independence in your own life to move, give up your job, your community? It's like you give up everything! So a lot of these people are too attached. Or they haven't really gotten the information how serious it is. Because it's *very serious.* It's fascistic. And Soen Sa Nim is a dictator!"

"Isn't *fascist* too strong a word to apply here?" I object.

She shakes her head. "Let me clarify for you what I mean by that. Basically it describes a situation where there's an inherent lack of democracy, where power comes from the top down, where decisions are often made in secret without a genuine process of consultation with the group as a whole."

And she goes on, "The lack of democracy can express itself in many ways; its essence is control which tends to be oppressive and dictatorial, in which the group's thoughts and actions represent or are heavily influenced by the will of the leader or in this case the 'enlightened master.' "

Many people have left the Cambridge Zen Center and the Empty Gate Zen Center, Loie tells me, and many of the old-timers from the Providence Center have moved to Cambridge or Providence proper, so that these centers are now peopled with newcomers. Many of the new people coming in don't know about the teacher's sexual behavior.

"One of the biggest issues for me is if people don't know what's going on, then you're abusing their ability to make decisions for themselves. So people are thinking once again that Soen Sa Nim is celibate, when he's not. If he really believed in himself and what he was doing, he could say, 'Well, I dress as a celibate monk, but what I really am is single, which means that I'm not married and I don't have attached relationships.' So someone can ask, 'Well, is five years' continuous relationship with somebody not attached? What do you mean by attached? Why is it okay for you to do this, and why do you still wear the robes of a celibate monk?' "

Loie finishes her breakfast and drinks her coffee. Then she begins again.

"It's not so much the action—I don't care about what he does: I mean I don't want him to *hurt* somebody, but abstractly I don't care if he's celibate or not. But I *do* care that he misrepresents himself, that the community doesn't know. I mean you don't have to get on rooftops with megaphones, but people in the *same house* don't know."

Loie herself is no longer a Dharma teacher and no longer lives at the Empty Gate Zen Center. She has sent back her robes and bowl with a statement of withdrawal. (She meditates with Maurine Stuart Roshi and Toni Packer[3] when they are on the West Coast.) And she is examining her own motives.

"Ultimately, I have to see what in me, what in all of us, drew us to these communities, to these teachers, and allowed us to stay there for years. How much of it was idealism, natural wisdom? I'm very fond of Soen Sa Nim as well as thinking very negative things about him. It's not all simple, that he's a horrible person. And there's a way in which he expounds the Dharma—I've gotten a tremendous amount. It's changed my life. And I've learned a lesson. Since I left it's been a great time for me to reexamine my whole life, my psychological makeup—it's a very yeasty situation. I think it's going on in our culture generally, so many people seeing our addictive patterns, how we plug into abusive situations. The people who are willing to look at that are going to have to distinguish: What's the Dharma, what's the truth, and what's all this other garbage that makes up the community or the form of what we've participated in?"

And as we leave the restaurant, she speaks of the effects the hypocrisy has upon teachers themselves in keeping them from seeing the significance of their actions. One woman at the Providence Zen Center was sexually approached by her Western teacher during a meditation retreat and began an affair with him that was disastrous for both partners and their spouses. "Even to this day this man, who has practiced all these years, still hasn't really *gotten it* that his mistake was to *tamper with a student's practice* by going with his own impulses and desires. What he did with her was very serious. He indulged himself and was not being the cor-

rect teacher. He has never come out and said that. Soen Sa Nim
has never come out and said that. The school has never said it."

And she concludes, "The response to the teacher's proposition-
ing of that woman tells me this school and these teachers have
nothing to teach me. And I wish they would learn from the students who have left, because *these* are the *real practitioners.*"

Having been approached by some of the people who are still
members of the Kwan Um Zen School, who were anxious about
the effect the disclosure of their teacher's sexual behavior might
have on the school, I spoke with five women. One who is a longtime, loyal student of Soen Sa Nim said she did not feel disturbed
or affected by the prospect of his behavior being commented
upon in my book, explaining, "It's *his* karma." Another told me
she did not consider his sexual behavior important and was not
concerned with protecting his reputation. A third, having read
Sonia's and Loie's comments, said "There's no problem here. It's
just the truth." But she asserted that, in her opinion, Sonia was
very much in the minority in feeling used, and that Soen Sa Nim's
affairs had not been hurtful to the women involved. She also said
that she understood that Soen Sa Nim himself had been going
through a process of change in response to the uproar, and that
he had softened considerably. In Chapter 7, "Living Together,"
in the short portrait of the Providence Zen Center, Shana Klinger
gives her view of developments there, pointing out her own and
other students' unrealistic expectations of their teacher.

Then I received a letter from a woman who had achieved some
status in the Kwan Um Zen School, demanding to see every mention of her school and her teacher in my manuscript so that she
could check it for "libelous content." This woman, with whom I
had always had cordial relations, was obviously acting out of fear.
I wished I had thought to communicate with her earlier about the
content of the criticism of her teacher and her school, but I had
been told that she was assiduously maintaining the secrecy and so
I had not known how to approach her. Now I answered that I
would be very happy to receive from her a statement of her own
experience and views on this matter, which I would include here
as a balance to Sonia's and Loie's remarks. She never replied.

Finally, I was approached by a student of Soen Sa Nim in the San Francisco Bay Area. She said she wanted to come to talk with me. This woman I knew to be very committed and supportive of her teacher. When she arrived, we took a walk and talked for several hours.

First, she spoke with me about the character of Soen Sa Nim, his personal and cultural background, and the good he has accomplished since coming to this country. She cited the enormous effort he has put forth to bring the Dharma to the United States, and she expressed her gratitude for this gift. Her depth of feeling was obvious.

While she had been disturbed by the disclosures of Soen Sa Nim's liaisons, she had not terminated her relationship with him or the Kwan Um Zen School, since she believes commitment requires that one stay through the hard times and support the teacher in his struggles. She cited some differences between the Korean and American cultures to explain and excuse Soen Sa Nim's actions. Again and again she returned to the question of what was at stake: the many Zen centers, the hundreds of Zen students whose practice would be disrupted by including the criticism of Soen Sa Nim in this book. And she told me that the people at the Providence Zen Center had been extremely upset when they learned about this section called "Secrets."

Why is it important to bring this material out and talk about it, she asked me, when the incident is over now, has been "dealt with," and when the disclosure, in her opinion, would be harmful to the Kwan Um Zen School?

So I asked myself, again, what is at issue?

The sexual affairs were apparently not abusive or hurtful to the women. By all accounts, they were probably strengthening and certainly gave the women access to power. (However, no one can know if other women were approached by Soen Sa Nim, said nothing, and may have been hurt or at best confused, and left silently.) No one questions that Soen Sa Nim is a strong and inspiring teacher and missionary, wholly committed to spreading the Dharma, who has helped many people by his teachings and by his creation of institutions in which they can practice Zen. In his organization he has empowered students, some of them women, by giving them the mandate to teach and lead. And he has speculated, in a positive vein, on the coming empowerment of women in religion and government. Even his critics describe him as a dynamic teacher from whom they learned a great deal.

On the other hand, former students point to secrecy, hypocrisy, an organization in which the people on top have power and information that they do not share with those farther down.

I remember reading, in Robert Aitken's *Mind of Clover* (p. 90) a quote from Soen Sa Nim:

The one who praises you is a thief.
The one who criticizes you is your true friend.

And I wondered if he believed those words and if he would share the anxiety some of his students were expressing.

My visitor told me that the members of the Kwan Um School have confronted the fact and implications of Soen Sa Nim's sexual liaisons and have achieved resolution on this matter. She said she herself went through a process of coming to terms with the information in which she had to examine her own complex and uncomfortable feelings, and she has reached a larger understanding of her teacher and herself.

I invited her to communicate this process and this insight in these pages by writing a statement that I would include as a balance to the critical statements.

At first she was enthusiastic about doing that, but later she called to say that she had decided not to write the piece. It was "too personal," she indicated, and besides she had little faith that the readers would be sympathetic to it. It was neither appropriate nor in good taste to address the issue, she added. Zen, she instructed me, is *not* about issues. And she asked me once again to reassess my motives in making this information available to my readers, and to consider leaving it out.

I took this challenge very seriously and spent a number of restless nights and preoccupied days examining this ethical dilemma, especially pondering the potential harm to students of Dharma. I sat with the question. As I mentioned in the introduction to this section, I had reached some clarity before beginning it as to its importance. Now I was plunged once again into this process, drawn by this woman's earnestness and her concern for the Dharma. For the first time I asked myself, would it be possible to simply leave out the "Secrets" subsection? Five days later I awoke one morning with the answer to that question.

I was sorry that, when offered a forum in which to express their views and present their teacher and their school in a favorable light, both of the women most passionately protective of him and his institution chose to remain silent. And as much as I liked this woman who came to share her experience with me, as much as I felt and understood her urgency, I could not do what she wanted me to do.

Why not? Because we belong to a community larger than any one Zen school. Because it is only by looking at our mistakes that we can find our way in American Buddhism. We need all the information we can get, from all the Buddhist institutions: What has worked? What went wrong? Where did we make mistakes? How might we do it better next time? With open inquiry and a generous spirit we can bring about healthy change. If we cover up our mistakes, minimize or justify them, and then hide the process of our dealing with their consequences, we benefit no one. If, as Bobby Rhodes of the Providence Zen Center says, they are just "people learning to live as a community" and their teacher is "just trying to learn the same thing," then what is there to hide? Wouldn't it be better in the long run, for the sake of the Dharma in this country, to open up our process, to share our changes, admit to our confusions, and call upon the support of the larger Buddhist community in finding new ways to organize our communities and relate to our teachers?

As to Soen Sa Nim's sexual behavior, which some of his supporters say is simply his own business: If a teacher is being presented as a celibate monk, and if he in actuality engages in sexual liaisons with women in order to accomplish the building of Zen centers, then that is information any woman studying with him or planning to study with him should have, because (1) as a woman, she might some day be approached sexually by him; (2) his behavior indicates a particular attitude to women that surely affects his nonsexual relations with female students and his counseling of female and male students in matters involving intimate relationships. And finally, students who must suppress information about their teacher in order to protect him are being asked to behave in contradiction to the purpose of Buddhist practice, which is apprehension and expression of the truth of existence.

Both those who criticize and those who defend speak out of real needs and desires. Let them express these openly so that the Buddhist community as a whole can benefit and students, particularly women students, can be informed of the conditions they may meet in any particular Buddhist institution.

DEFINING THE CONTEXT

Outside *Carla Brennan*'s windows lies a Massachusetts spring landscape where I have just walked, seeing the pale slender trunks of birches, pink-white apple blossoms massed above black bark, scarlet and yellow tulips cupping the residue of last night's rain. A mile down the curving road is Belchertown, a community harboring some of the college people from Amherst, others who commute to work in Springfield, and a few old-timers who grew up in that tiny town.

Carla, who has written a penetrating critique of sexual power abuse by spiritual teachers, lives in an apartment in an old farmhouse set in a sweeping lawn, with an ancient barn decaying out back. She works here as a painter and illustrator, and today, even though she has a debilitating cold, she is at work on a painting commissioned by the town of Belchertown.

Putting down her brush, she comes to sit with me in the living room next to her studio. As we talk, she is serious without being heavy handed, and sometimes a self-deprecating laugh punctuates her speech.

"Since I was in high school, I've called myself a feminist," she says, in answer to my question. "Even when I was in grade school I remember being angry that women aren't treated equally. Then in my first year of college I read Robin Morgan's *Sisterhood Is Powerful* and other feminist writings. I suddenly realized there was a whole culture created by feminists. For me, feminism is part of my spiritual practice, in the sense of understanding oneself, increasing consciousness, breaking free of conditioning, and realizing one's potential."

It was this attitude that led her to question the procedures and assumptions governing life in the two Buddhist centers she belonged to and brought her up against the entrenched sexism there. Later, in her indignation at the sexual abuse of power perpetrated by Buddhist and New Age teachers, and her recognition that many so-called spiritual people did not show concern over this problem, Carla Brennan wrote an article (originally published in *Kahawai*) analyzing the situation with considerable insight and common sense.[4]

Now, at age thirty- two, Carla knows well that many people do not share her inclusion of feminism in spiritual practice. She lived for 1 1/2 years in the Cambridge Zen Center (founded by Soen Sa Nim's students), where she was housemaster for a time, but she found that discussion of issues affecting the group was discouraged, and she tired of the "jargon and rules" governing the place. Then she began to sit at the Theravadin Buddhist center, Insight Meditation Society, in nearby Barre, Massachusetts, and eventually she was asked to join the staff. As a staff member she confronted what she considered to be the power dynamics operating there. It was clear to her that the power structure placed men at the top, but when she questioned this, she was met with denial.

"Somebody was leaving the board," she gives as an example, "and I suggested that we should consider a woman for the position. The response was, 'We should consider who's qualified— not whether it's a woman or not.' And I was sitting there wondering, Is this 1960 or what?! If this was the police department in the town of Barre, they couldn't say that! It was really politically behind the times. And not only about feminism, but racism and other social and political issues. Many people felt that these issues were someone else's problem. They believed that these problems didn't exist *there,* where everyone is supposedly open and fair. Some people also felt that political issues are separate from spiritual practice and should not be discussed in a spiritual setting."

She points out that this was 1980 and 1981, and that much has changed at IMS since she left. But while she was there, "The more I spoke up the more I felt I got shunned. Some people tried to dismiss me by suggesting that my dissenting opinions were not relevant and were the product of my own personal problems and lack of understanding. This was a painful experience: I'd talk to some of the staff and we'd all agree that there was an important issue that needed to be discussed with the teachers. We'd go to a meeting and everyone would remain silent except for me and sometimes a few others. Often no one would back me up. Those kinds of experiences were so painful that it just got to be too much after a while."

"You were ahead of your time," I suggest.

"Yes, there were a number of women who came after me who were outspoken and had similar experiences. Then eventually the staff became more solid and were not so influenced by the teachers. When I was there the staff was often intimidated by the teachers."

In her article, Carla particularly challenged the view of the teacher as infallible or superhuman, and she placed the sexual abuse of power of Buddhist teachers in the context of sexual power abuse as it is generally manifested in the world of business offices, psychiatrist's offices, and universities. Especially she urged that people in religious communities acknowledge and investigate sexuality rather than avoiding the subject. Now she tells what motivated her to write the article.

"I had heard so many stories over the years about teachers initiating sex with students, not only spiritual teachers but also teachers from all sectors of the New Age community. I was appalled by the lack of *concern,* by people *not speaking out,* and by the lack of awareness about sexual abuse. When I left IMS I was fed up with the indirect manipulation of power by teachers who denied that they had any power at all or that it was an issue. Although there are many types of power abuse, I felt that sexual power abuse was the most insidious and at the core of the others. I had thought about writing something for a long time, and then the scandals with Baker-roshi and Muktananda came out.[5] Then I went to the Providence Zen Center, where Susan Murcott did a workshop to talk about these issues. When I was halfway through my article there were allegations of an incident involving Munindra at IMS.[6] There was much confusion about what was happening in many Buddhist communities. But *I* felt some clarity, partly because I didn't have an ideal image of teachers. I also had done some research on sexual harassment cases in the secular world and was struck by the similarities between those situations and what many spiritual teachers were doing. I didn't think sexual misconduct was something so mysterious, I thought it was pretty ordinary, actually, and I knew there was a lot of information available that would help people understand the problem."

The major contribution of "Sexual Power Abuse: Neglect and Misuse of a Buddhist Precept" is its demystification of this problem. Businessmen sexually harass secretaries, male psychotherapists seduce female patients, and professors sexually approach students. In the secular world, Carla points out, this activity is punishable by law, and every day suits are filed in the courts for sexual harassment.

She emphasizes that the trauma and pain and sometimes long-term damage done to the women involved in these situations is often discounted. Carla speaks of the often uncontested power that some spiritual teachers enjoy and points to the myth of infallibility that surrounds them. She writes also of *women's* responsibility to "step out of the patterns that perpetuate sexual abuse."

In her conclusion she states,

Some people have avoided dealing with the problem of sexual misconduct because they fear that it would threaten their spiritual community and the establishment of Buddhism in the West. What does this say about our real priorities? If, under the guise of spreading the Dharma, we allow behavior that is dishonest and exploitative, then perhaps we have begun to lose our way. We need to reexamine the original purpose of Buddhist communities and decide exactly what we are trying to establish and why."

We talk about Carla's one experience of suspecting that she was being approached sexually by a spiritual teacher, which followed the classic model of the teacher pretending that nothing unusual is happening and thus confusing the woman and ensuring her passivity. During a sesshin, the Venerable Sasaki Roshi began to touch and hug her during the frequent interviews. As he became more aggressive, she began to suspect that his actions were motivated by sexual desire and not out of concern for her progress as a student. But it was not a simple situation.

"It gave me a lot of insight into the complexity of those kinds of sexual initiations," Carla tells me. "For me there were feelings of not wanting to offend, not wanting to cause problems, cause a ruckus. Hugging in our culture is fairly innocuous. But it so easily slips beyond that, and the line is often unclear."

Carla stops to think, to pull up the words.

"*He's* not acknowledging that anything funny's going on; so if *you* acknowledge it, suddenly there's this big thing in the room. There's a certain embarrassment or shame in bringing that out in the open. I think that's a woman's common response."

And she tells of the rationalizations students sometimes use to justify the teacher's behavior.

"I'd heard a number of stories of people saying, 'Well, maybe we just don't understand what the teacher is doing and the sexual relations is a spiritual teaching.' 'Maybe he knows that this woman has sexual problems and he's trying to . . .' " She bursts out laughing. "I've heard that so many times. Oh my god!"

"That's what some of the teachers themselves say afterwards, that it was for the women's spiritual good," I put in.

"Isn't that presumptuous?!" Carla asks, her eyes outraged. "Those men think they have"—and again her own laughter interrupts—"helped all these women by sleeping with them!"

Now we talk about the process of rethinking and transition in which she is engaged. She has begun to be more involved with women's groups, and she feels she cannot work with a male teacher. Sitting with a group of women, with no men present, she says, seems simpler and more honest. But she is leery of becoming heavily involved with any group.

It was in part the response to the allegations concerning the Indian teacher Munindra at IMS that soured her on groups. Carla was disturbed because, while there was general disapproval of what had happened, there was not an understanding that this incident related to larger issues in the spiritual or Buddhist community concerning power, authority, and the relationships between women and men. Despite her and other students' efforts to point this out, the affair was treated as an isolated incident.

"Much of the problem stems from the avoidance of sexuality," Carla says. "Sexuality is negated or ignored within most religious traditions, and you can't suppress something so basic and integral and not have it come out in some other way. When deeply repressed, sexuality often expresses itself in abusive and exploitative patterns. I think that's a real failing in the teaching."

And she adds, "There's a relationship between the suppression of women and the repression of sexuality. Women are the symbol of sexuality for men, so repression breeds that classic view: woman as the temptress who must be controlled."

"How do you think it *should* be dealt with?" I ask.

"I don't know," she admits, "but from observing our culture at large, I believe that sexuality is one of the most misunderstood and most explosive issues we must deal with. I would like to see people in spiritual communities *acknowledge* and accept sexuality. I'd like to see us try to *investigate* and understand it instead of just sweeping it under the rug."

COMMENTS ON AN UNCONVENTIONAL TEACHER, BY HIS STUDENTS

A Buddhist environment in which sexuality *is* pursued and discussed openly is Vajradhatu (the religious community) and Naropa Institute (the teaching institution) in Boulder, formerly led by the Tibetan Buddhist teacher, Chogyam Trungpa Rinpoche. This man, a former monk who became a husband and father, was until his death in April 1987 undoubtedly the most notorious of the Buddhist teachers who have sexual relations with their students. His community in Boulder numbers over a thousand participants. There it was common knowledge that Trungpa Rinpoche drank to excess and propositioned his female students, and that he maintained continuing relationships with a number of women, who were referred to as his consorts. This behavior took place within the context of an ancient, elaborately articulated, and colorful Tibetan Buddhist lineage in which the convention of "crazy wisdom" and outrageous behavior is strong.

Because neither Trungpa nor his students ever made a secret of his affairs and his drinking, his behavior did not pose the same kind of problem for his students that the secret affairs of Zen roshis have for theirs. Still, it was not an easy reality for most women to confront, and the Boulder women with whom I talked (most of them connected to Naropa Institute) had usually gone through an internal process to move from disapproval and dis-ease to acceptance of their teacher's actions. One problem that *was* acknowledged among them is students' imitation of the teacher's behavior, so that drunkenness and promiscuity have been viewed by many practitioners as desirable. Out of this problem has grown an Alcoholics Anonymous chapter within Vajradhatu itself to help the students whose use of alcohol has become destructive. Since my visit there, according to one Naropa woman, there is much more of an emphasis on work with addiction and codependency.

Women of the Boulder community, as a group, are presented in Chapter 7, "Living Together," but their comments on their own attitudes to their teacher's behavior belong most appropriately here. Following are the responses of seven women (given before Chogyam Trungpa's death) when asked the question: "Are you bothered by your teacher's excessive use of alcohol and his sexual liaisons with students?"

Irini Nadel Rockwell, dancer, director of the movement studies department, Naropa Institute (Naropa is known for its programs in art, poetry, and dance):

"I don't have any distress about that. I *did,* but as I practice more and get into more of the Tantric practices [see Glossary] I have begun to realize that his manifestation is totally brilliant. Not that I understand it, but that I understand not-understanding. I realize that he is working in realms that I only have a vague inkling of. I accept him as a totally enlightened vajra master, and so it makes sense to me that he does what he does.

"My first meeting with him was a real turn-off. I mean, I didn't want a guru who did things like *that!* The irony was that I had left my *other* Tibetan Buddhist teacher partly because he was coming on to me. And I just couldn't handle it. And Rinpoche is very much into alcohol and having girlfriends. *Now* it makes total sense to me.

"When I took the Bodhisattva vow from him, I remember saying to myself, 'I don't understand what this man is doing, but I trust him.' And it's been an incredible path."

Barbara Bash, artist, instructor at Naropa Institute:

"What I have to go back to is the feeling I'll never forget at the Women in Buddhism conference here in 1982 when the topic came up—the whole question of him sleeping with lots of women. I remember getting this sensation, like a knife in my chest, it hurt so much. It was like an old, old feminine hurt that was just there in the room. Something that couldn't be healed over was opened up and aired maybe, a bit, but certainly not resolved.

"I'm thankful, for myself, that he sees me as someone to work with, so that I have a relationship with him that is fun, that has a lot of inspiration. I also feel that being around him, around any true teacher, is like the ground falling out from under you, and sometimes even though I love that working relationship, the feminine thing comes up, like, 'Why am *I* not attractive to him?' It's a very vulnerable spot in me. I feel glad that I haven't had to make that kind of choice, but I also feel very exposed around him. I don't condone his doings, but I ask, 'What's *my* experience when I'm with him?' At the Women in Buddhism conference, I was in a discussion group with a number of women who weren't in the community, and they said, 'Well, what is all this?!' I just had to come back to: 'I'll tell you what *my* experience is of being around him.' "

Vicky Fitch, cofounder of Dana Home Care, an organization providing comprehensive and innovative care for the elderly (*dana* means generosity):

"I was Rinpoche's servant. I emptied his chamberpots, tied his shoes, cleaned his toilets, and did all that kind of work. And I just don't have any problem with anything he does. Which is not to say I see it as a guide for other people's behavior. For Sharpassana, which is the Buddhist alcoholic group, this is a crucial issue, because these are people whose life experience has taught them that they can't drink, that the AA guidelines are the only way to go in terms of getting sober. And here they have this teacher who's drunk every night, and how can they possibly make any sense of this? And the more I get into it the more I see that there's really no problem. When people get into quibbling about those kinds of things I always wonder what else is going on.

'I've seen Rinpoche in outrageous postures, and yet every time I've seen that it's made sense to me, actually being there. Hearing about it would not make sense. But I've never known him to be anything other than kind. He is infinitely kind and infinitely delighted, completely playful, not bound by conventions or traditions but completely rooted in Buddhism. There's nothing he does that is without discipline or sloppy. That's my personal experience."

Dennis Ann Robertson, administrator, Naropa Institute:

"I think there's a teaching in his drinking, for us; I thing it's a direct reflection of us. I know his drinking has certainly encouraged all of us to drink more. When I got here, that was a main thing, every party you went to it was considered not only okay but a good thing to drink too much. So it probably encouraged me to drink too much and to perpetuate the thing I had already gotten going with alcohol. But I see it as a reflection of *us.* And if he's forced the issue enough that there's a group formed and there's a context to go look at it, I frankly think that's better than the other extreme of his saying no alcohol at all and everybody would have had to be sneaking.

"I'm a very judgmental person, but I don't feel at all qualified to judge him. I see the qualities that he genuinely has and shares. He's so generous with himself. He certainly doesn't do anything to hide. He has the qualities that I admire in a human being, the gentleness and the warmth and the openness and the spontaneity. He doesn't fit into any of the categories that I usually lay judgments out for. I don't see him being stupid or rude or stingy, I don't see him not practicing what he preaches."

Susan Edwards, writing instructor and Tarot reader:

"He's great. I love the fact that he works on his problems the way he does. He doesn't hide it. He drinks, and it's almost killed him. So, he's working on it. I find that great. People will use him as an excuse for drinking, and he says, 'Don't use me as an excuse. This is *my* karma. Don't make me into a Buddhist Jesus Christ. I'm working on my things, you work on yours.' And when the drinking group formed, he was really happy. He gave it all his support.

"If I had seen the option that alcohol could be in a sacred, or at least a respectable, environment, I'd be a different person today. The idea is to educate people about it.

"About his sexual affairs, well, I went through a lot of things with that. Ultimately, I would say, it's my feeling about *women,* not about him. There's two things about him: one, he really likes women, not just sexually, but really *likes them.* I'm gay, he knows

I'm gay. I am a somewhat untypical woman but I feel that he accepts me as a woman. I don't feel that from a lot of men, that kind of acceptance. So I say, 'Okay, at least he's not a woman-hating man.'

"Then there are women who want to go to bed with him. At seminary people say, 'Oh, I went to bed with him,' and brag about it. And some women *wouldn't* do it. It's their choice. Some women want to do it to say they've gone to bed with a teacher. It's complex. Why is the woman saying *yes*? In this particular sangha I feel people are smart enough to say yes or no. So I'm looking at the *woman*, and if you're saying yes, then say yes. He's gonna *ask*, and if you say no, he's not going to kick you out. He might keep calling you up—'Please, please, please'—which he was doing to a friend of mine at seminary. She just said, 'No!' and he'd send his guards over to knock on the door, and she'd say, 'No, leave me alone!' And he'd say, 'Oh well . . .' He was very sweet about it. So that's when I started wondering what are the *women* doing, what are *they* getting out of it, and do they think it's a badge or status?

"A lot of women are consorts of Rinpoche. The Tibetans are into passion, they think sexuality is an essential energy to work with. You don't reject it. So it's a whole other perception of sexuality anyway."

Ina Robbins, psychologist, instructor at Naropa Institute:

"I certainly have had my problems with this. It's been a very rich part of my path, working with that, because being a Tibetan Vajrayana practitioner, the central part of my path is relationship to teacher. So it's been unavoidable, to relate directly to who he is, what he is provoking, what he is providing, what he is inspiring. It's been real juicy and scary and irritating and all of that. My conventional conceptual mind objects and protests and waves red flags about some of the things I've heard and seen. And at the same time, when I have been in his presence, what I experienced is tremendous gentleness and tremendous wakefulness. So there's always this flicker of what I think should be happening and what really is happening. So more and more I'm regarding what I experience in relation to him as part of the teaching, that it's instruction, or it shows me my mind, or it shows me my concepts, my aggression, whatever. It's not comfortable at all.

"I have a better sense of humor about it, which I think is a real good sign for me, because it shows much more willingness to be surprised and shocked rather than to hold so fiercely to things."

Bonnie Rabin, therapist, cochair of the Sangha Care Council:

"A teacher who came to talk to us last year said, 'You relate to the guru's mind, you do not need to question what he is doing.' There's always a segment of the community that wants Rinpoche to stop drinking or wants this or wants that. The teacher said, 'He knows what he's doing. You relate to his mind.' That was very helpful. I am a woman, but I trust what he's doing and I don't feel that in any way he is hurting anyone. I mean, any of these women, if he wants to spend time with them, can say no.

"But there is the flip side of this: if the teacher can do this, why can't his students do this? We've had a lot of that in this community. That's why, this teacher coming in and talking was extraordinarily helpful. You know, you relate to the teacher's mind, you know you have your family blah de blah, and you don't *imitate* the teacher, that's what he was saying.

"One thing that I have always been impressed with is the enormous kindness of Trungpa Rinpoche. It can be ruthless compassion—it isn't going to be idiot compassion—but the kindness is always there. That's my experience."

A MIRROR OF THE FAMILY

In 1983 the San Francisco Zen Center exploded into the center of the storm that rocked the larger Zen community and shook the foundations of other Zen institutions in other parts of the country. Even now, five years later, the damage caused to the institution and its members by the behavior of its roshi has not been fully repaired, and some of its most active women students are reluctant to speak of their own experience of dealing with and reacting to that crisis.

San Francisco Zen Center was begun by students of Shunryu Suzuki-roshi, author of *Zen Mind, Beginner's Mind*. Between 1967 and 1972, the city center, Tassajara Zen Training Monastery, and Green Gulch Farm opened. Their purchase and development, as well as the establishing of the various Zen center businesses, were due to the brilliant entrepreneurship of Suzuki's young American successor, Richard Baker, and the tireless efforts of hundreds of dedicated Zen students. Baker-roshi, a charismatic and powerful leader, jetted around the world to conferences, hobnobbed with politicians and business tycoons, and captivated his students.

A married man with a family, he demanded strict moral conduct from his followers and was the model of propriety while practicing in the meditation hall. Because of the enormous gift of the teaching that he gave, the opportunities within the many arms of Zen center, and the excitement of working with so gifted a master, his students tended to overlook his considerable expenditures to maintain a lifestyle far above their own and antithetical to the spirit of Zen. Rumors of his sexual liaisons with various women over the years floated around the Zen center but were squelched by the most devoted students. Most people believed he *was* the person he presented to the world.

Then in 1983, the board of directors of the San Francisco Zen Center was provided with so much evidence that it had no choice but to confront Baker-roshi with his sexual adventuring and financial excesses. He left the center. When the news of his affairs and extravagances reached his students, some of them who felt betrayed by their leader and bitter at having been exploited by him quit in outrage. Others chose to follow him as he went off to found another such institution in New Mexico. The organization itself was profoundly damaged, both spiritually and financially. The San Francisco Zen Center, even now, is still struggling to put itself back together, to learn new ways of working that will prevent a similar debacle from happening, to heal itself.

At the time of the disclosure of Baker-roshi's misdeeds, a number of articles were published setting forth the conditions within the Zen center that had allowed this situation to develop and the possibilities for restructuring and rethinking that existed among the people who chose to stay and work within the institution. One of the most thought-provoking was written by Katy Butler, a journalist who had practiced at the Zen center. Her "Events Are the Teacher: Working Through the Crisis at San Francisco Zen Center" appeared in *The CoEvolution Quarterly.* Through such exposure the events at the Zen center became public knowledge.

My interest is not to go back over those events or summarize that commentary but to bring out the experience of some of the women involved, both those who stayed with the institution and those who left it. I was told by a number of people that the San Francisco Zen Center and Green Gulch were trying to restructure themselves so that no one would ever be in the position to act as Baker-roshi had. Previously, said my informants, the system had been stiffly hierarchical and repressive, with Baker-roshi definitely controlling what went on there. Now the people at SFZC and Green Gulch are having to take responsibility themselves for decisions pertaining to the center. It was difficult for them to communicate openly, because there had been a closed system with management of information, that is, information being provided or withheld according to the judgment of the roshi. Many people mentioned, also, that Baker-roshi had insisted that news of Zen center affairs not be given to the press or the public.

I made an appointment with *Yvonne Rand,* one of the people most intimately involved with the development of the San Francisco Zen Center. She had worked with its founder, Suzuki-roshi, and cared for him in his dying. Over the years she held many posts inside the Zen center and traveled to raise funds, usually working closely with Baker-roshi. Her family life had been interwoven with the life of Baker and his wife and family. Over time she saw him engage in destructive affairs with a growing number of women, saw him abuse the trust of his students and misuse the money they had earned and/or given to the Zen center. She suffered tremendous mental anguish and even physical illness because of this knowledge, yet for many years she kept his secrets, because she felt it to be in the best interests of the institution as a whole to do so. Eventually, however, she changed her mind, and she was one of the people who participated in bringing his behavior to the attention of the board of directors. Yvonne Rand is still involved with Green Gulch Farm as a practice leader who gives Sunday lectures and leads retreats. (See Chapter 4, "Lighting the Way.")

"Richard Baker is a charismatic and powerful teacher," she told me. "Consequently he lived deeply in many of our lives. It was too easy to project a host of desires, hopes, fantasies—both psychological, emotional, and spiritual—onto him. So we, together, made a life which was not sustainable or healthy for any of us."

The disclosure of Baker-roshi's misconduct brings up the issue of who gets chosen to be a roshi. What are the implications of Suzuki-roshi's having picked someone like Richard Baker to succeed him? I ask.

"Suzuki-roshi loved him," Yvonne answers. "He didn't know how to read this person from another culture. He saw Dick Baker as being an organizational genius, as able to make the institution which would be a vehicle for carrying the teaching of Buddhism—and he was right. I think it throws up serious questions about lineage and Dharma transmission. If you look at people whose practice has some quality of authenticity, it has nothing necessarily to do with Dharma transmission. It has nothing necessarily to do with how many sesshins people have sat, or whether you're a zazen student or not. Being awake is being awake! Being in the zendo every morning like a good boy or girl doesn't necessarily mean you are not hiding."

As Yvonne points out, the students at the Zen center were behaving as people do in a nuclear family, in which the father holds power and is supported and protected by his wife and children even in actions that are destructive to them. Some former members of the SFZC, in examining their motives for participating there, look at their conditioning as women and their behavior within the family.

"Men and women do have different styles of ego," says *Barbara Horn*. "The women's scenario has a lot to do with deferring, with yielding, with giving up of self. A good chunk of my practice at the San Francisco Zen Center was giving up myself, when I hadn't even *found* myself. It was a lot of garbage. I was hiding behind 'Let's be generous, let's be compassionate.' First of all it's unhealthy, because it's repression and avoidance, and secondly it's not really having a full and rich practice."

Barbara Horn spent seven years as a monk-priest trainee at San Francisco Zen Center and Tassajara. When the Baker-roshi crisis erupted, she "fell apart," she says, "because my life commitment was there. My intention was to be a priest and to stay in that community and be ordained.

"It was profoundly confusing. I felt how mixed up everything was and how hard it was to sort anything out. And I felt the bigness of the community, so many people there; the lack of intimacy really struck me. And the lack of any interpersonal growth and development, and the resistance to being involved in groups with facilitators. When we first started to have community meetings there was a lot of pooh-poohing going on about therapy.

"But the clincher was, I realized I was functioning just like I functioned with my brothers and sisters. And that really did it for me. It wasn't shocking that I was *doing* it, but it was shocking that I was *getting away with it.*"

Another woman who points to the family dynamics being played out at SFZC is *Meredith Cleaves,* who is engaged in examining her motives for having chosen Baker-roshi as her spiritual teacher. "With a lot of help from other people, I have set about trying to find out what it was about me that caused me to choose this person who has very deep problems. It was through a process of a year and a half that I came to understand that basically I hadn't worked out my childhood, which was profoundly violent."

Meredith Cleaves lives around the corner from the San Francisco Zen Center, where she was an ardent student for eight years, and she still works at the restaurant owned by the center.

"There was alcoholism in my family, and I'm an incest survivor. The alcoholism and the incest have more than anything shaped who I am as a person and as a woman. I was addicted to Richard Baker, and in the Zen center I followed the same patterns that I created as a kid in terms of how to relate to a group, to a family. At Zen center I had a twofold personality, just as I did as a little girl. The public personality was very similar to what I did as a kid, and the situation was very similar. It was very emotionally repressive and rigid, and everybody was apparently happy and very terrified, and there was a lot of suppressed anger, because what was happening was a pain in the ass."

When she began to question rules and practices in the Zen center, she came up against strong disapproval, and, eventually, "I felt the longer I stayed at Zen center the less welcome I was, because I was a woman who was furious. I think I was one of the most actively questioning women. I *had* to, my mind was *brimming with pain.* I mean, when I was librarian, it was not all right to have a women's section in the library. This was in the *early eighties!* I came to feel that the negative response came from fear and antagonism. It's pretty simple, and it's very political. I feel like religious training places are where medical training places used to be a hundred, two hundred years ago for women.

"I really think this particular center was one of the most sexist. Women who competed with each other to be more masculine than each other were given positions of authority. That is destructive."

She pauses to think for a moment and then returns to describe the Zen center once again as a family, and to characterize its former leader.

"The Zen center approximated my family in that it was centered around a man who was profoundly insecure and didn't feel capable of doing what he felt he needed to do—and he had been asked to do more than he could possibly do. My family was addicted to alcohol, Richard Baker was addicted to power. Both my father and Richard Baker were tremendously out of touch with what's usually called the 'self,' and that was disguised. Both were charming, handsome. Both exceedingly bright. I mean, this goes along with being a sociopath, actually. Richard Baker is a much better actor than my dad. Very hard to see through. Almost no feminine energy. And just a devastating misuse of everyone— men and women, teachers and students."

In the effort to present the perspective of women who had chosen to stay in the institution after the disclosures about their teacher, I called the practice leader at San Francisco Zen Center, who is a woman; she refused to talk with me. A longtime resident of Green Gulch agreed to speak with me, but we missed connections and I was too busy to set up another appointment. Then I was able to arrange an interview with a woman high up in the administration. It is no paltry responsibility to be an administrator of this Zen center, one of the largest Buddhist establishments in the United States. The San Francisco Zen Center includes the practice and residence center in San Francisco, located in a beautiful old residence club on Page Street; Tassajara, a monastery and summer retreat center in the Los Padres National Forest down the coast; Green Gulch Farm, a community farm in Marin; and various businesses such as the elegant Greens restaurant, Tassajara Bakery, and Green Gulch Greengrocers. Millions of dollars in property and business are involved; many people live, work, and study under the Zen center aegis.

This woman, who had *not* known of Baker-roshi's affairs, even though she had worked and lived closely with him for a number of years, spoke of the deep distrust of authority that had been created by his behavior. No one, now, wanted to allow someone to take responsibility, for fear that person might abuse his or her power in the way Richard Baker had done. (We spoke before the new abbot, Reb Anderson, had been named.) She described the ways in which the people in the Zen center were gradually teaching themselves to step forward and take responsibility for particular tasks or events. Her remarks were carefully considered and quite supportive of the Zen center, while admitting to the difficulties the members were facing.

I remember thinking at that time that I admired the people who had chosen to stay at the Zen center after Baker-roshi left: people who, in my view, saw Zen practice as more important than any single teacher.

However, when I showed the interview to her, she said that while she "stood behind" everything she had told me, she did not feel comfortable having this published because as an officer of the Zen center she had to consider the welfare of the institution as a whole and was afraid this information might damage it. I asked her to show it to others, saying I did not think people would respond negatively to it but rather would see it as an honest account of an institution's struggle to change. She called me back several days later to say that although several people to whom she had shown the piece felt fine about its appearing in a book, a number of others urged that it not be published as they thought it would be strongly detrimental to Zen center's attempt to heal the wounds of the past.

There followed several months of negotiation, in which I communicated with her in the hope of including at least some of her experience and insight in these pages. Finally I had to give up, realizing this woman's profound ambivalence about sharing her experience with people outside the institution and her fear of the effect it might have on people inside the institution.

The process I engaged in with her was discouraging and instructive. I wondered whether it indicated that Baker-roshi's legacy of secrecy is still alive at the San Francisco Zen Center.

Eventually I returned to Yvonne Rand, surely one of the people most centrally involved in and committed to the San Francisco Zen Center and Green Gulch, to ask: What has been learned from the group experience here and the great turmoil and anguish of 1983? She said she would think on this question and write me a letter about it.

Her letter said, in part:

"In my time at Zen Center with Richard Baker I had a big investment in his being the perfect teacher that he wanted to be. We both wanted it. So when each of us had real problems and difficulties, we couldn't turn our attention and energy and capacity of investigation to those difficulties as they actually were. I gave away my personal authority partially out of my deep longing for someone to be perfect in the world; I became involved in a kind of cover-up, keeping secrets. And of course what becomes so deeply troubling in such a process is one's own capacity to *not see* what one is doing: to be out of touch with what is actually going on. Now I have a number of peers who give me response and criticism on my behavior. And having this feedback system, even when I don't like what I am hearing, is crucial.

"We are all corruptible. That includes me. So it's absolutely necessary to tell the truth in every picky detail of my daily life—especially to myself. And this means telling the truth even about those matters which cause me fear, discomfort, or shame.

"The question confronting us as a group is: Can we keep our vision before us of what Zen Center might do and be in the world, while being fully awake to our own dark and potentially dangerous or unhealthy possibilities?

"We at Zen Center need to examine more carefully the kind of cloudy and confused thinking that seems to arise within a residential community where people live and practice and work for too many years at a time. More of us need to go away to study with teachers elsewhere, to have some perspective on Zen Center and its culture.

"The board of directors is now elected by members of Zen Center. For years the board members were appointed by the previous board members. So to have an elected board feels like a big change. But we still have a long way to go in developing a structure which is truly American and democratic in style and form as well as in tone, and which includes more participatory ways of solving problems."

Lane Olson, who was guest manager at Green Gulch Farm when I spoke with her, came to San Francisco Zen Center in April of 1983, in the very week the announcement was made that Baker-roshi was leaving. While she is a relatively new and somewhat peripheral member of the Zen center community, her view of the situation since the crisis is important as it is not laden with the many complicated feelings engendered by contact with Baker-roshi, and it is informed by a developed feminist consciousness. Lane sees the changes made and the strong female influence that emerged just after Baker's leaving as hopeful, but she now notices the slipping back into the old forms.

"Within the first year after Baker-roshi left, everything loosened up," she says. "They started going into more and more American translations of the chants, and they added more walking periods and discretionary periods, in which you could choose whether to sit or walk or even sleep, during one-day sittings and seven-day sittings, which to me was a lot more feminine, for some reason. It was caring more about the people as opposed to putting on this ritualistic schedule.

"Now there's what I consider the right-wing pullback into a more strict Japanese-chanting much more stringent schedule."

Lane continues, "One thing that the whole Baker-roshi thing did do was shake everybody up. When I first got here to Green Gulch Farm there were probably eight to ten families, who had lived here for many years and weren't ready to budge. Now I think there are only four families left. And there's a whole question always about, What are we? Are we a practice place, are we a monastery?—we've got all these kids here—are we a Buddhist community? Are we just a commune? There is a lot of feeling against having the kids and the families, and yet I think the mothers are some of the strongest people in the whole Zen center. Like Wendy Johnson and Kathy Fischer. They're the most grounded, have the clearest overall picture of what it's like to be a woman and a mother and Buddhist and worker and sometimes priest. Their experience is so well rounded in all these areas that they have a much wider picture of what's going on."

Women have significant roles here, she tells me, as head of zendo, gardens, and kitchen. Lane herself is guest manager.

Yet, in her view, the residue of Baker-roshi's sexual affairs implies a compromised role for women. Disturbed by this, Lane is looking for female role models, asking "Where do we go from here?"

"I'm adamant about questioning these senior-priest women who have been around for ten-fifteen years, just saying, 'Where are *you* in all of that?' Because what I want to know is, 'What's happening with our concept of ourselves as women?' "

But the situation is not simple, she emphasizes.

"There *is* a feminine side to Zen center that I think nurtured people. It certainly came up right after Baker-roshi left. The women just got together and there was this incredible blanket of support in the community, the married women and senior priests that were female—*I* felt it anyway. But some of that, I'm sure, just came from their having been so repressed for so long."

She describes one aspect of this support. "There used to be a women's meeting. Apparently it was a very vital group a number of years ago, when there was a feminine spirit. They used to meet down at Mayumi's.[7] We had one meeting since I've been here, and I was the only woman from Green Gulch to go. Then, recently, we had another one. Mayumi and I just threw one together, and I think there were only maybe three Green Gulchers and the rest were all women in their late thirties to early fifties who had lived here at some point or had been at Tassajara and now were out. They were struggling with integrating practice—and they were still very much into practice, every one of them—with living on the outside. I was really impressed with them. But I was amazed by the lack of response from the community itself."

She tells about confronting the female practice leader in the city center, who was not speaking or giving instruction during a sesshin, as the male leaders were doing. The woman's silence troubled Lane. When questioned, the leader said she had to come from a place of "perfect balance" in order to give instruction. "Bullshit!" Lane explodes. "I was in tears! I was so angry and frustrated." (After their conversation, however, she reports, the woman did begin to speak.)

Lane ponders this incident, shaking her head, and sums up the situation. "I just think that women are so far behind at San Francisco Zen Center and Green Gulch that it's going to take an awfully long time to catch up."

As I was writing this section, a member of San Francisco Zen Center called to inform me of a bizarre incident involving the present abbot, Reb Anderson, that once again compromised the organization. Anderson had just been arrested for brandishing a pistol in a public housing project. He had been robbed of $20 at knife point, had gone to get the gun that he had hidden in the Zen center garage, and had driven around the neighborhood looking for the robber. Seeing the holdup man go into a housing project, Anderson followed, waving the gun. The robber disappeared and police officers, probably called by neighbors, arrived to arrest the abbot. Asked how he had acquired the gun, he revealed that he had found it lying next to a corpse he had discovered in Golden Gate Park four years before. Rather than reporting the death and turning in the gun, he had decided to sit with the body (a Zen tradition) and had gone back for several days to do so. Then he had taken the gun and hidden it. When asked why he took the pistol he could not explain himself. Later—on June 15, 1987—this story broke in the *San Francisco Chronicle* with a front-page headline and the text prominently placed on page two.

Anderson offered to resign his post as abbot, but the SFZC board did not accept his resignation; he then took a six-month leave of absence from his duties. (He agreed to perform thirty days of community service work for the misdemeanor charge of brandishing a weapon in public. Charges for taking the gun— theft and tampering with a crime scene—could not be pressed as the three-year statute of limitations had run out.)

When an institution has been set up on strict hierarchical lines and has functioned that way for over ten years, and the system of Dharma transmission based on the Japanese male model is still in use, can the institution's members, even with the best of intentions, alter the structure to allow for open communication, egalitarian governance, and women's leadership? The San Francisco Zen Center suffered the stunning consequences of an authoritarian structure when its former roshi abused his power in a way that was destructive to both the institution and to his students. Having been given this dramatic lesson, they were struggling to change their attitudes and procedures. Did they, dragged down by their own history and the power of inertia, sink back into the kinds of assumptions and behavior that created the unrealistic expectations and immature actions operative in that first crisis?

Now, once again, the board and members of San Francisco Zen Center have to confront the unacceptable actions of their chosen leader, in this case violent and erratic behavior. At this writing, months after the incident, the board of directors of SFZC are still trying to find ways to restructure their organization, and members and board alike are torn by conflicting attitudes to the behavior of their abbot.

NOTES

1. From "Sexual Power Abuse: Neglect and Misuse of a Buddhist Precept," in *Not Mixing Up Buddhism*, edited by Deborah Hopkinson, Michele Hill, and Eileen Kiera.

2. An article called "Vicissitudes of the Self According to Psychoanalysis and Buddhism," by John H. Engler, Ph.D., in *Transformations of Consciousness: Conventional and Contemplative Perspectives on Development*, by Ken Wilbur, John H. Engler, and Daniel Brown, had helped her understand her experience.

3. Toni Packer, head of the Genessee Zen Center, is a Zen-trained teacher who now pursues an independent form of inquiry.

4. "Sexual Power Abuse: Neglect and Misuse of a Buddhist Precept," as reprinted in *Not Mixing Up Buddhism*, edited by Hopkinson, Hill, and Kiera.

5. Baker-roshi, head of the San Francisco Zen Center, was found to have engaged in many destructive affairs with his female students and other women, as well as in other abuses of power. Muktananda, a Hindu teacher, was accused after his death of having sexual relationships with his students, including young girls.

6. Munindra, a Vipassana teacher from India, was alleged to have had some kind of compromising sexual encounter with a woman while teaching a retreat at IMS.

7. Mayumi Oda is creator of a book of paintings and prints called *Goddesses*, and a longtime Zen student. Her "Goddess Hears People's Needs and Comes," a depiction of the Buddhist Kannon or Avalokitesvara Bodhisattva, appears on the cover of this book.

Jan Chozen Bays

Denah Joseph

Sonia Alexander

Loie Rosenkrantz

Carla Brennan

Meredith Cleaves

Lane Olson

6.

Bridges: The Link Between Buddhist Practice and Political Activism

In 5 A.M. darkness, people shuffled about in the spare room, pulling on their clothes, rolling up their sleeping bags, putting aside anything that might get broken or lost in the demonstration. In half an hour we would pile into a van to drive out the highway to the Lawrence Livermore Laboratories, where nuclear weaponry is designed under the sponsorship of the University of California. Now we gathered in the living room to sit in a circle, men and women, ages twenty-five to seventy, and one woman led us in a metta (loving-kindness) meditation: "May you be free from enmity, may you be free from grief and disease, may you be happy." This we wished first to ourselves, then to people close to us, then to people with whom we experienced difficulty, then to the University of California police who guard Livermore, and to the employees of Livermore Labs, finally to all creatures everywhere. This metta meditation both steadied us and allowed us to expand our sense of connection with others. Hours later, in the stress and confusion of a demonstration in which thousands participated and hundreds were arrested, that meditation kept us aware of our reason for being there and strengthened the nonviolent tenor of our actions. Against the production of nuclear weapons, the threat of nuclear holocaust, we placed that wish for all beings: May we be free from suffering, may we be happy.

That demonstration was an attempt to express the wishes of the people in the face of the power of military and business interests. Among the participating groups was an organization of Buddhists whose concern is creating peace in the world.

Another Buddhist group works to alleviate the suffering of laboratory animals and farm animals raised in inhumane conditions. Many Buddhist women, as individuals, are active in support of various social causes and sensitive to the political implications in particular settings. Looking at the Buddhist experience and the nature and intent of political action, one can see a rationalization for this activity. Politics, as I have come to understand, concerns itself with who has the power in any given situation and how that power is wielded. A political way of thinking leads one to see the effect of world events "out there" on one's daily life, to understand the responsibility one bears for the health of one's community, to perceive the potential power of each member of the body politic if she joins her efforts with others.

Buddhism, based as it is upon an experience of the interconnectedness of all life, can complement or even awaken the desire to engage in social and political action. Despite the popular stereotype of Buddhists as socially unconcerned, it is important to recognize that Buddhism and nonviolent social action are not mutually exclusive or inimical to one another; the quality of compassion evoked by Buddhist practice can engender an active caring and involvement. The famed "detachment," so often misunderstood to mean indifference, can in fact clear the way for an intensely committed participation in life. As we step away from attachment to the things that bind and limit us, we can begin to see deeply into both inner and outer conditions and to move in harmony with the demands of the moment.

Important in this respect is the existence in Mahayana Buddhism of the ideal of the Bodhisattva, who out of compassion for all beings, human and otherwise, chooses to stay in this world and work to help them gain enlightenment. This figure provides a powerful institutional role model for unselfish action.

Some well-known Buddhist teachers work for social causes, expressing their sense of responsibility to their fellow beings. Perhaps the most influential is Thich Nhat Hanh, the Vietnamese monk who is a member of an order of monks and nuns who demonstrated and labored for peace in war-ravaged Vietnam, and for whose work the term *engaged Buddhism* has been coined. Robert Aitken Roshi in Hawaii has for years participated in peace and antinuclear efforts. The Theravadin Burmese master U Ba Khin, who as Accountant General of Burma ran three federal agencies simultaneously, turned his executive suites into meditation rooms and conducted Vipassana sittings at lunch hours for employees, while teaching meditation at his own temple in the evenings. The British Theravadin teacher Christopher Titmuss consistently expresses a social/political message in his teaching.

In my own experience, my Buddhist practice and my political activism have formed a loop, carrying me out into action and back into meditation—the one informing the other—and at some moments the two are one. In jail after antinuclear demonstrations, my Buddhist practice helped me to tolerate, and at times transform, the frustrations and indignities.

But the question of who has the power and how it is used reaches further than the areas of peace and social action and animal rights work, which we normally think of as "political"; it pierces into all aspects of our experience, awakening our responsibility toward our environment. A particularly interesting project that has taken shape in Asia may serve as a model for us in environmental work. Called the Buddhist Perception of Nature Project, it was originated by an American, Nancy Nash, who is its international coordinator. This group of scholars and religious leaders such as the Dalai Lama and Thai woman scholar Dr. Chatsumarn Kabilsingh promotes research into Buddhist teachings about the natural world and the assembling of these materials for use as educational tools. The project's initial researches have been gathered into a book called *Tree of Life: Buddhism and Protection of Nature.*[1]

Many American Buddhists are beginning to discuss crimes against women. The treatment of women in society and relationships, a complex web of issues, reflects the power dynamics that function in other oppressive situations. Rape, then, is seen as an act in which the rapist abuses his power by violating and damaging his victim. The same holds for childhood sexual abuse, where an all-powerful adult uses a child for his sexual gratification without regard for the physical and psychological well-being of the child. A number of female Buddhist teachers now seek to discover a method of healing for the victims of these crimes. Such crimes occur within a political context in which children are a powerless class, imprisoned and victimized by families where men exercise social, economic, and physical dominance. Some abused women need psychotherapy in order to work with their experience; some find other means to confront the problem and make changes in the conditions that allow it to continue. Clear parallels exist between the ownership and objectification of children and that of animals.

There are power issues involved, also, in realities of class position and racism; where it is obvious that middle- and upper-middle-class Americans have more time and freedom and access to Buddhist teachings than working-class white people and most people of color. In Sri Lanka, a social movement based on Buddhist principles and involving Buddhist monks and nuns, as well as laypeople, addresses the actual physical needs of the poor people in the villages. In Thailand, South Viet Nam, and Japan, as well, not only is the religion accessible to the ordinary people, but Buddhists are engaged in social action affecting the broad base of society. Here in this country, however, Buddhism is, as yet, a religion of the privileged; its centers are sometimes endowed and supported by the very wealthy; its adherents are overwhelmingly middle to upper middle class and white. (I do not know the class breakdown of the all-Asian immigrant sanghas.) Perhaps this elite phase is necessary until Buddhism becomes fully established; in all the confusion and searching of this early period, practitioners may not be in a position to make the teachings available to a wider range of people. Still, this exclusivity as to race and class has real implications for, and consequences in, the daily life of Buddhist communities, where the assumptions governing behavior may limit access for working-class people and people of color, as well as implicitly support the classist and racist bias of society at large.

One Buddhist denomination that has stepped past this class and race bias is the Japanese-originated Nichiren Shoshu Sokka Gakkai. In cities across the United States Nichiren Shoshu has involved thousands of people of all backgrounds and races in a strong practice. Nichiren Shoshu is viewed with distrust by most other Buddhists, an attitude based at least in part on class prejudice. And while the Nichiren sect does have certain questionable characteristics (like its claim that it alone is "the true Buddhism"), still it provides many thousands of people, often black and/or working-class women, with a way to transform their lives in a wholesome direction.

The issue of the uses of power permeates our lives and calls upon our Buddhist insights in response to conditions that cause suffering to human and other beings. Some Buddhist teachers counsel their students not to engage in political action, and some Buddhist women think it is inappropriate to work to change the world. But the individuals and the organizations presented here bear witness to a vital strain in American Buddhism of people concerned about their environment, their fellow human beings and animals, about nuclear war and the other issues confronting the modern world.

ENGAGED BUDDHISM—THE UNITY OF MIND AND WORLD: BUDDHIST PEACE FELLOWSHIP

"The feminine is not only the domain of folks in women's bodies, the feminine ideally is an energy. I would suggest that we have always, in our Western minds and our non-Buddhist minds, viewed peace work as *doing*. What are we *doing*? What Buddhism has to offer is peace work as *being*, both being and doing. So in its very essence, it is already in the realm of the feminine."

These words are spoken by *Ruth Klein*, president of the Buddhist Peace Fellowship. She is a New Yorker who lived and practiced for four years at the Providence Zen Center. It was there I met her, a curly-headed, engaging woman in her late thirties, and talked with her in her small room at the back of the building, where from her window we could see the resident woodchuck waddling across the lawn.

We talk the second time in Oakland, where Ruth has come to attend a Buddhist Peace Fellowship (BPF) board meeting at Harwood House, the home of Vipassana teacher Jamie Baraz, another BPF board member.

So what then *is* the Buddhist definition of peace work? I ask, and answer my own question, "Presumably it covers everything from writing a letter to a member of Congress to going to jail."

"To just being peaceful within ourselves," Ruth completes my thought. "Since Buddhist practice is to be awake and to be at one with ourselves, to be whole and not to be caught in opposites, automatically then the practice *is* peace. Is *being peace*. It's like the sign the Buddhists who sat at the UN carried. It said, 'We are sitting to be peace.' So outer peace and social peace is a manifestation of our inner peace. There is no difference. For some people that is manifested in different ways in the world, whether it's in relationship, parenting, or in antinuclear work or in work with the hungry."

She quotes from the Vietnamese monk Thich Nhat Hanh, whose Tiep Hien Order in Vietnam was the prototype for engaged Buddhism. "In the past, we may have made the primary mistake in distinguishing between the inner world of our mind and the world outside. These are not two separate worlds but belong to the same reality. Notions of *inside* and *outside* are helpful in our practical daily lives but can become an obstacle preventing us from seeing ultimate reality. If we are able to see deeply into our mind we can simultaneously see deeply into the world. If we truly understand the world, we also will understand our mind!"

When I ask Ruth about the nature of the organization she heads, she answers, "One of the main reasons for the existence of the Buddhist Peace Fellowship is to afford people an arena for dialogue on how to take a stand against oppression and injustice without engaging in partisan conflicts, on how to check it out and look at where we are and what our experiences have been. To really offer support to each other in what we're doing. So it's a place to come together with people who are struggling with the same issues."

The Buddhist Peace Fellowship is a national group affiliated with the Fellowship of Reconciliation,[2] with chapters in thirteen U.S. cities, in Canada, Australia, and England. Inspired by the work of Thich Nhat Hanh, it was founded in 1978 by Zen master Robert Aitken of Hawaii and several of his students. They hoped to identify Buddhism as a way of peace and to raise the issue among American Buddhists, who at that time did very little peace action or work for social change.

"Now it's this large growing organization," Ruth explains, "and it's a way to say, 'It's okay to be a Buddhist right now in the United States of America and engaged in social action.' The question is, how do we do it? How do we manifest our Buddhist practice in our work? I know that many people say this, and it's certainly true, and when I began to really get into my practice five years ago, a big question I had was, 'Can I do anything socially? How do I get involved in politics, or in changing the world in a way that isn't just going to be manifesting a dual vision?' And for myself with my Zen practice, that has been one of my actual living koans, a koan being something that I hold as a question in my life. I keep holding it as a question, and the correct actions for me just manifest."

Ruth's own spiritual quest began in the midseventies after she left her job as a psychologist and went on the road for two years. During that time she lived with a group of American Indians at an intertribal spiritual camp in Nevada. She also met the Korean Zen Master Seung Sahn (Soen Sa Nim), who so impressed her that she eventually moved into his Providence Zen Center and began to practice Zen.

Ruth is silent for a few moments, fingering the handsome beaded Native American style medallion she wears, which she herself made. Staring from behind her glasses she gathers her thoughts.

"Recently because of the turn of events in my life, I have been very keyed in to the *dying process* as a way to manifest peace work," she says. "When my father was dying, he was enraged much of the time. It was total rage, his anger and his explosion of words were complete. There was no place where he stopped. And when it was over, it was over. And there was something *even in that* which was peaceful, because of the harmony within him. And in a way the disharmony in that situation wasn't created by *him* but by my own fear. *I* brought the barrier, because I was just so afraid of that expression. But *within himself* it was *complete*. I have a big question about anger, I have had for a long time. It seems if we just *be it* completely we can go beyond it. My father was an example of a man who was angry and kept his anger within parameters his whole life. And then in his last days he was able to completely explode with no limits, and that afforded him a peaceful dying."

During Thich Nhat Hanh's recent tour of the United States, Ruth worked as a coordinator of his appearances. (He lives and has a peace center in southern France.) Another recent project of the BPF was cosponsoring the conference called Strategies for

Peacemaking at Naropa Institute in Boulder, Colorado. As Buddhist Peace Fellowship board members are scattered across the country, they communicate and handle business by phone and meet together once a year. At a recent meeting, Ruth Klein was elected president.

She reflects on her role, noting that the board is examining several organizational aspects and functions. "Up until now nothing has been clear, like what does it *mean* to be board president? I intend as president to network and help other people define their roles. I have the board's full support in this. If I felt like my job were to be sitting at the top of a hierarchy, then what the hell am I doing here and I'd better step off. But I don't see myself like that at all, I see myself as maybe being something of an orchestra conductor."

We return once again to the relationship of spirituality to peace work, and Ruth says, "It's all just the same! Because the Buddha way is the way of compassion, so how can that be separate, that *is* peace work. Just opening our hearts and getting out of our own way."[3]

In the Minneapolis Institute of Arts in Minneapolis, Minnesota, I meet *Catherine Parker,* curatorial assistant in the department of Asian art, Zen Buddhist at the Minnesota Zen Center, and former president of the Buddhist Peace Fellowship. She is a thirty-four-year-old woman with deep-set green eyes and reddish-blond hair, who took part in a unique peace demonstration several years ago.

With another Zen center member named Beverly White, Catherine set up a Minneapolis chapter of the Buddhist Peace Fellowship. Then in 1982, plans were being made for Zen practitioners to go to New York for the United Nations Special Session on Disarmament. They would sit zazen in Ralph Bunche Park across from the United Nations. Jane Dallinger Taylor of the Minnesota Zen Center was organizing the action. The roshi, Katagiri, who does not usually support political causes, encouraged Jane to invite members from all the other Zen centers in the country to come to New York to sit. And when it was time to go, he helped them make the signs they would hold.

Catherine describes that demonstration.

"It's the first time I had ever done zazen in public, with people looking at me, which is kind of a strange thing. But really it wasn't as hard to concentrate as I thought, even though it was six lanes of traffic near us and all these people walking by. What it made me realize is that zazen itself, just the posture, seems to have some kind of language that people *get*, they just catch on. People didn't make any hateful remarks. One guy yelled out of a car one time, 'Hey, get the bowling ball!' like we were bowling pins. So there were a few crackpot remarks like that, but there weren't any upset, angered, threatened reactions.

"We were sitting around the statue in the park and facing the UN building where the people were talking," she explains. "I had never been to New York City before, so I was feeling the power of the city, and I was getting a sense about the UN. I love the UN, I think it's this wonderful place. It was good just to sit there."

The participants, some of whom wore rakusus over their regular clothes, stayed for three days, sitting thirty-minute periods and then walking in a circle, then sitting again.

"It felt like we were sending a little teeny bit of this *something* to the building," Catherine comments. "It just seemed like what we were doing and the message we were sending were the same thing."

At the Zen center she finds that people are receptive to the efforts of the Buddhist Peace Fellowship to bring them information about world conditions. Recently the board of the Zen center voted to give money to the annual Mother's Day Peace March in Minneapolis. She emphasizes that she appreciates the need to keep the zendo apolitical and has never sought to promote any kind of faction but simply to inform people. In discussion here of the nuclear threat, she points out, one of the impediments has been the "taboo on feelings." She explains, "We're always kind of cool and collected at the Zen center." Grimacing, she admits, "*I'm* so not like that!" (This echoes Ruth Klein's observation about both the Native American camp and the Providence Zen Center that "If you want anything you say to be respected, you must not get emotional.")

Of the connection between Buddhist practice and peace work, Catherine says, "I've had a couple of talks with Katagiri Roshi, and one question he asked me is, 'What kind of peace do you want?' And that's staying with me, because I don't know. Because

of Buddhist practice I consider my search for peace to be a lifelong occupation, and it doesn't matter if I'm in the Buddhist
Peace Fellowship or at the museum or as union steward here or
with my neighbor who's just asked me to move out and how do I
keep my friendship with her. The practice is a grounding, and the
nearest thing I know for how to do peace work.

"But speaking just for myself," she continues, "I can't just
sit there and ignore stuff. I'm driven to know what's wrong.
People having wretched lives because of bad government and in-
harmonious human relations, I can't ignore it. I don't *want* to
know this stuff, and it hurts, but I have to know. And I'm thinking
I may have to live in the Third World at some point to know
what's going on." She admits that prospect frightens her. "But I
feel this huge push, something saying, 'Get out there, it's your
job.' "

I find another member of the Buddhist Peace Fellowship in Los
Angeles in a huge beige apartment building near the bustling
Vietnamese Buddhist Temple. *Jenny Hoang* takes me into the bedroom to meet her mother, a tiny old woman dressed in brown,
who nods when Jenny introduces me and peers from black eyes.
Jenny and her mother are Vietnamese. I notice the small Buddhist shrine next to her mother's bed.

Back in the living room, it is hard for me to believe Jenny when
she tells me she was born in 1931, for this would mean that this
smiling youthful-looking woman is in her fifties. But as we talk,
Jenny intensely focused, speaking again and again of suffering,
laughing often, her wisdom lets me know she has lived a great
deal. A member of the Buddhist Peace Fellowship, Jenny has
served on its board and devotes herself to work for peaceful
transformation.

She came to the United States in the sixties as wife of a Vietnamese diplomat, and she did her best to be a perfect wife and
mother, until she "realized that in the life I was living I didn't use
anywhere near my potential as a person."

Jenny sits on the couch, leaning toward me, gesturing. She is
tremendously alive, her whole being animated by her words.

After leaving her husband, she says, she plunged into the bohemian life of the lower east side of New York, with "the crazies, the theater people, the weirdos." She participated in anti–Vietnam War demonstrations, in which, she noted, the demonstrators often perpetrated anger and violence. Having met Swami Muktananda, the Hindu yoga "saint," in New York, she went to live in his ashram in Austin, Texas, and then in Los Angeles. It was there that she found the Vietnamese Buddhist Temple in 1977, went in, got involved, and began to work for the temple.

"I consider myself a Buddhist," she says, smiling. "The spirit of Buddhism is in me. My yoga training opened the world of Buddhism to me in a vast, real way. Yoga, in its deep essence, is the awareness that God is *you*—and that opens into Buddhism. I came full circle to Buddhism, as a fish returns to water. The first pool I swam in, growing up in Vietnam, was Buddhism, Taoism, Confucianism; then there came Western philosophy and psychology; then yoga; and now I've come back to Buddhism."

I glance from Jenny around this room with its heavy stuffed furniture, its brown-patterned flounce decorating the doorway to the dining room. On the mantel are a bouquet of artificial flowers and a green growing plant. Three small figurines of Asian patriarchs stand near a Buddha with figures of small children climbing on him.

I ask Jenny how her peace work began, and she tells me that after she had started to work at the Vietnamese Buddhist Temple, she read about Thich Nhat Hanh. She also read about Martin Luther King, Gandhi, and other nonviolent activists. Then when Thich Nhat Hanh came to town, Jenny was assigned to take care of him, and this contact encouraged her to take an active role. In her work with the Buddhist Peace Fellowship, she is interested in the cooperation of different groups and nationalities.

"My peace work comes out of my own personality," she explains. "I want to share. I give a lot of attention to companionship *with everybody.* I live life *now, fully.* I want the children alive now to grow up, and I hold that intention for myself, and if I die tonight, it's okay."

She laughs, and I believe her, and I have the sense that I am sitting here with someone quite extraordinarily connected with the essence of life. Earlier she had spoken of how in meditation "you sit, with the stillness, and the waiting, and from this you understand that you hurt and so does everyone else. Women by nature are closer to that reality of suffering, because we suffer every month, and especially in the distortion and wrenching of childbirth. Going through the pain is the process of healing. The other side of vulnerability is strength. We are very strong. If we can be ourselves we can change the world."

We speak of the participation of women in Buddhism, and Jenny expresses her opinion that our generation of Buddhist women is "a sacrifice. We have to stand up! Even if we die tomorrow, the next generation will have a stepping-stone. That's fine. I understand that the suffering is not mine; it's ours, it's humanity's. That's how you get the connection. Animals hurt, probably plants hurt, probably rocks hurt. The more you go inside and be sincere, the more *you* hurt, and you know that everyone does. That's not just *my* pain. And everything changes anyway. We must *allow* it to change. I want to share the joy. Why reject the pain? I take the whole package."

And she gives me her philosophy of change. "The evolution of consciousness moves like a spiral, moves up in circles, lifetime after lifetime. Patience is the essential quality. And don't quit! The Buddhist Peace Movement seems like the slowest one around. But that's Buddha's way. We don't want to be another institution. Sometimes it may seem like we are, but we're not. It's making friends, it's spreading beneath the surface, very slow and very solid."

Jenny's mother, in her brown dress and slippers, comes out of the bedroom now. Jenny gets up to fix dinner for her mother, and she says good-bye. Outside their door, in the hallway of the apartment building, I stand for a few minutes absorbing the effects of our encounter. While Jenny spoke to me I received from her such deep love, such tenderness toward life, such caring, that several times I had felt myself near to tears. As I walk down the stairs and out onto the street to my car, something in me says that Jenny Hoang is a Bodhisattva. This is not a thought I have entertained about very many people I have encountered. I keep it and let it go at the same time, simply glad that Jenny and women like her work for the cause of peace.

DESPAIR AND EMPOWERMENT WORK—CONNECTING WITH THE GREAT NET OF BEING

In recent years some concerned people have begun to approach the nuclear threat through an investigation of the feelings it arouses. Their theory is that most Americans maintain their equilibrium by denying the fear and anguish created in them by worldwide nuclear buildup. This blocking-out of feelings has been named "psychic numbing," and they assert that it operates to make people passive in the face of nuclear devastation. "Despair and empowerment" work has been developed by several activists to confront that repression. It entails a group experience that gives participants the opportunity to go fully into their reactions of fear, anger, sorrow, and despair when confronted with the prospect of nuclear war, and it offers a way to transform those emotions into a resolve to act.

One of the best-known despair and empowerment spokespeople is *Joanna Rogers Macy*, a Buddhist with roots in the Theravadin and Tibetan traditions, who studied and worked in Asia where she saw spirituality manifest in action for the good of the people. Under the auspices of Interhelp, an organization she helped found, she travels the country conducting workshops and giving lectures and presentations. She is a member of the advisory board of the Buddhist Peace Fellowship. She has set forth the guiding principles of despair and empowerment work in her beautifully practical, thorough, and humane book, *Despair and Personal Power in the Nuclear Age*. A passionately committed and articulate spokeswoman, Joanna Macy asserts that the threat of the destruction of humanity through nuclear war or accident can be viewed as an unprecedented opportunity for spiritual growth.

She perches on the desk at the front of a classroom at the University of California, Berkeley, a woman in her midfifties, talking easily as if she is thinking out loud. Constantly she asks questions, eliciting the class members' ideas and feelings about the nuclear threat, the destruction of our environment, the hunger and oppression suffered by so many people in our world. She speaks forcefully, and we can see her wide-eyed disbelief as she describes our inability to conceive of the horror of a nuclear holocaust; we can feel her distress as she gives the statistics indicating the destruction of our environment.

Our pain for the world and our power to change the world, she tells us, comes from the same source, and she defines what she means by power: not the old concept of power-over, of defenses and invulnerability, of win/lose; but the radically different view of power that is emerging from our planetary predicament and the findings of modern science—power-*with*, the 'synergy' of interlinked, self-organizing systems, offering power from the bottom up and models of win/win, lose/lose.

I go to talk with Joanna Macy at her pleasant home in Sausalito, California, where she lives with her husband Francis. Out the window of her study is the blue expanse of Sausalito harbor, with sailboats leaning on its bright surface. We sit on a rug with a bold dragon figure woven into it, in a room alive with vivid colors. Joanna herself is intensely animated, often vehement, as she tells me about the central importance of listening in her work.

"The key thing is what you allow people—whether it's in a community gathering or door-to-door canvassing or what have you—what you allow people to *hear from themselves.* And then there's the *asking:* the gift of the question. Doing some canvassing last summer in connection with voter registration, I combined it with peace work; I went door to door and said, 'I'm doing voter registration and a survey of people's views.' So people talked. It was so moving to me, and it was so important to many of the people who talked.

"Sometimes in the workshops we do door-to-door house calls. I just did that in East Lansing, Michigan, where it was so cold and rainy that people were resistant, they didn't want to go out. But they came back transformed! They asked people, 'What do you think is the greatest problem facing the world today? What do you think of the chances of nuclear war? Is this something you feel free to talk about with your families or your neighbors or your employers? Where do you find hope?'

"And I ask *myself,* 'Whom does it serve that we're powerless? Whom does our despair serve? Whom does the nuclear arms race serve?'

"You see, what will liberate us is not the *answer* but the *question.*

Because the answer is *in us.* The question will help us bring that out."

Joanna has been asking questions all her life. Coming from a long line of Congregationalist ministers, she grew up as a religious person, and she did her undergraduate work at Wellesley in biblical studies. But in her senior year, finding Christianity "intellectually claustrophobic," she stopped being a Christian. Turning to politics for answers to her questions, she did graduate work in political science and studied the French Communist party. She married and bore three children, and then, in India, where her husband's work had taken them, she encountered some Tibetan Buddhist refugees. She worked with them, helping them to create an economic base through handicraft production. Eventually she was so impressed by their humanity, their radiant wholeness and freedom from bitterness, that she asked for and received the Buddhist teachings from their monks.

After living in Africa for a time and returning to the United States, she went back to graduate school in her forties at Syracuse University and earned a Ph.D., writing a dissertation that linked early Buddhist teachings with "general systems theory." This "way of seeing" presents a view of reality as a web of dynamic, intricately organized and balanced systems, each element part of a vaster pattern that connects and evolves by discernible principles. This theory, she says, has helped her reinterpret the distinctiveness of Buddhist teachings and to see what the patriarchal mind did to the Buddha's original teachings.

She also worked for a time with the Sramadana Sarvodaya movement in Sri Lanka, in which Buddhist principles guide an extensive program of social service. This movement was begun in 1958 by a young high school teacher, A. T. Ariyaratna, to encourage his students to work in the villages, helping the people with their practical problems. It soon spread to thousands of villages, involving many Theravadin monastics as well as laypeople, becoming a major social and political force. Joanna Macy describes this movement in her book *Dharma and Development: Religion as Resource in the Sarvodaya Self-Help Movement.*

This study and experience has combined to lead her to a strong perception of the great net of being connecting us all. I ask whether her identity as a woman has contributed to this insight.

"There's no question," she answers. "As Carol Gilligan demonstrates in her work, our moral development as women is based upon relationships rather than principle.[4] We're socialized to pay attention to others' feelings, others' needs. That tendency may be biological as well, because of the capacity to give birth, but certainly society trains us in that way."

Joanna's Buddhist study, her understanding of general systems theory, and her experience as a woman come together in her leading of workshops. This work grew out of her own despair as early as 1977 or 1978, prompted by the proliferation of nuclear weapons.

She explains. "That was when I conceptualized the notion of, rather than countering our despair with hope, to move *through* it. It's a Tantric move, actually. It's what I call 'the Tantric flip.' That if you can move with where the energy is, then you can flip it over." (The Tantric path uses all things good and evil and transmutes obstacles into the impetus for spiritual awakening.)

Joanna says that "feelings of pain for our world are natural and healthy," and that the experiencing and expressing of these feelings not only releases vital energy in us but connects us to "the larger web of life," showing us our interconnectedness with all other beings. By experiencing our pain, we can move through it to contribute to the interaction of all life, engaging and enhancing our own and each others' capacities. She cites the Buddhist principle of muditha or sympathetic joy, in which one is made happy by the good fortune of others, as a possible outcome of this work. Her book *Despair and Personal Power in the Nuclear Age* describes how one works with individuals and groups and gives specific exercises and directions for organizing and carrying out the workshops. It delineates the stages of the work: acknowledging and experiencing despair, the turning point at which one becomes aware of one's interconnectedness with all life, the recognizing of one's power and how to use it to become an agent for social change.

I ask Joanna about her contention that for the first time in history we are faced with the possibility that there may not be a future for the human race.

"Then we see that there's no private salvation," she says. "There's no place we can go and hide. We're all in it together.

That's becoming evident to even the most thick-headed. That is echoing the teachings of the great religious teachers and saints and messiahs through the ages who have said, 'It's either love or hell.' So there's nothing new in what the bomb is teaching. What's new is that we have to take it *seriously.* Because it's a matter of life and death. It's a wonderful time to be alive in that sense."

"It brings us up against the moment," I offer.

"That's right," she says. "To have us be present. Because we have been accustomed to assuming that we were continuing in this linear time. That's been taken away, just chopped off. And instead now we're thrown right into this moment, which is what people sit for years on the cushion to realize. The bomb is doing that *for us.*"

In the workshops she offers practices, and these practices, she says, are teachers. "The metta or loving-kindness meditation, for instance. And the meditations in the chapter called 'Spiritual Exercises for a Time of Apocalypse.' They are all derived from the Dharma, all great teachers."

Joanna manages to be intensely involved with the participants in her workshops, again and again, because she herself so deeply experiences the anguish of facing the nuclear threat, and because she lets herself learn from them.

"I want to walk with these people in the workshops and the lecture situations, and I only can if I allow myself to enter into their experience. So when a young mother worries about the best way to kill her children after a nuclear explosion, so the child will not die in agony from radiation, I know no response of integrity except to experience that fully with her. I don't *know* that she might not *have* to. I know that she's experiencing that now, which is horror *enough*, whether the bombs ever go *off.* This work doesn't require that anybody have a blueprint or an answer. If we had an answer, it wouldn't work. So it's a posture of radical *presence.*

"I'm moved and informed when I see what people experience when they move through this, and the kind of connections they make. It's awesome."

Leaving Joanna's house this day, I admire how tireless is her investigation of the possibilities for the true living of Buddhist principles. Wherever she goes, she speaks of our development out of the confines of the personal ego into a larger realm, as she did at the Balancing of American Buddhism conference at Providence Zen Center in 1985, when she said, "I suspect that this is a historic time for all of Buddhism, because— and I see this very strongly with the Sarvodaya movement—instead of emphasizing that in our enlightenment we move into a sense of sunyata, emptiness, there is stress now on moving into *fullness,* or moving into interrelationship, interdependence. That is what we wake up to. That is also what the Buddha woke up to under the bodhi tree. We wake up to our relationship with all that is."

BUILDING FOR PEACE—THE PEACE PAGODA

The Pioneer Valley of the Connecticut River winds through northwestern Massachusetts, its small towns nestled amid oak and alder and maple, each town square watched over by a white steepled church and statue of a revolutionary soldier or founding father. In the graveyards, their ancient trees spreading luxurious foliage above the graves, weatherworn stones from the late 1700s bear names like Noble Hannum, Amanda Woodbury, Horatio Gates Howe. But this valley is remarkable less for its historic aspects than for the proliferation of New Age and political groups and practitioners in its towns and countryside. "Western Mass," as it is referred to in Boston, meaning the Northampton/Amherst area—site of five colleges—is known as "Cambridge in the Country," or, more flamboyantly, "the Berkeley of the East."

Here, on a hill near North Leverett, stands a giant domed structure of dazzling white, its contours and towering ornate pinnacle created from a much different mind than the ones that envisioned the tall churches and bronzed cannon of the village squares. This is the Peace Pagoda built by young Americans led by Japanese monks and nuns of the Nipponzan Myohoji order of Buddhism. Pagodas or "stupas," built to house relics of the Buddha, are common in Buddhist countries. Nipponzan Myohoji monks have built more than seventy such pagodas in selected locations throughout the world to promote the cause of world peace.

I am here in North Leverett during the building of this monument where I discover that some of the most dedicated workers are women, and that in the midst of the labor of building and meeting survival needs, they must contend with cross-cultural differences and with the monks' traditional Japanese attitudes toward women. In this process both Asians and Occidentals learn from each other.

I stay with *Dr. Paula Green,* one of the major supporters of the project, in her house in the woods. Paula is a woman in her late forties whose warmth and energy seem boundless. A therapist and teacher, she is creator (with Carol Drexler) of WomanSpirit Works, an organization offering workshops and rituals to "celebrate the spiritual in women and gather the energy for transformation and peace work." A Buddhist practitioner who is on the board of directors at Insight Meditation Society in nearby Barre, Massachusetts, Paula works hard to bring her Buddhist understanding to her therapy with clients. She wrote her doctoral dissertation at Boston University on the relationship between Buddhist meditation and Western psychology. Her Jewish identity is also important to her.

We spend the day at the Peace Pagoda, which we see rising out of the trees as we approach, a huge inverted bowl of steel and wood latticed with scaffolding. The completed structure, Paula tells me, will stand 104 feet high and 140 feet wide. Just down the hill is the converted barn where the monks and nuns and some of the workers live. It also houses the kitchen, dining hall, office, and, upstairs, the meditation room.

Clearly Paula Green is much appreciated here, for she is welcomed with enthusiastic hugs, and a woman who is leaving today asks to be photographed with her. Paula does publicity for the pagoda, participates in the planning and direction of activities, and houses some of the people working here in her house. Such generalized and unselfish support has not only endeared her to the other workers but made her extremely important to the project.

The workers have gathered for lunch. Paula and I join them, sitting at a long table in the pleasant rustic room. Most of the people at the table are young American men. Three Japanese men with shaved heads, dressed in work clothes, are given special respect. These are the Nipponzan Myohoji monks. The Western workers are not necessarily Buddhist, for anyone is welcome to come and be part of the project. The two nuns, one American and one Japanese, bring the food from the kitchen to serve us. When I give Paula a quizzical look, she says that she herself chooses not to work in the kitchen here so that she can teach, by modeling, that women participate and serve in a great variety of equally important ways. "Once I've gotten my message across," she says, "I'll be able to cook and serve as wholeheartedly as I speak and write and organize."

Up at the work site the men and a few women crawl up on the scaffolding to begin their hammering. I climb up with them, looking from the dizzying height out over an expanse of hills furred with trees. This dome, a wood frame bound with steel bars, will be sprayed with five inches of concrete. When the shell has hardened, the framework will be removed. Most of the women work in the yard below, where I soon join them. They pour concrete into small square molds and insert nails to create round holes. These concrete pieces are used as connectors on the framework of the dome.

Lisa Groves, a twenty-two-year-old wearing a "nuclear free zone" T-shirt and a white cloth over her dark hair, does construction work and cooking here. At first she often worked alone with two male monks, she says, admitting that she "felt like a kid working with a brother and a father." When she did construction work, at first, they would laugh, because, as she says, "It was amusing and perhaps a bit shocking for some of them to see American women doing full-time construction work." And, she adds, "It was always my prayer throughout the whole project, that people working together with such a focus, from many different backgrounds, would aid in the healing of the imagined inequalities and misunderstandings among people, especially those between male and female. And I hoped that women's spirituality and integrity would come to be more deeply felt, understood, and respected by more and wider circles of people."

That the monks sometimes order the nuns around, become impatient, and speak sharply to them bothers Lisa, who has lived in a political household in Cambridge with feminist men and women, and who reads books on feminism and spirituality. But, she tells me, "The monks are beautiful in their effort to overcome negativity within themselves and to bring light and peace to the world. If they are sincere in this effort—and I do believe that most of them are—eventually they can't help but examine their attitudes about women and sexist ideology more deeply. Wherever they go in the United States they'll encounter growing numbers of 'feminist' people, and change is bound to occur."

When we go back to the converted barn for the afternoon service, I am reminded that I have heard this chant, "Na mu myo ho ren ge kyo," and the beating of the drum often at peace and antinuclear demonstrations. This chant, which represents the essence of the Lotus Sutra, Paula points out, "was devotedly preached by a thirteenth-century Japanese Buddhist monk called Nichiren, who was a political revolutionary in his time and who upset the authorities by his ideals of equality, social justice, and universal salvation." It is used by a number of Nichiren sects in the United States, including Nipponzan Myohoji, which is dedicated to walking the earth, attending demonstrations, and building pagodas in the cause of world peace.

After washing, we go into the upstairs room where we sit in rows before a beautiful red and gold altar. A photograph of the founder of Nipponzan Myohoji, Nichidatsu Fujii, stands in the center, surrounded by offerings of flowers, fruit, and candy. At the side stands a drawing of the completed pagoda. The Most Venerable Fujii died in January 1985 in his 100th year. Nipponzan Myohoji, Paula tells me, "is unusual among Buddhist orders in that the ordained are not seeking personal salvation or enlightenment but the removal of all weapons from the face of the earth."

I am handed a drum that looks like a large ping pong paddle and given a stick with which to beat it. The monks and nuns have changed their work clothes for immaculate white and yellow robes. They lead the chanting. For half an hour or so we beat the drums and chant "Na mu myo ho ren ge kyo." At first I feel awkward doing this, the activity and noise so different from my experience of Buddhist meditation or even chanting, but after a while I relax and soon begin to feel the power generated in this room by the drums and voices.

Downstairs again, I offer to help the Japanese nun, *Sister Jun Yasuda*, or Jun-san, in the kitchen, where she is chopping vegetables. She happily accepts, and I sit down cross-legged on the floor with her and take up some bell peppers to chop. Jun-san radiates joy and a bright clear energy. She grins impishly at me as she tells me she is not interested in attending the meeting to plan the inauguration ceremony. "All that talking!" she says, shrugging and laughing.

And I remember where I have seen her before. At an all-night antinuclear demonstration at the Federal Building in San Francisco the year before, we stood on the plaza chilled by a relentless bitter wind. Most people huddled behind their signs or turned their backs to the wind. But kneeling on a spread-out cloth was a Japanese woman in white and yellow robes whose determination seemed unshakable. She beat the drum and chanted in a strong voice. Others joined her for a time and then fell away, but Jun-san went on vigorously chanting, her body erect, her face, though red with cold, somehow peaceful.

Now, in the kitchen, she chops and smiles at me, her shaved head wrapped in what looks like a white dish towel. Jun-san is the veteran of many of the marches engaged in by Nipponzan Myohoji. She has forged particularly strong ties with Native American peoples, living with them in Oakland and accompanying them on their "Longest March" in 1980. We work together without talking much, Jun-san giving me dark strips of seaweed to chop.

When Paula Green and I return to her house that evening, I meet *Terri Nash,* one of the mainstays of the pagoda until now, who is recovering from an illness while living in Paula's house. We go upstairs to talk in the pleasant study where Paula sees her clients. Terri, a brown-haired twenty-eight-year-old who is a lesbian and former graduate student in soils and agronomy, tells stories with great enthusiasm, now and then breaking up into a hearty laugh.

Her involvement with Nipponzan Myohoji began when she went to Washington, D.C., to join their march to protest nuclear weapons and affirm a fully realized peaceful world.

"I've been at actions at the Pentagon, and it gets to what I call"—she speaks in a deep ominous voice—"*American nonviolence.* Just because you're not bashing someone over the head . . . you spout all these angry and violent things. . . . That deeply disturbed me. I've had my reservations about a lot of the nonviolent aspect. But these monks were bowing and smiling! The vibration of the chant and of the drums was just incredible.

"So I walked with them from Washington, D.C., to New York City. And the drum, and that vibration, would just draw me. And I realized the preciousness of the sound of the drum, how sacred the sound was."

She sits on the couch, wearing blue sweatpants and a white sweater, her long hair in a swatch over one shoulder.

"I could feel myself healing," she explains. "I could feel myself really walking through a lot of obstacles I had created in my mind. So I reached New York City and have been with Nipponzan Myohoji, have been with a Buddhist perspective ever since then."

At a pagoda site in Washington state near the Trident submarine base, she opted to stay and help build the temple. Three women and perhaps a dozen men lived at the site, all working a very rigorous schedule. They would rise at three or four o'clock in the morning, read sutras, chant, have breakfast, work all day, chant, go to sleep. Terri worked in the kitchen because she loved to cook, but she also worked outside on the temple. And she encountered a monk who told her to get back in the kitchen. "It became a meditation," she says, "how do I deal with the very traditional mind and still express myself as myself? One of the things that came to me was something Gandhi spoke about, that there aren't any slaves if the slaves change their minds and realize they aren't slaves. I realized that if I wanted to express myself in the kitchen, and if they wanted to perceive me as a good little servant because I like to cook, that was their problem . . . but I was going to continue to express myself hammering nails and splitting wood, because that was me too. I was just going to be who I was and not allow those kinds of thoughts to control me. And it was hard," she laughs ruefully, "because it didn't go over well."

In August of 1983, Terri came here to Massachusetts, where the head monk, the two nuns, and one other man had come to begin the pagoda. They lived in the little town of Hadley, where Terri cooked for everyone, scavenging food from dumpsters, getting up at four each morning and working until ten or eleven at night. They cleared the land with Japanese hand saws, tore down any barn a farmer did not want, and brought the wood to the hill.

Terri did crucial liaison work with the community. And while in the full throes of work at the pagoda, she had a singular satisfaction. She grins as she tells it.

"The same monk who told me to go back to the kitchen, in Washington state, came to help us take down a barn in Hadley, to get the materials. We were taking down roof rafters, carrying them and stacking them. They were huge. I was on one end and he was on the other, and I said, 'Do you remember a year ago when you told me to get back in the kitchen?' He laughed, and he said, 'Oh, American women, *mind so big!*' "

When I mention Terri's stories, Paula Green assures me that the monks' attitudes have so changed that the contributions of the women are now sought after. "A lesbian-feminist carpenter named Bonnie is building the room housing the relics of the Buddha in the Peace Pagoda," she tells me. "Another woman is fixing the community cars. Nipponzan Myohoji has been here in this culture only a few years, but it will never be the same again, and the changes are welcomed by all."

When we go again to the pagoda site, I meet briefly with *Clare Carter,* an American nun of the Nipponzan Myohoji order. She is a bespectacled thirty-six-year-old whose head is cleanly shaved and who wears loose white top and pants. While we talk, she is continually being interrupted with requests for help or information by the monks and the other workers. Finally we escape for a few minutes to a tiny room upstairs, behind the meditation hall, where Clare keeps her bed and her few possessions.

Clare speaks with a flat Boston "a." She grew up as a Catholic and after college worked in Christian organizations such as Ministers Concerned with Social Justice. She lived for several years in a women's commune. At a Nagasaki Day peace rally in Boston she met the head monk here and her interest in Nipponzan Myohoji was awakened. In 1980 at the ground-breaking ceremony for the pagoda, Clare met Nichidatsu Fujii, who was then ninety-eight years old; his dedication to world peace contributed to her growing desire to join the Nipponzan Myohoji order. In 1981, she went to Japan to be ordained as a nun.

Soon, she tells me, she must make a phone call, meet some visitors, help with travel plans for the upcoming trip to Japan by Nipponzan Myohoji sympathizers. Our discussion is disjointed, as she explains to me that she does not feel oppressed by the sexism of the males. "Each person is a universe. The struggle is *within.*"

"Isn't there a contradiction, then, in working for world peace?" I ask. "Wouldn't it be enough, in your terms, to find peace in yourself?"

Clare shakes her head. "War is the corruption of the self on a huge scale. There is great suffering in the world, and I must work to end it."

Before I can ask her more, she is called downstairs to handle a crisis, and from then until I leave she is busy with arrangements and phone calls, now and then sending me wistful glances as if to say, "I *wish* I had the time to talk with you, but . . ."

As Paula Green and I drive home that night, on a winding road beneath dark trees, the scent of leaves and earth filling the car, she tells me she will be going on the trip to Japan. We talk about how her work with the Peace Pagoda meshes with her meditation practice. She had been involved in radical social action in New York City in the sixties, had been married there and raised two adopted children, who are now with their father. Later, living in rural New Hampshire, she first worked at a small liberal arts college and later started a feminist therapy collective. When the college fired her for asking Angela Davis to speak on campus, she filed a sex discrimination suit and after four years won it. Here in Massachusetts, besides her WomanSpirit Works, she joined with two friends to start a chapter of the Buddhist Peace Fellowship. This chapter has helped Cambodian refugees find a new way of life here in the valley, has held vigils, supported work on the pagoda, brought in Joanna Macy to conduct a Despair and Empowerment Workshop.

"I continue to see myself as a person needing and choosing to be involved in social change movements," Paula says. "And although I feel that meditating on the cushion is very important for transformation, I don't feel that the planet can afford to wait any longer until we're all actualized before we go out and practice in the world. I think there is an emergency situation on the planet, and it requires our actions now even if they are less complete than they might be in five or ten years. I want to participate in the movements for peace and social justice with other people who are involved in spiritual practice, so that we are behaving very consciously and nonviolently and doing action that comes out of Dharma, out of the best that we can be."

Six months later, back in California, I receive from Paula Green a photograph of the completed Peace Pagoda taken at its dedication ceremony. It is a magnificently proportioned white dome with a lacy ornament rising from its top. A large crowd of monks and nuns from Japan, townspeople from the surrounding areas, and other visitors gather before it; flags snap in the wind, and the niche that holds the Buddha statue is draped with bright-colored cloth.

In her accompanying note, Paula writes, "I seem to be moving in ever closer to this work and practice. My trip to Japan with the monks took away whatever barriers I was creating for 'safe distancing.' I'm feeling very committed to this practice, to its peace and social justice values, and to the ordained and the community here in Leverett. Something here is very strong for me, very compelling. It continues to be a privilege to serve."

GREEN POLITICS AND BEYOND

Related to the peace and antinuclear movements is the effort to promote a sane relationship to our environment, to create a balance of social needs with natural resources. This ecological concern is naturally a woman's issue, as it involves the preservation of the earth, which supports all life. One Buddhist practitioner has worked particularly hard to address this imperative.

Charlene Spretnak, who grew up in a midwestern Catholic home and was educated in a Jesuit university, has forged for herself a strong grounding in Buddhist practice and women's spirituality, from which she articulates a vision of the survival of our country and our planet. Charlene is a key organizer in the arena of Green politics (a new approach to politics centered on ecological, holistic principles and goals) in this country, and author of two books on that subject. The Greens work for the development of ecological wisdom, social responsibility, grassroots democracy, and nonviolence. Charlene's Theravada Buddhist practice aids and informs her in that work.

I have known Charlene since the late seventies as a dark-eyed, intense woman who lived with her small daughter and seemed always to be working very hard. Indeed she *was* working hard, for in addition to raising her daughter and writing her books, she has supported herself by working as director of a writing program at the University of California, Berkeley. She has also taught at the Institute in Culture and Creation Spirituality, an institution led by theologian Matthew Fox, in Oakland.

I come to visit her in her modest apartment near the Graduate Theological Union in Berkeley. Her daughter is a teenager now, and Charlene is forty years old. The living room in which we sit is also her bedroom and her study, with a desk and bed and a wall of bookshelves. In a niche in the wall opposite the books stand three small goddess figures and a statue of the Buddha.

She leans back on the couch, dressed comfortably in jeans and a casual sweater. She graduated from St. Louis University, she says, and she laughs about her "sneaky Jesuit ways" in incorporating hidden Buddhist principles into her political writing. After a period of sixties activism and some graduate work at the University of California, Charlene went to India where she established a strong Vipassana practice with the Theravada Buddhist teacher S. N. Goenka, married an American student of his, and later lived in Japan for a year. They came back to this country with their infant daughter. After they separated years later, she came to California.

"Where do you see the intersection between Buddhism and the political work that you do?" I ask.

"On a personal daily level it's really necessary to keep grounded and centered," she answers. "Even though I feel the integrity of the people I'm working with in Green politics is high, there are still the usual psychodramas going on and all kinds of things to work out, and crises, and so it's really necessary to be able to center yourself and just clean out at the end of the day. So that's one level.

"But also, I feel that practice lets you get a little glimpse of what's possible, of the idea of your development into wisdom, and

I think Green politics is very much about values and development. E. F. Schumacher,[5] who contributed so much to social theory, said the idea of economics is to give people meaningful work that helps them develop and increase wisdom; it's not to accumulate a lot of commodities that you sell, that's a secondary thing. So to me the sense of what a *person* is in Buddhism—the process of purifying the mind and cultivating wholesome acts—is very much intersecting with these new values that we'd like to work out in Green politics."

She does, however, feel the lack in Buddhism of a connection with nature. "There's compassion for all sentient beings, but there's not the sense of learning from nature, watching the cycles of nature as a Taoist would and learning the lessons from that, which I think is absolutely necessary if we're going to have a sense of deep ecology as part of the new values. So I've had to supplement Buddhism, in order to deepen my own sense of nature, by looking at Taoism and Native American teachings."

The books Charlene Spretnak has written illustrate her interests. Her 1978 *Lost Goddesses of Early Greece* presented the original prepatriarchal goddess myths from pre-Hellenic times; *The Politics of Women's Spirituality*, which she edited, brought together the latest writings on this subject; *Green Politics*, co-authored with Fritjof Capra, investigated the issues and activists in the Green political movement in Germany; and *The Spiritual Dimension of Green Politics* proposed the role of spiritual values in the new politics. She was a founding member of the Feminist Writers' Guild and of the Committees of Correspondence, a group of Americans working to establish Green politics in this country as part of the emerging Green movement worldwide.

To all this she brings a Buddhist sensibility. Now I ask her to elaborate on that sense of what a *person* is that she has mentioned, and she talks about the sense of subtle awareness one develops in meditation. "The fact that everything is relationships and interconnections: you get closer to seeing that what's interconnecting is vibrations and patterns of vibrations: that's very exciting because you're getting down to the 'isness' of what's happening."

And she explains how that awareness carries over into the social/political domain. "Buddhist teachings emphasize wisdom and compassion, and you can apply that to society—school systems, economic systems, environmental laws. That leads us to more subtle ideas of relationship, that there is this possible progression into wisdom that we could decide to take as a culture."

We talk about how changes in social patterns come about, and she uses an example from Japanese culture. "When I lived in Japan, I saw the whole cycle of hating the next generation of women in that patriarchal culture. The bride had to move into the husband's home, and the mother-in-law was terribly dictatorial towards the daughter-in-law. When she finally died, the oldest daughter got to be the dictator and be mean to *her* sons' wives for the next thirty years. Incredible! To break the system, you would need just *one person* in that chain to have compassion and relate for thirty years with *love* for her daughter-in-law and then *they* would to theirs."

After the publication of *Green Politics,* Charlene found herself expected to take a key role in organizing a movement for Green politics in the United States. She worked with theorists and political organizers to create the Committees of Correspondence, a network that now consists of over seventy-five Green groups, organized in regional federations.[6] The platform of this group includes the values of ecological wisdom, community-based economics, global responsibility, future focus and sustainability, postpatriarchal values, social responsibility, grassroots democracy, and nonviolence.

"I've tried to play a role as a catalyst," she explains. "I worked very hard the first two years to get it going nationally and to get it started locally here. But what I really want to do is putter around in the corner of Green politics and help to figure out the spiritual dimension. That's what I love."

She spoke about this spiritual dimension when she delivered the annual lecture for the E. F. Schumacher Society of America in 1984, the text of which is published as *The Spiritual Dimension of Green Politics.* "We have a model for interfaith, religion- based social change activism in the Sarvodaya movement, which operates successful self-help projects in eight thousand villages in Sri Lanka. It combines the Gandhian model of a small-scale community-based economy with spiritually informed ethics, mostly Buddhist but also Hindu, Moslem, and Christian. As I was finishing writing this lecture, the founder of Sarvodaya, Dr. A. T. Ariyaratne, passed through San Francisco and I attended a reception for him. Afterward I asked whether he felt that a spiritually based social change movement could flourish in a country [like ours] with twelve hundred kinds of religious orientations. He first explained to me that Sarvodaya works with greater religious and ethnic diversity than I thought. Then he smiled and said, 'First you build a spiritual infrastructure for the community, based on everyone's having a personal practice. Then everyone will come to you.' "

Charlene concluded, "I don't know whether 'everyone' will ever come to Green politics, but I do believe that a 'spiritual infrastructure' is essential for a successful transformation of our society in postmodern and Green directions. A spiritual grounding would not only answer a deep hunger in the modern experience, it could also be harmonious with various Green tendrils that have already begun to sprout: the bioregional movement, which teaches us to 'live in place,' to know and appreciate the heritage and ecological character of our area; the evolving philosophy of deep ecology; the emergence of community-based ecological populism; the Green-oriented activism in mainline religion; the work of cultural/holistic feminists; the spiritual dimension appearing in discussions of global responsibility—and the worldwide network of Green parties and organizations."

Charlene and I are just finishing our talk when her daughter Lissa Khema (her middle name means "peaceful" in Pali) comes home from school. An eighth grader with huge eyes and her mother's dark lashes, she tells me she wants to be a singer with a rock band. Half-smiling, Charlene watches Lissa with a mixture of pride and protectiveness.

When Lissa has disappeared into the bedroom and I am preparing to leave, I remark that Charlene must live a very complex and demanding life, with her job and teaching, her political work, mothering, and writing. She simply nods matter-of-factly and says, "Overloaded at times, yes." Leaving, I am impressed by the breadth and depth of her concerns.

BUDDHISTS CONCERNED FOR ANIMALS

Instances of cruelty and power imbalance are nowhere as obvious as in the treatment of animals in this country. Animals raised for food and used in experimentation are seen as beings whose only reason for existence is to serve human needs. The suffering caused in these endeavors is enormous in scope and viewed by some perpetrators as unimportant. Some Buddhists, responding to the predicament of their fellow beings, the animals, have come together to form Buddhists Concerned for Animals, a group that sees the helping of animals as intimately connected with the quality of human existence, as well as important in its own right. This activity comes naturally, for the Buddha himself urged compassion for *all* beings; and in the Buddhist system of rebirth, lifetimes spent in animal form are not unusual.

Buddhists Concerned for Animals (BCA) was founded in 1981 by Bradley Miller, Bonnie del Raye, and Vanja Palmers, who were then monks at Tassajara Zen Monastery. BCA now functions out of the home of Bonnie and Bradley on a quiet modest street in San Rafael, California.

On a mild Sunday morning in May, *Bonnie Del Raye* and I sit on the second-floor deck outside her office/living room. The sunshine is bright on the trees in the yard. Wind chimes clink winsomely. In preparation for my visit Bonnie has amassed letters, pamphlets, and copies of the *Buddhists Concerned for Animals Newsletter* on the table that holds our teacups. Inside the glass doors, Brad Miller is working, and now and then he responds to Bonnie's requests for information or photographs.

Blue-eyed, with a gentle face and shy manner, Bonnie wears a purple T-shirt inscribed "Women's National History Week" and brown wooden prayer beads around her wrist. She speaks urgently, pointing out quotes and photographs in the material before us, telling me of the help she and Brad received from Elsie Mitchell when they first began. Mrs. Mitchell's Ahimsa Foundation has been one of their major supporters, offering crucial financial aid at the beginning of the project.

But why create another animal rights group, I want to know, when there are already so many?

"There weren't nearly as many organizations when we started," Bonnie answers, "and very little going on as far as grass-roots activism. We felt that Buddhists make the perfect audience and base of support for animal protection. People practicing Buddhism are sensitive to the suffering of others, but most had no idea of the extent to which animals are painfully exploited. We also felt, and still do, that Buddhism has a lot to offer the animal rights movement. Animal torture is a volatile subject and a very difficult realm in which to keep an equilibrium. Without a spiritual base, or at least some sense of nonduality, it is easy for activists themselves to become victims of this emotional minefield."

A native of Massachusetts, Bonnie studied Zen with Sasaki Roshi and later found her way to Tassajara. There she met Brad Miller, who had already begun working for animal rights. She was shocked by the material he had unearthed.

"The more we looked into all the different areas in which animals were suffering, the more I became overwhelmed," she recalls. "I had never been politically active. I would rather do my Japanese tea ceremony and sit quietly. But once I started reading *Animal Liberation* by Peter Singer, I couldn't help getting involved."

She, Brad, and Vanja Palmers began organizing at Tassajara, where they passed around the material they gathered. They took the name Buddhists Concerned for Animals, created an introductory letter and first issue of a newsletter, and sent those, along with a copy of *Animal Liberation*, to every Buddhist center in the country. The response was enthusiastic from Zen centers such as the Providence Zen Center, Shasta Abbey, and the Rochester Zen Center, whose roshi, Philip Kapleau, has written a book called *To Cherish All Life: A Buddhist View of Animal Slaughter and Meat Eating*.

Unable to keep up with this work while living within the monastic situation of Tassajara, Bonnie and Brad (now married) moved to the San Francisco Bay Area in order to formally establish the organization. Most of their effort after arriving here took place in the area of animal research, when they discovered the appalling conditions in the laboratories of the University of California, Berkeley, where animals were kept in situations of filth and disease, where experiments were duplicated unnecessarily, where the buildings were so carelessly maintained that sometimes laboratory animals or fish died by the hundreds.

Using confidential information brought to them by sympathetic persons inside the university, Buddhists Concerned for Animals published an exhaustively documented report, "Animal Care and Animal Care Policy at University of California, Berkeley, Animal Research Facilities." Brad Miller presented this report to the U.C. Board of Regents Committee on Educational Policy, seeking an end to the needless animal deaths.

"How did the regents respond?" I ask.

Bonnie's eyes spark.

"It was unbelievable! They just didn't want to hear it. It was a fight to even get on the floor to *speak*. The amount of money the university receives from the National Institute of Health for these experiments is phenomenal! It's a business, and the animals are simply a means to their organizational ends—objects to be experimented upon. Not for human health, as many people are led to believe, but for trivial, yet painful, psychological experimentation, military research . . . the list is endless."

Noting the passion of her reply, I begin to revise my estimation of Bonnie as a shy, quiet person.

When it became clear that the agent for the U.S. Department of Agriculture in this area had been instructed not to monitor the behavior of U.C. Berkeley by applying the standards of the Animal Welfare Act, Buddhists Concerned for Animals decided to sue. Because of their lawsuit, the University of California was fined $12,000. "Financially, it was just a slap on the wrist," says Bonnie, "but it was the first time the university had ever been penalized for abusing animals. This enabled us to block, for over one year, construction of a new animal research facility." BCA also managed to force the university to appoint an animal activist to its institutional animal care committee—an unprecedented concession at an animal research facility.

Now that many groups are working on the issue of animal experimentation, an issue BCA still supports, they have shifted their major focus to the plight of domestic animals on so-called "factory farms" where chickens, pigs, calves, and other animals are kept in conditions so unhealthy that they must be fed large doses of antibiotics to combat disease.

"I had known that chicken farms were atrocious," Bonnie says. "One of my friends had worked in one, and I went to see for myself. It was unbelievable. They have buildings larger than the size of a football field full of chickens in tiny cages. Each cage is about the size of a record album cover. In these cages they stuff four, five, even six hens. Their legs often become tangled around the wire mesh and they can't move. There's a pecking order with chickens— can you imagine what it's like locked in those cages where there is nowhere for the birds to run? Many of them get mauled to death. Egg collection, food, and watering are all automated."

Brad brings out some color photographs he had taken inside such a building. The pictures show chickens jammed together in excrement-encrusted cages, their deformed feet caught in the wire floor of the cages. These images seem even more grotesque juxtaposed with the beauty of this sunny morning in San Rafael.

"Because we were being asked many questions by the public about this," Bonnie goes on, "and because there hasn't been any effective effort on the issue of factory farming, we decided to move into that area."

They have formed a separate organization, the Humane Farming Association, to confront the issues raised by factory farming, and they are receiving support from doctors who are worried because some of their patients, having so consistently eaten meat from animals fed with antibiotics, have developed an immune bacteria and can no longer be treated with antibiotics in an emergency. Bonnie points out to me that almost 50 percent of all antibiotics manufactured in the United States are used in animal feeds. The immense profit for the pharmaceutical companies is over $435 million.

"What we did by creating this group," Bonnie says, "was to bring in many other people from other humane groups to work with us." She explains that Buddhists Concerned for Animals will still exist, and she tells of a visit she made in its behalf to a Tibetan Buddhist center in Santa Cruz. "I just went down to visit. Several lamas from Tibet were visiting at that time. Many of the people at the center eat meat. I didn't go with the intention of talking, I just went and handed out newsletters. But one of the lamas saw this and said, 'Who is this person?' He asked me to come up and talk— there were about a hundred people in the room. He said, 'Tell us about this,' and I started explaining the realities of factory farming. They were just shocked! People have an image of Old Mac-Donald on the farm, that the animals are happy and out there in the sun playing with other animals." She points to a picture in the brochure of a calf chained in a tiny box. "No, *this* is the way veal calves exist. They were very surprised."

BCA receives support from many different schools of Buddhism, not only the Zen communities. Bonnie says that she is impressed by the level of commitment BCA members have shown toward the work of the organization. She recalls the time a monk from Sri Lanka sent BCA fifty U.S. dollar bills in a reused envelope. "We were all very struck by this gift. Here is a monk living a life of economic poverty in an impoverished nation, and he mails fifty dollars to America to be used in alleviating animal suffering. The spirit of that gift is what keeps us working."

Although she and Brad are vegetarians, they realize it is unrealistic to approach people from a strict vegetarian stance. Instead they advocate better conditions for raising animals for food. "It's a beginning," she says. "We start by examining how it is farm animals are raised and the impact this has upon human health. I believe this inevitably leads people to give up meat altogether."

Previously, Bonnie has held various jobs in order to support her work with BCA. She was a nurse in convalescent homes, where she loved dealing with old people, and for a time she worked in the admissions office of a college. But now she is pleased to be able to give full time to her animal rights work. At the Buddhists Concerned for Animals/Humane Farming Association office, she processes all the mail, does the bookkeeping and some writing for the *Newsletter*, and manages the efforts of the many volunteers who come to help. While this work is demanding, it can take place within flexible hours, a condition Bonnie values, for she is pregnant with her first child and will need to coordinate her office work with the work of child care when the baby arrives.

I ask if she has found it difficult to be so active and so vocal out in the world—a big change from her former more cloistered life.

"No. It's been a real surprise to me," Bonnie says. "In fact, it's been giving me a lot of energy. In the five short years I have been doing this I can see a change in the way many people are perceiving animals and acknowledging the need for their protection. We still have a long way to go to free animals from the painful effects of human greed, hate, and delusion. But looking on the bright side—things can only get better!"[7]

INTIMATE ENEMIES—SEXUAL ABUSE

Rape and childhood sexual abuse have reached epidemic proportions in the United States, with 44 percent of adult women having experienced at least one completed or attempted rape, 38 percent of females having been sexually molested before the age of 18 (for boys the figure is 9 percent under age 13).[8]

The threat of rape is a reality all women live with, all the time. It represents the effect of patriarchal conditioning as men act out their aggressive impulses and often deep-seated hatred of women. Thus it is a political issue, an instance of power-over, and the invasion of, a woman's body as violent and careless of human rights and values as the attack of one nation upon another.

A comparable issue, which illustrates the status of children as possessions, objects, and in this case sex objects, is the outrage of childhood sexual abuse. In the last few years, a context of increasing openness of public discussion has allowed more and more women to unearth the memory of having been sexually abused as little children by their fathers or other male figures in authority, an experience so traumatic and so efficiently repressed that in many cases it lay dormant for years. This remembering may occur in the midst of the activities of daily life, in therapy or, sometimes, during Buddhist meditation.

The Buddhist response to this painful coming-to-consciousness is extremely important, for it opens the door for crucial changes in Buddhist attitudes and practice; it requires the humanizing and feminizing that will create the new Buddhism. The reality of sexual abuse demands that we scrutinize some prevailing attitudes such as the denial of feeling practiced in many Buddhist environments, the social/political passivity of some meditators, and the resistance in male institutions to addressing women's concerns. An appropriate Buddhist response to rape and childhood sexual abuse requires that we care about the victimization of women, allow emotional content in meditation, recognize psychological pain and damage, and work with the emotions in healing this, as well as act in the world to change the conditions in which these crimes occur.

Buddhist women are attempting to deal with sexual trauma in their meditation practice and to confront the crisis of sexual abuse from a perspective that honors their rage and pain while drawing upon their Buddhist insights. Does Buddhist meditation offer anything in particular to women to help them deal with these assaults against their persons? Rape is an act of violent aggression in which sex is used to subjugate and humiliate the victim. Can Buddhist practice help a woman meet this experience and integrate its effects later? In the case of incest with children, the man uses the little child as an object with which to satisfy his appetites or release his frustrations. Can a woman who is a Buddhist meditator, remembering this experience many years later, find the strength in her practice to help her weather the emotional storms occasioned by her discovery?

The two women whose stories follow both attempt to grapple with the reality of sexual assault.

RAPE

A Zen student, *Alice Ray-Keil,* speaks critically of Buddhists who adopt a neutral position vis-a-vis social action, acknowledging that rape is not an isolated or random act but arises from forces and attitudes in our culture. She comes to some startling conclusions and expresses quite radical thinking on this issue.

Besides being a Zen practitioner in Seattle where she lives, Alice Ray-Keil is a nonviolent activist who has worked to educate her community about violence against women. Writing in *Kahawai* (Winter 1982), on the occasion of her nine-year-old daughter's being sexually accosted, she struggles with the difficult questions of her own relationship as a Zen student to the acts committed and to the man who committed them, and she wonders what she can do to educate her daughter. "How do I share with her a personal consciousness that can offer some protection from a rape culture?"

She sets out a plan of action, urging parents to talk honestly with their children, to respect and accept them unequivocally, and to help them live free of the stereotypes and arbitrary distinctions that bind women and make them passive. And she urges Zen students to work to change the society. "Cultural consciousness must be transformed to the point that rape is, quite literally, unthinkable—and the practice of personal transformation must be accompanied by political action in order to experience the complete fullness of freedom.

"Zen talks about being beyond the distinction of one or many," writes Alice Ray-Keil. "Perhaps the greatest intuition that both Christianity and feminism have to offer Zen Buddhism is the realization that personal liberation without social action in the face of collective oppression is a fraud."

And she points to the Zen communities that maintain a stance of insularity and indifference toward social issues, asserting that "many Zen students withdraw from politics and give implicit support to patriarchal structures of ignorance, hatred, greed, and judgment."

She ends by proposing collective radical acts designed to express resistance and educate the public about rape, and she compares these acts to the documented outrageous actions of some male Zen masters down through the centuries, in their effort to break through illusion and reach to the truth beneath appearances.

"In one case, the action is individual, private, and personal; in the other it is collective, public, and political. In both cases, the object is simply to wake someone up. Yet, too often, traditionally in Zen communities, the action of the single, male roshi is revered, while the action of the collective, female community and its teaching is ridiculed or ignored. At some level, both actions suggest a solution to the koan that is rape." And she ends with a surprising idea. "I hope that we will begin to recognize civil disobedience, property destruction, and guerrilla theater as consistent with the often radical and unconventional actions of teachers down through the ages. It does not replace private teaching or insight; it augments and makes sense of it."

Judith Ragir, who lives in Chicago and practices at the Minnesota Zen Center, was raped in an alley near her work place just a few days after returning from a sesshin. She demonstrates a similar impetus toward activism in her effort to confront rape and to search for an authentic Buddhist response to it. In this she takes first steps toward her own healing, steps that may have social significance as a guide or model for other women similarly brutalized. In her prose poem called "Rape #1, #2, #3" (in *The Path of Compassion: Contemporary Writings on Engaged Buddhism*), she speaks first of venting her rage at the rapist, of tasting the shame of being forced to surrender. "Something so strong in me mourns, wishes I could have protected myself, fought for my rights." And she vows, "I refuse to turn against myself."

Then she ponders the actual physical details of what happened to her and calls upon several Buddhist texts for wisdom in situations of aggression. She writes:

To go towards the enemy, no resistance
to go towards and merge with the object and therefore to lose the subject
These things I had contemplated fully the week before at sesshin
at Catching the Moon Mountain Monastery.
In the middle of this horrible commotion,
still calm from sesshin,
I tried to go towards my enemy, even in rape.
To the ordinary mind, this is heresy,
This is the guilt that I didn't defend myself.
But who is there to defend?
only to become fully the situation
a woman amidst a violent crime,
where passivity and compliance gets her out alive.

And she observes, surprisingly,

Everthing is in reverse.
I see in one of Frieda Kahlo's paintings[9]
that the roots of a tree are coming out of a skeleton buried in its soil
death fertilizing life
as this rape nourishes my understanding
and suffering teaches our souls.
But this is so upside-down to ordinary mind.
How dare I say, in ordinary mind,
the rape is a gift . . .

The next part gives Judith's thoughts seven weeks after she was attacked, when she still remembers the rape several times each day, when she is afraid on the streets and in need of nurturing. She feels that she has been "totally rearranged" inside.

This rearrangement I've been calling a realization, which it is. Though I cannot pinpoint exactly what has changed in me, I know that I am different. I think the greatest realization of the whole experience was to see my spiritual practice in action. . . . I saw that the years of practice are built into my life; that I could not internally collapse, which would lead, perhaps, into an extended depression. Doing what I always do on a daily basis, I tried to maintain the most wholesome attitude of mind I could. There is nowhere to go.

And she ends by saying that she felt the support of the Buddha, Dharma, and Sangha in confronting her experience.

In many ways, my ordinary mind could not support the fact of rape. It was unwired. Only the Buddha realm as expressed by the Dharma could give me an attitude of mind that could embrace rape, and only through the love of the Sangha could I have the strength, will, love, and comfort to shed my ego and walk my path through this experience.

CHILDHOOD SEXUAL ABUSE

The idea of working within the context of Buddhist meditation on the effects of childhood sexual abuse on adult women is a new one. In the world at large, the reality of the use of children as sexual objects has become more and more a recognized fact. As information is made public, many women (and some men) encounter the memory of having been sexually abused, often repeatedly, as little children, in actions on a continuum from exhibitionism and fondling through the many variations of sexual behavior up to and including penetration of the body. In many Buddhist settings, this content would be given little attention, but as some women question traditional male-defined practice and struggle to include the realities of their own female experience in their meditation practice, they create a precedent for confronting their vicitimization. And from this examination may come the knowledge and will to protect others from similar abuse or to aid in their healing.

Whenever a woman teacher leads a women's retreat and asks people to talk during or after the retreat, there are always several women who report that while they sat in meditation, memories of childhood sexual abuse arose in their minds, perhaps for the first time, perhaps for the hundredth time. The teacher, the group, the woman herself, must meet this suffering in some way.

Brenda (not her real name), an experienced meditator, tells of her struggle with this issue and her extreme sensitivity in approaching it. She describes what it was like to experience the feelings and memories of incest while sitting at a long meditation retreat.

"The past three years or so have been a time for me of very intensely dealing with a history of sexual abuse. And so for me meditation and this dealing with sexual abuse kind of fit together. Somewhere inside of me I knew it was time to just stop and stand still and just try to be with myself in a way that I had never been able to do.

"I've had run-ins with one of my meditation teachers. We've disagreed mostly around incest stuff. Every time I've seen her I've told her about it. What's happened is that I've experienced a lot of impatience from her around the amount of time it's taken me to deal with this thing. At the same time I've experienced her growing a lot over the years I've known her. I mean I think she's changed and taken in a lot of stuff.

"One conversation in particular. I sat with her a few months before I was planning to go to confront my parents for the first time with the fact of my father having committed the incest. She thought that was a terrible idea, when I told her about it. I knew there was no way I was going to live all the rest of my life without doing this, so it wasn't a question of my being talked out of it. But what happened was that the conversation we had was really good—and we talked for about half an hour—because it pushed me toward being more open to my parents. You know, she stressed loving-kindness, just opening up that part of myself that has love for my parents, not getting totally caught up in the anger and the hurt."

Recently, Brenda has become deeply involved in her meditation practice and has done several three-month retreats.

"Before I began to meditate, there had been a period in my life when I had thought I was going to go off the deep end. Actually I think what was going on then was that I was opening up to the incest and it was beginning to claim its place in my life, its rightful place—right in the center.

"So I had that fear with me when I thought of doing the long retreat. And then what happened was that I went and confronted my parents finally, which was something I never thought I would be able to do. It was like the major miracle of my lifetime. When I confronted my father, he said he didn't remember it. I think that he actually doesn't. A combination of old age and repression and ill health all sort of work together to help him forget it. And my mother has no clue that it ever happened, although she accepts that I'm telling the truth and has always been there to talk to me when I've talked about it. Now as an adult trying to deal with this, it's a bizarre experience having two parents who can't give me any feedback on it. But somehow being able to walk into their house and say what I had to say just released some of this fear inside of me. And it was after I did that that I thought, Oh, I want to go sit the three-month retreat.

"Going in with this incest stuff, I just really got in touch with the enormous power of the mind. I got in touch with what, as a child, my mind must have done to deny the reality of what was going on for me, so that I could survive psychically, to the point where I *still* cannot remember the details of what happened to me, even though I feel like so much of me is open to it, to remembering it and dealing with it. I just remember enough to know that it happened."

An important aspect of the retreat, for Brenda, was the women's meetings held at its completion, in which she discovered there were many other women at the retreat whose meditation practice was deeply affected by their experience of childhood sexual abuse.

"We had several women's meetings at the end of the retreat, and what came up there, which was stunning to me, was that there were ten to twelve women—and probably not everyone for whom this was true even spoke up—who identified themselves as having been sexually abused and identified that as having been a really important part of their practice, you know, what had been going on for them. For me, even though we don't use koans in Vipassana meditation, I identify the incest as being my koan always. It was wonderful after seventy days of silence, to come together as women and share some of that stuff and sit together."

She wonders how therapy and meditation can work together, therapy offering the opportunity to deal with emotional issues and the particulars of one's life, meditation giving a way to let go of the story or details of an experience and just be present for the feelings and sensations in the moment.

"It was really fascinating to me to talk with other women at the retreat who had also been dealing with incest. I think probably a lot of people go into meditation who've had a lot of pain in their lives. So they have a lot of stories they're trying to work through in some way, and meditation is part of the path. But how do you deal with the *details,* which are very important to me. Can I learn to let go of the details and at the same time really honor and acknowledge them? It's a huge question, and particularly important for women."

A young woman who has recently begun to teach meditation at Insight Meditation Society in Barre, Massachusetts, is coping with the issue of childhood sexual abuse in her own life. She expresses the newness of this and its significance within the Buddhist world, particularly as it illuminates how, in our culture generally as well as in Buddhist environments, one is discouraged from experiencing one's emotions, and how this in turn implies a rejection of the body. As women are considered to be more identified with the body, this tendency illustrates a bias that can oppress and silence women, deny our experience, and relegate us to a marginal and compromised position. In speaking up against this she acts politically, challenging established power and assumptions.

We talk in Oakland, California, where she is visiting a friend in a wood-paneled garden cottage, with the fresh green of leaves outside the glass-paned door. *Michele McDonald,* at age thirty-three, has masses of dark wavy hair and large dark eyes. Child of a Catholic family in Massachusetts, whose mother died when she was thirteen, Michele later lived for years in a farming community in northern Maine. She taught nature study and worked for the Audubon Society in addition to teaching children with learning disabilities and working with people just released from mental institutions. Having developed a deep bond with nature and a sense of aloneness, she turned to Buddhism for a technique to deepen her meditation, and for guidance in it.

Now at Insight Meditation Society, where she studies and teaches, she finds herself in the center of the changes taking place there. Talking about this, Michele is soft-spoken and emphatic at the same time.

She tells about her discovery that she had been molested repeatedly as a small child by a family friend. For several years she had been having serious back problems, which she attributes to the repressed information about this sexual abuse. Then she did a three-month retreat with a Burmese teacher.

"I went into that course only able to sit once a day. My back was still very bad, and I didn't know if I could do the course. I started out very gently, and yet I did the instructions as fully as I could. And during my three months, I started having very horrible memories of when I was five years old, of being raped. Mostly my perspective of it during the course, was . . ." She laughs, shaking her head. "It might be hard to believe, but I was seeing things molecularly. It was very much the perspective of not-self. I was seeing things in terms of heat and pressure. It's pretty hard to explain, but I was remembering very much in terms of the elements, and there wasn't much even of an ability to distinguish him or me.

"There would be crying at times, but the emotional impact of the whole experience that I had had as a child didn't completely hit me. What happened was that I worked very hard in the course, and many other things happened in it, and I came out of the course right into teaching the women's course. And I literally had no skin! The whole feeling of the memory seemed to have ripped open my system, and emotionally I was pretty much a five-year-old. I think basically most of us are really there anyway. I mean, I had no defenses. And I had a very difficult time learning how to *be* outside of my little room. I taught the women's course, I taught the three-month course, I taught the Christmas course from that place.

"It was real important for me to know that I could keep going. There was something that I don't understand now but it was important for me to finish what I wanted to do that year. And I'm glad I did. And yet when I finally stopped, which was when I decided I needed a couple of days to take it easy, my back went out again. And lots of memories surfaced of being molested when I was three. It's like I went to a three-year-old level, with no defenses again. And I really decided to not hold it together anymore. I decided to let it all come out. I would never recommend anybody to do it this way, but I really didn't have much of a map. I felt like I held my nose and jumped." She laughs at the image. "I feel very lucky that I didn't drown. I got some good help. I was seeing a therapist."

But many therapists, she points out, do not know how to work with a person deeply engaged in meditation. Rather than needing to open up more to her situation, she needed to integrate what she had discovered. It was the depth to which she had gone in meditation and the strength derived from it that allowed her to open to the emotional pain of her childhood.

We sit on the floor of the cottage, Michele on a matress, I on a pillow, while birds rustle in the branches outside and the sound of the nearby freeway is a faint rumble in the background. Michele is controlled yet strongly emotional and tells me about what she has been discovering as she has come to terms with her terror.

"We have not accepted that it's okay to have feelings! It's like, here we are, we've been on this planet quite a while, and we haven't accepted that we're human beings. You know, they get sad, they get angry, they get happy, they feel joy. There's this wealth of feelings that come from being on the planet and relating to each other, and most of us can't even feel like that's *okay.* To me that comes from that whole thousands of years of message that the body is bad, the whole devaluing of *connection.* Connection implies *feeling,* and detachment doesn't necessarily mean that connection is wrong. The religions that we've inherited in most of our cultures at this time, which include Buddhism, have been out of balance. Our conditioning is such that the masculine part of ourselves isn't honoring the feminine. Within this context, often detachment has been interpreted to mean one shouldn't connect. Whereas really each of us has to work to balance connection with detachment."

With Christina Feldman, another Vipassana teacher, Michele had for the past several years been leading the women's retreats that are offered as yearly events at Insight Meditation Society. In these retreats, besides meditation practices, the teachers use group discussion, movement, and chants. Michele says that she has seen the need to integrate into her teaching the lessons learned from confronting the issue of sexual abuse.

"I've had to learn a lot from women who have been doing this work for longer than I have," she says. "From what I have learned, it seems to be a lifelong koan. I've had to explore very hard feelings and accept them. To feel those fully is what will heal. Mostly, in meditation, a person is encouraged to stay on the process level and not to think about or investigate the story or content of what has happened. For women and men who have been sexually abused, especially as young children, there is so much denial, there is usually so much inability to look at or even remember the story or content. I have found that meditation can be helpful to balance that denial. The detachment that one can learn in meditation can help a person finally have the strength and courage to face the truth and the feelings that arise from facing the story. By honoring the content, in this particular context, I find people can go more deeply into the perspective of not-self that I talked about earlier and also begin to understand the karmic perspective and eventually not have to feel like a victim anymore—which is ultimately very freeing.

"I feel like anybody could come to me with any depth of rage or fear or anger and it wouldn't shake me too much at this point. I feel strong from that. It's like a fearlessness that doesn't come from honoring it, or come from having aversion for it or pushing it away, but it's really like, how do you be a flower with all this, and how do you open to it rather than tighten up? It's a gradual process. It's like a spiral, in which each time the fear arrives it seems like I have a new perspective to bring to it and I can open up to it a little more. And that seems to be what freedom is.

"The hardest thing is that I really love the person who molested me, and if I didn't really love him it wouldn't have been nearly as painful. And so I've had to go through all that rage, but also underneath that is the incredible hurt and love that was there. Trying to understand that brings about a lot of compassion for all of us. Because the pain and the joy that's connected to sexuality is something that I don't think has been explored very well. It's very scary to most people to look at the history of their own sexuality."

She speaks urgently, gesturing with a long-fingered hand.

"We have to learn to integrate what we call spiritual with what we call emotional. To me emotional *is* spiritual, I don't see any difference anymore. But if we really take a good look at this, what's been taught and what's been lived out for thousands of years is this *split*. You have to look at a teacher's life for that, you can't just look at what's coming out of their mouths.

"If a person's feeling like, 'Well, I wash the dishes or I go shopping or I'm playing with the children and this is *secondary* to my spiritual practice,' then there's that split going on, and one's feeling like, 'I can't wait to get done with this.' I don't feel like I'm going to be *done* with the sexual abuse stuff. That whole idea of getting rid of something or being done with it, or being over it, has always implied aversion and that that's not really spiritual but something separate and secondary. I've been investigating how all of that comes from *aversion to the feelings,* the belief that somehow if we were *really* spiritual we wouldn't be connected and we would't *have feelings!* I get very emotional about this!" She laughs, and adds, "It's been a long struggle for me to begin to see the split *in myself,* and it's by no means eliminated."

I ask what kind of response she gets from the other teachers.

"I have been trying to focus more on the work I have to do on myself and my teaching work with students, than on what kind of response I get from other teachers, the last few years. I feel that some understand and most are open to listening. But also I respect that we all have different things to do in our lifetime and different conditionings and, most important, different qualities to offer students. It took me a long time to have the strength to look at what I needed to look at, and I wouldn't want to be judged for not being able to do it five years ago. And so we all open the way we do."

It's clear that Michele's facing of her own truth has made her brave, for several nights later I see her stand up publicly for what she believes. A panel discussion on spirituality and sexuality features three well-known people in the Buddhist world—one teacher and two authors—and a woman teacher from another tradition. The event takes place in the sanctuary of a church in San Francisco and is attended by hundreds of people. In response to questions from the audience about sexual behavior in relation to spirituality, all of these spiritual guides speak of the positive value of having one-night stands, multiple relationships, of not possessing people, and so forth; not one of them mentions commitment or responsibility in relating. Finally Michele rises from her seat in the audience, goes to the front to climb to the stage, and speaks into a microphone set up for questions. Her voice trembling, she says she wishes to bring forth a viewpoint that has not been presented: the situation in which two people care deeply about each other and express that sexually, which im-

"I loved it. I was very happy with that job, and it was a good way to live. I really felt that the element of service made it different from a job. You got a stipend once a month rather than a paycheck. There was a sense of family, and a sense of a whole bunch of people working toward an end that we all believed in."

She points out that the makeup of the staffs at IMS has changed, now being comprised of more older people who have savings to tide them over and cars to drive. "When I was there, most of us were very poor, and a stipend meant everything. For many years it was a certain amount of money; then we on the staff really needed it to be more, and the board thought it was obnoxious of us to ask for more money. There was kind of a labor-management event going on there. It's a white, middle-class scene, so it's hard for people to understand any kind of poverty. Oh, it's talked about. There's the Oxfam, which is an organization that distributes food to starving people. Once a year IMS people fast, if they like, and the money IMS could have spent on that day's food gets sent to Oxfam. It's usually during the three-month course, so there's a lot of people and a few hundred dollars ends up being donated. So they see poverty on that extreme level of starvation, but as far as people just plain being poor, there's no consciousness."

Jo's parents ran a small farm in eastern Massachusetts, and their land happened to be situated in a neighborhood of upper-class white people. Her father made six or seven thousand a year, while the parents of the children she went to school with had access to at least forty or fifty thousand a year. Every summer, while her schoolmates went off on luxurious vacations, she worked on the farm. "Now I'm very grateful to have had that background of working on the land," she says. "My strong connection to the earth definitely came from that." But at the end of her childhood the disparity between her experience and opportunities and that of her schoolmates caused her extreme pain.

She admits that as a staff member of IMS she had "a lot of trouble with the money scene. I arrived there with fifty dollars. I'm *very* willing to work, but I need to get something for it. Once I realized I wasn't getting enough, I joined with other people to voice that. We said, 'This isn't enough.' And there was incredible resistance to us from the board. That shocked me!"

The issues of livelihood and sexuality are central, she believes, to the phenomenon of American women's participation in Buddhism. But she does not find much willingness, at least among the Theravadin teachers and practitioners she knows, to look at these areas. "Supposedly the Dharma is everywhere," she says adamantly. "That means you look at *everything*, you don't just pick certain things. I find a lot of resistance to looking at those newer issues that definitely exist in the West.

"The part that people don't look at, with the monastic traditions, is that someone is footing the bill. I consider monastics to be a privileged class. Irregardless of how wonderful monasticism is for the inner growth of anyone, that issue is being ignored. The nuns don't get too many of the bennies, but the monks definitely do! I have watched Westerners jump into it in the East and return here with incredible chauvinism around their robes. They expect privilege: 'I am a monk, aren't you going to do this for me?' even if it's not spoken. Especially expecting *women* to hop, skip, and jump. And so many Western women are ready to do that. That was my experience at IMS, with one teacher in particular and some of the men who were on staff or would come through. It was definitely a class situation, and they were on top."

NICHIREN SHOSHU SOKA GAKKAI

In this book one will find a number of Asian woman but very few black women and no Latinas. I was tempted, when interviewing, to make great efforts to seek out the few black women peripherally or tentatively engaged with Buddhist practice, so as to have a fuller representation, but this effort, I recognized, was in itself racist: seeking out token blacks to make the situation seem more integrated than it is. The truth is that in all but one of the many Buddhist gatherings I attended, I saw almost no people of color except for Asians.

In the meetings and ceremonies of the Nichiren Shoshu sect, the situation was entirely different. The first meeting I attended was held in a small apartment on Divisadero Street in San Francisco, in a largely black neighborhood. Of the twenty-five or thirty people crowded into the living room before the laquered shrine, perhaps half were blacks, and black people were running the meeting. There were at least four or five people of obviously Latin extraction, some Asians, and the rest white people. The meeting began with vigorous chanting of "Nam-myoho-renge-kyo," after which individuals stood up to testify as to the benefits they received from doing this chant regularly. One black woman spoke of her difficulties in relating with her husband and said that after chanting for a period of time and "taking it to the Gohonzon" (the Gohonzon is the scroll to which Nichiren followers chant), she found that she and her husband became more harmonious and began to enjoy each other. A Latin man said he had been using drugs heavily but through chanting had managed to clean up his life and get a job. Another black woman spoke, saying that she had had an alcohol problem, which she had beaten through chanting. A young white woman stood and gave a short inspirational talk on the power of the chanting in her life. The meeting had the nature of a pep rally, with, at one point, some members of the young women's division punching out a song with tremendous gusto and exaggerated cheerleaderlike arm movements. Finally a Japanese woman, who was introduced as an official in the women's division, superintended the efforts to sign up each of us new people and offered the fulfillment of our desires if we would chant every day for ninety days.

This is one of hundreds of such groups in the United States, often directed by Japanese-Americans, under the aegis of NSA (Nichiren Shoshu Soka Gakkai of America). Nichiren Shoshu means "orthodox school of Nichiren"; Soka Gakkai refers to its lay organization of believers. The *Encyclopedia of Religion*, edited by Mircea Eliade, sets forth a most intriguing description of the philosophy and aims of this organization: "Soka Gakkai (Value Creation Society), a Japanese 'new religion' stemming from Nichiren tradition, presents an understanding of Buddhism as the 'Third Civilization,' which can overcome the opposition of idealism and materialism in thought and, when applied to the economy, can bring about a synthesis of capitalism and socialism."

According to NSA's literature, there are organizations in 115 countries across the world, with seventeen million people participating. NSA's stated goal is to introduce its brand of Buddhism to America, and its larger goal is to "promote peace, culture, and education." It sponsors myriad activities and groups through its men's and women's divisions, young men's and young women's divisions, including study groups, shows, pageants, parades, orchestras, and marching bands. It strongly promotes family values. Its members function at a high level of energy and commitment.

In order to make Buddhist teachings accessible to everyone, Nichiren Daishonin, the thirteenth-century founder of Nichiren Shoshu, rejected the traditional meditation practices and devised a practice of chanting "Nam- myoho-renge-kyo" from the Lotus Sutra, plus a few other chants. After the defeat of Japan in World War II, when the nation was wartorn and seeking after peace, there was a great flowering of Nichiren Shoshu. It was formally introduced into the United States in 1960.[10]

The Nam-myoho-renge-kyo chant is the same one used by the Nipponzan Myohoji monks of the Peace Pagoda (with a slightly different transliteration), who trace themselves back to Nichiren Daishonin as well; and there are other Nichiren sects in Japan; but Nichiren Shoshu recognizes no other sects but itself. It considers Zen to be a depraved religion based upon a misinterpretation of Shakyamuni Buddha's doctrines, and it warns its followers against other Buddhist practices and groups.

Many people in the world of American Buddhists are leery of Nichiren Shoshu, seeing it as a pseudoreligion in which people "chant to get a Cadillac," and they are repelled by Nichiren's aggressive recruiting tactics. It is also said that Nichiren is "political" in some ill-defined but presumably sinister way. (Actually, in Japan, Nichiren Shoshu has a political party of his own, but it has not been known to operate politically in this country.) People in Nichiren *do* chant to get a car, a house, a job, a better life. It is also true that the majority of people in this country practicing the other forms of Buddhism already have access to those things and so can comfortably choose to renounce them. The proselytizing offends middle-class sensibility.

Race and class are inextricably linked in American society, as people of color tend to earn less money and have less power than white people. The appeal of Nichiren to many black people, thus, is not surprising. (I do not mean to give the impression that all Nichiren members are working class and/or people of color, but only to point out that Nichiren is much more accessible to these groups than the other forms of Buddhism.) In *Essence* magazine in January of 1986, a young black woman named Harvette Nelson says of her involvement in Nichiren Shoshu,

Buddhism is a universal teaching, and I'd recommend it to anyone, but especially to Black women. We have so much to grapple with in our lives. Through chanting you can realize inner power you never knew existed, so you don't go around feeling like the world is out to get you or the job is rotten or that relationships with men are difficult. It's about controlling your destiny by taking responsibility for your own actions.

The most famous black woman practitioner is spectacular rock singer *Tina Turner,* who swept the 1985 Grammy awards and hit the top with her record, "Private Dancer." Interviewed in Japan, Tina told of the developments in her fourteen-year commitment to Nichiren chanting, in which she was able to leave an abusive husband (in the process losing the opportunities she had earned as half of the rhythm-and-blues team Ike and Tina Turner), weather the lean years after that, and eventually make a dazzling comeback as the most celebrated singer in America in 1985.

Of her beginning practice, while she was still married, she says, "I continued to practice my faith . . . As a result, I began to develop the strength to change what I knew I had to change."

She speaks of the internal transformation that took place because of her Buddhist practice. "Even if one desires and prays for a car or a home, there may be times when such prayers cannot be immediately realized. But there are times when benefits appear internally, before they appear materially." And she adds, "Eventually it seemed as if a different sort of human being was emerging within [me] and I became convinced that I had changed a great deal."

In 1982, at a low point in her career, she performed at the "Aloha" rally of Nichiren Shoshu Soka Gakkai in Washington, D.C., an appearance she claims was a turning point in her practice and her career. A year later her song "Let's Stay Together" became a best-selling hit, and in 1984 the smash hit "What's Love Got to Do with It?" catapulted her to extravagant success. Tina Turner credits some of this upturn to the Nichiren teachings on perseverance, saying, "This particular guidance I was really able to engrave deeply in my heart, and I have made it an important part of my life."[11]

Dianne Douglas is a thirty-seven-year-old white woman who has found Nichiren Shoshu practice beneficial. Manager of Public Relations for Computerland Corporation, Dianne's first ambition, while in college at San Francisco State University, was to become a professional jazz musician. In 1971, a male friend took her to an NSA discussion meeting, where she saw "many Japanese people and some weird Americans." But she responded to the chanting of Nam-myoho-renge-kyo, joined NSA by receiving a Gohonzon, and began to do the daily practice regularly. In nine months she had found a job as a musician and, as she puts it, "got many of the things I had been chanting about."

Dianne talks enthusiastically of the "culture festivals" held each year by NSA, and I recall the movie made of the culture festival in Hawaii that I saw at the Ninth Women's Division General Meeting of the San Francisco Territory. Ten thousand people had come from all over the mainland to Hawaii to participate, as well as two thousand from Japan and three thousand Hawaiians. The parade featured twelve thousand American flags and such spectacular stunts as a four-story rolling pyramid propelled by young male roller skaters. Determination and unity were repeatedly mentioned in the performance, as it was the result of many months of preparation and rehearsal time by all the participating members. The gigantic stage show headlined a pageant of Japanese, Hawaiian and U.S. history performed by a cast of hundreds, with original music and many special effects, including an exploding volcano. The mostly nonprofessional singers and dancers performed with surprising skill and boundless energy. And the theme of the show was "No more Pearl Harbor, no more Hiroshima, no more war."

Dianne Douglas played in the orchestra at the Ninth Women's Division General Meeting held in a San Francisco concert hall and attended by about a thousand women. On the stage sat the fifty chapter heads wearing white suits with blue blouses: Japanese-American, white, and black women. They rose to report on their chapter's progress, to express their appreciation and determination to accomplish even more next year. All this was done with much gusto and was met with enthusiastic applause. The theme was stated: "Let us protect world peace, sinking our roots in the great earth, as queens of the mystic law." (The word *myoho* in the chant refers to mystic law.) Two men sat in places of honor on the stage. In their speeches they spoke of women's many roles in society, in the family, and as mothers, raising the young, nurturing life. They urged each woman to take full responsibility for her life, to develop a seeking mind, to realize her own human revolution by contributing to the goal of world peace, starting with her own environment.

While she plays in the NSA orchestra, Dianne Douglas no longer works as a musician. About nine years ago she changed her mind about her profession. She increased her chanting practice to three hours a day in the effort to find out what she wanted to do next in her life. She thought about the public relations business, interviewed people in the field, and got an entry level job in an agency. After that, as if she had achieved a particularly beneficial rhythm, several jobs at computer companies followed, each one better than the last, culminating finally in her excellent position at Computerland Corporation. She credits her chanting with the opportunities that opened to her. But beyond that, she attributes to her practice an inner sense of happiness and confidence and a feeling that her life is making a difference towards creating a more peaceful society and world in which to live. Dianne's husband, Sean, also practices Nichiren Buddhism.

In the lobby of the Herbst Theater at the Ninth Women's Division General Meeting, I met a woman named *Fay Christian* and took her picture with a Japanese-American woman named Tomiko Costello. Several months later I visit Fay in her apartment in the Ingleside section of San Francisco, a few blocks from City College.

Fay is a generously proportioned, thirty-seven-year-old woman with rich brown skin and a ready laugh. She meets me at her door and takes me into her living room where African carvings stand on the mantel. Opposite them is her Gohonzon in its black case, a small altar with candles and incense holder arranged before it. We sit on the couch before the picture window.

Born and raised in Seattle, Fay lived for nine years in New Jersey before moving to San Francisco, where she works as an investigator for the Equal Employment Opportunities Commission. She lives here with her husband and her teenage daughter, who is also a participant in NSA.

Fay remembers that when she was first approached by a new San Francisco friend in 1980 about Nichiren Shoshu, she thought, "Oh here's another Moonie group." But after hearing out her friend, she became interested. The word *Buddhism* caught her attention, because in Seattle she had lived near a Buddhist temple and had been curious about it, and she remembered as a high school senior, while researching an essay on world religions, that she had read about Nichiren Shoshu.

At her first NSA meeting, which she found through the community center near her (NSA maintains such centers in many neighborhoods), she was impressed at how friendly everyone was. "I went to that first meeting and I was hooked," she says. With regular chanting, she found that certain aspects of her life began to shift.

"There are things that change in you that sometimes you are not even aware of until someone else mentions it to you," she says. "For instance, I grew up being deathly afraid of the dark. I would never admit it to anyone, even to myself. I spent a number of years going back to night school, and I never got past the first month. I would always drop out, because I was afraid to go out in the dark. I received my Gohonzon April 28 of 1980, and that following September I went back to school, I went to City College. I guess it was October or November that we had a blackout in this area. I had parked my car in the reservoir across the street. Well, naturally all the lights were out, there and on the campus. And I had walked completely through the reservoir and was walking to the other side of the campus when I realized that *it was dark!* And I wasn't *afraid!*"

Fay chants one hour in the morning and one hour at night and sometimes participates in activities at the community center. Her husband, who does not chant, is supportive of her practice, she says. At first, however, her daughter very much opposed Fay's taking up Buddhist practice. She had gone to a Catholic school in New Jersey and was frightened by this exotic religion.

"When she found out that I was going to become a Buddhist, she was very resentful, because she saw it as some type of cult," Fay explains. "Later she told me she could just imagine me drawing all the money out of the bank and moving out to live in some commune. After a while our relationship started to change, it got real bad. And a lot of it had to do with her opposition to my practice, even though I wasn't forcing her to do anything. Our relationship deteriorated so rapidly, and it got so bad that my daughter had a real crisis. Naturally afterwards we were seeing a counselor on a weekly basis. And in the very beginning I didn't see it as part of *my* karma or *my* problem. This was all *her* problem. 'Cause I hadn't changed anything, I hadn't done anything! And even as we were seeing the counselor the situation just kept getting worse and worse. We had gotten to the point where we would actually *fight*."

Fay tells about how she eventually decided to use her Buddhist practice to help with the problem.

"The day that I decided to challenge that, to go to the Gohonzon, we had gotten up that morning and I had told her to do something and she didn't do it, and then later on I said something to her and she laughed at me, and I hit her. And she turned around and laughed at me again. And I hit her so hard that second time that it knocked her glasses off, and she fell to the floor. Well, she got back up and laughed at me—like, you know, 'You crazy fool!' And when I came to my senses I was choking her."

She sits forward tensely, her dark eyes on mine, as she describes what happened next.

"I got up, I walked away, she left the house, and I said to myself, 'Well, I know what I'm going to do about this, I'm going to leave both the child and my husband and forget the two of them ever existed!' I said, 'But before I do that, I'll go to the Gohonzon and chant to be able to find an apartment today.' " She laughs at herself. "Well, when I got down to do my morning prayers and I started to chant, I *didn't* chant for that. I started asking 'Why is this happening?' And it was then I began to realize how I had felt about *my mother* when I was growing up. And it was the exact same thing, only my *daughter* had the courage to stand up to *say* the things *I* had *felt*—she was verbalizing hers while I had always held mine in.

"And from that point on, things began to change. That evening was the first evening in months that she had come home and said, 'Hi, Mom, how was your day?' After what happened that morning! And the following week when we went back to see the psychiatrist, she couldn't *believe* the change in the two of us. And by the second meeting, well, I had noticed the change in my daughter's appearance, I mean she looked like a completely different person, she looked much happier. By the time we went to that third meeting, the psychiatrist said we didn't need to come back."

She relaxes into the couch cushions now, smiling broadly.

"From that morning on, I had continued to chant that we could get closer, and within almost a month's time our relationship was better than it had ever been. And maybe a month or two after that my daughter asked if she could go to a meeting with me, and I said, 'Sure, if you want,' and from that point on she continued going to meetings. Then she decided to join, herself. And she's been practicing ever since. She uses the practice, If she's having a problem at school, or with a friend, understanding homework—she takes it to the Gohonzon. We've been very close ever since."

I go to my friend *Dayna Lea* to ask what it is about the Nam-myoho-renge-kyo chant that is so stabilizing and energizing. She is an Oakland resident whose fuzzy hair and patterned headscarf, bare feet, and silver toe ring do not fit the stereotype of a Nichiren woman. A Jew who grew up in Los Angeles, Dayna looked approximately this way for the five years she was an NSA participant, and her appearance aroused some disapproval among the more straitlaced members.

"Nam-myoho-renge-kyo is a powerful mantra," she says. "How it was explained to me was, it puts you in harmonious vibration with the vibration of the universe. I got that. When I chanted I could feel I was in sync. So I think that's why it works, and why it has these effects."

For Dayna as a naive teenager, Nichiren Shoshu Soka Gakkai offered a place to belong.

"It was in the late sixties. Everything was up for grabs, and I wasn't prepared to grab at anything that was there. I wasn't into doing drugs or being sexual, so it was kind of a safe harbor for me. And the idealism—you know, We do this and we're going to achieve world peace. And it was exotic, because at that time it was still primarily Japanese and it was still very small, with a lot of access to the Japanese leaders. I liked that part a lot.

"Also," she says, gesturing broadly, "I wanted to be *happy!* I was pretty depressed. My energy was low. Nichiren was all rah-rah. Some people chanted for cars and jobs and places to live. I just chanted and wanted more the emotional rewards."

"Did you get them?" I ask, and Dayna nods vociferously.

"The first thing that happened to me: I had always had this tremendous fear of death, all my life. And the first real proof that Nichiren worked was that that fear was lifted, really fast. I think it was, basically, getting into the Buddhist philosophy, just of the cycle of life and death; there was some quality of what I was being given that alleviated the sense of just the void where there was no return. So I didn't feel as terrified. That's the first thing I remember. I think that's what kept me there. That was a real gift to me."

Dayna plunged into the activities in the young women's division. "I joined the young women's fife and drum corps. Those long-suffering Japanese women! They were so sweet, those young ones: they would teach us. I started out on the piccolo, and I moved on to the flute. We'd have parades, and we'd wear these little marching uniforms with boots and the whole thing. I think it was Sunday morning that we would practice. It was so far from my sense of who I was that it was just ludicrous. And I couldn't play the piccolo, so I faked it most of the time. I hated the uniforms and marching in the hot sun. But there was something in it I must have liked, because I did it. It was the idea of unity. Many bodies, one mind. Doing something together for the higher good. And the showing, I mean, if we did a parade, it was to affect the whole community, not just for us. So it was participating in this cultural thing. And it was developing young women's spirit—there was a lot of stuff about spirit."

Dayna was strongly involved in the recruiting efforts of Nichiren. She tells about it with great zest. "We'd go through these campaigns in which we'd have five meetings a night. Like in Westwood. We'd have a meeting, and we'd go into Westwood Village, round people up, go into movie lines, people walking down the street, they'd get into our cars with us, they'd come to meetings, we'd have a half-hour meeting, you know, just rah rah rah, and sign them up and hit the streets again.

"It was a good time to do this, because there was so much burnout from drugs, we'd get a lot of hippies in. The Japanese liked that, cleaning up the hippies."

How many of those people actually kept on practicing? I want to know.

"A lot of them *did* hang in. . . . It all depends on how you take care of them and help them practice. The really hard part is learning the daily worship service, learning how to chant the sutra. The discipline is a lot of work. People who have trouble with the sutra have a hard time hanging in, because that's a drag if you can't recite it."

The "very fifties Midwest morality" of Nichiren at that time in Los Angeles was severely challenged when a number of lesbians began to join, Dayna says. She herself came out as a lesbian while she was an NSA member. Still, the leaders saw her as promising, and she went three times to the head temple in Japan. While she was there on her third trip, she received news that her mother had been killed in an automobile accident.

"God must have gotten me to Japan," she says, "because I don't know how I would have handled her death if I hadn't been there practicing. It was really a gift to be in that setting and have that kind of support and just really focus in on the practice."

Not too long after that, however, she began to think of stopping her involvement in NSA.

"I went from feeling 'This is where I'm going to be for the rest of my life and isn't it wonderful, I don't have to make any decisions' to pretty much burning out. When I finally left, in 1972 when I was twenty-two, partly I was starting to hear about feminism and looking at the organization and what was going on in terms of the chauvinism and how women are treated. Like, know your place and serve the man and be the pillar. Women are the pillars to hold up the man. But it was mostly that I couldn't play the game anymore and wanted to know what else there was of me besides being a Buddhist. So that was the final straw."

Dayna emphasizes that since she left there have been changes in awareness of gay people and the roles of women, but that in those days it was still pretty traditional. "Eventually I asked too many questions," she says. "They always used to tell me not to ask questions. I always wanted to know *why.*

"Something else that was hard is that they say anything but this kind of Buddhism is heretical. I mean, Christianity and other stuff were kind of like discounted, but they *totally* discouraged exploration into *any* other form of Buddhism. They were all 'less than' and heretical and would harm you. They would tell these horror stories of people who went into Buddhist temples and this or that thing would happen to them. They made it so very terrifying that it took me a few years after I quit to open to exploring other forms of Eastern philosophy."

But she tempers her objections.

"I don't regret those years at all. My involvement was probably very wise because I wasn't prepared to deal with the kinds of decisions that I might have had to make for my life, and I think it really protected me until the women's movement came along so that I'd have someplace to go. I got a lot out of it in terms of learning how to relate to people. It forced me out of myself. To go talk to total strangers on the street, you know . . ." She laughs, and mimics, smiling sweetly, " 'Do you want to come to a Buddhist meeting? Have you ever heard of Nam-myoho-renge-kyo?' Listen, I tried to recruit Barbra Streisand! I swear to god, I did!"

Dayna plays with her bracelets, ponders for a time, then says, "The basic intention is good. It's a positive thing for people who need to feel they belong somewhere. It gives a feeling that you're belonging and really participating, and *doing service*."

NOTES

1. Information about the Buddhist Perception of Nature Project can be obtained from Dr. Chatsumarn Kabilsingh, Faculty of Liberal Arts, Thammasat University, Bangkok 10200, Thailand.
2. Fellowship of Reconciliation is an international organization that opposes war and works to achieve a just and peaceful world community.
3. Information about the Buddhist Peace Fellowship can be obtained from P.O. Box 4650, Berkeley, CA 94704.
4. Carol Gilligan, *In a Different Voice: Psychological Theory and Women's Development*.
5. E. F. Schumacher authored *Small Is Beautiful, A Guide for the Perplexed, Good Work, The Future is Manageable, Roots of Economic Growth*, and other books.
6. In the Revolutionary era in this country, Committees of Correspondence designated the secret grass-roots political groups all over the colonies. The term has been used several times since then.
7. Buddhists Concerned for Animals is located at 300 Page Street, San Francisco, CA 94102.
8. These figures from *Sexual Exploitation: Rape, Child Sexual Abuse, and Workplace Harassment* (1984) by Diana Russell; and *Child Sexual Abuse: New Theory and Research* (1984) by David Finkelhor.

9. Frida Kahlo was a celebrated Mexican artist known for her series of powerful and sometimes macabre self-portraits. Her name was originally spelled Frieda, as Judith has it.

10. Information from *Nichiren Shoshu Sokagakkai* (Tokyo: The Seikyo Press, 1966).

11. All quotes from the NSA *World Tribune*, Monday, January 13, 1986.

Ruth Klein

Catherine Parker

Jenny Hoang

Joanna Rogers Macy

Peace Pagoda under construction

Peace Pagoda dedication ceremony

Paula Green

Lisa Groves

Sister Jun Yasuda—"Jun-san"

Terri Nash

Sister Clare Carter

Charlene Spretnak

Bonnie Del Raye

Michele McDonald

Jo Palumbo

Dianne Douglas

Tina Turner

Nichiren Shoshu Soka Gakkai
women's chorus

Tomiko Costello and Fay Christian

Dayna Lea

7.

Living Together: The Integration of Buddhist Practice with Family Life, Job, and Community

One could easily devote a whole book to the discussion of the relationship of Buddhist practice to the rest of a woman's life: her responsibility to children and spouse or lover, her search for right livelihood, her experience of living with or otherwise relating to a particular sangha. Grappling with these issues is seen by many women as the essence of their practice. The changes which arise as women learn to coordinate their practice with their family responsibilities are crucial to the evolution of American Buddhism, for in better accommodating the needs of mothers, Buddhist groups and centers will tap into a source of vital energy and humane direction, and allow for the full flowering of female gifts within Buddhist experience.

Problems for American householders in integrating practice with their daily lives often stem from the male monastic root of Buddhism. While groups and communities are experimenting in combining monastic practice with lay life, problems continue. Some mothers are bitter because their needs are not addressed by the male-biased groups with whom they've practiced. Some women who plunged deeply into practice when their children were small now feel guilty for having neglected their family responsibilities; others chose to sacrifice formal practice and sought to realize mindfulness within the performance of their domestic duties and their work to earn a living. A few women speak of motherhood as a path in itself.

The history of Buddhism in this country is one of communities comprising both men and women in contrast to the Asian model of all-male monasteries. As Maurine Stuart Roshi pointed out, Zen koan practice in America began with Mrs. Alexander Russell and her family in their own San Francisco home. In the Buddhist communities that came together in the succeeding decades, women are equal in importance to men, often functioning as the prime organizers and maintainers of Zen, Tibetan Buddhist, and Theravada centers. These communities, as they exist today, may consist of laypeople who come periodically to the meditation center for sittings and retreats with a particular teacher; they may be ordained people gathered around a teacher, who live together, pursue their practice, marry, and raise families. Communities take many forms from city centers to remote country retreat houses, from semimonastic situations to family centers. In all of them women are central; women often run the physical plant and take care of residents and guests, but rarely are encouraged to assume religious leadership.

The communities presented in this chapter are quite distinct from each other, and the women in them have different concerns and perspectives, but the major themes of care for children, search for right livelihood, and the insistence on acknowledgement and dignity in relating to a group are shared. All but one of the communities presented here are headed by male teachers of Asian background; the exception is run by a team of American male and female teachers. The Buddhist centers founded and headed by women are presented in "Lighting the Way" and "Nuns, Monks, and 'Nunks.' " Male-run centers are much more numerous, given the history of Buddhism in the United States. This reality can be viewed as problematic or may be seen as an opportunity for women to draw from experience in these centers to create visions and plans for the institutions they may someday build.

The tension between monasticism and the demands of job and family arises in Buddhist centers as people test how best to manifest the heart of Buddhist practice while honoring lay experience and responsibilities. Questions of celibacy versus relationships come up. Strict hierarchies exist in most centers, operating both to empower and to repress. The issue of how to manifest Buddhist practice in the earning of one's living absorbs many women. Lesbians encounter mingled acceptance and prejudice in the groups with which they practice. Residents and participants in these centers are testing Buddhist practice in the crucible of daily life, and in the process they are shaping the direction of American Buddhism.

MOTHERS

Central to the process of the acceptance and evolution of Buddhism in this country is the experience of women with children. In this new practice that involves laywomen and families, Buddhist groups are finding ways to accommodate the needs of mothers, to honor the special experience they gain in nurturing small human beings. While a common Buddhist prescription for the awakening of loving-kindness is to think of all beings as one's children, in the actual practice of Buddhism in this country so far, the perspective of women with children has rarely been valued. Often, by virtue of the structures set up in practice situations, mothers have been denied access to formal training, have been forced to choose between their duties with their children and their spiritual quests, and have sometimes been treated as lesser beings whose struggles and needs were irrelevant to Buddhist practice.

In the following section, mothers speak of their attempts to pursue their practice while raising their children; they admit to the emotional fallout from this usually frustrating endeavor, and describe the particular quality of their spiritual practice that resulted. Mothers' voices echo throughout this book and are gathered especially here in order to emphasize the importance of this phenomenon for American Buddhism. Undoubtedly, many mothers who were sincere Buddhist practitioners gave up their practice in the face of overwhelming stresses and lack of support from their sanghas. The loss of these women's input and wisdom from Buddhist groups is incalculable. On the other hand, the difficulties experienced by the women who persisted caused them to develop a particularly realistic and quintessentially Buddhist relationship to their spiritual practice. Both those who gave up their practice and those who persisted have much to teach us.

Jan Chozen Bays, who was a priest and teacher at the Los Angeles Zen Center, admits, "One thing I feel now is that I wish I had spent more time with my children when they were growing up. In my very intense drive to go into Buddhism as deeply as I could, to practice in a traditional way, I really feel I missed something with the kids. Now I'm trying to make it up. I don't feel horribly guilty about it, it was what happened. My children, interestingly, do not feel they were neglected. Kids are sometimes happier to have their parents out of their hair. But I do feel for a few years I really did neglect my family. I don't know if I would do it again. I probably would."

Jan Bays's choice was necessitated by her being in a relatively traditional Zen center set up on the basis of Japanese rules, an institutional setting in which she found it difficult to fully attend to mothering while passionately pursuing a practice.

"In Japan, if you have children," Jan says, "you wait until they're all gone and you're eighty and then you enter the nunnery. But I was too impatient to do that. This drive was too strong within me, and so I had to plunge in.

"We did some things that worked fairly well. We had three families with children, and for a sesshin we would combine those children, and one mother or mother-and-father pair would take care of the kids for the duration of the sesshin. The other two families could sit. Some kind of communal child care is good. I think it is too hard for women with this very deep need to put it off until after their grandchildren are grown."

Dahlia Kamesar, who lives in San Francisco with her husband and small son, speaks of the stresses placed upon a Zen family both in a city center and in a country monastery that emphasized monk, not lay, practice.

"My husband Jack and I started sitting one afternoon a week, two afternoons, three . . . at the Page Street Zen center here, which is a ten-minute drive from home, and gradually—it had to be slow because we had a house and a child—we increased our involvement, until five years later we were yo-yoing back and forth to Zen center from here. Going to meditate every morning, going to lectures, going to meals—sort of not-there and not-here, trying to bridge our lives, our work, and friends with a residential Zen community, and never quite being able to bridge it." They were raising his child from a previous marriage, and soon she gave birth to a child of their own. "Then it worked out with our children that we could go to Tassajara [Zen training monastery]. Our older son was graduating from high school, and our younger son was four. Jack went first for a three-month practice period, then I joined him and we were there for two years with our four-year-old."

A dark-haired, green-eyed woman in her late thirties, Dahlia speaks with tremendous animation about those years at Tassajara.

"The people on the staff at that time were not parents. For the first three months my son Elan was the only child there, and then a boy two years older than he came. The way Jack and I practiced was we took turns watching him, and also the cabin was right by the zendo and we'd leave him there. He has a lively imagination, and he just spent lots of time alone playing with his Leggos and drawing mandalas.

"I would read books to him. The reading I did with him and the time I spent with him was very high quality time. And I appreciated that. But I couldn't quite follow the schedule of meditation sessions and work. [The schedule at Tassajara is a rigorous monastic routine, with little free time or flexibility.] We were sort of set apart from the rest of the people."

"Did anyone help you with your son?" I ask.

"Well, they tried to do what they could, but nobody really understood—especially the people who were making the decisions—what it was to practice with a child there. I was trying not to ask for anything special, as a parent, from the community. We were trying as much as we could to follow the schedule. When this other woman and her son came, we sort of had a little more strength, so we pressed for some things. Then in the summer it was easier, there were more children and families."

She ponders this, her eyes thoughtful. "I wanted to participate fully in the community, and because I was a parent I was set apart. Because no one who made the decisions was a parent, they couldn't quite understand what our situation was."

The return to city life, Dahlia says, was tortuous, as there had been a dramatic change in the Zen center community's leadership while she and her husband had been at the monastery. They went to family therapy for over a year.

"We spent quite a lot of that time asking, 'Where have we been, what have we been doing?' Elan was quite traumatized by his experience there actually. He had had no peers at Tassajara and had felt a lack of privacy. When he went to school in first grade here, he had a hard time; he'd missed something. The experience wasn't good for our family, for our marriage. But also it was something we'd shared, and some commitment, something we believed in together. And when that fell away, it was, like, 'Okay, what do we share now? What can we develop together?' We're working through that."

And there was another difficult facet to the return, for Dahlia had found that she didn't want to leave Tassajara.

"I had given Jack three months to be there alone while I took care of Elan, our home, and our livelihood. Then *I* wanted to be there alone, not as a parent. So that I was really horrified when I realized, No, I was *not* alone, I could not abandon Elan. It would not have been a good decision. Elan and I were so close in our relationship. If I had stayed there and he had come back here with Jack, who was equally traumatized, it would have been difficult. But I felt really cheated that I couldn't have that time to just settle in there and be quiet and not have a child to take care of. So I didn't feel ready to come back."

Now that she has been back in the city for a few years, she is not involved with the San Francisco Zen Center. But in her job and mothering and other activities she feels that "I'm following through with my practice, of exploring *in* the world, on my own. When I came back from Tassajara, I just felt empty. You've been away, out of history, in outer space, and you come back to ordinary life. It was like gathering threads, just what would come, taking a thread and following it until I had a little bundle. And I feel very engaged now. I have a lot more energy."

It is possible to view motherhood itself as a spiritual path. It provides a rich opportunity for practice in its requirement of caring for other beings before oneself and in its focus on tasks of creating and maintaining a home, preparing food, adjusting to the constant changes of developing human beings. This vision has been articulated by several women in this book who have stated that their children were their teachers.

Laura Kwong, of the Sonoma Mountain Zen Center, came to

view her own mothering of four sons this way, not by choice but by necessity. She was just twenty-one years old when she had her first baby, and it was hard for her to give up her opportunities, her image of herself as worldly and intellectual, for a life of washing dishes, scrubbing floors, and taking care of an infant.

"At that time I felt very inadequate," she says, "because I was so anxious about being in the home and being a mother. I was active at Sokoji Temple in San Francisco in 1960, before the San Francisco Zen Center was formed, but I was not yet sitting regularly. Suzuki-roshi didn't encourage me to sit. First of all, he probably knew I had this baby. Then, another thing, on my own I felt that since it was being at home that I was afraid of, I should *stay there*. That's how I perceived it. And not because I wanted to be the model parent or anything like that: I stayed there because I experienced anxiety there. That experience was very important to me; I used that as the beginning, as spiritual initiation actually."

I am talking with Laura Kwong at the tree-shaded Zen center headed by Jakusho Kwong, her husband, in the yellow hills outside Petaluma. She is a dynamic, articulate Chinese-American woman in her late forties whose pixie-cut hair frames a face both intelligent and kind.

"You know, for some people motherhood comes real easy," she continues. "For me it didn't. I was afraid I was going to lose myself to being in this house, to being nothing but taking care of this baby. If there is Buddha nature in everything, what is there to lose? Right? But it sure *felt* like I was going to lose something! But anyway, I trusted it. Suzuki-roshi said, 'Buddha nature is everywhere.' So I felt, I have to remember that, and I'm going to test it to see if it is so.

So then I gradually learned how to do it—not meaning I learned how to do the household things—I learned how to *give up* my idea of self. Not for this baby, not for this husband, but give up so that there's something else that comes up to take care of this matter. That was my first experience learning how to give up the self."

Although with several babies and a part-time job she was not able to attend many sesshins, Laura did get up to sit in the morning and found this along with other directed activities valuable.

"Practice, meaning some kind of spiritual foundation and

meditation, was very important in how I was *able* to have a family. I felt like I did a lot of mindful practice, like going to work, being with the kids, now I do this, now I do that—moment after moment. If it were not for that, it would have been horrendous. When I was twenty-one years old with one baby, I could hardly *go to the store*, because I couldn't think straight, couldn't focus. But because of sitting and that feeling of being present or living my life completely wherever I am, it helped me to just take care of the babies, take care of the house, do the cleaning, with that feeling of devotion. And it became very easy because of that."

Sitting with us is *Sylvia Kincaid*, who lives at the Zen center and is responsible for the guest program, running the store, tending the garden, and managing the house, as well as sometimes leading the chanting. She is a forty-five-year-old woman with gray hair in fluffy waves and a gentle, quiet-spoken manner. Sylvia too is a mother, who for years lived nearby, worked at a job, and raised her children while pursuing her Zen practice here. She tells how she managed that.

"I have two daughters and I was raising them alone, and having to work outside and take care of the family and also come up here." She laughs. "All at the same time! I was just determined that wherever I was would be practice. At my work, that would be practice, at home it would be practice, and here it would be practice. So it didn't matter if I was here or not, but something kept bringing me here.

"Also that same something asked me to take care of my life— which was going to work, cleaning my house, washing the dishes, taking care of the yard. When I was supporting my daughters I mostly worked as a waitress because I could make more money doing that. So in order to bring the practice into that, I thought of it as serving, just serving without expecting anything. It made the job wonderful. I was happy to be there and happy to do it. It was the same feeling as at the zendo serving. You don't actually bow, but you *feel* the bow when you're serving."

I ask Laura Kwong what it's like to be the wife of the roshi here, and she answers earnestly. "There was a time, when we first moved up here and my husband was the teacher and all this, I was very confused by it. It took me awhile to know where I am."

Suddenly she is grinning.

"That's my practice *now*. That's my koan. Every day. Sometimes I'm yelling at the husband, sometimes I'm bowing to the teacher." Sylvia and I laugh, as Laura warms to her subject, straight-faced now but with sparkling eyes. "I'm never bowing to *my husband*, I always *scold* my husband and then I bow to the teacher. I have to keep that straight!" Finally she herself begins to sputter with laughter, and she adds, "Sometimes I scold the teacher!" And we all lean forward, guffawing.

"I used to have a very difficult time," Laura says when she has composed herself. "I have a sense of humor about it now because I think I have it pretty clear that this situation was given to me for some reason. I do believe there's a reason for whatever is given to you, in our perfect universe. I used to think of it as such a problem, but now *I* decide how to use it and not become the passive victim of other people's projections.

"When you have kids it's the same. I mean, it's a problem, right? Then pretty soon, you say, 'Hey listen, I've got four kids for some reason!' " She laughs. "So you get up and decide to *do something* instead of be in that state of being victimized."

When I ask about the participation of women here at Sonoma Mountain Zen Center, Sylvia Kincaid answers, "I think it's kind of hard to tell about women. I think if they are sincere they're practicing in whatever they're doing, but it might not come out in sitting or attending the sesshins regularly. Men have more of a one-pointed direction, women are more involved in the whole environment.

"The men are the builders and the women are the tenders. So it doesn't show as much. It doesn't come out as being spectacular. But the practice is there, it's happening, and it will show itself over time."

Laura nods, agreeing, and expands on this idea. "Although I am very grateful for the buildings that were put up by the men in the first few years we were here, right now I am very grateful for the last five years of tending. The daily life here has been more focused. Before it seemed like the men would go out and build things, but the dishes didn't get washed, the kitchen was dirty, they didn't see those things. To me, the women are more conscious. Your being here," she leans to Sylvia, "and my being here has a lot to do with it. Also the other women who have been more active. It's that tending and that daily kind of practice that I think is Buddhist.

"Now the work is all very even. There are men who cook, who dust, who work in the garden. We're talking about change between the seventies and eighties. There's a definite change. There's less of that male-female separation.

"So in that way I feel that the ongoing kind of practice here from about 1980 until now is more daily, more even, more *real* actually."

Sylvia tells what practice has become for her, over the years.

"Less of an idea of what practice is, and more of just a feeling. In some ways much more difficult, and in some ways easier. It's difficult in having to accept everything just as it is. Before, I was saying 'Not-this, Not-that, Not-that.' Now, I say, 'Everything.' And to me that's harder, in a way, because you have to get very adept at guiding yourself through all the rough spots. And easier in the sense that there doesn't seem to be any fear of getting lost."

Laura speaks of her own deepening process, which she links to living in community.

"Some of the change is life experience, but then I value the opportunity for being in a community practicing together. Living in a community, practicing in a sangha daily, it's the irritation that to me has been major in the changes I've experienced in myself as a person and in my practice. It *had* to go deeper. Irritation, disappointment, discouragement, having to work with different people and to open up to people you might not open to in your usual private life. I'm confronted with actually asking myself, 'Do I see all human beings as having Buddha nature?' You know, it's *real*, it's not a conceptual thing."

MINNESOTA ZEN MEDITATION CENTER

Minnesota is a land of wooded lakes bordering majestic Lake Superior, a territory originally inhabited by the Ojibway and Dakotah nations. French, English, and Spanish explorers mapped and claimed the area. Later, Swedes, Norwegians, and Germans flooded in to farm the land, run the dairies, log the forests. Thinking of Minnesota one sees the image of a canoe on a still lake, feels the chill of bitter northern winters; going to visit, one finds an optimistic, industrious populace.

In Minneapolis, center of Minnesota industry, education, and culture, a group of Zen students in the early seventies invited Katagiri Roshi, a Japanese Zen master based in San Francisco, to be their teacher, and they established the Minnesota Zen Meditation Center. Women played an important part in the founding of this center, and its first board president was a woman.

Now the center is housed in a gracious mansion on the shore of Lake Calhoun, one of the many lakes dotted throughout the city. A cream-colored stucco building with dark brown trim, it stands among old trees and commands a view, on summer days, of the colorful sails of windsurfers tilting on the sparkling surface of the lake, of bicyclists and roller-skaters rolling past on the sidewalk. Only Katagiri Roshi and his family live in the Zen center, although many members live in the neighborhood so that they can walk to sittings and services. The center is supported by about 120 members and others who contribute.

A certain maturity characterizes the sangha here, where some members have been practicing Zen for ten or fifteen years while raising families and working in the world. Katagiri Roshi has encouraged his students, both women and men, to give Dharma talks and take responsibility and authority in the center. He advises students, in their lectures, to draw upon their own experience, an attitude one woman finds positive and familiar. "I've appreciated his advice in telling us to speak about our own lives," says Karen Thorkelson, "because it's so similar to the wisdom we have as women. When you look at women's literature, at what women have to say, they're often speaking out of their own experience. He tells us that *is* what we have to say, both as men and as women." There has always been a strong lay practice at the center, but now that the country monastery, Hokyo-ji, is being developed, there is increasing emphasis on ordination and monastic practice. Some members resent this shift; others welcome it and are striving to understand how to manifest a monastic commitment in a Western setting.

Nancy James, one of the founding members, now in her early fifties, sits daily at the Zen center and has always found the meditation useful and illuminating, but she is not drawn to monastic practice and does not like ritual. "I'm a very practical person," she says. "It just seems kind of silly." At first there had been very little ceremony involved with their practice, but after a while, she says, Katagiri Roshi added lay ordination for his students and ceremonies for various specific occasions such as Buddha's birthday. "My involvement here," Nancy says, "is being in touch with what's meaningful to me and trying to ignore the rest, which," she adds, "there isn't that much of."

Her down-to-earth, very Western approach extends to her teacher, whom she sees in a realistic perspective.

"One of the things that attracted me philosophically about Zen," she explains, "was that the training, the techniques, the philosophy, all the things that made it a religion, were the reason a person got involved. It was not that you were following a guru. So I felt that when Katagiri died or left, the Zen center should be prepared to go on and find another teacher, just like a Christian church would. But it has seemed to me more and more that people are following individual teachers. Many people come here because they've heard of Katagiri. I'm glad they come here and I'm glad they've heard of him, but I don't want us to be in the position of Katagiri having a cult following—that if he goes, they go. The firm foundation we should be laying is the *practice*, the teachings, regardless of who the teacher is."

Some women, unlike Nancy, have ordained and are committed to finding a way to live their priest practice in their daily lives. In this endeavor, many issues leap to prominence, including such seemingly superficial questions as whether to wear robes, which when examined tap into deeper considerations of the role of the priesthood.

Joen Snyder gives her reason for valuing the robes. "I've always felt that robes were really important, because they mark you as someone who is there to give him- or herself to others, that there is someone who has vowed to stop and take care of other people. So it's important to me to be marked like that. And it's a burden to be marked, but that's the burden you bear when you become ordained. So you choose to *consciously* bear the burden of suffering."

She goes on, "Priests have been, traditionally, responsible for the transmission of the Buddhadharma from generation to generation—caring for it with great mindfulness, with great compassion and wisdom. So the priests are the caretakers of the religion. I felt such devotion for this flame that I knew I had to devote my whole life to taking care of it, not only for me but for my children and their children, and I felt this great more-than-feeling that I had to align myself with this flame and to look after it, to take care of it, to support it, to handle it."

She pauses, searching for another simile, drawing upon her own experience as a mother. "It's like a woman who sees an abandoned child in the middle of the road. Her whole being would go out to pick up that child. No mother I know could stop herself from going and giving herself to being sure this child was given the best situation. And that's how I felt. My whole being just went to taking care of that Dharma child. So that's what being a priest means to me."

From the beginning, Joen admits, she was "totally fanatical" about Zen practice, not a convenient passion for a mother of small children.

"It was very hard, because I wanted to do every sesshin and be in the zendo. I would do sesshin and run home during breaks and nurse the baby, and then run back. First I had to drive across the city, during a break, nurse, drive back, sit. I felt as if I had no choice, I was just *pulled*. My husband was very nice and understanding for years, but finally it was too much. He was a Zen practitioner too, but *I* was the one who was crazy, who was driven, not only to practice but to study. He got to the point where he hated to see me with a Buddhist book. So it was very very hard, and I know it was hard for my kids too. But I really felt like I would die if I didn't do it. I felt like I had been in the desert for lifetimes and I was at an oasis and I had to drink fast before it disappeared."

Now she has grown in her understanding of how to manifest the practice, and she expresses her experience of integrating it with the thousand tasks and frustrations of daily life. A part-time teacher of learning-disabled adults who shares in the raising of her two daughters in addition to maintaining her practice, Joen says life is simpler now that she is divorced and doesn't "have a marriage to take of." Yet at the same time she is discovering depths in her practice that do not fit her previous models. "I've been thinking lately about what this Mahayana practice means," she says, "what it means to practice as a Bodhisattva, who has vowed to save all sentient beings before myself. Zen Buddhism is very young in this country, and it seems that in the first few years of practice we became very excited and wanted to forget everything and submerge ourselves in this beautiful clear lake we found. We wanted to swim across and back again, practice our laps. And we didn't want to stop—no interference. No children allowed, no pets allowed, no husbands allowed. But at some point-–and maybe that's the *true* beginning of practice—we realized that stopping and taking care of all these difficult situations is *it*, that that's the path! *That's* the path of compassion, of wisdom."

One of the founding members of the Minnesota Zen Meditation Center is *Sekijun Karen Thorkelson*, who, while she is a priest, is very committed to her work as a Jungian-oriented psychologist in private practice and to the raising of her young son. I first read Karen's name in *Kahawai*, where she wrote an article about being in a primary relationship with another woman and the effect of that commitment on the context of her Zen practice.[1] I had been impressed by the maturity of that piece, its acknowledgement of prejudice, and its resolve to "speak up."

In Minneapolis I stay at Karen's house. We talk of many things during my stay there, and she says she has gotten the reputation as the sangha member who "talks about women's issues all the time. People make jokes about that, even. '*We* know what Karen is going to lecture about.' "

She is a thoughtful woman in her midforties who, after her initial reticence dissipates, radiates a warm nurturing quality. I can imagine that her clients find her a helpful therapist. She combines her Jungian background and insights with her Zen training in her investigation of the elements of her own life.

Both in Zen and in Jungian therapy, in the last few years, Karen has noticed a conservatism that she hadn't been aware of before. "I got into both Zen and studying Jung about the same time," she explains, "which was kind of the hippie era, and I assumed a lot of freedom in both, and a lot of openness." And I've run into a lot of conservatism in both, as they've become established in this country. With Zen too I'm seeing the conservative side and the rigid side and wondering what to do with it for myself. There are many beautiful things about Zen, and yet when it looks as if it's going to be just like the other patriarchal religions, and it's just promoting rigidity, I get really turned off. So I'm trying to get back to a place where I'm practicing out of the joy of it, just to be in it without letting it run me and without getting caught by the rigidity myself."

Karen tells me that she wants to broaden her contacts with all kinds of Buddhists, and in this effort she attended a Buddhist-Christian conference in Vancouver and the Women in Buddhism conference at Providence. After many years of extensive participation in the Zen center, as a board member and in other capacities, she now is changing her relationship to the center to incorporate new attitudes and interests.

In addition to the Minnesota Zen Meditation Center members who live in Minneapolis, a number of members live in other midwestern or eastern cities and maintain their practice by traveling long distances to attend sesshins. These people, not as tied in to the dynamics of the community, have a somewhat different view of their practice.

Many now come to attend sesshins and longer training sessions at the country property in southern Minnesota. These 280 acres are reached by driving on a rutted dirt road through thick woods, until one arrives at an open cleared area where several low structures built of raw wood stand, and small tents are pitched on the grass. This is Hokyo-ji, which consists, so far, of a meditation hall, cookhouse, and cabin for the roshi but will one day be a full-fledged monastery. When I arrive, a sesshin is about to begin, to which people have come from as far away as Massachusetts.

One woman here, who lives in New England and came of an intellectual atheist background, was leery of religion and when she first started sitting, considered that she was doing Zen, not Buddhism. "Now it's become more and more clear that it's Buddhism," *Caroline Warner,* or Cary, says. "Now I find myself, *god forbid,* a religious person, and it shocks me. It has been much harder to accept my religious direction, to let go of the shibboleths, my lifetime's encrusted assumptions, in this area of spirituality, than it was to come to terms with my lesbianism when that came up many years ago."

Cary speaks of how significant Buddhism has become to her. "Practice has become bigger and bigger in my life. It becomes an orientation to every act, every moment. Zazen is the central act of practice perhaps. Every moment is practice. Katagiri Roshi says if a peace activist comes to you and says they're putting their life on the line, and what are you doing? you want to be able to say that you offer your life and death moment by moment into the intimacy of this. Only this year have I begun to have a glimmer of what a life of practice means. And it feels right to me. It's terribly hard to keep that attitude all the time, but that's the lodestone."

The year after this interview, Cary and her longtime partner Joan Goldsmith moved to Minneapolis so Cary could study with Katagiri Roshi on a more regular basis.

Another Zen student, who comes from Chicago to sit with Katagiri Roshi, recently experienced a profound shift in her life, partly due to a deepening in her practice and partly to a traumatic event. Up until this time she had been a dancer.

"In sesshin two years ago," *Judith Ragir* tells me, "I had one of the deepest experiences I've had, highest or deepest, I don't know, but it was a very changed experience for me. And I went back home to Chicago and the next day I got raped. Dealing with that violence deepened the experience I had the week before. So I really felt totally changed by the combination of sesshin and then having this rape experience.[2] It cracked my world open. The whole structure changed. And then I came for my first four-week training period, and I really healed up a lot about the trauma of the rape, but also it was then that I realized that my world was completely broken apart by these two experiences and if I wanted to change my life now was the time I could do it, because it was already in total shambles. So that's when I stopped dancing and made a deep commitment toward Buddhism. And then I asked, 'Well, what's right livelihood now?' And that's when I went to acupuncture school. It was a lifestyle issue. I needed an occupation that was conducive to Zen life. The lifestyle of a dancer wasn't conducive, for me. Basically acupuncture is from an Asian point of view and is much closer to what I'm doing here. I wanted something where I could be quiet. And now, when I'm working on people, especially if I'm using my hands, I feel in my body exactly the same as when I'm doing zazen. So it's just like continuing my sitting practice."

Perhaps because she has been distant from what she calls "the womb of the sangha," her practice has been quite eclectic, including therapy and Alcoholics Anonymous experience. She searches out female teachers and is grateful for the periodical *Kahawai Journal of Women and Zen*. "I just feel very strongly that I want and need women who are ahead of me to be there for me too," she says. "Not only my male teachers. I think Katagiri is really terrific. He's not real gender-y. He's very feminine, and very male, he's both things. Although I haven't been in the daily life of the sangha. I might have a different relationship with him when I move here. But I don't have very many good examples of women who own their own power but are also extremely gentle and compassionate. Sometimes I get afraid of my power, or afraid of who I am, and then, when I'm afraid, that's when I start doing things to undermine myself. Then I see a woman like Pema Chodron, who can go up in front of a group in her orange robe, full of the Dharma, not back down, and yet she's so gentle and funny. I just did a three-day sitting with her at Dharmadhatu in Chicago. I would go out of my way to sit with her. I checked out Toni Packer when she came to Chicago. I always go and see them if they're women, to see what it's like." And, she adds, a lot of the women here at the sesshin are very important to her, of equal value in her life as the women teachers.[3]

The Minnesota Zen Meditation Center has given American women an opportunity to practice Zen in a receptive environment with a scrupulous and sensitive roshi. No hint of scandal has ever attached to Katagiri Roshi: his students trust him implicitly and benefit both from his teaching and his example of deep practice. The Zen center offers a setting in which the relationship of monasticism to lay life is vividly at issue and is being tested by priests and laypeople alike.

INSIGHT MEDITATION SOCIETY

One of the proudest and more tragic struggles for religious freedom took place in Massachusetts, where in the Puritan colonies of the late seventeenth century women spoke out, challenging the authority of the church and its ministers, calling into question the ascendancy of their husbands over them. Anne Hutchinson took her authority to preach from God himself, without reference to the male ministers who surrounded her, and when she was brought to trial for heresy, she asserted that God had revealed to her that the clergy of Massachusetts Bay were not competent ministers. In this female insubordination she was joined by other brave and inspired women. Not isolated eccentrics, these religious women represented widespread female dissent against the strictures of Puritan life.[4]

The women at Insight Meditation Society benefit from this heritage, and they live in an atmosphere of free thinking and experimentation nurtured in nearby college towns Amherst and Northampton. In the countryside outside the little town of Barre, Massachusetts, among green fields, picture-book red barns, and old stone fences, the Insight Meditation Society found an unlikely home in a former Catholic monastery. It is a distinguished red brick building with white columns at its entrance, set on a sweeping lawn. This building and its annex, a concrete block dormitory, can accommodate over a hundred people for the Vipassana meditation retreats offered regularly.

Insight Meditation Society was the first Theravada Buddhist center of its kind: a retreat center for the teaching of Vipassana meditation by many different teachers of varying backgrounds. That it was founded not by an Asian master but by young Americans allows for a kind of equality and flexibility not usually present in other Buddhist environments. The center is run by a board of directors, a number of teachers working together, and a rotating staff. Visiting teachers also come to lead retreats. The only hierarchical distinction is that between staff and teachers, two groups whose interests sometimes conflict. Some decisions at IMS are complicated by the relationship of the institution to Asian Theravadin teachers who come to teach, and whose strict asceticism and orientation to women often conflict with American mores.

IMS has become an important place for women to explore their relationship to spirituality, with Ruth Denison having given its first women's retreat in the late seventies. Later, teachers such as

Christina Feldman and Michele McDonald offered regular women's retreats for a time, and Christina leads a family retreat, which includes children. Group therapy is available to the staff members some months out of the year. Most staff members say that besides being provided with an excellent environment for meditation at IMS, they have been encouraged to relate as honestly and deeply as possible with other staff members and teachers.

While the board deals with financial matters, the "guiding teachers"—Joseph Goldstein, Sharon Salzberg, Jack Kornfield (who has moved to California and is founding Insight Meditation West), and Christina Feldman—are responsible for implementing the teachings within the context of student and staff life at the center, for keeping the center aligned with its stated purpose and vision, and for guiding IMS activities outside the center. IMS regularly hosts other teachers such as Ruth Denison, Christopher Titmuss, Jamie Baraz, and Michele McDonald. Periodically, Eastern teachers such as U Pandita and Munindra, both men, and Dipama, a woman, are invited to teach. That many teachers having different training and styles of teaching work together here distinguishes IMS from other centers. All the teachers meet together annually to share their ideas and experience with practice and teaching.

Ten to fifteen people at a time work on the staff at IMS. They are responsible for the day-to-day operation of the center. Using their understanding of the Dharma as their reference point for living at the center, they are committed to supporting the intensive practice environment for the yogis (meditators), to supporting each other in their own practice, and to working with the visiting teachers.

In the world of Vipassana meditation, IMS, or "Barre," as it is often referred to, is known as one of the major places to go for retreats, especially for the three-month course held each autumn. The IMS community is comprised of hundreds of people who come from all over the U.S. to meditate, as well as the teachers and the staff. As the usual length of time for a person to serve on the staff is one year, probably most of the staff members I mention here have moved on and been replaced by now. This very transiency is revealing of IMS, and while I do not know if this particular group of staff members is representative, I trust that the issues they bring up reflect the ongoing concerns of the women of successive staffs.

Among these is the issue of sexual activity in the meditation center. People participating in retreats at IMS are asked to remain celibate for the duration of the retreat, and staff members are also asked to refrain from sexual activity in the retreat center. Since the opening of IMS, the rule regarding staff has been periodically challenged and has recently been the subject of meetings of staff, teachers, and board members. "It's an issue that has required many hours of meetings," says *Jeanne Ann Whittington,* one of the managers. "It finally came down to an unanswerable question: Does sexual activity by staff members have an effect on the atmosphere of safety and simplicity that we want to provide for retreatants? Even after hours of discussion, some felt it mattered and others felt it didn't. But since the guiding teachers felt strongly that the rule should be maintained, we finally decided to take a new tack on the issue, look for a way that both sets of needs could be met—both the guiding teachers' decision to maintain celibacy in the main building, and the staff's need to have freedom to make choices in their personal lives. We undertook a brainstorming process that resulted in the creation of a number of staff living spaces outside of the main building, and we also set aside some reserve funds for new construction. It was a process that brought up a lot of strong feelings, but ultimately I think we did a good job of finding a creative solution that respected all the major concerns."

An added dimension in the approach to problems like this is IMS's strong ties with Asian Theravadin teachers, whose views must be considered. When IMS seeks to define itself, one of the pressures that is exerted from the conservative side is the necessity not to alienate the Asian teachers.

Among the women generally there has been strong reaction to the Asian teachers and to the monks who sometimes stay at IMS. The monastic rules create a strict hierarchy and specifically prohibit certain kinds of contact with women, making for inconvenience; but more important are the attitudes from which these rules stem, which view women as evil temptresses, to be avoided. Theravadin monks are adherents of the most ancient lineage, be-

fore the changes in Mahayana doctrines described by scholars Jan
Willis and Diana Paul. Particularly women who have known only
the American version of Theravada Buddhism are shocked to encounter its Asian misogynist character.

Julie Nelson tells of her experience of the Burmese teacher U
Pandita when he taught at IMS. "I found it difficult to connect
with him. I was very resistant, because he's so traditional. I could
hardly listen to the talks. After one of his talks the women all
came out and said, 'We have to have a meeting with him. Let's
schedule one, to talk about women.' He had told some story about
a monk who was being seduced by all these women. It was very
negative, like who are these women up there *seducing this monk?!*
So we met with him, and we addressed our issues. Essentially what
he said was, 'It's one of those times where if your practice is deep
enough, it doesn't make a difference if you're a man or a
woman.' "

She pauses, frowning. "It's this attitude of 'Stay away from
women, don't touch them, don't look at them, they are hindrances'—so how could we feel good about ourselves under the
tutelage of something like that?!"

Carol Tierney, a cook, says that her experience of the retreat
with U Pandita was devastating, even though she found "a lot of
beauty" in the man personally and enjoyed serving him his meals.
It was what U Pandita represented that repelled her.

"When I went to his talks, I'd go in and I'd try to sit up straight,
and I'd find myself quivering, I was just overcome by these trem-
ors. The attempt to focus on the sound of his voice speaking Burmese sent these waves of revulsion through me. Something about
the intensity of the effort, I think, is what brings it about. But
there was also a lot of intense aversion to what he represented: to
the message, to the centralization of authority. U Pandita puts out
a message that, in crude form, is 'Life is bad, the body is gross, get
out of it as fast as you can. Do this practice and it'll get you out.'
The little experience I have of the very rigorous form that he
teaches, I know it is very deep, capable of probing layers of psychological conditioning. And so I respect that. But coming from
the cultural background that he does, he couches the message in
what seem to me very crude terms. To some extent I think he
feels that way himself, and in another way I think he talks down to

people. The message is, do this technique and you'll get it, just march along like a good soldier looking neither right nor left."

Perhaps her instinctive aversion echoes the resistance of those early Massachusetts women to male-instigated religious tyranny. Thinking this, I am reminded of the remarks of Barbara Horn, a staff member who had come from Zen practice at the San Francisco Zen Center to IMS and was confronted for the first time with the strictures of Asian Theravadin Buddhism. (Barbara appears in Chapter 3, "Nuns, Monks, and 'Nunks.' ") She was especially appalled by the measures taken to accommodate the monks.

"One thing that happened when I came here," Barbara told me, "was that I stepped into the stone age! I couldn't *believe* what goes on in this tradition. The men monks are not allowed to ride alone in a car with a woman, so when we go to arrange doctor rides for them we have to find a guy. I said, 'I'm just not doing it. I don't believe in it, to me it's sexist, and I don't think that's what Buddha meant, and if it *is* what he meant, it's wrong!' It comes from: Women seduce men.

"Another example, the housing thing. You know if there's a woman under the same roof the monks are not allowed to lie down, even in a room on another floor. So there is some talk about changing part of the annex into a facility for them. So I said, 'If we really feel that we have to uphold this part of the tradition, then how about offering comparable accommodations for the nuns.' See, the nuns aren't bound by the same rules, they're not given the same regard in Burma, so there's no money or interest in building housing for them. I insisted that the only way we can give some dignity to it and Americanize it in the sense of being equal is that if we're going to offer special treatment for the *men*, we have to do it for the *women* too. So let's take the women to the doctor with just a *woman* driving. If we're going to *do* this craziness, be courteous all the way around, even though the rules don't say you have to be."

Insight Meditation Society has gone through many changes since its founding by Joseph Goldstein, Sharon Salzberg, Jack Kornfield, and Jacqueline Schwartz in 1975. These young people, fresh from India and Thailand, at first saw the place simply as a retreat center to which people could come to sit and then go home and form a sangha. Gradually their view of it changed. According to Sharon Salzberg, "It took quite a number of years to realize that it wasn't only that: it was an energy center and a primary focus of attention for a great many people. It was the focus of some people's *lives,* really, just as a place—as a symbol, an embodiment of what that meditation experience meant for them. So we had to assume a very different level of responsibility for it, which of course is still evolving: to try to have IMS itself express what we consider the values of the practice."

Jeanne Anne Whittington speaks of some of these changes and her role as manager. "IMS is an organization that perhaps is in its adolescence," she says. "It's definitely not just starting anymore. It has a reputation and its vision is defined to some extent, but it's also examining itself and constantly processing new input, because so many people come through here, and the teachers change, and their feelings about things develop and shift. And so we as managers are in the middle of coordinating the communication and the organizational definition between the teachers and the people who are out there in Houston, Texas, writing in saying, 'Keep doing what you're doing.' "

There are fourteen people on the staff now. With her comanager Carol Wilson, Jeanne Anne directs the operations of the staff, but there is not a boss-to-employee relationship. Staff and managers receive the same monthly stipend of one hundred dollars and are very much peers, with most decisions made by consensus. All staff members are allowed five days a month for sitting, and some staffers sit daily in the huge meditation hall or in their rooms.

The economics of IMS are of interest as they affect the staff members. The teachers, following the Theravada custom, do not charge for teaching and live entirely on donations. Staff members find it hard to live on a hundred dollars a month, even when room and board are provided. Jeanne Anne Whittington says, "There's only one staff person now who is able to live with the hundred-dollar-a-month stipend. Everybody else is either borrowing money or living off savings. You can do it, if you don't have a car, if you never go anywhere that costs any money, if you don't buy anything."

On the one hand, staffers work here in order to offer service to this place which has given them so much. On the other hand, they encounter hardships while doing it and many are in debt when they leave. Jo Palumbo, a former staff member, points out the class bias in this situation, the assumptions that one will have other resources or can afford to go into debt, when many people *have* no other resources and must earn a decent wage for their labor. This is another issue, like that of celibacy in the building, that periodically warrants a great deal of discussion in meetings. (Jo comments upon her experience from the perspective of social class in Chapter 6, "Bridges.")

Jeanne Anne, who herself completely depleted her savings while at IMS, points out that the staff makes it perfectly clear to prospective staff members that they will need either to live very frugally or have access to savings. "It's worth it to be here," she says, as IMS provides a very special opportunity to practice and a unique situation in which to be with people. Carol Tierney echoes this estimation.

"Just to be among these people who are committed to recognizing as often and as consistently as possible the truth in their experience, in having to communicate on that level with people," she explains, "just day after day all day long to have to live and work with the same people really wakes me up in ways that as soon I go and stay with my parents, for instance, I notice how quickly I slip into sloppiness in communication."

And *Ellen Mooney,* the bookkeeper, appreciates the support she finds at IMS from people who have a shared commitment to Dharma practice. "You can be afraid in a meeting and say, 'I'm really afraid to say this and I'm going to say it anyway.' It's so helpful. You are trying to be aware of what's going on, to look at yourself and understand what's true. Because everyone is involved in that questioning, situations are not so hard or solid. You know how people can get very rigid about how they want you to behave, or what they think is important? Here two people can go into a discussion, each having a different idea of what is important, and both can lose that fixedness to their own ideas. They can be open to understanding each other as well as themselves."

Teaching methods at IMS range from traditional to innovative.

The original woman teacher, *Sharon Salzberg,* is a traditionalist who attempts to transmit the teachings in their classical form and eschews a political focus.

Sharon distinguishes herself from her close friend, Jacqueline Mandell (formerly Schwartz), with whom she taught at IMS, and who resigned in 1983 because she could no longer represent a tradition that denied women equal opportunity. (Jacqueline's comments appear in Chapter 2, "Strong Voices for Change.") Sharon says she can understand why Jacqueline resigned, and goes on to describe her own very different relationship to the tradition. "A friend of mine who has been involved in the Native American church had a good way of putting it. She said there are certain people in the movement who are traditionals. Their role and their manifestation is to uphold and preserve and keep intact the integrity of the tradition. And there are other people in the system whose role is to shake things up and look for new directions and extrapolate and stretch boundaries. I have a strong personal sense of wanting to uphold the tradition. I feel protected by the tradition. In connecting to it I'm bonded very deeply to something that is 2,500 years old. When I take responsibility for someone's life, when they open up so completely to me in the course of doing meditation, I feel protected by that connection. I don't feel isolated, like I'm just a human being with my own frailties with this person, but I'm there with all my strengths and frailties plus all of that larger thing I'm connected to. So it's very important for me to maintain and deepen that bond."

We speak about the difficulty inherent in the Theravada system as it has been transmitted to this country, in that it is mostly pursued in intensive retreat settings, which are not a viable option for most people. Some instructors gear their teaching to help people realize the benefits of practice in daily life. Sharon views the issue this way: "What has been deepest in my heart, and the thing that gives me the most joy in teaching, has been trying to foster an in-depth experience, *knowing* that sometimes people have difficulty integrating it into their lives. *I* had difficulty integrating it. It still gives me the greatest joy because I think it's so unique, to be able to go very deep and still and cut through all the layers of who we think we are and come to the most profound experience possible, of breaking through all of that convention and illusion.

"People are demanding some reality-testing for this tradition and saying, 'Is this real? Is this relevant to what I face each day?' There are many teachers who are inspired to look and see what's happening in the area of integrating practice into daily life. It's an essential question, I don't want to diminish it in any way, but my teaching reflects more of where my own passion is."

Insight Meditation Society has been offering all-women retreats for years now, and some of its women teachers "extrapolate and stretch boundaries," as Sharon puts it, especially with respect to practice in daily life. There are some women teachers whose attitude to their teaching is a revelation for students used to the usual male methods. Michele McDonald is one of these teachers. *Jenny Taylor,* who works in the office, tells of an important encounter she had with Michele at a retreat. "I remember being flabbergasted when I walked into an interview with Michele one day and tried to explain, without really talking about images or thoughts or memories, that weird things were happening for me. She understood. Though I was not specific, she had an understanding from her own experience of what might be going on there. I was in tears, I was very raw, and I felt as though she could just read everything that was going on. She said, 'Okay, what's the story?' I was shocked. I had thought I was not supposed to talk about the content of my thoughts, herstory, or feelings while on retreat. I'm sure other people do all the time in interviews, but it hadn't crossed my mind that I could relate as a *human being* to her, that I could ask for a hug. I'd mainly worked with male teachers before, and that certainly wasn't an expectation of mine."

Michele McDonald is the teacher most mentioned as receptive to women's concerns and respectful of women's process. (She appears in Chapter 6, "Bridges.") She is a relative newcomer to IMS. Ruth Denison has been teaching in original and innovative ways at IMS for years, and she pioneered the women's courses there. (See Chapter 4, "Lighting the Way.") Christina Feldman also teaches from a consciousness of women and offers the women's retreats. One woman in the community who has experienced these retreats says that besides meditation they include discussion groups, music, and sometimes even dancing on the lawn, all in an attempt "to help women feel fully included in the practice and fully accepted for our value and different way of knowing." This searching for new directions is part of what goes on at IMS as some of the women students demand more flexible practice and a few of the female teachers respond by experimenting with forms that can include more female experience. In the last few years a number of women are being trained as Vipassana teachers, on the east coast, the west coast and in England, and their influence will certainly be felt at IMS.

Recently, one staff member, *Iris Marchaj,* created a multimedia slide show of the women at IMS as an assignment for a college class. It presented both teachers and staff members. In her words, "When I showed it here, I think what most touched people was the beauty of their own lives and their journey into the heart."

It is significant that IMS can tolerate disparate views, even in the area of practice. This allowing, plus the input of many teachers, staff members, and students, and the willingness to work with the issues that arise, to go back again and again to meetings in order to find a solution that will benefit most participants, offers the hope that IMS can be a Buddhist institution that continually stays current with its students' concerns and needs. Mitigating against this is the fact that while some participants push for change, the decision makers may resist it. In the opinion of former staff member Carla Brennan, the teachers were unwilling to accord issues such as sexual power abuse their full importance. Others have noted the dominance of male teachers as well as the coming into their own of some women teachers. All this is true of Insight Meditation Society, a Buddhist community fully in the throes of the process of American Buddhism's changing.

PROVIDENCE ZEN CENTER

Fifty acres of Rhode Island woods and fields surround the large gray frame and shingle building with its many wings that is the Providence Zen Center. A former nursing home, it is a hive of corridors and rooms, with a huge, dark-beamed meditation hall in a spacious wing built by the students. Outbuildings have housed a pottery shed and a sculptor's studio; and up the hill in back stands a beautiful blue-tile-roofed Korean-style temple where the few monks stay. But the pulsing heart of the building is the Dharma room where each morning the members, dressed in gray robes, gather to perform 108 bows and chant lustily in Korean and English to the "tock" of the wooden knocker. This is a center where hard practicing and communal action are highly valued, where intensive daily meditation practice together with all residents is combined with shared meals and community work.

The Zen center is home to a fluctuating number of people— from ten to fifty—including some families with children. They are led by Korean Zen master Seung Sahn (addressed as Soen Sa Nim) who has established Zen centers in twenty-two cities in this country and abroad and superintends fifteen more affiliated Zen groups that fall under the umbrella organization of the Kwan Um Zen School.

The Providence Zen Center is important to the development of women's participation in American Buddhism, because its members, both male and female, hosted several conferences on that topic. With efficiency and openheartedness, they provided the opportunity for women to share their experience and to hear and study with women teachers. The tradition of enthusiastic involvement is strong in this school; and women's participation has always been important. A number of the students are mothers, and families and children have a place here. The hierarchy, with Soen Sa Nim at its head, empowers people as Dharma Teachers and Master Dharma Teachers; members are continually working with Soen Sa Nim to develop forms rooted in the Korean monastic tradition but appropriate to American life.

Within the last two years, disclosures about their teacher have caused difficulty for some Kuan Um Zen School participants and have led to the resignation of a number of longtime students from the affiliated Cambridge Zen Center and Empty Gate in Berkeley. (A partial description of this event appears in Chapter 5 in a subsection called "Secrets.") All of my talks with PZC women took place before this crisis. Since then, the population of the Providence Zen Center has dropped dramatically with all but one family and a number of individuals moving out. The reasons for this are many and complex, having to do with the evolution of the women's needs in relation to their Zen practice and environment rather than because of the disclosures about the teacher. However, even though they live elsewhere now, their contributions give a sense of what it is and has been like to be a student at the Providence Zen Center.

First among the qualities noticeable at PZC are the industry and discipline of students, who are encouraged by the example of Soen Sa Nim to work hard and practice hard. Perhaps most strictly exemplary of this dedication is Master Dharma Teacher *Barbara Rhodes,* one of the founders of the center.

"I've spent a majority of my adulthood with Soen Sa Nim," she says. "When I first came it was just a day-by-day thing, I never thought of leaving *or* staying. It's like having a good friend, you just enjoy them every day you know them. Now he's gone most of the time, and I don't even notice when he comes and goes. That's his teaching. Clear mind is universal mind. So he said, 'Whenever your mind is clear, I'm with you.' "

She first met Soen Sa Nim in 1972 when he had just arrived from Korea, and she moved with him and a few other students into a rented apartment in a ghetto neighborhood in Providence to establish a small Zen center. Soen Sa Nim worked full-time in a laundromat and took night classes in English. He was a missionary who had come to bring Korean Zen to America. Bobby Rhodes, at twenty-four, was the oldest person in the center. She worked at a job to bring in money, washed the kitchen floor, cooked the meals, kept the books. "And it wasn't a sexist thing at all," she says, "it was that I was willing and capable of doing it. He would help cook, you know. I saw it as training. Because in all the books I had read the male monks were doing all those jobs too. The men had a lot of other things they were doing. They were students and I wasn't, so I had more time."

Now her duties as a Master Dharma Teacher include leading one weekend retreat a month, sometimes more than one, here or in centers in Lexington, Cambridge, Kansas, and other locations. Often she takes her daughter Annie with her on her trips. She also does koan interviews with students and counseling.

Bobby says she enjoys routines and regular practice. She describes the hundred-day retreat she did in 1978 in a cabin in the woods. With Soen Sa Nim she worked out a schedule of one thousand bows a day, chanting and sitting, that she followed scrupulously and that kept her busy all day. A gregarious person, she did suffer from loneliness, but nothing kept her from honoring her commitment.

"It was really important to me to stay with the schedule. I just kept it going for one hundred days. That's a significant thing, I guess, about my personality and why I've been nurtured by Soen Sa Nim. He really believes in scheduling and commitment and keeping busy. It was the kind of retreat I felt like I needed. I said I would do it and then I had to do it. That's the way I practice now. If I say something I try to follow up on it. I try to do the 108 bows each morning. Like last night I spent the night with my brother, and I got up and did the 108 bows."

For Bobby and other women at the center, motherhood has required a different relationship to the practice than is available to their childless fellow students. *Suzanne Bowman,* a former director of the Providence Zen Center, Head Dharma Teacher, and member of the board of directors, who has been associated with this center for eleven years, is the mother of two teenage boys, one of whom lives at the Cambridge Zen Center where her former husband is director. Her sons were the first children to live in the Providence Zen Center, and both of them grew up there. Now in her midforties, Suzie was thirty-one when she moved in, older than most of the people there; and she had come from living as a housewife and mother in the suburbs. Zen center life was good for her older son, she says, because he had learning problems but was accepted in the Zen center, where he could work on construction projects and have friends.

"The first priority for everyone was practice," she says. "I was the only one who wasn't in the Dharma room every night, because I had kids. I would put the kids to bed and I would hear the chanting coming up the stairs. People really felt they needed an arduous training period, and I knew that I had to do it more slowly because I had children already. None of the others were married or had children at that time. So they all sort of went through their monk period first, whether or not they actually became monks. Seven of us lived in the first center. After two years my husband and I moved next door. At first the other residents were really upset about that, but I felt at that time that the Zen center could survive financially without us and it was really necessary for our family and for the kids. We kept coming to do bows every single morning. Other residents did child care so that I could come."

Barbara Rhodes speaks of the conflicts between the demands of practice and her motherly duties. "I did a strict practice until I had my daughter, practicing every day twice a day. It was wonderful, I mean I wish I was over there right now! It's wonderful to sit down for an hour every day and to chant with people you live with. After she was born, I had to stay here with her. So it's been very hard. I still get very torn. Today I was out walking when the bell rang at seven o'clock, and I always . . . it's not settled for me at all. But I want her to know I'm available to her and to be home in the evenings. My husband and I go every morning at a quarter to five, and we have a different babysitter every morning, which is no problem for Annie, because she's sleeping, and even if she wakes up, she knows each person well. She doesn't mind that it's a different person, because she's been raised like that."

A woman with a very different perspective is *Shana Klinger,* who characterizes herself as a translator of the practice into daily life. She sees her baby daughter Mae as providing her with a uniquely powerful opportunity to practice. "For seven years I practiced twice a day and did many retreats, and I saw that my ignorance was so immense that sitting barely touched it," she explains. "Then I saw the limitation of practice. At a certain level it becomes a way to be okay. I felt I had to do something to blow my mind. Having a baby has been that for me. It puts me up against how conscious can I be in each moment?"

When I was finishing this book, Shana felt the need to communicate with me. She emphasized that while she no longer lives in the Zen center, she still considers herself a Zen student and is grateful to Providence Zen Center and to the sangha that was PZC for the "sincerity of practicing spirit which made the process of being there worthwhile." She detailed the reasons so many longtime students had left the Providence Zen Center and described some of the changes over time that the Zen center had gone through, as follows:

"Largely it [the exodus from the center] is related to the type of commitment that PZC asked of its residents and the effects that had on the community when some residents were exempted from that commitment. In offering 'hard practicing' and 'together action' [the intensely communal lifestyle set up by Soen Sa Nim for his American students] to its residents, PZC asked for a very strong commitment to shared daily practice and shared community work. Over time it became clear that the time and energy needs of families and the personal priority choices of individuals in different phases of their lives were in essential conflict with this commitment.

"Over a six- to seven-year period, PZC experimented with numerous variations in participation in order to reconcile these conflicts, but there was always an imbalance. Loosen things up for the families and the 'together action' spirit of the rest of the community suffered. Tighten things up and the families found it impossible. Around 1985–86, a natural conclusion to this tension seemed to be reached, as families left and the Zen center returned to a narrower and more rigorous focus.

"Another factor in this process was the vacuum in strong teaching leadership to take Soen Sa Nim's place as he absented himself more and more from PZC to teach internationally. Each of his American Master Dharma Teachers was sincerely growing and experimenting in their own lives with practice, but hardly willing or able to step into the shoes of such a charismatic teacher. They also lived and practiced with everyone else in the community in a fairly equal and extremely intimate way, so that their human failings and particular personality quirks were, like everyone else's, common knowledge. . . .

"Some might say that it was/is simply impossible to accommodate too many diverse needs at once in an institutional setting. Perhaps this is true. But there did seem to me to be a certain inflexibility in our mode of thinking about PZC that prevented more transformational and inspiring solutions to the conflicts about family practice. Another way of saying it is that in the absence of strong new teaching leadership, the old forms and definitions of Zen practice were stuck to with inertia. . . .

"Which brings me to what I believe to be another underlying reason for the cycle of growth and decline which I have described at PZC: the tendency of students—like myself—to have idealistic and perfectionist hopes/expectations of their teachers, their community, and themselves. This is a very large subject which touches directly on other issues such as the difficulties caused in sanghas when Zen teachers' sexual activities have been made public. To state it simply, I had many, *many* illusions and unrealistic hopes about the fruits of Zen meditation practice for myself, and similarly unrealistic expectations for how Zen teachers and a Zen community ought to be. I must honestly say that I saw the same pattern of inflated and idealistic thinking in every one of my fellow students, including the Master Dharma Teachers.

"Personally, it took me four years to even begin to own these ideas as *my* projections and desires and another two or three years to 'digest' my feelings about them. It continues to be an ongoing process for me. It is no accident that by the time I had put to rest a lot of the perfectionist ideas I had about Zen practice and Zen teachers, I was ready to leave the Zen center. I think that there was a similar sort of time bell curve for many students at PZC which coincided with the expansion and contraction of the population there."

It was out of the experience of living with family in the Zen situation that the need for a conference on Women in Buddhism was first recognized. Another motivating factor was desire for new forms and forums for sharing emotional and intellectual expression. As Shana Klinger put it, "The hierarchical setup of the Zen center and the traditional Oriental [Korean] interpretation of Zen practice did not encourage psychologizing or self-expression of an emotional nature." Ruth Klein, a resident of the Zen center for four years, noted a tendency there to suppress emotions and commented that if one wanted to be listened to it was not wise to become emotional. (Ruth Klein was very generous in helping me to get to know the Providence Zen Center. Her views appear in Chapter 6, "Bridges.") Suzanne Bowman, organizer of the first two conferences, says, "Our community had always erred on the side of not meeting our needs as human beings, in terms of communicating and expressing our feelings."

This being the case, when Suzie's marriage ended and she felt desperate, there was little receptivity to her emotional needs. She felt that she might totally collapse, that her life was crumbling, and she turned to the practice for strength, but she also needed to communicate with other women. "I was still director and I became Head Dharma Teacher—that overlapped for a month—and I started sitting with Maurine Freedgood [now Stuart] in Cambridge—because I always had jobs to do at the retreats at PZC and so I could not fully participate in the sitting. So I'd sit one retreat a month at the PZC and one retreat a month with Maurine. We started communicating more and we started a women's group, which was just incredible. As director I had people come to speak, and I had Susan Murcott come and Toni Packer, fall of 1982. That really opened people up to communicate. Susan Murcott did communications groups, in a format so that everyone was really talking together, and people liked it and decided to do it again. And we'd started a women's group at the center and talked a lot about how we hadn't been communicating. One other mother and I were always the two people who spoke up about issues, asking for more nurturing for families, and we were seen as selfish, or taking time away from the Zen center, because our Zen center had been so monastic for so long.

"So the women's conference. Here were all these people who really felt support for their practice for the first time, felt support for those issues that a lot of women feel in terms of time and nurturing relationships, children, jobs, sitting. Those were the issues that I'd go to Soen Sa Nim about in 1973 and he would sit there in interviews and say, 'Your children, your job, your practice are not separate.' I'd sort of spend two years digesting that. But the issue for me by the time I got this conference going was more communication and nurturing relationships within a practice framework. What happened was that people came from all over the place! They were sitting on their own, their husbands didn't sit, or their lovers, all those issues started coming out for people."

After Suzie Bowman had moved out of the PZC, the next conference on women's issues, in 1985, was organized by *Ellen Sidor*, a sculptor and mother who tells of her own demanding schedule in doing her art, pursuing Zen practice, and raising her two daughters.

"When I first came here I worked for the Zen center on the maintenance crew. I'm a pretty fair woodworker, I did a lot of carpentry and used to go around and order the electrical stuff.

Just helping out any way I could, just getting my feet down. And then that turned out to be physically too demanding, and I decided I wanted to get back into my carving. I've had this studio on the grounds since I came. So I've gone through cycles of being out there full-time, half-time, no time. And I'm back in the stage now where I'm trying to get out there half-time." Wanting to be useful to the community, two years ago she took on the job of editing the Kwan Um Zen School's international newspaper, *Primary Point*.

She does as much practice as she can manage, scheduling her mothering and other work to allow for that.

"I go to practice every morning, unless my ten year old is here. It's harder then, I have less energy, she's a real bombshell. She was here last week, and when she comes I usually have a friend of hers come, so I have two ten year olds living in my room plus my fourteen year old plus trying to get the quarterly out the last week of production, with people getting sick, oh it's crazy. I get up at a quarter to five every day and do bows and sitting; and I do the first three chants; and then I come over here because it's then time for my daughter to have breakfast and go to school. I like to see her for half an hour before she leaves. Then I eat breakfast and go to work at the school office. I work in the morning only unless we're in a real production whirl. Then in the afternoon if I have energy I get some sculpture work done, if I don't have other things I have to do like dentist appointments; you know, it's typical motherhood, laundry, housework, all that. Then I get to evening practice on the average of four times a week. So it's a heavy schedule."

(Since we talked, Ellen has moved to Providence so that her daughter, who goes to school there, will be able to participate in school-related activities. She has bought a house and has established a Zen group in her home.)

Under the direction of a charismatic and hard-driving Zen master, the students at the Providence Zen Center and the other centers connected with the Kwan Um Zen School have accomplished a great deal toward the introduction of Buddhism to this country. In the opinion of those who have left Soen Sa Nim's centers because of the recent revelations about his sexual behavior, as well as other related issues, Soen Sa Nim and his institutions have lost some credibility. Barbara Rhodes perhaps speaks for those who have stayed at the Kwan Um Zen School when she says, "Staying with a group and teacher can come from having patience with all of our human error. I just want to keep trying to be a part of people learning to live as a community and not leave my teacher because he too is just trying to learn the same thing. We all make mistakes. The important thing to me is that we learn from them."

SAKYA CENTER

One stop away from Harvard Square I come up out of the subway into a tall glass-enclosed station in which a huge mobile hangs, turning slowly. Outside, the intersection throbs with traffic noise. Just around the corner, I climb up to the apartment that serves as the center of the Sakya Order of Tibetan Buddhism in Cambridge.

The Sakya lamas are the most recently arrived of the representatives of the four schools of Tibetan Buddhism, ten years behind the other Tibetan teachers in their impact on Americans. In this cramped, noisy city environment, a small band of dedicated students comes to do long individual retreats. When the teachers are here, the place fills with monks and perhaps a hundred practitioners. Otherwise, about fifteen people come regularly to sittings and about thirty come "fairly often." The center recently purchased 180 acres of land in Barre, Massachusetts, on which to build the future seat of the Sakya Order of Tibetan Buddhism in America. Among the teachers who will come there is Jetsun Kushok Chime Luding, the highest ranking woman lama of the present day, who lives in Vancouver, Canada. There are Sakya centers in New York and Los Angeles, and a small group has come together in Minneapolis. A large center in Seattle was established by a different teacher than the one who established this Cambridge center.

Students here are very intent upon practice, often staying for months at a time in one of the small sleeping rooms in order to do the elaborate Tibetan Buddhist rituals. Their appetite for practice is so keen that inconveniences such as street noise are simply accepted. *Susanne Fairclough,* manager of the center, who has spent up to four months in seclusion here, admits that it can be difficult to do retreats in the city.

"One time I did it in New York City at 125th Street where the elevated goes by constantly. It was very noisy. Then I've done all the others at this center, one during the construction of the subway, when there were jackhammers going constantly, and blasting. Then there's a train that goes behind the house and in the summer there's the kids in the alley shooting off fireworks. In a way it's been good for my concentration. In the beginning I used to be very irritated by people 'disturbing my practice.' And it just blew all of that out of my mind. So I could probably sit and practice anywhere—you know, in the middle of a train station— and not be much influenced by what was going on."

Susan Campbell, a former actress and singer, was first a Zen nun before coming to Tibetan practice. While she had loved Zen, she says that within Tibetan Buddhism she feels liberated. "Nothing is denied, even wrath. Everything is usable." Now Susan does temporary office work to support herself while making Buddhist practice the center of her life. We talk about the seemingly endless repetition of actions in Tibetan Buddhist practice, in which practitioners do one hundred thousand full prostrations and other physical and verbal observances over a time period that may stretch to years. One is changed by these practices, Susan says, offering an example.

"When I first met Deshung Rinpoche [head of this center] I sat down in front of him and I saw a nice old lama, a nice old man. I liked him a lot. Nothing special. And then I did prostration retreat where I did fifty thousand prostrations to the triple gem [Buddha-Dharma-Sangha]. And the day that I was coming back to the center and I knew I was going to see Deshung Rinpoche, for some reason I couldn't wait to see him, I just felt so excited, like seeing your dearest friend after a long time or something. I walked into the room and did my bows in front of him and sat myself down, and he looked at me and I looked at him and I just *loved* him, he was my teacher suddenly. And I think that came about because of this retreat I had done. It *set* something."

When I talk with her, she has just completed a three-month retreat. I look around the little room, hearing the acceleration of a truck in the street, imagining what it was like to be in here for three months, constantly practicing. Susan did four sessions a day of 1 1/2 to 2 1/2 hours of chanting and prostrations. She says she feels very fortunate to be here. And, leaning toward me intently, she speaks of her perception of what she is doing.

"Buddhism, the more you get into it, is so slippery. There isn't anything you can really lay your hand on. It's *you!* There isn't anything outside you, you've got to find that thing. The Buddha set forth the path and you get on it and you start finding out all these things, and Buddhism starts disappearing as you begin to realize that *you're it!*"

(Since this interview, the Sakya students have closed their Upland Road center and meet in private homes, as they work to establish their new center in Barre.)

VAJRADHATU AND NAROPA

From the streets of Boulder, Colorado, one looks up at the snow-dotted peaks of the Flagstaff Mountains and the Flatirons. Here at above five thousand feet the air is thin, exhilarating, and the water in the taps comes cold and clear from a municipally owned glacier. The town's Gold Rush origins are echoed in Old West motifs in shops and restaurants. Dominated by the University of Colorado, Boulder teems with tanned young students who look as if they just pushed off a ski slope.

In this hearty environment exists one of the largest, strongest, and most controversial Buddhist communities in the United States. About a thousand people pursue their Tibetan Buddhist practice through Vajradhatu, meditating at Karma Dzong; studying Buddhism, the arts, and psychology at Naropa Institute; sending their children to Alaya Preschool and Vidya Elementary School, perhaps working at the bookstore or in other related businesses. Shambhala training offers lay instruction toward the establishment of an enlightened society. There is a flower arranging group, an archery group, a theater group, a group of translators, and even an in-house Alcoholics Anonymous group. Other centers, called Dharmadhatus, are strung from Berkeley to

Vancouver to New York City and Europe. Reigning over this elaborate complex until his death in April 1987 was Chogyam Trungpa Rinpoche, a man of great spiritual power, whose behavior since he came to this country had been consistently surprising and often outrageous.

The structure of Vajradhatu was extremely hierarchical, arranged in the style of a kingdom, with Chogyam Trungpa at the top, under him the Vajra Regent, the Ministers (all male), the Ladies of the Court, the Consorts, and so forth. Some women are fairly high up in this organization. The issue of hierarchy and its uses is often examined by the practitioners, especially women who have come from more feminist and egalitarian environments. As is always the case in Vajrayana Buddhism, devotion to the teacher is central to the practice; students scrupulously followed Trungpa Rinpoche's directions and took their inspiration from him, sometimes with unfortunate results, as in following his example of alcohol abuse and promiscuity. (See Chapter 5, "Conspiracy of Silence," for Boulder women's views on this matter.) It is considered an honor to serve as domestic help in his household or that of the Regent, and to be received "at court."

Naropa Institute was host in 1981 and 1982 to the Women in Buddhism Conference, the first forum of its kind in this country. There were surprises for the visiting Buddhists in the environment at Naropa, where most people dressed like conventional businesspeople, the men in dark suits and ties, the women in conservative dresses, hose, and heels. Many practitioners smoked and drank a great deal—shocking behavior from a traditional Buddhist perspective—and there was an air of electric energy, as if everyone had just gulped down six cups of coffee. We women who had arrived from all over the country to attend these gatherings were joined by only a few of the Vajradhatu women themselves, who, in effect, boycotted the conferences.

The conferences had been organized almost single-handedly by one feminist woman, without much support from the community at large, in which issues of concern to women were not give importance and a feminist perspective was looked upon with suspicion. While some Vajradhatu women had come from past experience of political activism, they had changed their priorities upon entering the Vajradhatu or Naropa community. As *Judith*

Simmer-Brown, organizer of the Women in Buddhism conferences, puts it, "The primary interest in this community is practice and the influence of practice in our daily life, and insofar as you are on the bandwagon about something, maybe to that extent you haven't related to your practice." (There are exceptions, notably in the area of peace work, in which a few Boulder women have become active.) Yet despite this lack of interest by the community, in the conferences themselves much significant work and communication took place. (See Judith Simmer-Brown in Chapter 2, "Strong Voices for Change," for a description of the conferences.)

The women of Vajradhatu and Naropa are extremely energetic, intelligent, and creative people whose effort to bring their Buddhist practice into all aspects of their lives, and particularly into their work, is impressive. They take their Buddhism out into the Boulder community through dance, poetry, graphic arts, psychology, care of the aged, financial counseling, administration, and other businesses and services. The bringing of inner work to its manifestation in the world engages these women, who are always experimenting with how to activate their Buddhist perspective in their art, teaching, and jobs.

In Boulder, I spoke primarily with Naropa Institute women. The community is so large, with so many types of subcommunities, that one questions whether any brief sampling could be representative of Vajradhatu as a whole. However, the comments that follow give some sense of the concerns and attitudes of at least some of the women who constitute that whole.

The women I spoke to, while not actively pursuing feminist goals, sometimes as individuals express a developed consciousness of women's issues. They have chosen not to work for their own interests in any obvious way but to trust in the wisdom of their guru in providing for their needs. In this situation mothers especially have suffered, as was made clear in a 1981 women's conference panel of mothers who said that they found little support in the sangha for their needs. Progress in this area has been made, yet single mothers still have a difficult time trying to survive, raise their children, and find time to pursue a spiritual practice. While hierarchy is strongly criticized by feminists as perpetuating oppression, some Naropa women find the hierarchical arrangement natural and conducive to spiritual growth. A few have questioned women's role in the hierarchy, wishing that women might be represented among the ministers.

One woman who came from a past of sixties political activism has changed her orientation to social action through her experience of Buddhist practice. *Lila Rich,* former Director of Shambhala Training, wife of the Vajra Regent, and a woman often referred to as "Lady Rich," says, "This *is* my political sense. Because I came to understand that in order to realize my political aspirations, spirituality had to be incorporated. Internal warfare is the first thing to work on and help others work with. It's the most direct path. I don't feel that I've removed myself from politics in any way, or social action. I think this *is* social action—I mean the whole practice, Mahayana Buddhism, Shambhala teachings."

Lila goes on to tell me, "I do have passion for women's issues. I get very hot under the collar over things that I see women suffering under, such as whether they have the model appearance physically. It hurts me a lot to see women feeling unconfident due to their body types! I'm willing to say that I have a lot of passion for those issues and other issues like that."

I mention a young single mother I spoke with today who is not receiving much understanding or support in the community, and I offer, "It would be a developed feminist consciousness that would open a space for those women and say, 'Okay we have to provide child care, we *must* provide child care, no matter what.' "

Lila answers, "I think the Vajracharya [Trungpa Rinpoche] has just got other ideas of how to get to the heart of the matter, such as giving empowerment to women, and perhaps it's that the women practitioners need to realize more compassion. It's our responsibility to help each other to practice, and if we're not fulfilling that responsibility, that means that our own discipline is weak, our realization is too shallow. Of course, then there's some kind of division of labor. I could feel like I would like to work on organizing something that would be helpful to women practitioners, but I'm not doing that, I'm doing *this* work."

"That's a telling point," I comment, "because if the organizing of something for single-mother practitioners were seen as important, somebody *would be* designated to take care of it."

Lila nods. "That's probably true." And she tells me about the Office of Health and Social Well-Being, an agency created to help alleviate problems within the community, saying that single motherhood is an issue that group will probably address.

A young mother speaks of the period when she was studying for a degree at Naropa, working at a job, raising her child, and trying to find time to do her Buddhist practice. "I've been through lots of resentment," asserts *Susan Gillis*, "about how hard it is to be raising a child alone without any support or any help, and looking at how easy other people have it. Naropa didn't offer me any kind of help. They gave a thousand dollar scholarship to some guy because he was from Canada. I was so furious. They never really gave me a break."

She shakes her head. "In Vancouver, I lived in the Dharmadhatu there for a period. It was run by these younger men, who would do things like telling me, 'You haven't met your sitting requirements for the month,' and I would say, 'You can babysit whenever you like, I'd love to sit.' It was like Catch-22. They were so arrogant! And then I got the same thing when I moved here to this community."

Judith Simmer-Brown, whose husband is a teacher at the Vidya School, has noticed a change in the past five years to more sympathy and accommodation to the schedules and needs of parents, but she points out that the community has far to go on this issue.

"There are a couple of situations," Judith says, "of Shambhala training for instance, in which Lila Rich has insisted on the scheduling of the talks and the timing so that parents with children are considered. She's probably the strongest voice in that way. The women who are single parents who've spoken up about these things have had some response. I think the delek [neighborhood group] system has been very effective for bringing information to the top. [All of Boulder has been divided by Vajradhatu into a grid of neighborhoods in which sangha members live. Representatives from these neighborhoods meet monthly to form a network of care.] The problem is that the habits of the community are very, very deep. It's going to take a while for a community this size to change and to really accommodate those things."

Poet and teacher *Pat Donegan* has met with some problematical attitudes among Vajradhatu practitioners. "I'm not a person who carries a flag, but I've never hidden anything in this community either. A lesbian lifestyle is really underground here, though there are some other women besides myself. Gay men are underground too, but they're more accepted and blatant in many respects just because of the fact they are men and they have more power in the community. Even though this community is probably one of the more liberal places, Buddhists here have more stereotypes and prejudices in their minds about gay people and women's roles than they think.

"Especially the sexism is painful, because if people are practicing you think maybe their behavior might be a little more enlightened, which is not necessarily the case. They may be working toward that and show some hint of it, but when it doesn't happen or when you find the old stereotypes cropping up, it's all the more painful."

"As a last word, I would like to say that I've never felt held back from my personal meditation practice because of the fact I am a woman, and Trungpa Rinpoche always encouraged women to go forward as much as possible and even said it was becoming time for great American women teachers of meditation. But it is the sexism of practitioners in the community and the innate trappings of hierarchical sexism in Buddhism from cultures like Tibet and Japan which have to be cut through and worked with in American Buddhism for women practitioners to truly flourish in the communities."

In regard to hierarchy, at least one woman sees it as a logical expression of the differing capacities of individuals in any group situation. *Susan Edwards,* writing teacher at Naropa, says, "In the women's movement, it was 'No hierarchy!' And we ran this newspaper, *Lavender Woman,* and I said, 'It's impossible not to have a hierarchy here. This person's better at this, and of course, I'm a leader, and I'm going to get assassinated, aren't I?' No matter what I did to play it down, everyone knew that I was a leader and attacked me for it. So, getting rid of the hierarchy's not the answer. Men didn't invent it, I decided. Hierarchy could be 'natural.' You're who *you* are, I'm who *I* am. I could be put in the wrong *place* in hierarchy, or I could not do my *best* in the place I *am*, that is true; but the fact that you're better at doing this than I am, or that I'm better than you, that's life! Hierarchy's great because it brings up those personal issues. You can really work with your particular ambition."

A less enthusiastic assessment is given by *Bonnie Rabin*, a psychologist, who reminds me, "In Tibetan Buddhism, you *do* need a teacher. The rest of the hierarchy Trungpa has certainly worked with to have it be uplifting rather than oppressive. The whole idea is that you help the next person come up. But the members of the hierarchy are not enlightened. It used to feel a whole lot more oppressive than it does now, from the point of view of women, because there have been a lot of men in the hierarchy and not a lot of women. I personally have never felt particularly oppressed by it. I think there has always been room to speak up. That's my personal experience."

Some events at which women come together at Vajradhatu along with men to communicate and share their lives are the twice-monthly Vajrayogini feasts. (Vajrayogini is one of the foremost dakinis or manifestations of the primordial feminine in Tibetan Buddhism.) Both Susan Gillis and Judith Simmer-Brown speak of this gathering as a welcome opportunity to relate to their sangha peers.

Judith says, "The Vajrayogini feasts are a replacement for personal friendship in a lot of ways, in the sense that the closest group within our community is the group of Vajrayogini practitioners. The feasts are a tremendous celebration of our connection with each other. They are given at the shrine room and last six to seven hours. That time is mostly practice, but there is a section when we eat and drink together. The whole practice is designed to be a celebration, and at the end of the feast people stay and talk. There are around 350 advanced practitioners in Boulder, people who do the Vajrayogini practice, and the feasts usually have 150 people. These feasts are the glue of the community. They provide some real ground to share. People come to town and come to the feast. It's where heart connections are made."

The Naropa women are impressive in their efforts to achieve

right livelihood by manifesting the fruits of their Buddhist practice in their work. In this endeavor they innovate, investigate, experiment, and their strength shines out most visibly.

Irini Nadel Rockwell, a dancer who came from Berkeley, says she finds the women here different from her former friends. "There's something about the women in this community, something about this combination of spiritual practice and career women that has bowled me over. There's an inner strength but an outer vitality as well. They're not people who are particularly withdrawn into their practice but rather—and I think this has a lot to do with the emphasis of our teaching, which is manifestation in the world—they see the *real* practice as being in the world.

"I have been struck by the feeling that the men in the community don't *get it* as well as the women, somehow. That doesn't mean that there aren't a lot of very strong men, but what really has hit me is how many strong women there are. This combination of inner life and outer manifestation: there are not many places for it to exist in our society."

Particularly in the fields of psychology and the arts women are active. Naropa Institute offers programs in both, as well as in Buddhist studies; and some women who work in business or social agencies also teach there. Naropa's approach to psychology, called "contemplative psychotherapy," emphasizes that the patient is basically healthy, that confusion obstructs his/her access to that health, and that psychology should work to remove those obstructions. It is not a technique as much as an attitude, says *Ina Robbins*, who is one of the psychologists working to define and disseminate this viewpoint.

Bonnie Rabin is cochair of the Sangha Care Council, which seeks to provide creative in-house solutions to family problems within the community, and a therapist at the Boulder County Mental Health Center. She tells how she brings the Naropa perspective to her work by viewing the client as a whole, healthy person and by emphasizing description in the presenting of cases rather than interpretation. "Now in the adult treatment team at the county we present cases that way. You say, 'The person is so-and-so tall, has brown hair and green eyes,' you know, on and on, and how they speak and how their mind works, and by the time you get to talking about what their predicament is, it's as if they're *in the room* and it's very lively. Rather than the traditional way—a 'thirty-four-year-old Caucasian female.' That has no life to it. And there isn't this whole hierarchical 'I'm well and you're sick' thing. It's an exchange. And that comes out of our practice too. The person doesn't feel threatened, and they begin to click into some kind of wholesomeness about themselves.

"People really are intrinsically healthy," she says and tells about her alteration of language on the Sangha Care Council. "The one phrase that I coined—I said, we are not going to use the word *problem*. We are going to use *current opportunity.* This has changed our whole way of looking at situations. The reason to use it as current opportunity—you know, obstacles arise on the path to enlightenment, so you use the obstacle as an opportunity to see more clearly. This reoriented even *our own* thinking, because we're so used to saying *problem*. So it's a 'current opportunity' and it's fun. And that change we communicated to the heads of the deleks [neighborhoods] too."

Ina Robbins brings to her clinical work an emphasis on eating disorders, conventionally a women's issue. "Eating disorders has been my specialty for about eight years now," she begins. "That has been a valuable vehicle for me to integrate my Buddhist training with my professional training, because being eating-disordered is a *practice*. There's a ritual and a sequence. Probably initially it is a mind-*less*-ness practice, but it has all of the elements of practice than can flip it into a mind-*full*-ness practice. So what I usually do with women is first have them recognize that they have access to their awareness, and increase their perception of that, and then begin to see how they can interrupt their habit patterns by using that moment of awareness as an opportunity to make a choice. And one of the things I emphasize is that growing sense of empowerment that comes from choosing. All of my work with women seems to have a lot to do with power, and how to be a powerful woman and still feel one's womanness."

Work with battered women also confronts power issues, and can arouse tremendous anger. Susan Gillis, who helps run a safe house for victims of domestic violence, and who graduated from Naropa, says of this anger and that of the abused women themselves, "I'm starting to see more and more that rage is significant as a healing stage for, for instance, battered women: being angry is much healthier than being beaten." However, in her work now she is searching for a model that will allow for compassion for the battering male as well as the battered female. "There does seem to be some kind of mutual fear of aloneness, mutual grasping for rescue, and mutual low self-esteem, in the men and the women. And it's easy to make value judgments that hitting is not nice and being hit at least you can sympathize. But I think it's really important to be sympathetic equally to the perpetrator and the victim.

"It's just that feeling that you can't solve anything by making a problem outside of yourself. I mean, there *is* a problem of violence, and I can provide shelter here from violence, but part of the problems these women are working with is their own dependency. I would like to make a *big* difference! I would like to see the *whole thing* cleared up."

Vicky Fitch manifests her practice in a particularly innovative and useful way in her work with the elderly and their families. As cofounder of Dana Home Care, Inc., she has discovered that old people are not merely vegetating but are performing what she calls "the tasks of old age," and she and her coworkers seek to create an environment conducive to the performance of those tasks. "Old age is enforced renunciation—a gradual slowing of physical and psychological processes, not necessarily a diminishment but a slowing, and it takes a Buddhist, trained in meditation, not to be afraid of that, to allow that slowing to be okay," she says.

She emphasizes that her work with the clients of Dana Home Care is not therapy but environmental care. "It has to do with the very simple truth that how your environment is affects your state of mind. With our older people we both learn a great deal about them from their environment and often care for them by caring for their environment; work with their state of mind by cleaning their kitchen, or by tidying the table in front of them. We have a mutual learning relationship."

Dana Home Care was begun in 1979 when Vicky Fitch and her present partner Ann Cason were asked to help out an old woman who was ill but did not want to leave her home. Vicky is a nurse's aide with experience in psychiatric nursing. Since their working with that first client, Dana Home Care has grown to employ 150 and include Chicago and Boston branches. Besides the usual housekeeping, meal service, and personal care offered to elders, Dana Home Care seeks to provide a sense of extended family and what Vicky calls a "constellation of care." She elaborates, "There are all these people in your world—the postman, the cashier down at the drugstore, the minister, the trust officer, the neighbor next door who will come over and do shopping. How to bring in all these people who are already connected to you karmically and teach them how to help you if you need it."

Naropa Institute is a unique teaching institution, bent upon combining contemplation with instruction, providing an environment in which students are encouraged to explore their own mental processes while engaging with the subject matter. Its departments of dance and poetics are known throughout the country, and people come from distant cities to study at Naropa, where one's usual ideas of learning or performing are challenged. Women are strong in the curriculum.

Dennis Ann Robertson, who studied at Naropa and now works in the office there, describes her experience of the class work. "Every instructor had a somewhat different way of helping you learn about yourself—whether that was Tai Chi and just making you stand in one position for five minutes at a time, or sitting meditation itself, or really rigorous Dharma study, or even music or writing classes—they all had that quality of making you look inside at your own motivations and the meaning behind the words you were putting out in response to a question. It was the first educational experience I had run into where they *didn't* want you to memorize all this stuff and then spit it back out. They wanted to know, 'Do you really *mean that?* Do you *know* what that means? Is that what *you* mean? I think that is really incredible."

Even one summer of work at Naropa can substantially change an artist's approach. Irini Nadell Rockwell, who is now director of the movement studies department, describes her first touch with the program.

"I think a lot of what Naropa did to people, and *still* does to people, is create turmoil within their life. It brings everything up. I came to Naropa thinking that this was going to be a serenely meditative community, and it was completely the opposite. It just stirred everything up. After I went back to Berkeley, in about a year I abandoned my repertory company and started to work much more personally with material and to evolve a form that I now call 'movement theater.' It is basically an improvisational form and has a lot more to do with processing and working with the full person, rather than the more stereotyped, more physically oriented idea of what a dancer is. So professionally that's the turmoil that coming to Naropa that first summer put me in."

Dance training at Naropa is different from the usual, Irini tells me, in that it is a contemplative discipline, and honoring this perspective they have also developed a dance therapy program. "The element of dance therapy that has come into the department has become very interesting because in some sense we're just as aligned to dance therapy as we are to dance as art expression. I'm very interested in an approach to movement somewhere in between the client-therapist-in-the-institution dance therapy and big establishment art dance: an approach where the process has the fruition of performance and the creation of art, but its integrity is never lost in terms of genuineness of personal expression."

We talk about the practice of mindfulness, which is basic to Buddhism, and its integration into movement work. "The biggest challenge for us as faculty is how you actually *do* this," Irini admits. "One of the classes is called Contemplative Dance, and it most specifically deals with this. We sit for forty-five minutes, then we do a personal warm-up just to get the body moving, and take that practice of mindfulness-awareness into actually moving. You can move, or you can speak, or you can do a solo or people can join you, or whatever, but it's very much the sense of being on the spot with whatever is coming up. Over and over again for students that class seems to be the place where they not only get their own processing going but also get the feeling of what contemplative education, contemplative dance, is really about, which is becoming centered and then moving."

The art of calligraphy is expressive of spiritual practice, explains *Barbara Bash*, artist and codirector of the book arts program at Naropa. She points out that calligraphy was important in all the world religions, in the copying of the texts, the communication of the sacred word. And in Buddhism it has retained its significance. But, more intrinsically, its practice takes on a spiritual significance.

"First, it's a practice of immediacy. Calligraphy is defined as 'beautiful writing.' It's not letters that are outlined and filled in, which is another area of lettering arts. Calligraphy is specifically writing that is done on the spot, immediate, not touched up. So there's a kind of life there that's essential. Because it's just *of that moment.* And this makes it beautiful, not that it's refined or smooth but just that it's fully what it is. So that's what makes calligraphers so wonderfully paranoid about what they're doing: you feel enormously exposed. Your calligraphy is like your face—*out there.* It has a quality of vulnerability in it that keeps it honest and makes it inherently a spiritual discipline, because of that exposure to oneself."

Susan Edwards, codirector of the book arts program and teacher of journal writing, speaks of her own process of beginning to teach, after coming to Naropa to help administer the poetics department.

"The students would ask me, 'What do you write?' and pretty soon I'd be teaching them—because the poetics department focus was on being a good poet—it's what I call cranked-up a little bit. I'm not interested in cranking anything up, because I can't do that, I just want to know how the person is doing; and if they have writing as part of their lives they should have something fun to do with it and they don't have to be Shakespeare. At the same time, they should respect literacy. So I started working with students and they started working with me, and before I knew it I was teaching it. The student is working on him- or herself through language. I have people do hermetic exercises, I have them write about colors, planets. I say, 'There's all these things you can learn about, and if you can mix your words *with* this, you'll know more than you did yesterday.' I have people make lists about their lives. I have people work on relationships. They are presented with a lot of different exercises."

The poetics department at Naropa is famous for its association with the beatniks, represented by its director, Allen Ginsberg, and for its extremely masculine orientation. A few women poets have survived there, one being Anne Waldman, an old crony of Ginsberg, another Pat Donegan (faculty from 1976 to 1985), whose lesbian and feminist orientation set her slightly outside the prevailing perspective. Still she appreciated Naropa and her time spent there.

Her Buddhist practice has had a profound effect on her poetry, she says, and Chogyam Trungpa Rinpoche helped her move toward more freedom in her work. "Buddhism and poetry co-emerged," she notes. "Haiku is a poetry that is in-the-moment, straightforward, simple, and has a lot to do with feelings at the same time. In true haiku you have both heart and objectivity, that balance, which I think is a life's path. Meditation practice is still a profound influence on my poetry, because it has so much to do with being centered, being clear, being vulnerable to my world. My writing is also a meditation practice."

Tibetan Buddhism took her further into the spontaneous tradition of poetry, she says. "To just cut through the conceptual mind, to be on the spot, in the moment and not worry about what comes out. Trungpa Rinpoche was a big catalyst for me. When I was at seminary [three-month training period] in 1980, during the Vajrayana section, out of the blue he just called me up before hundreds of people and asked me to compose a four-line poem on the spot. Fortunately, I was able to say something. This happened for about a week, many nights in a row. It was a very traumatic experience but also a very important learning experience for me. It was like a transmission of teachings. Not only did my poetry and teaching of poetry change after that, but also my daily life. I was able to be much more spontaneous and right there, not so self-conscious. I'm still working on it."

Her 1985 book *Bone Poems* speaks of mortality, strength, joy in poems like these:

> I can speak only
> a little while about bones
> before I am bones too.
>
> > Gandhi's bones
> > overcame
> > steel.
>
> No bones in Hiroshima
> but outline of a man
> heat imprinted on stone steps.
>
> > I remember her naked in the bath tub
> > her white breasts against white porcelain

like pure bone—
this was our intimacy.

Contradictory, challenging, home to many strong women, Vajradhatu and Naropa serve as goads to intense practice and creativity. Important for its hosting of the early Women in Buddhism conferences, for its innovation in the arts and psychology, Naropa sparks in its women students the desire to manifest Buddhist practice in their teaching, working, earning of a living.

NOTES

1. "Speaking Up," by Sekijun Karen Thorkelson, in *Kahawai*, vol. 6, no. 4 (Fall 1984).
2. Her prose poem about this experience, "Rape #1, #2, #3", appeared in *The Path of Compassion: Contemporary Writings on Engaged Buddhism*. See Chapter 6, "Bridges," for quotes from this poem.
3. Teijo Roberta Munnich and Catherine Parker of the Minnesota Zen Center, whom I also interviewed, are presented in, respectively, Chapter 3, "Nuns, Monks, and 'Nunks,' " and Chapter 6, "Bridges."
4. A description of these events, with actual documents from the period, is given in *Women and Religion in America*, vol. 2, *The Colonial and Revolutionary Periods*, edited by Rosemary Radford Ruether and Rosemary Skinner Keller.

Dahlia Kamesar

Sylvia Kincaid and Laura Kwong

Nancy James

Joen Snyder

Karen Thorkelson

Caroline Warner

Judith Ragir

Jeanne Ann Whittington

Carol Tierney

Julie Nelson

Ellen Mooney

Sharon Salzberg

Jenny Taylor

Iris Marchaj

Suzanne Bowman

Susan Campbell

Barbara Rhodes and Annie

Susanne Fairclough

Ellen Sidor

Shana Klinger and Mae

Lila Rich

Susan Gillis

Denny Robertson and
Susan Edwards

Bonnie Rabin

Irini Nadel Rockwell

Ina Robbins

Pat Donegan

Barbara Bash

Vicky Fitch with her children Covina and Jesse

8.

Two Women on a Hill: A Vision

THE YEAR 2015—A BUDDIST CENTER IN A WESTERN CITY

The morning is raucous with birds calling and swooping in the nearby oak grove. Here where she sits on the grassy hill, Alyssa can see down into the courtyard where children are just coming sleepy-eyed from their beds in the adjoining houses, where men and women move purposefully about. The female and male monastics have just finished morning service and are mingling with the others in the yard. Outside the compound walls, traffic gathers and flows on the streets, moving toward the freeway, taking the city's inhabitants to work. Soon Alyssa too will join that migration.

Now she looks to her companion, a woman much older than she, whose straight back and peaceful face attest to her many years of practice. In the morning, June often comes to sit up here on the hill, touching earth and stone. Sometimes Alyssa sits with June. After they have grounded themselves in the sensations of the body, precisely observed, have penetrated to an awareness of matter and mind as process, as energy that vibrates in the universe, and stayed in that understanding and communion for an hour; after they have chanted their gratitude for this; June, who sometimes grows testy in the bustle of the day, becomes gracious and willing to talk with Alyssa.

Others simply live this moment, but Alyssa nurtures a fervent curiosity. She needs to reach back, to the time of her birth and before, in order to make sense of now.

June smiles as Alyssa questions her. Once again Alyssa appreciates the beauty of June's coarse gray hair, her eyes so dark the pupils meld with the irises, her skin a warm tan, and remembers that June's ancestry is a merging of several races.

"So you think all this we've built is new, but in 1988 when you arrived screeching into the world, everything we have now, existed already. Yes." June lifts an emphatic hand. "The seeds had begun to sprout. In an individual here, in a center there, in a group across the country, in two friends who talked and sat together. Nuclei of energy, of vision. We had to trust that we *knew* what to do, because we had begun to do it. We were creating in increments and in microcosm the new Buddhism."

"Does that mean we have the future in us now, as well?" asks Alyssa.

"We're only just groping toward some maturity," June says, gazing out past the grassy curve of the hill to the windows of the city flashing in the sun. "Back then we thrashed around in a painful adolescence. Some would say infancy, but I think that sheltered time was past. Suddenly nothing fit anymore. We outgrew our forms, our teachers, our ideas about practice and life. We stomped around in too-small clothes, or went without, beset by our ignorance and limitations, yet most of us knew that the heart of the Dharma would always serve and protect us."

"My mother told me," Alyssa says.

June clasps her hands, remembering. "Yes, some quite innocent people were hurt. Often it happened to those who were young and ardently trusting, who believed their teachers to be perfect. It was just the kick in the pants we needed. Those who had been dreaming woke up and looked around."

Alyssa leans back on her elbows, glancing down once again into the courtyard where people bustle about. Her own small son and daughter are there, cared for by others this morning; and her mother and father live nearby, coming each day to the center to practice.

"So how did we heal and grow again?"

Scratching her head, June looks speculatively at Alyssa. Another morning she might brush off the question, claim to be busy, get up, and walk away, but this day it feels right to answer it. Alyssa and she share a special bond. The young woman is in some sense an apprentice to June, receptive to her knowledge, understanding much without having to be told. June settles herself more comfortably on the grass, tilts her head, thinking.

"There have been three major stages of development since the late eighties. First came the five years or so of *communication.*" She emphasizes the word. "It began to happen all across the country in many ways. Women interested in Buddhist practice met in sitting groups and study groups, in local and national conferences where we began to know each other, to share our concerns, our relationship to the Dharma, our pain and joy. One early conference in particular made a breakthrough and empowered us. It was, first of all, a celebration that brought together Zen women, Theravada women, and Tibetan Buddhist women as well as those women who practiced the Buddha's path without affiliation. The conference was political, a place for women to define the issues that concerned us as Buddhist practitioners and to discuss these, to devise ways to confront and work on those issues. It fully acknowledged each woman's potential: instead of relying on teachers and authority figures to give us their wisdom, we met mostly in small groups, adopting forms that would honor and elicit the wisdom of each participant. It included practice periods drawn from all three of the traditions. This conference became a model for other such gatherings all over the country.

"We communicated through newsletters and pamphlets and books, urgent communiques, mimeographed speculations, computer formulations—sent by mail, phone, car, bicycle, crystals, modems—until there was a net of information reaching across the country and from up in Canada to Mexico, until no one was isolated in her little corner anymore but connected up to all those with similar concerns. We created a group-mind and began to think together, like the individual cells of a brain functioning with all the others.

"At first we communicated the efforts that had already been made by women and groups, so that we could all benefit from what some had experienced in their innovation: the altering of the language of chants and sutras to eliminate male bias, the insistence that women equal in number to men be allowed to give lectures and perform religious offices, the creation of support structures to give mothers the opportunity to do their spiritual practice, the incorporation of body movement into practice situations, the allowing of psychological content as a useful point of focus in practice, the integration of group therapy into the schedule of activities of a center, the very *acknowledgement* of therapy, individual or otherwise, as useful; the recognition of autonomous women teachers and the establishment of women-led centers and retreats.

"Those who particularly understood the synthesis of Buddhism with Native American beliefs communicated their awareness, for it was realized that the native religions connect us to our land, a heritage that is ours because we live here as well and draw our sustenance from this particular patch of earth. Others brought their knowledge of the women's movement, as even male teachers and students knew that the uniqueness of American Buddhism derived from the more autonomous role of women in this society, a product of our long struggle for freedom. We reflected on, and learned from, our heritage of movements for liberation, such as the break from colonial rule, the abolition of slavery, the populist and labor struggles, and civil rights activism.

"All this information and speculation came together, forming an immensely rich stew. Everyone—women and those men who cared—ate to satiety. And from this nourishment syntheses were made, plans and visions issued. People began to see how the Dharma could be lived out and transmitted in ways more beneficial than before. The group-mind became a womb and began to give birth."

Alyssa feels her own excitement rising to meet June's enthusiasm as she talks. She tries to project herself back to that time when she was a baby, when all this was happening around her.

"You make it sound as if it came about pretty smoothly."

June grins, the sun full on her face now. "Well, it did and it didn't. There were many people—teachers and students—not all of them men—who thought that this activity was not appropriate, who thought that it would lead to a watering down of the Dharma, as they said, or who retrenched in order to preserve the male power in their centers and groups. So we were criticized by some; efforts were made to discredit and prevent us, and some women *did* shut up and go back to the old ways of doing things. But," and she leans toward Alyssa, raising her blunt-fingered hand to make her point, "there is such a thing as a historical moment. When all the preconditions have been created for some change to occur, it will happen despite opposition. In that sense it *was* easy, for each new endeavor—each publication or conference or group—came together almost effortlessly and drew more and more women into its context of investigation. For women were hungry to know, and they were dissatisfied with much that had been imposed upon them before.

"You know that in other countries where Buddhism has taken root, the marriage of Buddhist practice with the cultural needs of the people has been accomplished by a particularly compelling teacher or teachers. In our country, while teachers have been and are indispensable, this task of acculturation is being accomplished, in keeping with our egalitarian orientation, by the practitioners themselves. But I am getting ahead of myself."

She pauses, thinking, looking out to the horizon and up at the sky, then to Alyssa. Alyssa likes to see June this way, her dark eyes concentrated, her mouth firm, as she begins again.

"After that most vibrant initial stage of communication, when all the secrecies and provincialisms were blown away, and a true group-thinking began, there came the second stage. This was the time of *building* and *teaching,* which lasted ten years or so in its most intense aspect, and is still going on now."

June sits up straighter, wrinkling her forehead. "How can I describe to you the complexity of this, the creativity in it, the willingness to innovate, to invent, while holding firmly to the basic truths set out by the Buddha? There aren't that many truths, you know, and they make perfect sense if you test them in your own experience. We took those and asked ourselves, 'Now in what sort of observance can we manifest these truths while fully honoring what we know of ourselves as American women?' We looked deeply into our original religious heritage—in most cases Christian or Jewish—and asked ourselves at what point that touched the truth the Buddha gave us. We remembered our native people's reverence for the earth and all its inhabitants and elements. We followed the guide of women's spirituality to our deepest female knowing and studied the female aspects in our Buddhist heritage as they existed particularly in Tibetan Buddhism. We explored the ancient myths of descent and renewal that mirror the seasons and provide models for the cycles in our human lives. We allowed for the basic investigation of Vipassana, the beauty of Zen, the elaboration of Tibetan practice. Music came to us. Movement happened. Gradually we developed a practice fully grounded in the Dharma and conducive to the enlightenment of women."

She pauses, looking down at the grass, frowning again. "I don't want to give you the impression that this was a matter of simply combining one practice with others, though at first that was sometimes all we could think to do. At first we were awkward, sometimes we went wrong, sometimes we wound up with a hodge-podge rather than a synthesis. But as different groups and individual women created rituals and shared these, the artificial mergings began to fall away, and gradually the real power began to manifest itself and to guide us. The casual, the superficial, the inappropriate, were discarded, and we began to *know* what to do: which gestures, words, sounds, movements carried our deepest meaning and aspirations. From this has come the practice followed in our centers throughout the country.

"As you know, we now honor the great life changes of menarche and menopause. You have experienced the ritual solemnizing your first period. You know that menarche and menopause are times of great power and vulnerability in a woman, when she is more spiritually open, a time to pierce into the truth of impermanence and experience oneness with the life flow. We have created psychic/emotional environments in which the adolescent girl and the menopausal woman can fully experience and enlarge her capacity through ceremony, practice, and study.

"Along with this, of course, there was the building of centers and living accommodations, the establishment of practice and work schedules that allowed for family life and employment. Some people actually lived at the centers but most, as now, lived in the community and came to the centers to practice and socialize. The care of children became formalized as a central practice, especially for men, as it was seen to work against their training and to teach them the consideration for the needs of others more usually present in women. The men were found to be very good at building and maintaining the physical plant, keeping the books, running the computers, and such tasks; and they were taught to take care of guests and children. Because it is we women who bring forth life and are more strongly connected to the heart of all livingness, we naturally were recognized as the spiritual teachers, and we took up our responsibilities as such. The men's supportive work allowed us more time and freedom to pursue our practice and develop our teaching capacities. Of course, one of our great lessons for the men was what we had learned by following the practice amid the tasks of our daily lives, and we made certain that we kept that knowledge alive in ourselves as well."

"Is it really true," asks Alyssa, "that, before I was born, most of the teachers were *men?*" And she goes on, thoughtfully, "A few years ago, when some men began to be teachers, I first wondered about that. The men just seemed so good at what they were doing that I never thought of them as capable of teaching."

June looks sternly at Alyssa. "We had to right the balance. The pendulum had swung so far to the male side that we had to swing it all the way back and for a time allow only women to be teachers. Only now when the men have had some decades of training to broaden themselves can they begin to be thought of as potential teachers. You must remember, Alyssa, that in those early years of your life there were the nuclear accidents that killed thousands of American citizens. It was a devastating time, and in this crisis for humanity the awareness came forth that the male way, the linear, narrowly focused, logical mind that built the weapons and sent them off in rockets had set us on a course of self-destruction that promised to decimate the planet. People reacted by opening themselves to the more welcoming, allowing, nurturing qualities usually ascribed to women, which of course include wisdom. They began to be suspicious of the male way and sought out female teachers. This was a period of the coming to ascendancy of many women teachers, who for the first time were given full material and psychological support.

"But it had also been learned from the example of the male spiritual teachers that the very fact of having a single teacher at the top of a hierarchy invited corruption, so no woman teacher was given exclusive responsibilities. There were always two or more teaching together, checking each other, keeping each other honest. Among the students generally, too, there were structures devised to promote the confrontation of issues rather than avoidance of them, because we understood that this empowers people to reach to deeper concerns, creates understanding and respect, and frees the mind to concentrate on practice. And, furthermore, the limitations of teachers had become painfully clear, so that an arrangement was instituted in which the teacher could be both leader and student, alternately performing the duties she performed best and then merging back into the group to allow someone else to lead. The lines between teachers and others blurred, in this way, until there came an acting-out of the truth that we are all teachers to each other, each of us embodying Buddha nature."

June pauses, smiling at Alyssa, and they share the recognition of how they have instructed and informed and supported each other over the years of Alyssa's growing up and young adulthood.

Then June resumes her telling. "One other great shift was in the area of monasticism. Some women gathered and made the decision to drop the rules imposed on female monastics in the Asian countries. They called themselves the New American Order of Buddhist Monastics, and they followed the Buddha's example in establishing the first monks' and nuns' orders: they started with no rules at all except the precepts, and, just as he had done, they devised the regulations one by one as situations arose requiring some guidance, the goal being to create an environment conducive to intensive practice and harmonious living. They dealt with clothing, comportment, rituals, domestic arrangements, and all other behavior requiring guidelines. Some decisions were made and written down, with the agreement of the sangha to follow these rules. Provision was made for mothers to pursue intensive practice for periods of time while maintaining satisfactory contact with their children. When all this was in place, the female monastics opened their doors to men wishing to become monks and allowed them to ordain.

"During this time also, there began to build a literature of Western women's enlightenment and wisdom. Poems were written and published. Students put together books of the teachings of especially acute and articulate spokeswomen. Gradually there built up a library that *you* know and have studied, which didn't exist when I began Buddhist practice."

"Who were your models then?" asks Alyssa.

"What an effort we made to find them! You see why it all had to change."

"And now? Where are we now?"

Leaning back to breathe deeply, June looks out, her eyes making a sweep of the city and returning to gaze down into the court-

yard where now few people move, as most have gone to work or
school.

"Don't you have to go to work now?" she asks Alyssa.

"In a few minutes. I want to hear about this . . . third stage."

"But you've *lived* it. You were a teenager when it began."

"Yes, but I haven't heard *you* tell it."

"All right, briefly then." June sits up straighter.

"In those years of building and teaching, we set down deep
roots in the Dharma and established institutions that would transmit the teachings and provide both security and opportunity for
people. Then, for these last ten years that you know best, the task
has been to make what we do accessible to more and more people,
especially women, and to express our concern for all life.

"Through all we had learned in the preceding fifteen years, we
had developed a distinct state of mind. Our sharing in the condition of all phenomena became very clear to us and awakened a
sense of responsibility for the world, both the world of human beings and that of all other beings, and the earth and water and air
too. This connection that we felt more and more strongly led us
out into the social, political, and environmental action that you
know so well. By now it is required that students give part of their
time to such causes, which are understood to be practice."

Alyssa nods. It is well known now that Buddhists function
among the strongest laborers for peaceful change and social and
environmental justice. She herself has given many hundreds of
hours to this work, most recently helping to staff a prenatal clinic
in a low income neighborhood where infant death rate is high.

"In instances of injustice or wrongdoing," June goes on, "we
have learned not simply to concern ourselves with the motives or
ethical deficiencies of the wrongdoer but to ask, 'Who has been
hurt?' and 'How can that person or group be helped to regain
physical and psychological well-being?' That allies us with the suf-
ferer, asks us to feel that pain and then do all we can to alleviate it.
When this has been accomplished, then perhaps we can turn our
attention to the perpetrator of the deed, who also suffers. One of
our primary goals has been to heal the psychological damage
done to women in a male-defined and controlled society. It is a
matter of priorities and of a particular cast of mind. To you, of
course, this is a given, as you grew up in that consciousness, but it

was a profound shift from the dominant thinking of thirty years ago.

"In this spirit, we have learned to stretch ourselves in making the Dharma accessible to the spectrum of people in this society. The many hundreds of Buddhist centers and groups in every city in this country attest to our success, and the relative racial and class diversity in them really does let us know that we have left behind what one early teacher called the 'hothouse phase' of American Buddhism.

"But you know all this, Alyssa, and especially the problems and the failures in it. *That* we could talk about for another hour."

Alyssa waits, while June looks thoughtfully at her, knowing her friend's penchant for symmetry, her need to complete her thoughts.

"It's only a moment in time," June laughs, raising that sturdy hand. "This is only 2015—not even a hundred years since Buddhism began to be known to many people in the United States, only a paltry thirty years or so since women began to investigate and communicate and take leadership."

"But so much has been done since then!" Alyssa bursts out.

"Indeed," June says, looking full into Alyssa's eyes. "More than beginnings now. We've made it ours."

NOTE: This projection into the future is offered in the hope that you will make your own vision, imagine what you want to come about.

"We are what we think," said the Buddha. "All that we are arises with our thoughts; with our thoughts we make the world."[1]

Sandy Boucher

NOTE

1. From *The Dhammapada: The Sayings of the Buddha.* Trans. Thomas Byrom (New York: Vintage Books, 1976), Verse 1.

Glossary

AVALOKITESVARA. Bodhisattva of compassion.

BHIKKHU or BHIKKHUNI. Monk or nun in Theravada lands. The Pali word means "mendicant," as Theravada monastics traditionally beg for their food. Bhikshu and Bhikshuni are the Sanskrit forms.

BODHISATTVA. The religious ideal in Mahayana Buddhism: an enlightened being who postpones his or her Buddhahood in order to save all sentient beings. In Theravada Buddhism the term means simply one who is set upon the path to enlightenment.

BODHI TREE. The pipal (fig) tree under which the Buddha was sitting when he experienced his enlightenment.

BUDDHA. One who has awakened, i.e., who has direct understanding of the truth. Usually refers to the historical Siddhartha Gautama (Shakyamuni Buddha), founder of Buddhism.

BUDDHADHARMA. The Buddha's teachings.

DAKINI. In Tibetan Buddhism, a manifestation of the feminine. She may appear as a human being or a goddess, may be benevolent or wrathful, or may be perceived simply as energy moving in the world of phenomena.

DHAMMA DENA or DHAMMADINNA. A member of the original order of Buddhist nuns, who became a great preacher.

DHARMA or DHAMMA. The truth of the teaching of the Buddha; reality, doctrine. The term with a lower case d and usually in the plural is also used to indicate the smallest elements of which the universe consists.

DHARMA HEIR or DHARMA SUCCESSOR. One who has received Dharma transmission from a teacher.

DHARMA TRANSMISSION. A ceremony in which the Dharma or truth is passed from master to student, giving the student permission to teach.

DOGEN KIGEN (1200–1253). Founder of the Soto Zen school in Japan.

DOKUSAN. In Japanese Zen, the formal interview between teacher and student.

HARA. The region of the body below the navel; sometimes used to symbolize the core of one's being. In Zen it is viewed as the natural place of meditation.

HINAYANA BUDDHISM. Another name for Theravada Buddhism.

JAINS. Members of Jainism, a religious system that arose in sixth century B.C.E. India (as did Buddhism). Mahavira was a Jain saint.

JIZO. Japanese patron saint of children, farmers and common people.

JODO SHINSHU BUDDHISM. A type of Pure Land Buddhism popular in Japan.

KALI or KALI MA. The "Dark Mother," the Hindu Triple Goddess of creation, preservation, and destruction.

KENSHO. In Japanese Zen, an enlightenment experience.

KOAN. Question posed to a student by a Zen master in order to help the student break through to her or his own true nature. Also can mean any problem or obstacle in daily life that the student must confront, examine, and transcend. Rinzai Zen emphasizes formal koans; Soto Zen emphasizes the naturally arising koans of ordinary life.

KUAN YIN or QUAN YIN or KWAN YIN or KANNON (AVALO-KITESVARA). A famous celestial Bodhisattva, the personification of compassion, usually portrayed as female.

KYOSAKU. In Zen, the long supple stick employed during sitting to awaken a student who is sluggish or sleepy. The student is struck sharply on the shoulder or back.

LAMA. A Tibetan or Mongolian monk or layperson deeply learned in Buddhist doctrine and/or Tantric practice.

MAHAYANA BUDDHISM. "Greater vehicle," one of the two great divisions of Buddhism. Dominant in northern Asia. Mahayana stresses compassion, active love, and wisdom, and its ideal is the Bodhisattva, who vows to save all beings.

MERIT. In Theravada Buddhism, one accumulates merit toward a fortunate rebirth by practicing, supporting the community of monks and nuns, and doing good acts. This merit can be transferred to or shared with other beings.

METTA. Loving-kindness. Basis of a particular meditation in the Theravada school of Buddhism.

MUDITHA. A feeling of joy in the good fortune of others.

NICHIREN SHOSHU OF AMERICA. A type of Japanese-originated Buddhism with many followers in the United States.

NIPPONZAN MYOHOJI. A type of Japanese Nichiren Buddhism whose practitioners build peace pagodas and demonstrate for world peace.

NIRVANA or NIBBANA. The state of final enlightenment or at-one-ment, liberation from the round of rebirth.

PRACTICE. The attempt to maintain constant awareness throughout all actions of daily life as well as in formal meditation sitting.

PRAJNAPARAMITA. Perfection of Wisdom. Wisdom that is beyond discriminatory thought, arising naturally from meditation and diligent training. Often personified as a goddess. In the Perfection of Wisdom sutras she is described as the mother of the Buddhas, for she produces the highest enlightenment.

PURE LAND BUDDHISM. A form of Buddhism in which the practitioner chants the name of Amitabha Buddha in order to be reborn in the Pure Land, from which she or he can become a Buddha.

RAIHAI TOKUZUI. A chaper of Dogen's writings (in his *Shobogenzo*), which speaks of the complete spiritual equality of men and women and relates stories of famous female Zen masters.

RAKUSU. An abbreviated version of the kesa (priest's robe), worn like a bib around the neck.

RINPOCHE or RIMPOCHE. A Tibetan title, meaning "the Precious One," accorded to high lamas and to tulkus (incarnations of previous Lamas).

RINZAI ZEN. The second largest school of Zen in Japan, known for its use of the koan technique of meditation.

ROSHI. Zen master.

SAMURAI. Member of a military class in feudal Japan.

SANGHA. Originally, the company of enlightened beings, but, more generally, any community of people practicing the Buddhist way.

SESSHIN. In Zen training, a period of intensive meditation, usually lasting seven days.

SOTO ZEN. The largest school of Zen in Japan, which emphasizes the unity of training and enlightenment, the keeping of the precepts, and meditation in the activities of daily life.

SENSEI. Teacher.

SUNYATA. Emptiness, the void that underlies all existence.

SOKKA GAKKAI. The lay organization of Nichiren Shoshu Buddhism.

SUTRA. Scripture. One of a collection of discourses attributed to the Buddha.

TANTRA. A Hindu or Buddhist mystical path, distinguished by its "wealth of techniques for utilizing all things good and evil . . . Obstacles are transmuted into instruments for providing the tremendous momentum needed. Most other paths require a turning away from dark to light, whereas Vajrayana [i.e. Tantric] yogins welcome both demons and angels as their allies" (from *The Tantric Mysticism of Tibet* by John Blofeld).

Tantra is also distinguished by its use of sexual symbolism, with the "thought of awakening" identified with semen, wisdom with a woman waiting to be inseminated. This symbolism apparently derives from ancient mother-goddess sources, in which fertility rites were utilized.

TEISHO. In Japanese Zen, the formal lecture given in the meditation hall.

THERAVADA BUDDHISM. "The Way of the Elders," one of the two great divisions of Buddhism. Known as the "Southern School," it is found mostly in Southeast Asia. Theravada teaches gradual progress toward individual enlightenment.

THERIGATHA. A collection of enlightenment verses believed to have been composed by early Buddhist nuns.

UPAYA. Skillful means.

VAJRADHATU. "Vajra," all that is pure and indestructible; "dhatu," elements; sometimes translated as "indestructible space." In this country, the headquarters (in Boulder, Colorado) for a network of Tibetan Buddhist meditation centers.

VAYRAYANA BUDDHISM. Tibetan Buddhism.

VAJRA VARAHI. In Tibetan Buddhism, one of the major embodiments of female energy, who, in the words of Tsultrim Allione, "springs out of the cosmic cervix, the triangular source of dharmas, burning with unbearable bliss, energy in an unconditional state."

VINAYA. The monastic rules formulated in India during the life of Shakyamuni Buddha.

VIPASSANA. Insight meditation, a training in mindfulness in which one pays meticulous attention to one's body and mind while not identifying with them. A type of practice developed and followed principally in Theravada Buddhism, but also sometimes used in the other forms of Buddhism.

ZAZEN. Formal Zen sitting practice.

ZENDO. Meditation hall.

Bibliography

Aitken, Robert. *Mind of Clover.* Berkeley: North Point Press, 1984.

Allen, Paula Gunn. *The Sacred Hoop: Recovering the Feminine in American Indian Traditions.* Boston: Beacon Press, 1986.

Allione, Tsultrim. *Women of Wisdom.* London: Routledge & Kegan Paul, 1982.

Blofeld, John. *The Bodhisattva of Compassion: The Mystical Tradition of Kuan Yin.* Boston: Shambhala, 1978.

―――. *The Tantric Mysticism of Tibet.* Boulder: Prajna Press, 1982.

Boucher, Sandy. "The Healing." In *Hear the Silence: Stories by Women of Myth, Magic, and Renewal,* ed. Irene Zahava. Trumansburg, NY: The Crossing Press, 1986.

Butler, Katy. "Events Are the Teacher: Working Through the Crisis at San Francisco Zen Center." *CoEvolution Quarterly* (Winter 1983), pp. 112-123.

Capra, Fritjof, and Charlene Spretnak. *Green Politics: The Global Promise.* New York: E. P. Dutton, 1984.

Christ, Carol P. *Diving Deep and Surfacing: Women Writers on Spiritual Quest.* Boston: Beacon Press, 1980.

―――, *Laughter of Aphrodite: Reflections on a Journey to the Goddess.* San Francisco: Harper & Row, 1987.

―――, and Judith Plaskow, eds. *Womanspirit Rising: A Feminist Reader in Religion.* San Francisco: Harper & Row, 1979.

Daly, Mary. *Beyond God the Father: Toward a Philosophy of Women's Liberation.* Boston: Beacon, 1973.

―――. *Gyn/Ecology.* Boston: Beacon Press, 1978.

―――. *Pure Lust.* Boston: Beacon Press, 1984.

David-Neel, Alexandra. *Magic and Mystery in Tibet.* New York: Dover, 1971.

―――, and Lama Yongden. *The Power of Nothingness.* Boston: Houghton Mifflin, 1982.

Donegan, Patricia. *Bone Poems.* Boulder: Chinook Press, 1985.

Endo, Shusako. *Silence.* Rutland, VT and Tokyo, Japan: The Charles E. Tuttle Company, 1969.

Engler, John H. "Vicissitudes of the Self According to Psychoanalysis and Buddhism: A Spectrum Model of Object Relations Development." In *Transformations of Consciousness: Conventional and Con-*

templative Perspectives on Development, by Ken Wilbur, John H. Engler, and Daniel Brown. Boston: New Science Library, Shambhala, 1986.

Eppsteiner, Fred, and Dennis Maloney, eds. *The Path of Compassion: Contemporary Writings on Engaged Buddhism.* Berkeley and Buffalo: Buddhist Peace Fellowship/White Pine Press, 1985.

Falk, Nancy A., and Rita M. Gross, eds. *Unspoken Worlds: Women's Religious Lives in Non-Western Cultures.* San Francisco: Harper & Row, 1980.

Fields, Rick. *How the Swans Came to the Lake: A Narrative History of Buddhism in America.* Boulder: Shambhala Publications, 1981.

Finkelhor, David. *Child Sexual Abuse: New Theory and Research.* New York: Free Press, 1984.

Friedman, Lenore. *Meetings with Remarkable Women.* Boston: Shambhala, 1987.

Gilligan, Carol. *In a Different Voice: Psychological Theory and Women's Development.* Cambridge: Harvard University Press, 1982.

Gross, Rita, ed. *Beyond Androcentrism: New Essays on Women and Religion.* Decatur, GA: Scholars Press, 1977.

———. "Buddhism and Feminism: A Personal Synthesis." In *Not Mixing Up Buddhism,* ed. Deborah Hopkinson, Michele Hill, and Eileen Kiera. New York: White Pine Press, 1986.

———. 'Buddhism and Feminism: Toward their Mutual Transformation." *Eastern Buddhist* vol. 19, nos. 1 and 2 (Spring and Fall, 1986).

———. "The Feminine Principle in Tibetan Vayrayana Buddhism: Reflections of a Buddhist Feminist." *Journal of Transpersonal Psychology* vol. 16, no. 2 (1984).

———. "Feminism From the Perspective of Buddhist Practice." *Buddhist-Christian Studies* vol. 1, no. 1 (Fall 1981).

———. "Suffering, Feminist Theory, and Images of Goddess." *Anima: An Experiential Journal* vol. 13, no. 1 (Fall Equinox 1986).

———. "Three Strikes and You're Out: An Autobiography at Mid-Life." In *A Time to Weep and a Time to Sing: Faith Journeys of Women Scholars of Religion,* ed. Mary Jo Meadow. Minneapolis: Winston-Seabury Press, 1985.

———. "Women's Access to Dharma." *Vajradhatu Sun* (October-November 1982). Excerpts published in *Kahawai Journal of Women and Zen* vol. 3, no. 4 (Fall 1981).

———. "Yeshe Tsogyal: Enlightened Consort, Great Teacher, Female Role Model," *Tibet Journal* (forthcoming).

Guggenbuhl-Craig, Adolf. *Power in the Helping Professions.* Dallas: Spring Publications, 1971.

Haddad, Yvonne Yazbeck, and Ellison Banks Findley, eds. *Women, Religion, and Social Change.* New York: State University of New York, 1985.

Hopkinson, Deborah, Michele Hill, and Eileen Kiera, eds. *Not Mixing Up Buddhism: Essays on Women and Buddhist Practice.* New York: White Pine Press, 1986.

Horner, I. B. *Women Under Primitive Buddhism.* Delhi: Motilal Banarsidass, 1930.

Iglehart, Hallie. *Womanspirit: A Guide to Women's Wisdom.* San Francisco: Harper & Row, 1983.

Kahawai Journal of Women and Zen. C/o Diamond Sangha, 2119 Kaloa Way, Honolulu, HI 96822.

Kapleau, Philip. *To Cherish All Life: A Buddhist View of Animal Slaughter and Meat Eating.* Rochester, NY: The Zen Center, 1981.

Kennett, Roshi Jiyu. *How to Grow a Lotus Blossom.* Mt. Shasta, CA: Shasta Abbey, 1977.

———. *The Wild White Goose.* 2 Vols. Mt. Shasta, CA: Shasta Abbey, 1977 and 1978.

———. *Zen is Eternal Life.* Emeryville, CA: Dharma Publishing, 1976.

Khema, Ayya. *Be an Island unto Yourself.* Parappuduwa Nuns Island, Dodanduwa, Sri Lanka, 1986.

———, *All of Us: Beset by Birth, Decay and Death.* Parappuduwa Nuns Island, Dodanduwa, Sri Lanka, 1987.

Macy, Joanna Rogers. *Despair and Personal Power in the Nuclear Age.* Philadelphia: New Society Publishers, 1983.

———. *Dharma and Development: Religion as Resource in the Sarvodaya Self-Help Movement.* W. Hartford, CT: Kunarian Press, 1983.

Meadow, Mary Jo, and Carole A. Rayburn, eds. *A Time to Weep, A Time to Sing: Faith Journeys of Women Scholars of Religion.* Minneapolis: Winston Press, 1985.

Mitchell, Elsie. *Sun Buddhas Moon Buddhas: A Zen Quest.* New York and Tokyo: Weatherhill, 1973.

Miura, Isshu, and Ruth Fuller Sasaki. *The Zen Koan: Its History and Use in Rinzai Zen.* San Diego, New York, London: Harcourt Brace Jovanovich, 1965.

NIBWA (Newsletter on International Buddhist Women's Activities). C/o Dr. Chatsumarn Kabilsingh, Faculty of Liberal Arts, Thammasat University, Bangkok 10200, Thailand.

Nichiren Shoshu Sokagakkai. Tokyo: The Seikyo Press, 1966.

Paul, Diana Y. *Women in Buddhism.* Berkeley: Asian Humanities Press, 1979.

Perera, Sylvia Brinton. *Descent to the Goddess: A Way of Initiation for Women.* Toronto: Inner City Books, 1981.

Ross, Nancy Wilson. *Buddhism: A Way of Life and Thought.* New York: Random House, 1981.

———. *The World of Zen.* New York: Random House, 1960.

———. *Three Ways of Asian Wisdom.* New York, Simon & Schsuter, 1966.

Ruether, Rosemary Radford, ed. *Religion and Sexism.* New York: Simon & Schuster, 1974.

———, and Rosemary Skinner Keller, eds. *Women and Religion in America, A Documentary History.* Vol. 1, *The Nineteenth Century;* Vol. 2, *The Colonial and Revolutionary Periods;* Vol. 3, 1900–1968. San Francisco: Harper & Row, 1981, 1983, 1986.

Russell, Diana. *Sexual Exploitation: Rape, Child Sexual Abuse, and Workplace Harassment.* Beverly Hills: Sage Publications, 1984.

Sidor, Ellen, ed. *A Gathering of Spirit: Women Teaching in American Buddhism.* Providence, RI: Primary Point Press, Kwan Um Zen School, 1987.

Spretnak, Charlene. *Lost Goddesses of Early Greece: A Collection of Pre-Hellenic Mythology.* Berkeley: Moon Books, 1978.

———. *The Politics of Women's Spirituality: Essays on the Rise of Spiritual Power Within the Feminist Movement.* New York: Anchor Press/Doubleday, 1982.

———. *The Spiritual Dimension of Green Politics.* Santa Fe: Bear & Co., 1986.

Stanton, Elizabeth Cady, and the Revising Committee. *The Woman's Bible.* Seattle: Coalition Task Force on Women and Religion, 1974.

Starhawk. *Dreaming the Dark: Magic, Sex, and Politics.* Boston: Beacon Press, 1982.

———. *The Spiral Dance: A Rebirth of the Ancient Religion of the Great Goddess.* San Francisco: Harper & Row, 1979.

Stone, Merlin. *When God Was a Woman.* New York: Harcourt Brace, 1976.

Suzuki, Daisetz T. *The Awakening of Zen.* Boulder: Prajna Press, 1980.

———. *Zen And Japanese Culture.* Bollingen Series LXIV. Princeton: Princeton University Press, 1959.

Tree of Life: Buddhism and Protection of Nature, published by Buddhist Perception of Nature, 1987. Contact: Dr. Chatsumarn Kabilsingh, Faculty of Liberal Arts, Thammasat University, Bangkok 10200, Thailand.

Walker, Barbara G. *The Woman's Encyclopedia of Myths and Secrets.* San Francisco: Harper & Row, 1983.

Women & Buddhism, A special issue of *Spring Wind—Buddhist Cultural Forum,* vol. 6, nos. 1, 2, 3. Zen Buddhist Temple—Toronto, 46

Gwynne Avenue, Toronto M6K 2C3, Ontario, Canada; and Zen Buddhist Temple—Ann Arbor, 1214 Packard Road, Ann Arbor, MI 48104.

Zahava, Irene, ed. *Hear the Silence: Stories by Women of Myth, Magic, and Renewal.* New York: The Crossing Press, 1986.